What Reviewers Are Saying About
The Traveler's Medical Guide

Outside Magazine
"One of the most recent and most useful health-care manuals written especially for travelers. It's readable, understandable (with lots of checklists and quick-reference charts), and comprehensive, covering pretrip preparations, first-aid kits, preventive measures, diagnosis and treatment of specific maladies, and more — but it's still slim enough to take along."

Islands
". . . not only a basic manual to healthy traveling, but a disorder-by-disorder guide to virtually every kind of exotic ailment an independent traveler is likely to encounter . . . including specific, up-to-date medications — and what to do when medical care is not available. Stash it in your backpack, and save a copy for your doctor if a strange fever breaks out after you return."

Travel & Leisure
"If you're . . . more at home in a Brazilian rain forest than a Paris boite, pick up a copy . . . there are sections on immunizations, jet lag and first aid kits, but the emphasis is on responsible self-care for far-flung adventurers who might be days away from modern medical facilities. You'll learn how to diagnose and treat a range of ailments (from minor skin wounds and insect bites to intestinal disorders) and how to determine whether you can handle something yourself or need professional help."

Footprints
". . . by far the most comprehensive and detailed self-care manual available for travelers . . . the authors did it exceptionally well . . . Any traveler would benefit from

this information especially in the area of preventive health measures. And if problems do come into play, detailed, educated information is available."

Journal of Wilderness Medicine
"The format used certainly is more practical for the average tourist traveling abroad than that of other self-help books . . . I would recommend *The Traveler's Medical Guide* specifically for persons traveling to areas where medical help will not be available, and/or immediate medical evaluation might be required."

Library Journal
". . . comprehensive . . . advises readers on how to prepare for serious health hazards that may be encountered when traveling... Focusing on the needs of people planning extended trips or travel outside modern urban areas, it covers first-aid kits, dental remedies for emergencies, and prescription medications. The book also includes extensive food and water guides, quick reference charts to help diagnose common illnesses . . ."

International Travel News
". . . a thorough, self-doctoring guide for travelers . . . the best part of this book is the field-guide-type diagnosis and treatment sections, which compose a major part of the book. . . . you don't need to be a doctor to understand the symptoms and undertake treatment if there isn't a good doctor around. Even medicines are listed in their generic equivalents - important since trade names sometimes change from country to country but generic names never do. (*** Excellent)"

San Diego Peace Corps Association
"Don't leave home without one."

The Traveler's Medical Guide, 3rd edition

The comprehensive self-care source for all aspects of healthy global travel.

Gary R. Fujimoto, MD,

Marc R. Robin, ANP,

Bradford L. Dessery, RN

Prairie Smoke Press
St. Paul, Minnesota

For ordering information write to:
Prairie Smoke Press
7125 Willow Lane
Brooklyn Center, MN 55430

Internet ordering:
www.prairiesmokepress.com

Manufactured in the USA
10 9 8 7 6 5 4 3 2 1

ISBN: 0-9704482-5-2
Library of Congress Control Number: 2003105371

Printing History:
1st Edition printed August 1990;
2nd Edition printed August 1992;
3rd Edition printed July 2003

Contents

Charts
Pre-Trip Planning

Quick Reference Charts:

General Charts:

Acknowledgements

The authors wish to express their gratitude to the following people for contributions to the latest edition of this guide: Mike Kelly, Rachel Andersson, Chris Lafferty MD, and Sue Grogan. A very special thank you to our index goddess, Kathy Dessery.

Disclaimer

The Traveler's Medical Guide has been written by applying standard medical principles for the general public. It's meant to help you plan in advance for possible medical eventualities in the area of the world you are visiting. While planning your trip, consult your physician before implementing recommendations in this book, especially if you have any pre-existing or chronic medical problems.

Medical treatment is constantly changing. We urge any reader who is ill to seek medical help if it is available before utilizing the medical recommendations or suggestions contained in this book. The authors and publisher emphasize that this book is not a substitute for the medical advice of a physician, and disclaim responsibility from adverse consequences or effects resulting from use or misuse of the contents of this book.

Guidelines have been included to help you determine when medical care is mandatory. The Traveler's Medical Guide provides resources to help you find competent medical care in a foreign country should you need it. It will also alert you to some potentially harmful medical practices in a few countries, such as the use of dangerous medications that have been banned elsewhere.

Preface
The Traveler's Medical Guide
Jay Keystone, MD

Sherwood Gorbach, an eminent infectious disease specialist, once said, "Travel broadens the mind, but loosens the bowels." Although travelers' diarrhea is undoubtedly the most frequent ailment of travelers, it is certainly not the only medical problem that travelers face. Health risks are a fact of life for all travelers, whether the intrepid backpacker crossing Africa by truck or the sun worshipper lying on a beach in the Caribbean. Fortunately, most travel related medical problems are preventable and the rest are usually treatable. How you prevent and treat unexpected illness or accidents is exactly the basis of this comprehensive and very useful guide.

Marc Robin, Brad Dessery and Gary Fujimoto are experienced travel medicine practitioners who not only provide pre-travel advice, but also travel to those remote areas where such advice is most needed. This unique combination of medical expertise and personal experience provide a wealth of medically sound and practical information for the newest edition of this book.

The key to remaining healthy during travel (and hopefully afterwards) is "preparation." Unfortunately, most travelers think of preparation as pre-travel health advice only. In fact, an equally important aspect is being prepared to identify and manage medical problems that arise unexpectedly. Why do you need to know how to identify and manage your own medical problems? Two good reasons: 1. The standard of health care provision is not the same high quality everywhere in the world, particularly in developing countries, and 2. You may find yourself in a remote location in which you do not have access to any healthcare.

This book not only addresses preparation, it will also help you to identify health risks in advance, allowing you to take the necessary steps to avoid them. The real strengths of this book, however, are the tools that the authors have provided to enable you to self-diagnose and treat illnesses or injuries. The quick reference charts are wonderful, and the section on medications and how to use them is unique in the travel medicine literature. Useful information including uses, doses and side effects are at your fingertips and written with a minimum of medical jargon (amen!).

Whether you are traveling to Burma, Bangladesh or the Bahamas, or whether you are sun burned, bitten or bedridden, this well-written, easy to understand, pocket sized manual is an excellent guide to preventing, identifying and managing illness in the field. This is one book that should be in the backpack or bag of every traveler to the developing world whether the travel is first class or "no class." I hope the authors send me a free copy to use on my next trip!

Dr. Jay Keystone is professor, Dept. of Medicine, and director, International Health Programs, at the University of Toronto, Ontario, Canada. He is also a staff physician at the Center for Travel and Tropical Medicine at the Toronto Hospital. He is past president of the International Society of Travel Medicine, the American Committee on Clinical Tropical Medicine and Travelers' Health (of the American Society of Tropical Medicine) and the Canadian Society for International Health. He is a frequent lecturer in the fields of travel and tropical medicine and Senior Editor of the Traveling Healthy Newsletter. Dr. Keystone's research interests include leprosy, travelers' diarrhea, and intestinal parasites, with field research in southern India.

Foreword
The Traveler's Medical Guide

Elaine C. Jong, MD

Expanded and updated since originally published as **The Medical Guide for Third World Travelers, The Traveler's Medical Guide** is an invaluable and practical health guide for international travelers. This book is geared towards persons who spend significant time traveling, such as repeat and long-term travelers, or the traveler who plans to go to remote areas. Fundamental principles of prevention and self-care are applied to the common health problems that occur during international travel, and are extended to cover exotic diseases and hazardous exposures, as well.

Although consultation with a health care professional is always advised in case of serious illness, actual health scenarios will help travelers to go as far as they can with self-help efforts, and give them an idea of when to bail out. The self-diagnosis and treatment guides will help the traveler to assess the appropriateness of medical care abroad, and even how to initiate first steps when illness strikes in areas remote from professional care. Detailed drug treatment regimens are given to help the traveler to become aware of the options for various medical problems.

An attractive feature of this book is the continued inclusion of the "Quick Reference" charts that help to diagnose common ailments. New sections in this edition address the health concerns of special groups, such as children, women, and corporate travelers.

The contributing authors are themselves experienced adventure travelers as well as health care providers. Readers will be pleased by the clearly written text, the definitions of medical terminology, and extensive coverage of the health questions that frequently occur among international travelers. In my opinion, this book is among the best currently available for the intrepid international traveler.

Elaine C. Jong, MD is Clinical Professor of Medicine, University of Washington, Founding Director, The Travel & Tropical Medicine Service at the University of Washington Medical Center and an International Travel Medicine Consultant. She is an author of *The Travel and Tropical Medicine Handbook*. (W.B. Saunders & Co., 3rd edition, June 2002).

Introduction

How To Use This Book _____

Anyone living or traveling outside the developed world - whether for work, business, research, vacation, volunteer work, or adventure - will encounter increased and unaccustomed health risks. These new risks are a challenge, requiring increased responsibility for your health and well-being. The information in this book will help you stay healthy and cope with illness, whether traveling for 2 weeks or 2 years. It should enable you to assume responsibility for a substantial part of your medical care when the need arises, whether in a large city or isolated area. Travel, even to remote rural areas of the world, need not entail major health risks. Both the hazards and anxiety of new, possibly exotic locations, can vanish with proper preparation.

Part I

Pre-Trip Medical Planning

Preventing illness is the key to successful travel outside the developed nations. Understanding the health risks enables you to avoid and minimize them. Part I will help you identify potential health problems and prepare appropriately. From immunizations to first aid kits, health insurance to birth control measures, physical exams to food and water precautions, we'll help you get ready for your trip. Special chapters address the needs of women travelers and parents traveling with children. Read Part I before your departure, and know the preventive measures to follow during travel.

Part II

Diagnosis and Treatment of Medical Disorders

In spite of precautions, illness and injury may occur. Part II will help you interpret symptoms and identify commonly encountered illnesses. Use the table of contents and the index to locate specific information quickly. To identify possible causes and find relevant information when you know only the symptoms, consult the Quick Reference guides in each chapter. A guide to identification of a mysterious rash, for example, will be found at the end of Chapter 7, "Skin Problems." In addition, there are guidelines to help you determine when medical evaluation must be obtained.

We provide treatment schedules in Part II for use when medical care isn't available. When care is available, use this information to ensure that the medications prescribed for you are appropriate and safe. These dosages are for adult use only as children have specialized medical needs beyond the scope of this book.

Part III

Medications and How To Use Them

Part III helps you safely evaluate and use a variety of pharmaceutical tools. You'll find information on contra-indications, as well as how to maximize the effectiveness — and minimize potential side effects — of medications. Read this information before taking any medication we or others recommend for use while traveling. You'll also find the generic equivalents or chemical compositions of brand name medications we mention in the text. Throughout the text we capitalize brand- but not gener-ic- names.

Appendices

You will find an extensive list of web resources as well as weight and temperature conversion charts, high alti-tude destinations, and travel clinic contact information.

Part I

Pre-Trip Medical Planning ___

Preparing for any trip depends on several factors. These include the length of the trip, your general state of health, and your destination — urban or rural, temperate or tropical.

It's essential to allow sufficient time to complete all the necessary immunizations and medical preparations. Many travelers to developing countries will need **2–4 months** and some may need up to **6 months** to adequately complete their immunizations. Make the best preparations possible, and you'll be well on your way to a healthy stay abroad.

Wherever you travel in developing countries, you must take measures to safeguard your health. Food and water precautions are essential. Vaccinations, insect precautions, sun protection, malaria prophylaxis, and other preventive measures depend primarily on your destination. The first aid kit you assemble and the medical or dental checkups you obtain depend mainly on the duration of your stay.

Use the checklist on the next page for travel planning, and for quickly locating specific information.

Medical Checklist:
Planning Your Trip

All Travelers (including travel to urban areas for two weeks or less)
❏ first aid kit (pp. 46 – 51)
❏ food and water precautions (pp. 67 – 82)
❏ health and evacuation insurance (pp. 53 – 57)
❏ insect precautions and repellents (pp. 39 – 44)
❏ jet lag (pp. 21 – 24)
❏ locating health care while traveling (pp. 57 - 59)
❏ motion sickness (pp. 25 – 26)
❏ prevention of malaria (pp. 32 – 36)
❏ prevention of traveler's diarrhea (pp. 44 – 46)
❏ sun exposure and sunscreens (pp. 28 – 32)
❏ traveling with prescription drugs (p. 26 – 27)
❏ vaccinations (p. 20)
❏ water purification (pp. 71 – 77)

Special Individual Needs
❏ allergies to stinging insects (pp. 99 – 101)
❏ altitude sickness precautions (pp. 90 – 91)
❏ birth control measures (pp. 114 – 125)
❏ travel with children (Chapter 5, pp. 144 – 167)
❏ medical alert tags (p. 99)
❏ pregnancy and travel (pp. 130 – 141)
❏ prevention of sexually transmitted diseases (pp. 86 – 89)
❏ diabetes (pp. 168 – 171)
❏ traveling with prescription glasses and contacts
    (pp. 103 – 104)
❏ Travel Clinics (p. 460)

Vaccinations and Other Preventive Measures   1

Vaccinations

Your travel itinerary determines needed vaccinations. Immunizations may be legally required to enter a country. Other vaccinations are recommended to prevent illnesses commonly found in a country or region of the world.

Almost everyone gets the routine childhood immunizations necessary to attend public schools, such as polio, measles, rubella, tetanus, and diphtheria. If you didn't get them, by all means obtain them before departure. Certain childhood vaccines may need to be boosted as an adult prior to travel to certain parts of the world. To determine which other vaccinations you need, consult The Centers for Disease Control and Prevention (CDC) either on their internet site at *www.cdc.gov/travel* or tel. 1-888-232-3299, or a local travel medicine clinic (see p.468. In general, travel agents are not reliable sources of information about your health needs. This is not their area of expertise, nor their responsibility.

Start immunizations early. Certain vaccinations can not be given together. Others require a series of injections at intervals of a week or more. If you need a vaccination while traveling, use a reliable clinic listed by IAMAT (International Association for Medical Assistance to Travelers) at 1-716-745-4883 or *iamat.org*, the

International Society of Travel Medicine at *istm.org* , or obtain a name from your local embassy. Be certain all vaccinations, as well as any other injections you obtain while traveling, are given with sterile, disposable equipment. You should request that the syringe and needle are unpackaged in your presence, or in certain circumstances take your own sterile, disposable syringes (see below, p. 19, 21).

Documentation

Carry documentation of your vaccinations, but Yellow Fever vaccine must be recorded on a yellow *International Certificate of Vaccination*. Each injection should be properly entered and signed by the medical provider or their representative. You must show this book on request at international points of entry. Keep it with your passport. It's a good idea to keep a photocopy of these documents separately.

If for medical reasons a legally required vaccination can't be given, obtain documentation from your medical provider. A signed and dated statement on letterhead stationery is sufficient. It should explain the medical reasons why you are unable to receive the vaccine.

Precautions When Obtaining Injections in a Foreign Country

If you require vaccinations or any other injectable medication while traveling, the syringes used must be sterile beyond question. Do not risk infection with AIDS, hepatitis B, or other diseases from contaminated equipment. Insist on sterile, disposable needles and syringes for any injection you receive while traveling.

How do you tell?

Syringes should be made of plastic, not glass, and come in an unopened protective wrapper with no tape around the outside. Needles, if separate from the syringe, should come in protective unopened wrappers.

Vaccination Schedules

Consult the Centers for Disease Control and other websites (see Appendix A, p. 457) or a local travel clinic to see if any of the vaccines listed in Group 2 or 3 are recommended based on your situation and travel plans.

Group 1: All Travelers
   Tetanus-diphtheria (Td)
   Hepatitis A (Havrix, Vaqta)
   MMR (Measles (rubeola), Mumps and
      Rubella (German measles)

Group 2: Special Situations
   Typhoid
      Oral (Vivotif) .
      Injection (Typhim Vi)
   Rabies, pre-exposure
   Influenza
   Pneumococcal pneumonia
   Hepatitis B (Engerix-B or Recombivax. Also
      Twinrix, a combination vaccine for
      Hepatitis A&B)
   Cholera
   Varicella (chickenpox)

Group 3: for Travel in Some Geographic Areas
   Yellow fever
   Japanese encephalitis
   Meningococcal meningitis
   Polio
   Tickborne encephalitis (available only in
      Europe)

We also caution against receiving injectable medications from previously opened multi-dose vials. Confirm that the vaccine or drug is from unopened single or multi-dose vials only. Medication vials will be glass and must be broken open or have a metal covering over a rubber stopper. The metal cover is removed and the sterile needle is then stuck through the stopper to pull the contents into the syringe. During the process of drawing up and injecting the medication, the needle must never come into contact with anything unsterile, such as a finger or tabletop. To confirm safe administration, you will need to ask that any injectable medication be drawn up in your presence.

For extended travel, you may want to ask your medical provider for syringes and needles to add to your first aid kit. If so, carry a written prescription for these items.

In developing countries, many injectable medications are available at pharmacies without a prescription. Frequently the pharmacist or their assistant will offer to give the injection. Do not take advantage of this service unless you can assure yourself that sterile technique is employed.

Several years ago, a Peace Corps Volunteer, stationed alone in a remote area of Honduras, managed to crawl to the local pharmacy after 5 days of intense illness. He was desperately sick, and the shopkeeper had just the thing. "Medicina fuerte — strong medicine," he promised. Obligingly, the injection was given. Too weak to protest, the unfortunate volunteer barely registered a vision of the needle being wiped off with a grubby handkerchief. He soon recovered from the original illness and — much later — from hepatitis B contracted from the contaminated syringe.

Other Preventive Measures

Jet Lag

Traveling east or west across 3 or more time zones puts our daily biological rhythms at odds with environmental cues. These rhythms are chemically regulated daily cycles of hunger, sleep, and wakefulness. They involve changes in hormone levels, kidney function, brain and heart activity, and body temperature. The chief environmental cue for these cycles is sunlight. Until your body reorients to sunrise, sunset, and the living routines of a new location, you are likely to suffer the discomforts known as jet lag.

Flying east generally produces the most severe, prolonged effects of jet lag. Daytime sleepiness and insomnia are the most frequent effects. Other symptoms include poor concentration, fatigue, indigestion, depression, irritability, slowed reflexes, headaches, and memory loss. It's worth noting that north-south travel does not produce jet lag.

After exposure to sunlight on 2 successive days, the body clock effectively resets following exposure to sunlight on the third day. Although the exact mechanism is unknown, the hormone melatonin apparently governs the biological rhythm. Light passing along the optic nerve affects its production in the brain. Consequently, most symptoms of jet lag disappear within 3 days. Travelers who spend daylight hours indoors may take up to a week to fully recover from jet lag symptoms.

There are many strategies to cope with jet lag. They may not all work for everyone, but they should help adjustment to new time zones in the shortest time possible.

Preflight

1. Fly east, fly early; fly west, fly late. Make reservations accordingly. This allows arrival at your destination with the least loss of rest due to the flight itself. It works best for flights of 6 time zones or less.

2. Change sleep patterns to fit more closely the destination time zone. Do this by adjusting your bedtime. For example, on westbound flights go to bed 1 hour later each night for 3 successive nights prior to departure.

On eastbound flights, go to bed 1 hour earlier for three nights before departure. This also works best for flights of up to 6 time zones.

3. If possible, plan to break up very long flights with one day layovers at locations en route to your destination.

4. At the airport, walk around before boarding the plane. Avoid sitting and waiting. Stay active.

5. Avoid overeating and drinking alcohol prior to the flight.

6. Set your watch to the destination time when boarding the plane. This may help psychological adjustment to local time upon landing.

7. Melatonin — at present there is no set schedule for melatonin. Try taking 2-5 mg. orally at bedtime. Start 3 days prior to departure, each night while flying, and for 2-3 days after arriving. Repeat the process when flying home.

8. Other remedies include the use of homeopathic treatments or diets.

In-flight

1. During the flight do stretching exercises in your seat. Walk up and down the aisles as permitted. Avoid cramped positions to help minimize fatigue.

2. Drink water and juices on the plane. Avoid caffeine and alcohol which, along with the dry, pressurized air, promote dehydration. Dehydration makes it harder to sleep at night and may make it more difficult for body rhythms to adjust. On flights from developing countries, drink only water that is bottled or purified.

3. Unfortunately, the quality of sleep on long flights is usually poor, rarely providing adequate rest. Use of sleeping pills is controversial, although many travelers

use them to increase the ease and duration of sleep. These should be used in the lowest dose possible, and only when there will be at least 6 hours of uninterrupted flight time. Don't use alcohol with sleeping pills, since this is a potentially dangerous combination. Some sleeping pills have been linked to retrograde amnesia. This type of amnesia allows you to function normally, but unable later to recall what transpired. The phenomenon is temporary and usually resolves without residual effects.

Postflight

1. Adopt local time and routines immediately upon arrival.

2. For the first 72 hours, allow plenty of time to sleep and rest to compensate for reduced sleep quality and to make the adjustment period easier. If you are using sleeping pills, use a short acting medication such as Ambien or Sonata. Do not use sleeping pills for more then 3 days. Avoid prolonged use of sleeping pills — they can be habit forming.

3. Take walks outdoors for several hours daily for the first 3 days. Sunlight exposure helps reset your biological clock for the new time zone. Following eastbound travel across 6 time zones or less, exposure to bright morning sunlight advances daily rhythms, preparing the body to accept an earlier bedtime. Westbound, exposure to afternoon sunlight appears to delay body rhythms so that the need to sleep comes later. For travel east or west across more than 6 time zones, exposure to midday sun appears to be most effective in resetting the body's biological clock.

4. Avoid critical decision making until you have accli-

mated.

Motion Sickness

Motion sickness is a common problem. On highways, even seasoned travelers may succumb to a combination of rutted roads, dead shock absorbers, and broken seat springs. Travel by several different modes of transportation can overwhelm balance centers in the inner ear and result in nausea, vomiting, fatigue, and loss of equilibrium.

Prevention

Preventing motion sickness is much easier than treating the symptoms once they occur. While medications to prevent motion sickness work fairly well, other preventive measures can be taken. If you're prone to illness, reduce your exposure to modes of transportation that cause you problems. On a bus, plane, boat, or train, it is often helpful to sit near the mid-section. If possible, lie back in a reclining position and close your eyes. Don't try to read. When looking out the window, look as far ahead to the horizon as possible — not to the sides. Eat only small amounts of light foods, and avoid fried foods, alcohol, and overeating both before and during travel.

Sea Bands

"Sea Bands" are light weight, elastic knitted stretch bands with a small, non-corrosive plastic button. Worn on the wrists, they apply pressure to an acupuncture site used to treat motion sickness. They both treat and prevent symptoms. They're a drugless alternative, ideal during pregnancy or conditions such as glaucoma because of the absence of side effects. They're worth a try if you are susceptible to motion sickness.

Medications to prevent motion sickness

Scopolamine — The medication of choice for preventing motion sickness, Transderm-Scop, is a small circular patch. Placed behind your ear, it works for up to 72 hours. Apply it at least 4 hours before the effect is needed.

After putting on the patch, wash your hands thoroughly to remove all of the medication. Otherwise if you rub your eyes, the pupils will become uncomfortably dilated. *Transderm-Scop should not be used by anyone with glaucoma or a history of urinary obstruction.* The patches may produce a dry mouth, disorientation or confusion and in persons over the age of 65 urinary retention. Travelers over 65 should use an over the counter motion sickness medication instead of the Transderm-Scop. patches. The use of $1/2$ of a patch can possibly reduce side effects and still prevent motion sickness in those who are sensitive to medications.

Antihistamines — Many drugs in this class of medications are also commonly used to prevent motion sickness. They include Phenergan (promethazine), Dramamine (dimenhydrinate), Marezine (cyclizine), Antivert or Bonine (meclizine), and Benadryl (diphenhydramine). The main problem with these, especially Benadryl, is that they may cause drowsiness. Start these medications 1–2 hours prior to travel.

Ginger- taken orally, ginger has been reported to help prevent motion sickness and is rapidly growing in popularity.

Treatment

"The only cure for seasickness is to sit on the east side of a barn in the country." The truth is that once vomiting from motion sickness starts, none of the preventive medications have much effect. If possible, stop traveling until symptoms disappear, then take preventive medications before resuming travel. If this is not possible, treat symptoms with a drug to stop vomiting such as Compazine or Tigan (see Part III, p.434). If you can't keep pills down, use the suppository form. It may also help you to get fresh air, focus on the horizon, find a quiet spot to sit or lie down and rest, or nibble on dry crackers.

Traveling with Prescription Drugs

Carry each medication in a container with a proper

prescription label. Don't mix different medications in the same container. These are legal as well as medical precautions. In some countries, carrying any kind of un-marked medication without a prescription is an invitation to harassment. However unjustified, local officials are sometimes in a position to delay travel, deny entry, exact a bribe, or even toss you in jail for smuggling. Proper identification of prescription drugs is a sound precaution.

Travelers who take medicine regularly should carry with them a sufficient quantity for the entire trip plus a small back up supply. Medications may not be easily re-placeable. They may be unavailable, unavailable in the correct dosage, outdated, or found only under a differ-ent trade name.

Carry a written prescription for each medication *sep-arate* from the medications themselves. It should contain the generic name of the drug, which may enable you to find an equivalent medication if needed. Trade names vary from country to country. If you have web access, find the trade name of a drug in any country at www.medicineplanet.com/translator.

During travel, carry medications on your person or in your carry on luggage. If checked bags are stolen or lost, you won't be caught short while awaiting replacement, which may take *weeks*. A travel medicine expert we know recently flew to India from Canada and accidently packed his antimalarial pills in his suitcase — which took an extended holiday in London while he flew to Bombay. Luckily, he didn't get malaria.

Liquid medications require spill-proof containers. If you are flying, leave space in the container for expansion of the liquid.

When traveling to hot humid areas of the world or on water for prolonged periods, protect your medications from moisture. Place them in a sealable plastic bag, keep them refrigerated, or add a packet of a drying agent such as silica gel. This is usually available where ammunition or camera equipment is sold. These measures will help prevent breakdown of the medication.

Sunburn

Excessive sun exposure is a potential hazard to any traveler, especially in the tropics. In addition to fried skin, other dangers include sunstroke, heat cramps, heat exhaustion (see p. 377), and dehydration (see p. 223). Longer term, there is an increased risk for skin cancer, premature skin aging, and eye damage.

Use sunscreens and other protective measures to avoid direct sun exposure. Drink plenty of fluids, avoiding alcohol, to prevent dehydration. Limit your physical activity, especially during the hottest part of the day.

Most of the skin damage caused by the sun is cumulative. Excessive exposure to sunlight results in degenerative changes such as wrinkling and skin aging. It may eventually cause precancerous or cancerous skin lesions. It's the ultraviolet (UV) portion of the light spectrum which is responsible for these changes, and for tanning as well as sunburn.

The spectrum of ultraviolet light is further divided into UV-A and UV-B. UV-A contributes to eye damage and skin damage (including skin cancer), and is the main cause of photosensitivity reactions from drugs. Severe sunburn on exposed areas of the skin characterizes these reactions. UV-B is the major cause of sunburn (as well as tanning) and chronic skin injury, including aging and skin cancer. UV-A and UV-B probably act together to cause skin cancer.

Medically speaking, there is no such thing as a "good tan" or "safe sun". Always minimize your sun exposure and use proper protective measures when outdoors during the day.

Factors Affecting Sun Exposure
Time of day
The earth's ozone layer, or what's left of it, filters out

ultraviolet light. When the sun is directly overhead more UV light reaches the earth's surface. Minimize direct sun exposure from 10 a.m. to 3 p.m.

Altitude

For every increase of 1,000 feet (305 meters), there is a 4% increase in ultraviolet light. The intensity of the sun at 6,000 feet (1,830 meters) is 24% greater than at sea level.

Clouds

Cloudy days cut exposure to ultraviolet light by about 40%. Since it's usually cooler, people stay outdoors longer and often by much more than 40%. Light overcast or haze is especially deceptive. Cloudy days warrant extra vigilance about sun exposure.

Reflective surfaces

Ultraviolet light reflects off white sand or snow by up to 20% and 85%, respectively. Near these surfaces, sun exposure often intensifies. Water also reflects UV light.

Protective Measures

To avoid sunburn, tan slowly — no more than 30 minutes sun exposure the first day. Increase exposure by 5–10 minutes daily thereafter. Use a hat with at least a 3 inch wide brim all the way around, light-colored protective clothing, and sunglasses to avoid overexposure outdoors. Make liberal use of sunscreens and sunblocks on exposed skin. Sunscreens are best applied at least 15-30 minutes prior to sun exposure and reapplied every 2 hours for continued exposure. Use protective lip balm with a sunblock. Be especially careful of sunburn during high exposure activities such as skiing, swimming, or snorkeling. In the water, people stay cool and often lose track of time while their sunscreen washes away.

Clothing

Clothing is not as protective as you might think. It may provide little more than a false sense of security. A white cotton T-shirt has a Sun Protection Factor (SPF) of only 7 when dry and 5 when wet, admitting as much as 50% of UV rays.

Because dark colors absorb UV light, opaque and dark clothing with tight weaves are the most protective. Dark blue denim, for instance, has an SPF of 1000. The problem of course is that dark tightly woven clothes absorb heat and are uncomfortable in hot humid weather. Clothing designed for comfort in the tropics, while still providing good sun protection, is now on the market. SPF ratings are often found on the label. These clothes are lightweight, vented, and dry rapidly.

Some manufacturers of sun protective clothing are:

SunGrubbies- http://sungrubbies.com/ or 1-888-970-1600.

Sun Precautions : 1-800 882 7860 or 1-888-solumbra. Web: http://www. sunprecautions.com.

Sun protective clothing: 1-800-353-8778 or http://www.sunprotectiveclothing.com/

Also try Rit® Sun Guard™ — a laundry additive that washes UV protection into your clothing, giving it the SPF equivalence of 30. It retains effectiveness through 20 washes.

Sunscreens

Use a broad spectrum sunscreen that blocks both ultraviolet A and B rays, with an SPF (Sun Protection Factor) of 15 or greater. SPF numbers from 2–50 or higher measure the degree of protection from a given sunscreen preparation. In theory, it would take that many times as long to produce a sunburn with the sunscreen as it otherwise would without it. SPF #2 provides minimal protection, while SPF #15 or higher provides closer to maximum protection.

In actual use sunscreens may not provide as much sunburn protection as expected from the SPF rating if you don't apply enough. Full body protection for an adult requires about an ounce of sunscreen, or 1/4 of a four ounce bottle. One way to measure is to apply 1/2 teaspoon to each of the following: head and neck, each arm and shoulder, each half of the torso, and one teaspoon to each leg. Don't forget to apply sunscreen to the tops of and behind the ears, to bald spots on the head, and to the back of the arms, legs, and neck. Bicyclists need to protect the low back where shirts may ride up.

Additionally, SPF numbers are meaningless if the sunscreen or sunblock washes off from bathing or sweat. Reapply sunscreens every 2 hours for maximum effectiveness, including those marked "waterproof", " very water resistant", or "water resistant". For continuous water exposure or immersion, reapply more often. Under such conditions waterproof or very water resistant products provide protection for 80 minutes, while water resistant sunscreens protect for 40 minutes.

Carry sufficient sunscreens and sunblock for your entire trip. Many brands are not available overseas. In very hot and humid climates avoid oil based sunscreens. These may increase the risk for heat related problems as they can prevent perspiration and affect internal temperature regulation. It's safer to use water based creams and lotions.

The best UV-A protection is provided by products with Parasol 1789 (avobenzone), such as Neutrogena Sunblock, "PreSun Ultra", or "Ombrelle". Protection from UV-A is especially important when taking medications such as tetracycline or doxycycline which may cause a photosensitivity reaction. A list of photosensitizing drugs is in Part III, pp. 417.

Some people may react to certain sunscreen ingredients such as PABA, particularly when applied to the face. Before using a new sunscreen, test it to make sure it won't cause a reaction. It's a good idea to do this before loading your suitcase with quarts of the stuff for 3 weeks in the Bahamas. Apply a small amount to an area of one arm and observe for a rash or itching. Hypoallergenic and PABA-free sunscreens are available if needed.

Sunblocks
Sunblocks are opaque products, available in many

colors, which totally block out sunlight and look like war paint. They usually contain either zinc oxide or titanium dioxide, and protect against both UV-.A and UV-B light. Use a sunblock for sensitive areas prone to burn, such as nose, ears, and lips.

Sunglasses

The sun's ultraviolet light damages your eyes just as it does the skin. UV light can cause corneal and retinal damage, increase the risk for cancer of the eye and eyelid, and contribute to the development of cataracts. To protect from UV light, sunglasses should be UV rated and labeled for both UV-A and UV-B protection, or endorsed by the American National Standards Institute (ANSI). Unrated sunglasses can often be tested for UV protection by an optometrist or at stores selling prescription lenses.

Sunglasses will also help protect the eyes from dust, dirt, and the glare which causes squinting. Lenses of green or gray plastic are best and should be dark enough so that the eyes cannot be seen through them. In areas of intense glare, such as snow, ice, water, and sand, use sunglasses with side shields to help prevent reflected UV and visible light from entering the eye. Polarized lenses will help filter out reflected light. They will not, however, reduce exposure to UV light unless they are also UV rated.

Artificial tears are a good addition to a first aid kit. They will help protect your eyes from dryness on an airplane, in the desert, or following prolonged exposure to the tropical sun.

Preventing Malaria
(*Malaria Prophylaxis*)

The red blood cell parasite "Plasmodium" causes malaria. It's spread by the bite of the female Anopheles mosquito. Infection can also occur from blood transfusion and congenitally from mother to fetus. Measures against malaria are not legally required for travel in any country. However malaria is on the rise worldwide and we *strongly* recommend the routine use of antimalarial medications and insect precautions.

Individuals with little or no previous exposure to malaria may rapidly progress to severe or sometimes even fatal illness. While you can't prevent all cases of malaria, you can lessen the risk of malaria with preventive measures and by immediate treatment when preventive measures fail. We can't overemphasize the importance of prophylactic medications and protection from mosquito bites for travel in malaria zones. All travelers should use them in any malarious zone, for travel *as brief as a single day*.

Check with your local public health department, travel clinic, or the Centers for Disease Control (CDC) malaria hotline (1-888-232-3228), fax information service at 1-888-232-3299 or website at www.cdc.gov/travel to see if your travel plans include a visit to a malarious zone. Areas of risk include parts of Mexico, Haiti, Central and South America, Africa — particularly in the region of the sub-Sahara — the Middle East, Turkey, the Indian subcontinent, Southeast Asia, China, the Indonesian archipelago, and Oceania.

There are 300–500 million cases of malaria and several million deaths yearly throughout the world, making it one of the leading cause of illness and death. Among U.S. travelers, 3,555 cases of malaria due to P. falciparum were reported during the period 1985-1998. 84% were acquired in sub-Saharan Africa, 7% in Asia, and 6% in the Caribbean and Central and South America. Of 47 fatal infections among US travelers, 78% were acquired in sub-Saharan Africa. Worldwide, malaria is the third leading cause of death from infectious diseases. Canada, Europe, Japan, and Australia are considered free of malaria.

Malaria Prevention During Pregnancy

See Chapter 4, "Women and Travel" (p. 136).

Travel in Malarious Zones

Preventing mosquito bites prevents malaria! This is just as important as taking prophylactic medications. Even while taking antimalarial medications it's possible to contract malaria, as antimalarials do not provide 100% protection. See mosquito precautions, p. 39.

Symptoms may develop as early as 6 days following exposure, or up to months and occasionally even up to 3 years after leaving a malarious zone. It's also possible for symptoms to develop after completing all recommended antimalarial medications.

> *Anyone who develops recurrent fevers, sweats, malaise, and headache during or following travel in a malarious zone should obtain medical evaluation as soon as possible, including blood tests for malaria. Notify your medical provider that you have been in a malerious area.*

Malaria is most effectively treated in the early course of disease. Delaying treatment may have serious or even fatal consequences.

Recommended Preventive Drugs for Travel in Malarious Zones

Recommendations for the prevention and treatment of malaria change regularly. Check with local public health department, travel medicine clinic, or the CDC (see above) for the latest updates. The existence of several species of Plasmo–dium and the spread of drug-resistant strains of the species Plasmodium falciparum complicates the prevention of malaria. The other significant species, P. ovale, P. vivax, and P. malariae, are generally not resistant to antimalarious medications, although resistant strains are now emerging.

Travel in nonresistant malarious areas

This includes Haiti, the Dominican Republic, Central America west of the Panama Canal, Mexico, Egypt and most countries in the Middle East, and parts of Peru.

Chloroquine (Aralen) or Hydroxychloroquine (Plaquenil) — Should be taken orally, after dinner, on the same day *once a week*. Start 1–2 weeks prior to entering the malarious zone, continue weekly during your stay, and for 4 weeks after leaving the zone. Plaquenil is significantly less expensive and is often better tolerated than Aralen.

If side effects do occur, try taking the medication with food, or take 1/2 dose twice a week. If nausea, vomiting, diarrhea, abdominal cramps or an upset stomach occur, instead of chloroquine take hydroxychloroquine sulfate (Plaquenil).

Chloroquine is not recommended for travelers with preexisting retinal degeneration. Chloroquine should be used cautiously by individuals with psoriasis as it can cause a flare-up, and by those of African ancestry as it may cause severe skin itching.

Travel in areas of chloroquine-resistant Plasmodium falciparum

Malaria caused by species of P. falciparum that are resistant to chloroquine is increasing worldwide. One of the following antimalarial medications is usually recommended in chloroquine resistant areas:

Malarone (Atovaquone/Proguanil) 250 mg. — Take one tablet orally once a day beginning 1 day prior to arrival in a malarious zone, each day while in a malarious zone and for one week after leaving the zone. Malarone is not recommended for use during pregnancy or for children under 24 pounds. Do not take Malarone within 10 days of finishing oral typhoid vaccine. Do not take with tetracycline, doxycycline, Reglan (metoclopramide), or rifampin.

Mefloquine (Lariam) 250 mg. — Take one tablet once

a *week* after dinner, starting one to two weeks before entering a malarious zone, each week while in the zone, and for four weeks after leaving the malarious zone. Avoid taking Mefloquine if you are taking Coumadin (warfarin) or cyclosporin, if you have chronic liver or heart conduction problems, a history of current or past psychiatric problems, or have been unable to tolerate mefloquine in the past.

Mefloquine resistance has been reported in the western provinces of Cambodia and in Thailand bordering Myanmar and Cambodia. Use of Malarone or doxycycline these areas is recommended.

Do not take the combination drug of mefloquine and Fansidar marketed as "Fansimef".

Doxycycline 100 mg. — Take one tablet orally once a day beginning 1-2 days before arrival in a malarious zone, **daily** while in a malarious zone, and for four weeks after leaving the zone.

Doxycycline is contraindicated for children under 8 years of age, and during pregnancy and breast-feeding. It may predispose to vaginal yeast infections. It's also photosensitizing and can result in severe sunburn. Taking the medication with dinner may decrease the risk of a photosensitivity reaction. Avoid taking it just before going to bed as it can cause inflammation of your esophagus (esophagitis). Carefully observe protective measures for sun exposure (pp. 28 – 32).

Chloroquine — Take weekly as prescribed for nonresistant areas, plus a daily dose of Proguanil (Paludrine). Proguanil is available over the counter in Canada, Europe (including London's Heathrow airport), and many countries in Africa. *This regime has a high failure rate and is not recommended.*

Emergency Self Treatment

When traveling in chloroquine resistant areas and using no antimalarial prophylaxis or using either chloroquine alone or in combination with daily Proguanil, it is recommended that you carry a self treatment medication. This should be used for any recurring unexplained fever, especially if accompanied by chills, headaches, muscle aches and fatigue, when medical care is not available within 24 hours. This is only a temporary measure and medical evaluation and treatment are necessary *immediately* after self treatment to establish the correct medical diagnosis and treatment. Use one of the following:

Malarone 250 mg. — Take 4 tablets orally at one time for 3 consecutive days (see Part III, p. 439 for side effects and contraindications).

Fansidar — *Do not use if sulfa allergic.* Take 3 tablets orally of Fansidar as a *single one time dose.* Be aware that use of more than 2 doses has been associated with severe, even fatal, drug reactions. Following such use there may be changes in the skin or mucous membranes, including *itching, redness, development of a rash, mouth or genital lesion(s),* or a *sore throat. These may be life-threatening.* Do not use combination medications containing Fansidar, such as Fansimef. Fansimef is available over the counter in certain countries.

Travel in areas with Plasmodium ovale and Plasmodium vivax

Unlike P. falciparum, P. ovale and P. vivax can persist in the liver. They may cause relapses for as long as 4 years after you discontinue preventive drugs. Making sure the type of malaria is properly diagnosed is imperative to appropriate treatment.

Travelers in malarious zones who develop symptoms suggesting malaria after returning home should seek medical help immediately. Report your travel history and the possibility of malaria to your doctor. If malaria due to ovale or vivax is the diagnosis, the drug primaquine can be prescribed. This medication acts against the liver stages of malaria, preventing relapse.

Use of primaquine preventively (without the diagnosis of P. ovale or P. vivax malaria) should be limited to Peace Corps Volunteers, missionaries, or others who will spend an extended period in a malariouszone exposed to either of these Plasmodium species. Prior to taking primaquine, a blood test is required to rule out a particular blood deficiency (G6PD).

If possible, take primaquine at home under medical supervision rather than abroad. This will be feasible for many travelers because the drug is taken once a day for 14 days, usually during the last 2 weeks of the chloroquine or mefloquine treatment following departure from the malarious zone.

Other antimalarial medications

Halofantrine has been used against chloroquine-resistant P. falciparum in other countries. This drug can cause serious heart condition problems — particularly when taking Mefloquine — and should be avoided.

Proguanil (Paludrine) — This medication is not available in the U.S. It is no longer recommended due to its high failure rate. The 200 mg. daily oral dose was taken in combination with weekly chloroquine as an alternative to other anti-malariousmedications in areas of chloroquine-resistant P. falciparum malaria.

Amodiaquine is another drug no longer recommended in chloroquine-resistant areas due to adverse and potentially fatal side effects.

Use of antimalarial medications during breastfeeding — No protection from malaria is provided by the breast milk to the infant. With the exception of doxycycline and Malarone, the use of antimalariousmedications is considered safe for infants who are breastfeeding. All infants and children should take antimalariousmedications if at risk for malaria.

Use of antimalarial medications during pregnancy-

see Chapter 5, "Women and Travel", p. 136.

Use of antimalarial medications for children see Chapter 5, "Travel with Children", pp. 162 – 164.

Overdose of Antimalarial Medications Never exceed the prescribed amount of medication. Overdoses can be fatal. Store medications, especially chloroquine, in childproof containers out of reach of children.

Mosquito and Tick Precautions

Besides causing itching and discomfort, insects carry a number of formidable diseases, including malaria, yellow fever, dengue fever, myiasis, Japanese encephalitis, lyme disease and tickborne encephalitis. The first line of defense is protective clothing, backed up by use of repellents. Many insects are active at dawn and dusk. The mosquitoes that spread malaria, yellow fever, and Japanese encephalitis are active at night and the mosquito which carries dengue fever is active during the day. Insect precautions can therefore be a 24-hour concern.

Clothing

When venturing outside where mosquitoes are active, avoid using scented preparations such as perfume, lotions, hair care products, or deodorants. Wear clothing that covers the neck, arms, legs, and ankles. White or light-colored clothing is least likely to attract insects. Avoid dark-colored clothing.

For maximum protection, treat clothing with a permethrin clothing spray or liquid. Permethrin both repels and kills mosquitoes, ticks, and chiggers upon contact. It's odorless and doesn't stain or effect the clothing. Spray on outer surfaces of clothing and allow to dry before wearing. This may take up to 2 to 4 hours in humid weather. The treated clothing retains its effectiveness through numerous washes up to 2 weeks. It can also be used on tents and mosquito netting.

Insect Repellents

Apply topical insect repellent evenly to all areas of exposed skin except around the eyes and mouth. Repellent can also be applied to clothing, including shoes, socks, cuffs, and caps. Repellents are not effective against stinging insects such as bees and wasps.

Repellents can be washed off by rain or sweat, or when swimming or diving. Repellent is also lost through absorption, evaporation from high temperatures or windy environments, abrasion from clothing, or wiping the skin. An increase of 10° C can cause a 50% reduction in protection time. *To maintain effectiveness, repellents must periodically be reapplied.* Lotions with DEET provide longer protection than other formulations. Sprays, with more alcohol, provide the briefest protection.

DEET

Of the many ingredients traditionally used in repellents, DEET (diethyl-m-toluamide) is without question the most reliably effective. It repels but does not kill a variety of mosquitoes, chiggers, ticks, fleas, and biting flies. On mosquitoes, it may work in part by interfering with the ability of the insect to home in on carbon dioxide and lactic acid.

DEET requires some caution. Most formulations are absorbed through the skin and, though very rare, have caused toxic reactions in children and allergic reactions such as itching, skin rashes, blisters, and swelling. DEET is an eye irritant, and can be fatal if ingested. For these reasons adults should use only insect repellents containing concentrations of 50% or less. Avoid inhalation and eye contact, and do not apply to areas of the hands likely to come into contact with the eyes and mouth. Do not apply DEET under clothing, or to cuts, wounds, or skin that is irritated, infected, or severely sunburned. If a reaction does occur, wash the DEET off thoroughly and seek medical attention. If care is unavailable, see pp. 196 – 198 for treatment.

When applying DEET be careful as it can damage plastics, such as cameras, watch crystals and eyeglass frames, rayon, spandex, and other synthetic fabrics, leather, and painted surfaces. It doesn't affect nylon, cotton, wool or other natural fibers. When applying DEET and a sunscreen, studies show it may decrease the effectiveness of the sunscreen by about 33%. Apply sunscreen first, then the repellent. If applying a combination formulation of sunscreen and insect repellent expect to get the sun protection factor stated on the package. To prevent unnecessary DEET exposure, do not apply combination products solely as a sunscreen. These should be used primarily as daytime repellents. Remember to avoid scented products.

"Ultrathon" is a formulation of 33% DEET in a polymer that prevents absorption into the skin and resists removal by exposure to sweat, rain, and water. It provides protection for up to 12 hours and still rates as one of the best repellents on the market. It can be obtained from Travel Medicine, Inc., 1-800 872-8633 or http://www.travmed.com. Sawyer also makes an extended release formula which is widely available.

Do not use DEET on infants younger than 2 months. Children older than 2 months should use no more then a 50% DEET repellent, although many effective products have 10% or less. Some made especially for children include Off! Skintastic (SC Johnson Wax, 1-800 558-5566), Repel 7% Gel or 10% Camp Lotion for Kids, (WPC Brands- http://www.wpcbrands.com) and Cutter   All Family pump (http://www.cutterinsectrepellent.com/).

How effective is DEET in combination with permethrin-treated clothing? An Alaska study demonstrated 99.9% protection with only one bite per hour over an 8-hour period, compared to unprotected volunteers who averaged 1,188 bites per hour! On a recent elephant trek in northern Thailand one of the authors and his wife, using both DEET and permethrin, were the only travelers in their group not to be eaten alive by mosquitos.

Other repellents

"BiteBlocker" is a plant-based formulation containing soybean, geranium, and coconut oils. It provides protection from mosquitoes and black flies (reportedly equal to DEET) for 3-4 hours. Test the product first on a small patch of skin as allergic reactions to soy and geranium oils have occasionally been reported. Available from http://www.biteblocker.com or on Ebay.

Avon has a number of repellents available. Products formulated without DEET, however, require frequent re-applications.

Citronella is the active compound commonly found in many herbal insect repellents. Studies report that citronella can be effective, but it provides shorter complete protection time than most DEET formulations. Use of citronella products requires applications at intervals of 2 hours or less depending on environmental conditions.

Some people claim that vitamin B1 supplements act as an insect repellent. Studies show that it neither decreases the frequency of bites nor the risk of disease.

Indoor Precautions

Houses and sleeping quarters may also need protection, especially in rural areas. Window and door screens, if present, must fit tightly. They must be free of holes, with a mesh small enough to prevent the entrance of insects such as mosquitos. Use a pyrethrum insect spray in living or sleeping areas during the evening and nighttime hours. After spraying, stay out of the room for 30 minutes until the spray settles. Remember that spraying kills insects already in the room but doesn't deter new ones from entering. Mosquito coils, burned in your room at night, will also help keep insects away. Be aware, however, that coils available in some countries may contain DDT.

Air conditioned rooms allows you to keep the windows and doors closed and insects out. Cool environments are less attractive to many insects.

In Central and South America, there is a risk of Chagas disease from bites of the nocturnal assassin or kissing bug. Avoid sleeping in thatched roofed huts, or use protective netting at night.

Mosquito Nets

In areas of mosquito borne diseases, mosquito nets for the bed are crucial, whether or not you have screens on the rest of the house. Treat mosquito netting with permethrin! It both repels mosquitoes and kills any that touch it on contact, preventing bites that might otherwise occur through the netting.

Rectangular shapes are preferable to cone shapes. Otherwise, skin contact with the netting might allow bites. Netting should have a tightly woven border so it can be tucked under a mattress. It should also be white so that insects can be seen against it or through it. A zipper is a nice extra, allowing easy entrance and exit.

Free standing, portable rectangular mosquito netting is available from IAMAT at 416-652-0137, 716-754-4883, or http://www.iamat.org/index.htm. "La Mosquette" weighs 5 pounds, adjusts to single or double bed size, and is easy to assemble and pack away. Nets impregnated with permethrin that remains effective up to a year are available from Thai Occidental, 5334 Young St., Suite 907, Toronto, Ontario, Canada M2N 6M2. Tel.: 416-498-4277 or fax 416-496-2490. These nets are strong, large enough for a king bed, weigh 2 lbs., and ship for about $70 Canadian.

If living overseas permethrin or deltamethrin liquid may be purchased for treatment of bed nets.

Netting with a minimum of 26 holes per square inch will keep out the smallest mosquito. Tears should be patched with needle and thread, or with tape (duct tape works well). Use the tape back to back, inside and out. Mosquito netting will also keep out spiders, ticks, beetles, flies, roaches, and assassin bugs. It will not, however, keep out sand flies. These insects sometimes transmit *leishmaniasis*. While sand fly netting is available, it's very hot and stuffy to use.

In summary, to obtain maximum protection from mosquitoes:

1. *use an insect repellent containing 50% or less DEET on exposed skin;*

2. *wear protective clothing treated with permethrin;*

3. *use mosquito netting treated with permethrin;*

4. *spray your room with either a permethrin or pyrethrum spray if needed.*

Other Precautions

Note that electrical or sonic insect devices do not repel or kill mosquitoes, and that mosquito nets may provide unintended benefits. A paramedic traveling through South America was sleeping outdoors unprotected. He awoke in the morning with blood on his forehead, puncture wounds, and an area of numbness. He realized he had been bitten by a vampire bat and wisely sought treatment for rabies.

If necessary, shake out your shoes and clothing before dressing in the morning. This will help prevent bites or stings from scorpions, spiders, and the like. In Africa, clothes or diapers left outside to dry should be ironed to kill the eggs of the tumbu fly.

Prevention (Prophylaxis) of Traveler's Diarrhea

Traveler's diarrhea is caused by a wide variety of infectious organisms, including bacteria, viruses and parasites. Nearly 40% of all travelers develop traveler's diarrhea. *Strict adherence to food and beverage precautions is the best prevention* (see pp. 67 – 81). These are summarized in the Nutshell Guide™ (see pp. 105 – 106).

Pepto-Bismol

For travel of 3 weeks or less, Pepto-Bismol can be taken as a preventive. The dosage is 2 chewable tablets, 4 times a day or liquid Pepto-Bismol, 2 tablespoons 4 times a day. Start one day before departure and continue until 2 days after your return. This regimen prevents traveler's diarrhea in up to 60% of cases in some studies. It also avoids taking antibiotics which are usually not recommended unless symptoms have developed. The problem is that the liquid, especially, is too bulky for practical use. The saying is "I need one bag for my clothes and one for my Pepto-Bismol." Some travel medicine experts recommend taking 2 tablets just before and 6 hours after a high risk meal although no data is available on this dosage regimen.

Pepto-Bismol contains salicylic acid, an aspirin-like compound. Don't use it if you are pregnant, have an ulcer, or are taking probenecid, methotrexate, tetracyclines, or anticoagulants such as Coumadin or aspirin routinely as treatment for a medical condition. Don't use Pepto-Bismol if taking doxycycline as an antimalarial. It can prevent or decrease the absorption of doxycycline and other tetracyclines. Avoid Pepto-Bismol if you are allergic to aspirin or your doctor has advised you not to take aspirin, or if you have gout or kidney problems (renal insufficiency). Diabetics on either insulin or oral medications should discuss use of Pepto-Bismol with their doctor. There is an increased risk of low blood sugar (hypoglycemia). Pepto-Bismol is not approved for use in children under 3 years old, and should not be given to children or adolescents who have chicken pox or flu-like symptoms due to the risk for Reye's syndrome.

Pepto-Bismol may turn the tongue and/or stools black and cause mild constipation. These are harmless side effects which disappear after stopping the medication. If ringing in the ears or a burning sensation in the stomach occur, immediately discontinue use.

Antibiotics

Once commonly used for prevention of traveler's diarrhea, antibiotics are usually no longer recommended. Adverse consequences include antibiotic-induced intestinal problems, vaginal yeast infections, medication reactions, photosensitivity and the emergence of drug resistant bacteria. See Chapter 4, p. 137 for information on treatment of traveler's diarrhea during pregnancy.

Several dangerous products once popular for treating diarrhea in western travelers **must be avoided**. These include Enterovioform, chloramphenicol, Clioquinol, Iodoquinol, Mexaform, and Intestopan. These medications can cause severe neurologic or other problems. Treatment of traveler's diarrhea is discussed in Chapter 8, "Stomach and Intestinal Disorders," pp. 226 – 231.

First Aid Kit

A first aid kit can be anything from aspirin and Band-aids to a miniature MASH warehouse. If travel will only be to major cities where doctors and pharmacies are available, take the basics. A rural Peace Corps Volunteer or New Guinea anthropologist will need something more extensive.

When preparing a first aid kit remember that in developing countries all types of medicines are available without prescription. They're often cheaper. There's no need to carry everything, or to carry large quantities.

Have your medical provider assist in planning the kit, particularly if you have any drug allergies, chronic medical conditions, or are pregnant, breast-feeding, or have other special medical needs. Write down specific instructions in the book.

Following is a list of recommended medicines and first aid kit supplies. You can customize the kit depending on several factors. These include the destination, length of stay, anticipated activities, and the local availability of medical supplies and care.

People living and working in rural areas face special problems when medical help isn't readily accessible. Some of the medications will be useful when medical help is not available, or if you choose to be your own doctor under certain conditions.

Basic CPR and first aid classes are highly desirable for all travelers. These are available through the Red Cross, the American Heart Association, and other organizations. The Red Cross has an excellent first aid book with information on the use of triangular bandages, Ace wraps, dressings, and covers other first aid skills. Such preparation is of particular importance for anyone planning to visit remote or rural areas for any length of time.

Parts II and III of this book provide information that you'll need in order to use the medicines in your first aid kit appropriately and safely. Part II also provides guidelines to help determine when medical care is mandatory. These guidelines, together with your first aid kit, will prepare you to cope with most medical contingencies even when help is not immediately available.

Finding Health Care in Foreign Countries

Falling ill in a foreign land can be a terrifying experience. Part II, "Diagnosis and Treatment of Medical Disorders," offers guidelines to help determine when medical care is needed. When it is, who do you turn to for help? Are they qualified? Do they speak English? How much do they charge? Depending on circumstances, there will be a lot of choices, or very few. But there will almost always be a way of locating medical assistance.

Finding Help Before You Go

By far the best way to locate help is to identify potential resources in advance. This can be done inexpensively through one of the following organizations:

Basic First Aid Kit

antacids

antibiotics for traveler's diarrhea

antimalarial medications (if traveling in malarial zones)

aspirin, acetaminophen (Tylenol), or nonsteroidal anti-inflammatories

Band-Aids

Benadryl or other antihistimine (for itching, allergies, or sleep)

Chapstick with sunblock

condoms (if any new sexual contact is even a remote possibility, or as a birth control option)

cotton swabs

dental floss

hydrogen peroxide

insect repellent (with DEET)

Pepto-Bismol and Imodium)

safety pins

scissors

sunscreen products

thermometer

topical antibacterial ointment

tweezers

water purification system (iodine, filter, or apparatus for boiling)

Basic First Aid Kit (Continued)

Optional:

anaphylaxis (allergy) kit if allergic to bee or other insect stings

antihistamines for allergies, artificial tears

"Extractor" for removing animal venom.*

motion sickness medications

medication to prevent altitude sickness (Diamox)

mole skin (for blisters)

mosquito net, permethrin clothing spray, knock-down spray (if needed for mosquitoes, insects)

Optional for women:

medications for menstrual cramps

medications for vaginal yeast infections

medications for urinary tract infections

tampons or sanitary napkins

Reminders: flashlight, Swiss Army Knife, sunglasses, extra prescription glasses, contact lens solution, copy of lens prescription, hearing aid batteries, contraceptives, soap, medications for chronic conditions, and your doctor's phone number. Keep prescription medications in their original labeled containers.

For travel in rural areas for less than 1 month, add:

Ace wrap, 3" width

CAVIT (a temporary dental filling)

adhesive tape, 1" width

cotton

Basic First Aid Kit (Continued)

antibiotics for bacterial skin infections

fine forceps for tick removal (in tick infested areas)

antifungal topical cream for fungal skin infections

aspirin or acetaminophen (Tylenol) with codeine for
   pain

Betadine swabsticks

butterfly bandages or steri-strips,

tincture of benzoin

hydrocortisone topical cream

muscle relaxants

oil of cloves (a dental anesthetic)

oral rehydration solutions

Sam splint**

sterile disposable syringes and needles***

sterile gauze, 2" x 2" and 4" x 4"

sterile gauze roll, 2" or 3" width

For travel in rural areas for up to 6 months, add:

antibiotics for bacterial respiratory infections (see
   Chapter 13)

Silvadene cream

If living or working in rural areas for more than 6 months, add:

antibiotics for eye and ear infections

medicines for intestinal parasites

Elimite

Basic First Aid Kit (Continued)

*We highly recommend the "Extractor" for travel in rural areas. It can be used in the treatment of almost all venomous bites and stings — except for venomous snakes. The "Extractor" is a hard plastic vacuum pump in the shape of a syringe, which creates very powerful suction. It is designed to remove venom through the injection site, whether a bite or a sting. Because of the strong suction, *no cutting is ever* needed. The "Extractor" is supplied with a variety of suction cups for bites to different parts of the body. Because suction is created by pushing in on the plunger rather than by pulling, it can be applied with one hand. The manufacturer states that it can be used to treat bites and stings from scorpions, bees, wasps, hornets, and spiders.

**The Sam Splint is a compact, versatile splint that can be molded into almost any shape and used on any part of the body. It is made by:
   The Seaberg Company, Inc.
   4909 S. Coast Highway, Suite 245
   Newport, Oregon 97365
   ph. 800-818-4726 fax: 541-867-4646
   web: http://www.samsplint.com

***The purpose of carrying syringes and needles is to protect yourself from having blood drawn or shots given with possibly contaminated equipment. This would increase the risk for both AIDS and hepatitis. If you carry these items you must have a written prescription to carry them and you may be hassled at customs.

1. IAMAT (International Association for Medical Assistance to Travelers):   417 Center St. , Lewiston, NY 14092 (716) 754-4883, or at 416-652-0137 (Toronto) or http://www.iamat.org/index.htm.

   IAMAT is the best known traveler's assistance organization. It's a nonprofit group that provides a worldwide directory of physicians, hospitals, and health care centers. If you become ill, locate the nearest IAMAT center in the directory. It will provide you with a list of approved English-speaking doctors, including those on 24-hour call. A physician does an appropriate medical workup, makes referrals if necessary, and even reports to your personal physician at home upon request. He or she will furnish a medical report if you need it for the remainder of your trip.

   IAMAT pledges that their physician referrals will meet a high standard of medical practice, adhere to a fixed fee schedule, and speak English. Furthermore, there is no charge for joining IAMAT, although they do request donations.

2. American Express Travel Related Services

   Tel.: 1-800 528-4800

   American Express has a telephone hotline referral service, "Global Assist", for their cardholders while traveling. It's a worldwide 24-hour emergency medical referral service. They'll also refer translators if needed and notify family members and your office upon request.

   If you already have an American Express card this may meet your needs. If not, you'll have to join. In addition if you have an American Express Platinum card, you may be covered for emergency medical evacuation (see below). Other issuers of premium credit cards have similar referral services.

3. Contact information for hospitals and doctors in some countries can be found on the web at: www.istm.org, *http://travel.state.gov/acs.html#em*r, and other sites (see Appendix A, p. 457.

Pre-arranged Health Insurance and Emergency Services

A variety of insurance plans provide medical coverage and emergency services for international travelers. Costs and coverage vary considerably. Some programs include emergency evacuation and 24-hour telephone hotline services to track down English-speaking doctors or provide quick medical advice. Other programs provide directories of English-speaking doctors, but may require treatment from an MD on their approved list. Some health insurance is available only as an option to comprehensive travel insurance, which usually includes trip cancellation, interruption, baggage loss, and other features. Such plans may or may not fit your needs.

When considering insurance, check the fine print. Many policies exclude coverage for accidents from skiing or other winter sports, skin or scuba diving, mountaineering, and other activities. Some policies exclude coverage in certain politically unstable countries. They may exclude problems related to pregnancy or illness diagnosed or treated within a period, usually 2–6 months, preceding your trip. Some limit medical payments to one or two thousand dollars, which would not be sufficient to cover hospitalization for serious illness or surgery.

Individual health insurance coverage for extended travel should be available for $5.00 a day or less. The following is a list of agencies with health insurance plans for travelers. An even more extensive list can be found on the web at *http://travel.state.gov/medical.html*. The first 4 companies offer policies that pay medical providers directly — an advantage. Most supplemental travel health insurance provides only for reimbursement of medical expenses.

1. Access America (World Access Service Corporation)
   PO Box 90315, Richmond VA 23286
   ph. 1-800-284-8300
   Covers Scuba diving injuries and complications of pregnancy

2. Health Care Abroad (Wallach & Co.)
   PO Box 480, Middleburg, VA 20118
   1-800-237-6615 or http://www.wallach.com

3. Medex International (TravMed Program)
   PO Box 5375, Timonium, MD 21094-5375
   ph. 1-888-MEDEX-00 or 1-800- 527-0218
   web:www.medexassist.com

4. Travel Assistance International (Worldwide Assistance)
   ph. 1-800-821-2828, http://
   www.travelassistance.com
   Covers complications of pregnancy

5. Travel Safe
   PO Box 7050, Wyomissing PA 19610
   1-888-885-7233

6. Travel Insured International Inc. (Travelers Ins. Co.)
   PO Box 280568, E. Hartford, CT 06128-0568
   ph. 1-800-243-3174 http://www.travelinsured.com
   Excludes Scuba diving and pre-existing medical conditions

7. Travelex Insurance Services, Inc.
   11717 Burt Street Suite #202 Omaha, NE 68154
   ph.: 1-888-457-4602 or 1-800-228-9792 ,
   Fax: 1-800-867-9531
   web- http://www.travelex-insurance.com
   Covers medical treatment and emergency evacuation

8. Travel Guard International
   1145 Clark St., Stevens Point, WI 54481
   ph.: 1-800-826-4919. Web- www.travel-guard.com

Covers medical, trip cancellation, baggage; excludes mountain climbing with gear, covers Scuba diving injuries.

9. AIGAssist Global Travel Protection
    1-800-382-6986   web: www.aigtravel.com

10. Travel Insurance Services
    2950 Camino Diablo #300, Walnut Creek 94596-3949
    1-800-937-1387   web: *www.travelinsure.com*

12. ASA, Inc.
    PO Box 50659, Phoenix, Arizona 85076-0659
    1-888-272-8288   web: *www.asaincor.com*

13. Petersen International Insurance Brokers
    23929 Valencia Blvd. Suite 215, Valencia, CA 91355
    1-800-345-8816 *or* 661-254-0006   web: *www.piu.org*

14. Credit Card Assistance (American Express Platinum Card)
    provides medical, financial, and legal assistance for Platinum card holders- tel.: 1-800-345-2639.

Air Ambulance and Emergency Evacuation Services:

15. Traveler's Emergency Network (TEN)
    1100 Pinellas Bayway, St. Petersburg, FL 33715
    1-800-275-4836   Fax #:888-258-2911
    Web: *www.tenweb.com*
    Arranges and pays for emergency evacuation to a medical center for care. No exclusions, except for mountaineering with equipment.

16. International SOS Assistance
    Eight Neshaminy Interplex, STE. 207 , Trevose, PA 19053-6956
    ph. 1-800-523-8662

17. Air Travel Card (for travel industry members only)
    1301 Pennsylvania Ave. NW, Wash. D.C. 20004-1707

1-800-222-4688
web- http://www.air-travel-card.com
Provides emergency evacuation for airline employees, travel agents, and other travel industry employees.

18. Medjet Assistance P.O. Box 610629
4900 69th Street North,
Birmingham, Alabama 35261-0629
1-800-9Medjet

19. IMA (International Medical Assistance)
6000 Stevenson Ave. Ste. 300, Alexandria, VA 22304
1-800-772-9111
web- http://www.universaltravelassistance.com/

Insurance for Divers

In addition to emergency transport, covers use of a hyperbaric chamber for treating decompression illness. .

20. Divers Alert Network (DAN)
The Peter B. Bennett Center
6 West Colony Place Durham, NC 27705 USA
1-800-446-2671 or 919-684-2948
web: *www.DiversAlertNetwork.org*
Their annual membership includes a magazine subscription of interest to divers. DAN enrolls nondivers as well as divers for emergency evacuation

21. Divers Security Insurance
PO Box 57007, Salt Lake City, Utah 84157-0007
1-800-288-4810
Covers decompression, air evacuation, and all water sports except jet skiing, parasailing, and boat racing.

22. PADI Diver Accident Program
c/o Vicencia and Buckley Insurance Services, Inc.
PO Box 4919, Cerritos, CA 90703-4919
1-800-223-9998 web- http://

www.diveinsurance.com/
*Covers disability and loss, medical expenses (including
air transport and decompression treatment) for diving related accidents.*

Finding Help Abroad

Web resources assume internet availability, usually
through local internet cafes or the larger hotels. All of
the telephone referral services, no matter how extensive,
assume you have access to a telephone. They also assume that calls can be put through to the U.S. without
difficulty. Obviously, this is not always the case. What
other options exist for finding help locally?

In Large Urban Areas

There are usually many alternatives in large urban
areas:

1. Your local embassy or consulate will have a list of
   medical services available in the vicinity. Information
   can be obtained during office hours, and frequently
   from a duty officer at other times. U.S. consulates provide names, addresses, fee schedules, and qualifications of local English-speaking physicians. In the U.S.,
   information on U.S. consular services, including addresses, can be obtained by calling

   1-202-647-1488.

2. Large hospitals, medical schools, or university hospitals will usually have English-speaking staff.

3. Major tourist hotels will usually have a list of English-
   speaking doctors available, or they may be able to tell
   you who to contact.

4. International agencies, such as the Red Cross, CARE,
   Catholic Relief Services, American Friends Service
   Committee, and other development or relief agencies,
   or their employees, may be able to make a medical referral — especially in an emergency.

5. Other Americans or foreigners living abroad, or English-speaking nationals are often willing and able to provide medical referrals. Find them by checking foreign-based U.S. companies, American church `, offices of international airlines, even telephone operators — or anywhere else you can think of.

6. In an emergency, head for the emergency room of the nearest large hospital.

In Isolated or Rural Areas

In small towns or rural areas you will be more on your own. Check locally with missionaries, Peace Corps volunteers, Red Cross personnel, or any other foreigners living in the area. Local hotels may be able to locate a doctor, although fees, language, and the quality of care could present difficulties.

If all else fails, check the local pharmacies. In developing nations, especially in isolated areas, the pharmacist frequently finds him- or herself in the position of community doctor. Though language and qualifications are problematic, the local pharmacist is in an ideal position to learn about and respond to the medical needs of the community. The information in Parts II and III of this book will be useful in conjunction with this approach.

In an Emergency

If an international phone line is accessible, call *The Overseas Citizens Emergency Center* in Washington, D.C., which is part of the U.S. State Department. In case of serious illness or other medical emergency, they will help find local medical care through the nearest U.S. embassy or consulate. They can also contact family and friends at home, obtain medical records and send them abroad, help with the transfer of emergency funds, or arrange a medical evacuation. Their phone number is:

1-202-647-5225.

In Case Of Death

Report the death of a relative or traveling companion in a foreign country to your nearest consular or embassy office. They will provide further instructions.

After Obtaining Medical Care

It's important to keep a record of any diagnosis made or treatment obtained while traveling. This information may be vital for follow-up or if problems occur upon returning home. Write down both the brand name and the chemical name of any unfamiliar medication taken. Save the original package or package insert if one is provided. When symptoms of illness occur after returning home, give this information to your doctor. He or she should also be informed of your itinerary, especially after visits to malarious zones or areas of high risk for other illnesses.

Preparations for Extended Travel 2

For trips exceeding 3 – 4 weeks, you may need more than just a vaccination or two to be adequately prepared. Take care of all medical and dental needs before departure. It could make the difference between a successful or disastrous trip.

Medical Preparation

Obtain a complete physical exam if there are any underlying medical conditions such as diabetes or chronic heart or respiratory problems. This is the time to have other health maintenance measures done if needed, such as blood work, a Pap smear, mammogram, EKG, breast, or rectal exam. Besides routine matters such as vaccinations, antimalarial medications, and a first aid kit, we recommend a TB skin test if traveling for 6 months or more or working in close contact with local populations.

With your practitioner, determine if any of the medications suggested in this book are contraindicated, particularly if you have known drug allergies or a chronic medical condition. Have the practitioner recommend alternative medications if possible.

Travel Clinics
Whether or not you have a personal physician,

consider making medical preparations for travel through a travel clinic. Travel clinics are most likely to be on top of changing health conditions worldwide and to know the latest CDC (Centers for Disease Control of the Public Health Service) and WHO (World Health Organizations) recommendations for travelers. Travel clinics can tailor their recommendations according to your health status, itinerary, duration of travel, and anticipated activities. They're also a good place to go for a post-trip medical evaluation, if needed. See Appendix B, p. 460 for a web based list of travel clinics.

Tuberculosis Skin Tests

Travelers who visit developing nations for more than 6 months or who work in areas of risk for TB should consider a TB skin test (PPD) 8-12 weeks or more after their trip. This will determine whether or not exposure to TB has occurred while traveling.

Skip the skin test if you have previously had a positive TB skin test. Obtain the skin test even if you have had BCG vaccine. BCG is a tuberculosis vaccine not routinely used in the U.S. or Europe, but which has been widely used in Asia and elsewhere. It may cause a positive PPD test result. Record all TB tests and their results in the yellow vaccination certificate. For more information on TB see Chapter 9, "Infectious Diseases," pp. 272–273.

Dental Preparation

Travelers face an increased risk of gum and tooth disease. Changes in diet, increased sugar consumption (soft drinks used as a safe water source, etc.), and potential nutritional deficiencies all contribute to the likelihood of dental problems. For these reasons we strongly recommend a thorough dental exam and completion of pending dental work before extended travel.

If nothing else, have your teeth cleaned and checked. One of life's more unendurable experiences under any circumstances is suffering from the pain of a relentless toothache. Imagine it striking on the way to an elegant banquet, or three days out backpacking in the Andes!

Buy dental floss and use it daily. Both flossing and brushing are required to thoroughly remove plaque. If needed, review flossing and brushing techniques with a dentist. Individual concerns, including potential dental emergencies, should also be discussed before travel.

For extended travel in rural areas, add oil of cloves, CAVIT, and possibly I.R.M. to the first aid kit. The first is a dental anesthetic, the latter are temporary filling materials available at dental supply stores. If the need arises, Part II of this book contains instructions on how and when to use them. Also consider taking along .4% sodium fluoride gel, which has proven effective in slowing cavity formation in adults. Not sold over the counter, it's available in the U.S. from dentists. It's difficult to find while traveling.

Foreign Cultures and Culture Shock

Learning to live in a foreign culture can be exciting, rewarding, and a great deal of fun. It can also be very frustrating and demanding. Adopting a new lifestyle, learning the language and customs, changing one's expectations to fit a new reality — all this can require much effort and energy.

Coping with the physical environment, including the health-related challenges, is only one of the problems. Most of us have inherent difficulties adapting to a foreign culture. One of these is our ethnocentrism — a widely shared and deeply ingrained assumption that the way our own culture does things is the way things ought to be done. This unconscious prejudice against other cultures is a major obstacle with which to contend.

Communication is another demanding challenge. Language may be a large part of this, but it is only a part. Whether you know the language or not, the problems of cross-cultural communication can be stressful and diso-rienting. Various symptoms associated with "culture shock" are frequently the result.

Adapting To a Foreign Culture

We offer the following suggestions. Some are obvious, not all will be practical or necessary for everyone, and none are altogether easy.

1. Approach the people and their culture openly. Avoid the trap of looking at foreigners as "underdeveloped" Americans or Europeans.

2. Extend a nonjudgmental attitude not only to native individuals, but to yourself as well. It takes considerable time to develop expectations about peoples' performance — including your own — which are realistic in terms of the new culture.

3. Be patient. Learning about a foreign culture takes time. The meaning of what you observe and experience will not always be readily apparent, but often emerges gradually.

4. Learn the language. If you don't have a working knowledge, this is a top priority. Many countries have language programs which allow you to live and board with a native family. This is an excellent approach.

5. Talk with the people — storekeepers, market vendors, neighbors, waiters, bank tellers — whoever you come in contact with. It is good language practice, and the interactions may help you learn many of the nonverbal cues and gestures used in communication.

6. Research the culture. Learning the cultural history can be invaluable. In addition, the last 30 years have seen a lot of published information on different aspects of cross-cultural communication. Much locally relevant material is floating around in foreign countries;

especially in the capitals. American and European private or government agencies, especially those concerned with economic development, might be of some help. Another place to look are the foreign campuses of American and European universities.

7. Before departure, talk with people who have been there. Once there, talk with foreign residents who have lived there a year or more. They may have insights or interesting anecdotes to share from their experiences.

Culture Shock

Culture shock is an emotional reaction to the experience of being unable to accurately convey or decipher many environmental and behavioral cues. These cues are primarily nonverbal, and normally operate *beyond conscious awareness*. For the foreigner plopped down in another culture, it is as if someone changed the rules — but no one can say what they are.

Culture shock doesn't appear overnight, but brews slowly over several months. It results from an accumulation of disconcerting experiences *which cannot yet be understood*, because the cultural context has not been learned.

Not everyone experiences culture shock. When it does occur, symptoms range from mild to overwhelming. Employment which requires working extensively and effectively with the native people is a good bet to produce at least some of the symptoms.

Symptoms of Culture Shock

Typically, there is a mounting sense of frustration with no tangible cause. Persons working with native citizens may feel discouraged and ineffective. The apparently sourceless frustration is often accompanied by confusion, anxiety, depression, or anger.

Behavior is often defensive. It's common at this juncture to hear criticism or condemnation of the foreign country, its citizens, its institutions, *ad. nauseam*. All aspects of the culture are apt to be vehemently disparaged, excepting possibly the beer. One's organization or employer may also be scapegoated.

Feelings can also run to intense depression and loneliness, with a sense of profound isolation. It's not uncommon to question one's motives for being abroad. Falling ill may elicit or intensify all of these feelings.

Severe culture shock can be a personal crisis — an opportunity for growth — but not without pitfalls. For one thing, it compounds the difficulty of adapting to the new environment. It may permanently sour one's attitude toward foreign countries, not to mention living abroad. One possible outcome is a quick trip home to familiar and comfortable territory.

Surviving the actual experience of culture shock may depend in part on helpful support at the time. The insights and experiences of fellow citizens who have "been there," or who may be having similar experiences, shouldn't be overlooked. The positive resolution of culture shock requires patience, openness to change, and time to accumulate and digest further experience. As the cultural context is gradually learned, adjustments are made.

Culture shock itself can be a strong motivation to understand the new culture and learn to work effectively within it. Like a mirror, the new culture may open up a different view of one's own. In the experience of culture shock also lies a germinal perception of the powerful role culture plays in determining the meaning and significance of our experience.

The Silent Language (1959), by Edward T. Hall, is still probably the best place to start an investigation of problems in cross-cultural communication. We highly recommend it.

Preventive Health Measures

3

The key to successful travel outside western, industrialized countries is adherence to preventive health guidelines. Preventing illness isn't difficult. Increased public health risks, real enough in many places, are largely a threat to people who ignore the problems.

It's easy to make recommendations that will minimize health risks from the environment. The incentives for a traveler to follow them, however, will vary. This is a risk versus gain area. Such factors as length of stay, inconvenience of illness, the availability of health care, and personal traveling styles affect one's decisions.

For maximum safety, adhere strictly to the guidelines summarized in the Nutshell™ Guide at the end of this chapter. In our own experiences, when illness occurred, it usually followed some conscious decision to disregard normal precautions. While it's sometimes appropriate for guidelines to be modified, this can be done safely only when based on knowledge of the potential risks and local health conditions.

The most important preventive health measures pertain to food and water, but there are other sources of infection to consider. Chief among these are skin exposure to contaminated soil or water, and the bites of various insects, especially mosquitoes.

Food and Water Precautions

The Risks

Contaminated food and water are the most common source of illness among travelers. Disorders range from diarrhea to food poisoning, hepatitis to typhoid, cholera to a virtual rogue's gallery of disgusting little (sometimes not so little) parasites. If there's ever any doubt about the safety of the food or water you're using, err on the side of caution. Avoid it. In certain social situations where you may be unavoidably exposed to potentially contaminated food or water, consider taking a dose of Pepto Bismol before and 6 hours after the meal (see p.230).

Contaminated Water

> "Water, water, everywhere
> Nor any drop to drink" — Coleridge

Tap Water

Because water delivery systems are unreliable, don't assume that tap water is safe — ever. *Assume that all tap water is unsafe,* no matter who says it's OK to drink. There are good reasons for this assumption.

Most major cities worldwide have potable water systems. In general they do an adequate job of purifying water much of the time. Unfortunately, the delivery of safe water to the tap cannot be assured *all* the time.

Even where chlorination and water treatment facilities exist, pure water cannot be guaranteed. Routine disinfection of water may not kill certain disease-producing protozoa, particularly giardia and amoebic cysts. Furthermore, contamination can occur at any point in the delivery system between the treatment plant and the tap. This is a problem wherever sewage is inadequately controlled. It's also a problem whenever water service is temporarily disrupted. When water pressure drops, the likelihood of outside contamination increases dramatically.

Another problem in many areas is the onset of the rainy season. Months of accumulated waste can be swept up and delivered to water intake and storage facilities all at once. This flood of garbage and sewage frequently overwhelms treatment and delivery systems. An increase in hepatitis A, typhoid fever, and dysentery commonly occurs at this time, all from tap water that may previously have been safe. This problem can occur during *any* heavy rainfall.

As you can see, there are many reasons not to trust tap water. Wise travelers don't even ask the question, "Is the water safe to drink?"

Rivers, Lakes, and Wells

In rural areas, local water supplies from lakes, rivers, and wells are also suspect. They are often contaminated with human and animal wastes. This is almost assured around small towns, villages, and farms. Even camping in isolated areas can have its surprises. One of the authors discovered he was sharing his source of water for morning coffee with a dead cow, as it came lazily floating by the riverbank. Do you know who your neighbors are upstream?

Ice and Frozen Confections

The rule is, "If you can't trust the water, don't trust the ice." This is a difficult rule for North Americans (not so much Europeans) to observe to the letter on hot, humid, tropical days and nights.

Interestingly, there was one study on the survival of bacteria in iced drinks. It showed that freezing did not completely eliminate any of the bacteria. However, freezing for more than 24 hours did significantly reduce bacterial counts.

Bacterial counts were further reduced when melting ice was exposed to high-proof alcohol, specifically scotch and tequila. By contrast, ice cubes melting in cola, soda water, or plain water showed little or no reduction in bacterial numbers. Finally, the longer ice sat in a drink melting, the higher the bacterial counts became.

One conclusion to be drawn from this study is that enough shigella or other bacteria can survive freezing to cause infection. Another — of dubious merit — is that if you do put ice in your drinks, they should be consumed quickly — using, of course, high-proof alcohol ("To your health, then! Bottom's up!").

Whatever can be said about ice cubes goes for snow-cones and confections made from shaved ice. We also urge avoidance of those mouth watering, succulent pop-sicles made with fresh frozen fruit (such as strawberries) and water. They are irresistible on hot, muggy days in the tropics, but can be lethal. They cost one of the authors five miserable dysenteric days in Mexico City.

Airline Water

Over the years, a number of travelers have success-fully avoided illness abroad only to fall prey to traveler's diarrhea upon returning home. As a consequence the water served by international air carriers on the return flight has fallen under a degree of suspicion.

Some airlines make special efforts to test the water that goes into the airplane holding tank. Water in the holding tank is usually replenished at stopovers on the plane's route, by topping off at major destinations. As we have previously seen, the problem with this water is that it can not be counted on 100% of the time. Even con-scientious spot inspections may fail to reveal a potential source of impure water.

It makes sense to avoid both the drinking water and ice cubes routinely served on flights originating from or with stopovers in developing countries. Either request bottled water from the flight attendants, or take your own bottled or purified water with you on board.

Other Sources of Contaminated Water

Avoid drinks such as smoothies or fresh squeezed juices if tap water has been added. Avoid using tap water for brushing your teeth, or rinsing your mouth or dentures or cleaning your contact lenses. Make sure that glasses, plates, and utensils are dry before using — not wet from washing. Water on the outside of cans or bottles may be contaminated. Always wipe off wet containers before opening them. One of the authors uses a bandana carried in his pocket to conveniently dry cans, bottles, silverware, cups, and plates when necessary.

Note also that the comments regarding tap water and ice cubes apply to all classes of restaurants and hotels, even the top rated, most expensive tourist facilities. Don't be overly reassured by prestige and high prices. Travelers have reported to us that a prestigious hotel in Nepal bears the nickname "Diarrhea Alley."

At this point your reaction might well be "What's left but thirst and despair?" You need not cancel your trip. There are many ways of ensuring that your water and other beverages are safe.

Safe Water and Other Drinks

Bottled Beverages

Canned or bottled beverages are normally OK to drink. They need to be wiped clean and dry before consuming. Internationally known brands of carbonated beverages are usually considered the safest.

Avoid local brands of bottled soft drinks. Local bottlers may use contaminated or unpurified water for their drinks. If so, the high sugar content can promote bacterial growth.

In restaurants, an excellent way to avoid tap water as well as sugar and caffeine overload is to order soda or mineral water. For variety, these can be flavored with limes or other citrus. The acidity from carbonation discourages bacterial growth. Carbonated water may be high in sodium, however.

Other safe beverages include beer and wine, and other alcoholic drinks (with tonic or soda water but not tap water). Tea and coffee are safe if made from boiled water.

Purified Bottled Water

Purified bottled water is usually safe, but not always. This appears to be especially true of bottled water in Nepal and India. Recent studies show that up to 80% of tested bottled water in Nepal is contaminated with bacteria that can cause diarrhea. There have also been reports of bad bottled water from Vietnam. It's also not unknown for delivery truck drivers to fill their bottles with tap water and pocket the proceeds. We suggest you distrust bottled water unless you break the producer's seal from the bottle yourself. Even then be careful. If the water smells or tastes peculiar or has particulate material in it, dump it. With the increasing number of reports of bad bottled water, you may want to filter or iodine even bottled water to be on the safe side.

Methods of Water Purification

There are three main ways of purifying water: boiling, chemicals, and special filters. Prior to using *any* of these methods, cloudy or dirty water should first be coarsely filtered. For this purpose an inexpensive commercial filter, clean cloth, or coffee filter is usually adequate. If none of these are available, the water can be poured after allowing the sediment to settle.

Boiling

Boiling is by far the most reliable way to ensure that water is safe to drink, and coffee, tea, soup, or other hot drinks made from boiled water are equally safe. Water boiling at 212°F (100°C) will kill all dangerous bacteria, viruses, and parasites. Their protein structures begin to denature at about 170°F (76°C). A small electrical immersion coil heater is a quick and practical way to boil water wherever electricity is available. You may need to purchase a plug adapter and possibly a current converter to make the coil compatible with available current.

Bring the water to a vigorous boil. Allow it to cool before drinking. If you are at high altitudes, remember that the boiling point of water decreases by 2°F (1.1°C) for every 1,000 feet (305 meters) above sea level. Boil the water for one additional minute for every 3,000 feet (1,000 meters) of elevation above 8000 feet. Many high altitude locations lack natural fuels, especially if hiking above the tree line. A pressure cooker can save time and fuel at all elevations.

If you have no available means of water purification it makes sense to use hot rather than cold water out of the tap. This is particularly true if you are trying to prevent or correct dehydration due to diarrhea. Any fluid is better than no fluids if you are dehydrated. Allow the hot water to cool to room temperature. Remember, this water may still be contaminated and should not be used regularly as a source of drinking water.

Chemical Water Treatment

Iodine or chlorine can be used to treat water of uncertain potability. However, neither one will kill cyclospora or cryptosporidium, two bacteria that may cause diarrhea. These organisms are not widespread, although the incidence of cyclospora is increasing worldwide. Boiling, use of a filter with an iodine contact system, or a combination of filtering and chemicals will kill these organisms.

Given a choice of chemicals, iodine is always preferable. Chlorine should be used only as a last resort, because- unlike iodine- it can not be counted on to kill parasites such as amoebas or giardia, or certain viruses that attack the intestinal tract.

Both chlorine and iodine alter the taste of the water, which initially may seem unpleasant. After the appropriate treatment time, taste may be improved by:

1. adding flavor with powdered drinks (such as Tang or Gator-ade), or juice from fresh citrus;

2. using a granulated activated charcoal filter;

3. adding 50 mg. or more of ascorbic acid (vitamin C),

available as granules or powder, to a liter/quart of water;

4. adding a few granules of sodium thiosulfate per liter of water (available at chemical supply stores). This changes the chemical structure of iodine and chlorine to iodide and chloride, eliminating both their taste and color.

Do not filter or add flavoring or chemicals to change the taste of treated water until after the recommended contact time.

Before using iodine or chlorine, always filter cloudy or dirty water through a clean cloth or coffee filter to remove sediment and particles of organic matter.

Iodine- should not be used by individuals who are hyperthyroid or have iodine allergies. It can be used safely during pregnancy for a maximum of 3 weeks. It's otherwise easy, safe, and effective.

There are 3 available forms — 2% tincture of iodine, iodine crystals, and tablets. Crystals and tablets carry directions on the bottle. Simply add the specified amount of iodine to the desired quantity of water, and let sit. For clear water at room temperature the manufacturer's recommended length of contact time is 30 minutes, but it is best to let it sit for at least one hour to be sure that all giardia are killed. For cold or cloudy water, the amount of iodine is usually doubled and the time increased. It's best to allow very cold water to come to room temperature prior to treatment.

Recent information shows that iodine tablets and crystals are only about 90% effective against giardia after 30 minutes of contact, and 2% tincture somewhat less than that. After 8 hours, however, all 3 are virtually 100% effective. If you mix your iodine and water at night, you'll be all set to go the following morning.

For extended trips crystals are preferable to tablets and liquid as their potency does not decrease with exposure to heat, air, moisture, and time.   Remember to check the expiration date. A bottle of "Polar Pure" iodine crystals makes about 2,000 quarts of purified water. The chemical name for the tablets is tetraglycine hydroperiodide; some brand names are *Globaline, Potable Agua,* and *Coghlans*. Both crystals and tablets are available at sporting goods stores and pharmacies in the U.S. They may be difficult or impossible to find while traveling.

Tincture of iodine (2%) is widely available. One disadvantage is that it will stain anything it touches if the container is spilled or broken. To purify water, add 5 drops per quart or liter of clear water, or 10 drops if the water is cloudy or cold. Let the solution stand for a minimum of one hour before drinking.

A 10% providone iodine solution (Betadine) has been used for *emergency* water purification by the militaries of some countries. This use has **not** been approved by the Food and Drug Administration (FDA) in the United States. The suggested dose is 8 drops per quart of clear water, 16 drops per quart of cold or cloudy water. Wait 30 minutes before drinking, or up to 8 hours for increased protection from giardia.

Chlorine — Don't use chlorine if water can be boiled or treated with iodine. If these alternatives are unavailable, use either Halazone tablets or standard liquid laundry bleach (usually 5.25%). Be sure to check the percentage of liquid bleach on the label. Use the following chart to determine the number of drops to be added to each quart or liter of water.

Determining How Much Chlorine To Use

percent chlorine solution	Drops per quart or liter of:	
	clear water	cloudy water
1%	0	20
4-6%	2	4
7-10%	1	2
unknown	10	20

Mix thoroughly and let stand for 30 minutes. A slight chlorine odor should be detectable in the water. If not, repeat the process and let stand for an additional 15–20 minutes.

Chlorine crystals produced by Sanitizer are frequently used for treating water stored on boats. The resulting high levels of chlorination help prevent algae and bacteria growth during storage.

Filters

Micropore filters may be the ultimate convenience in water purification for travelers. Most filters, though, have one drawback. They cannot filter out viruses, so they will not protect you against waterborne viral infections. These include hepatitis A, polio, and the viral causes of traveler's diarrhea.

Filters with a sufficiently small pore size will protect against bacterial and parasitic infections transmitted through water. Disease-producing bacteria average around .5 microns in diameter, and none are smaller than .2 microns. Protozoa such as giardia and amoebas and the eggs of other parasites are even larger, ranging from 5 to 20 microns or more. Therefore any filter with a pore size of .2 microns or smaller is more than adequate for anything except viruses.

When using a micropore filter, let cloudy water settle out or prefilter the water with a course filter, clean cloth, or coffee filter. If the filter contains a chemical element, heat cold water or allow it to come to room temperature before filtering.

Iodine Contact Filters

The most appropriate and easy to use micropore water filters for travel are those with an additional iodine contact system, which kills viruses. Some of the more popular water filters, such as the "PUR" and "Sweetwater," may no longer be available. Check the web or your local camping/travel store for the latest products with iodine resin technology. Among the iodine resin filters which may still be available are the Water Technologies Corporation's Puri-jug, Penta Pour Bucket, and Travel Tap Faucet Filter. These are good for hotel use and long term residency.

Use your filter on water from all potentially contaminated sources, such as rivers, lakes, and wells. Use it on tap water for drinking or for brushing your teeth. But remember that unless the filter has an iodine element, it will not protect against viral infections.

Charcoal Filters

Filters with granulated active charcoal (GAC)/ charcoal resin remove pollutants by absorption — including most organic and many inorganic chemicals, and radioactive particles. This can improve the safety, color, smell, and taste of the water, and eliminate the taste of iodine and chlorine. GAC filters do not, however, disinfect water. These filters should be used if there is concern about chemical or nuclear pollution of the water source. Use the GAC filter after first boiling the water, or following the appropriate contact time for chemical purification.

More Sources Of Pure Water

With some imagination and preparation, it's possible to travel almost anywhere and still ensure a safe supply of drinking water. One woman we met, a Bahai missionary in Honduras, traveled frequently to remote Indian villages by mule. She made a habit of picking fresh lemon grass outside of town. Upon visiting in the indigenous homes, she would offer the lemon grass with instructions to boil the leaves for at least 5 minutes. Stick cinnamon or any other herbal tea could be used the same way, thus ensuring a supply of water purified by boiling.

A wide variety of drinks are prepared by natives of local cultures, especially during regional fairs and festivals. If the drinks are boiled and served hot, they are usually safe depending on how hygienically the utensils or containers are handled. Again, this is a risk/reward area that requires individual judgement. The process of exploring a culture and getting to know its people sometimes requires a relaxation of customary precautions.

Food

Contaminated food is a major source of illness among travelers. Because impure water used to wash or prepare food is a source of contamination, most of the waterborne diseases already discussed can be passed along in food. Food handlers are another primary cause of contamination. Whenever handwashing is inadequate and intestinal disease widespread, the people involved in harvesting, transporting, preparing, and serving food are all potential sources of infection.

Contamination also occurs from irrigation water or fertilizer which may contain human and animal wastes. In markets and restaurants, flies or other insects may spread disease organisms to food.

In developed countries refrigeration is taken for granted in all aspects of food transportation, storage, and preparation. In the developing world this is often a luxury. Unrefrigerated, food spoils rapidly and even slight contamination can result in rapid bacterial growth, especially in warm or tropical climates.

It pays to take responsibility for the safety of your food in developing countries. Even restricting yourself to restaurants at 5-star hotels can be futile in preventing illnesses like traveler's diarrhea. Although the dining room is elegant, the kitchen standards may be lax. It's easy to imagine food preparers not washing their hands after using the restroom, holes in the screens or a back door left open admitting a host of flies, vegetables arriving contaminated from the local market, the cook dicing them after cutting up raw chicken on the same cutting board, and all the bacteria multiplying happily on food left unrefrigerated. Sitting down to a gourmet meal, you face an entire zoological horde incubating in your entree. Learn what foods are safe or unsafe- and congratulate yourself in advance on the illnesses you'll miss out on.

Safe and Unsafe Foods

Some foods can be eaten safely without cooking or special treatment, such as foods with intact skins that you peel yourself. This includes most fruits (but not berries) and vegetables such as onions or cucumbers. The same foods peeled by others in restaurants can't be considered free of risk.

Cooked Foods

Boiled vegetables served hot (not reheated) are safe. Steaming, however, isn't as reliable a cooking method as boiling. Not all surfaces are reached by the steam so parasite eggs may not be killed. Beans, rice, and other cooked grains and legumes are safe to eat as long as they are hot and steaming (in India, several travelers have developed cholera after eating cold rice).

Beef, pork, lamb, and fish are safe — if well-cooked (medium-well to well done) — and served hot. Avoid ordering meats "rare" or "medium- rare." In addition to bacterial illnesses, raw or insufficiently cooked beef, pork, and other meats, as well as freshwater fish, are a source of parasitic infections. Eating raw shellfish such as oysters also entails a risk of hepatitis and cholera. It's best to avoid all raw or insufficiently cooked meat and fish, including shellfish.

Menu items which use sauces for meat, fish, and vegetable dishes are best avoided as they can contaminate easily. The sauces are also sometimes used to disguise spoilage. Dishes prepared with mayonnaise, like potato salad, are a good medium for bacterial growth. The same is true of such high protein foods as chicken or eggs, including custard. If these dishes are likely to have been prepared well in advance of serving, such as at party or picnic buffets, they should be avoided. Foods such as lasagna, quiches, and casseroles may have been cooked earlier in the day and sat incubating bacteria. When served without sufficient reheating, these also pose a risk.

If you do your own cooking, consider investing in a pressure cooker. Not only will it save on fuel, but it's an excellent way to make sure food is thoroughly cooked and safe to eat.

Ciguatera fish poisoning — Some tropical reef fish, even when cooked, pose a hazard of ciguatera fish poisoning. Red snapper, grouper, barracuda, amberjack, sea bass, and other tropical reef predators can accumulate the toxin. Though infrequent, the potential for ciguatera poisoning exists in all subtropical and tropical areas of the West Indies, Pacific, and Indian oceans (see p. 390).

Canned foods

Canned foods are usually safe. Avoid cans with rust or swollen ends or sides. Once opened they should be consumed, refrigerated, or discarded.

Bread and baked goods

These are usually safe, but avoid pastries filled with cream or custard.

Milk and dairy products

Unless pasteurized, milk and all of its derivative products carry a risk of typhoid fever, tuberculosis, brucellosis, traveler's diarrhea, and other bacterial infections. Canned evaporated milk, condensed milk, or powdered milk are good milk substitutes if pasteurized milk cannot be obtained. In preparing powdered milk be sure to use purified water.

Raw milk can also be pasteurized by heating to 143° F (62° C) for 30 minutes. An alternative is to scald or "flash" heat almost to boiling for just under a minute.

Salads and green leafy vegetables

Fresh green leafy vegetables, radishes, and other ground crops used in salads are a problem. The water and fertilizers used to grow them are often contaminated, making them a source of disease. Yet green leafy vegetables are a major source of iron and B vitamins. One strategy often used is to soak leafy vegetables in chlorine or iodine solutions. The concentration can be slightly higher than that used for water purification. Unfortunately, this procedure is less than 100% effective, even using iodine. Thorough scrubbing and dipping in hot or boiling water is also unlikely to be completely effective.

Travelers who don't give up salads should probably use some combination of the above measures to clean their unpeelable vegetables. Use iodine rather than chlorine as a chemical disinfectant. Better yet, substitute cabbage for spinach or lettuce in homemade salads and throw away the outer layer of leaves. By peeling cabbage, onions, cucumbers, tomatoes, and the like, it's possible to minimize the health risk from fresh, uncooked vegetables.

Restaurants, Street Vendors, and the Market Place

Restaurants catering to foreign travelers may be more attentive to food preparation and handling. Certainly the very expensive tourist hotels and restaurants, and the international chains, have an interest in maintaining high standards. What about other places? It may not always be wise to assume the safety of a restaurant, just because it caters to the tourist trade. One of the authors took care of 4 (out of 10) elderly travelers who developed typhoid fever while staying exclusively at 5-star hotels in India. The quality of food and water may be better in a 5 star hotel, but the kitchen staff don't live in the hotel and can bring diseases with them.

To some degree, whatever risks exist may be shared equally by all local establishments. In many cities and villages, especially the smaller ones, restaurants share the same market sources for their meats and produce. They share the same water supply. Contamination by food-handlers may be as likely in one place as another.

However, an inaccessible kitchen may well be more lax in general health practices than a kitchen under public scrutiny. It's easier to throw the food you dropped on the floor back in the pot and to tolerate a horde of flies when the customers aren't watching.

Logic argues that it may be safer to eat where the kitchen is open to inspection. Where the cooking is accessible, it's possible to verify for yourself that there are no flies, that dishes are well-cooked and kept hot. You can point to the food you want, rather than select blindly from a menu. An inspection of prospective eating places will many times yield a market stall or smaller restaurant that has appetizing food and an acceptable standard of cleanliness. The prices are often cheaper and there may be a wider variety of native foods than the usual tourist menu provides.

When it comes to street vendors, food can be found that is obviously safe. Fresh corn-on-the-cob pulled from boiling water is a good example.

Certain street foods, no matter how tempting, must be avoided. Sliced fruit such as watermelon and pineapple is frequently kept moist by periodic dowsing from a bucket of obviously questionable water. Look for it and you'll find it. Also glasses, dishes, and other serving containers may be used by more than one customer without washing. Or, they may be washed on the spot in what looks like gray swamp water. The point is that in selecting food from either restaurants or street vendors, your own observations can serve as a guide to what is or isn't safe. This is simply not possible in most other establishments, including those that cater to tourists.

The same principle applies to the marketplace. Observing the market scene before buying, you can usually pick up enough clues to eat safely. A word of caution,

though — things are not always what they seem..
Friends of ours were forced to live in Morocco for an extended period of time after their van broke down. They
quickly learned to buy the meat in the marketplace that
was covered with flies. The flyless meat got that way by
repeated applications of insecticide, which many mer-
chants kept handily accessible under the counter.

Airline Food

On airplanes that are leaving developing countries,
avoid the salads. Food on the planes will be prepared in
the country you are leaving from. The same health risks
you would find in country may be found on the airplane. A few years ago a large number of travelers on a
US airline returning from Peru developed cholera from
the seafood salad.

The sacrifices made to adhere to food and water precautions may seem like a lot of trouble, but they will
help you avoid the most common sources of illness.

Safety Issues

Transportation Safety

Motor vehicle travel is the number one cause of accidental death in travelers. At least 750 Americans die
each year in overseas motor vehicle accidents. The risk
for death from motor vehicle accidents is 7-13 times
greater in developing countries. Careful selection of
your transportation can reduce the risk of trauma and
death. Motorbike accidents rank among the highest risk.
In Bermuda 92% of all accidents were due to motorbikes.
When riding motorcycles, bikes, or mopeds always use a
helmet. Use of a motorcycle or moped with the use of alcohol increases the risk of injury. Avoid night driving,
overcrowded public transportation, and flying on airlines with poor safety records. When renting cars always
check that tires and brakes are in good condition. Use
seatbelts when available. Risk increases greatly when

alcoholic beverages are factored in- do not drink and drive.

Water Sports Safety

Water sport accidents are very common among travelers, and drowning is a frequent cause of death. Swimming or diving under the influence of alcohol increases the risk for death or injury. Surfing poses a risk for lacerations, abrasions, puncture wounds and occasionally back, shoulder, and head injuries. Wounds or injuries from coral, marine animals, or trash such as glass or metal frequently lead to secondary bacterial infections. See p. 185 for wound treatment and pp. 386–391 for marine animal hazards.

Observe the following safety precautions when swimming:

1. Never swim alone or under the influence of drugs or alcohol.

2. Never dive head first into an unfamiliar body of water. Even familiar areas may be hazardous — swift rivers can move sandbars overnight. The shallow end of a swimming pool is *always* a dangerous place to dive into.

3. Beaches where no one else is swimming might pose a risk from rip tides, sharks, or in some areas even crocodiles- inquire about hazards with local residents. Corals, jellyfish, stingrays and other stinging sea life may be hazardous in certain areas.

Violence Related Injuries

Assaults, robbery and rape are a concern for all travelers. Avoid walking or traveling at night especially in unfamiliar areas. In Arequipa, Peru, a traveler taking a taxi at night to the train station was driven into a dark alley and robbed of everything he had. Do not wear expensive jewelry, flashy or inappropriate clothing, or show large sums of money. Avoid driving expensive cars.

Rental cars clearly labeled "rental vehicle" on the license plate or elsewhere may be more frequent targets of break-ins- avoid them if possible. Avoid buying illegal drugs. Check state department travel warnings and the consular information sheet for your region or country of travel prior to departure: http://travel.state.gov/travel_warnings.html.

Contact with Contaminated Soil

Hookworms are found in all developing countries. Hookworm eggs are passed in human feces and the hatched larvae enter the body through skin contact. They then migrate to the intestines where they attach to the intestinal wall and feed on blood and other substances. Major hookworm infestations result in a loss of blood and protein and can cause anemia. Hookworms passed in the feces of domestic cats and dogs don't cause intestinal infection, but can cause a skin rash called "creeping eruption" (cutaneous larva migrans, p. 200).

Prevention

Avoid going barefoot wherever there is a chance of soil contamination with human or animal feces. Avoid laying on beaches where cats and dogs roam. As a general rule, don't go barefoot outdoors in either rural or urban areas of developing countries. This not only protects against hookworm, but also bites of insects and snakes, and injuries such as cuts or puncture wounds that can lead to infection.

Contact with Contaminated Water

Bacterial eye, ear, and skin infections can all be transmitted by skin contact with contaminated fresh or salt water. Don't swim or bathe near sewage outlets in oceans or bays, lakes, streams, or rivers, or near towns where water is likely contaminated with human or animal feces. Swimming in chlorinated pools is considered safe; avoid swallowing the water. In some areas, skin contact with fresh water also poses a risk for leptospirosis and schistosomiasis, also known as bilharziasis.

Schistosomiasis (Bilharziasis)

An unpleasant parasitic disease, schistosomiasis is potentially quite dangerous and very widespread as some 200 million people worldwide are infected. Wherever it is prevalent all sources of fresh water should be considered potentially contaminated. This includes lakes, streams, rivers, and even irrigation canals. Since there is no practical way for the traveler to distinguish between infected and noninfected water, *all sources of fresh water in regions with schistosomiasis should be viewed as potentially infectious and avoided.*

Risk is particularly high in Africa, especially Egypt and the sub-Sahara and is spreading to many places where it was previously absent. Other areas include the Middle East, India, Indonesia, Celebes, Laos, Thailand, the Philippines- in fact, most of southeast Asia. Risk is high in parts of China, especially southern China. In the Americas, areas of high risk include the northern two-thirds of South America including Brazil, and some Caribbean islands including Puerto Rico, Santo Domingo, and Santa Lucia.

Prevention

Obviously, avoid swimming, washing, and bathing in fresh water in these areas. Stagnant or slowly moving water is especially risky. Wear high protective waterproof boots if skin contact is unavoidable, as when fording streams or rivers. Apply rubbing alcohol to areas of skin exposed to water and then dry thoroughly. If rubbing alcohol isn't available, immediate and vigorous towel drying will reduce the risk of infection.

Drinking contaminated water can also result in schistosomiasis infection. Purify fresh water for drinking or bathing by boiling or heating for 5 minutes at 50° C

(120° F), filtering, or by treating with iodine or chlorine as previously recommended. Water for bathing can be made safe by letting it stand in a container for at least 3 days. Filtering water with paper coffee filters may also be effective in removing the parasite.

Upon return from travel if you think you may have been exposed to schistosome-infected fresh water, see your medical provider to undergo screening tests.

Leptospirosis is a bacterial infection spread by water contaminated with the urine of wild or domestic mammals, including rodents. Exposure usually occurs from contact with fresh water, wet soil, or vegetation through mucous membranes or cuts in the skin. The risk is worldwide especially in the tropics, and increases after heavy rainfall or flooding. Swamps, ponds, flooded agricultural areas, and occasionally lakes and rivers are high risk areas. In 1997, nine white water rafters from the United States were infected during a river trip in Costa Rica. To prevent infection, avoid contact with fresh water and mud. Wear protective clothing, such as waterproof boots or waders, during recreational or work activities that might result in contact with contaminated water. Rafters in high risk areas need to carefully cover all cuts and abrasions. If thrown out of the boat, keep your eyes closed under water, avoid swallowing water, blow your nose, and shower as soon as possible. For symptoms and treatment, see Chapter 10, "Tropical Diseases", p. 297.

Insects

See "Mosquito and Tick Precautions," pp. 39 – 44.

Sexually Transmitted Diseases

International travelers may be at increased risk of contracting sexually transmitted diseases (STD's). For various reasons, travelers out of their normal environments are sometimes more sexually active.

To decrease the risk of STD's, avoid casual sexual encounters. Having multiple contacts with different partners is dangerous behavior. Especially risky are contacts with prostitutes, intravenous drug users, bisexual or homosexual men, or a person who has or had multiple partners. Avoid sex clubs and prostitutes as this is the main way that HIV infection is passed in most developing countries. As has been said, "sex could truly be something to die for".

All condoms will help protect both men and women from bacterial infections such as gonorrhea and chlamydia. Only condoms made from *latex* will also protect against herpes, HIV, and other viral infections. Make sure the product says "latex" on the package when you make your purchase.

It's unrealistic, however, to count on a condom for absolute protection. On occasion they may leak, break, or unknowingly slip off. In fact, condoms manufactured in developing countries have a higher failure rate than those produced in industrialized nations. It may be best therefore to take a supply of condoms with you. Keep some in your first aid kit, as the need for a condom may be a true emergency.

Other barrier methods of birth control for women offer some safety. Use of a diaphragm or cervical cap in conjunction with spermicide, for example, provides protection from many sexually transmitted diseases.

It goes without saying that certain sexual practices, especially involving the anus or rectum, spread infectious organisms. Avoid risky behavior. If you do have unsafe sexual contact while traveling, consult your medical provider for evaluation upon returning home.

AIDS and the Traveler

AIDS (Acquired Immune Deficiency Syndrome) or HIV (human immunodeficiency virus) infection has spread throughout the world. AIDS has been reported from more than 100 countries. The risk to travelers is determined less by their destination or itinerary than by their individual behavior. As frightening as AIDS is, it's a preventable disease.

There is no documented evidence of HIV transmission through nonsexual casual contacts, air, food, water, contact with inanimate objects, or through mosquitos or other insects. Travelers are at increased risk for acquiring HIV infection if they engage in the following behaviors:

1. sexual intercourse (heterosexual or homosexual) with an infected person;

2. use of unsterilized syringes or needles for any injections (intravenous drugs, tattooing, acupuncture, or medical/dental procedures);

3. treatment with blood, blood components, or clotting factor concentrates in countries that don't screen donated plasma or blood for HIV antibodies.

Travelers should avoid sexual encounters with anyone in a high-risk category for HIV infection. This includes IV drug users, prostitutes (male or female) or others with a history of multiple sexual partners, homosexual or bisexual men, and hemophiliacs. Avoid sex clubs, no matter how much will power you think you have. Latex condoms may decrease but not entirely eliminate the transmission risk of HIV. Use of a latex condom is encouraged for any new sexual encounter, whether the contact is vaginal, oral, or anal. Diaphragms in combination with spermicide may provide additional protection.

In many non-western countries there is inadequate testing of blood or blood products for HIV infection. Avoid locally produced blood clotting factors, immune globulin, and blood products for transfusion. Needles used to draw blood or administer injections should be sterile and disposable. Diabetics or others who require frequent injections should carry a supply of syringes and needles sufficient to last their entire stay abroad. Make an exception only when a foreign supply of sterile supplies has been confirmed in advance of travel. Carry a prescription and a letter from your physician detailing the medical need for these items.

High, Deep, and Dark Places

As Richard Halliburton discovered, new environments can lure us to exotic challenges as well as dangers. Unlike him, few of us will feel compelled by our first view of Mt. Fuji to improvise an immediate ascent — alone, and in the middle of winter! Yet few of us can resist the view from "just over there. . . ." New places tempt us, begging to be experienced, explored, and occasionally surmounted. This section covers the special hazards and requirements of high elevations, underwater environments (Scuba diving), and caves.

High Places: Safety at High Altitudes

There are increasing risks in activity as you ascend above 6,000-8,000 feet (1,800–2,400 meters). This is just as true for young, healthy travelers as for the old or infirm, although certain chronic medical conditions may require special precautions.

Chronic Health Conditions

Travel above 6,000 feet (3,660 meters) may aggravate some medical conditions. Prior medical consultation and consent is strongly recommended for travelers with:

1. chronic lung conditions such as asthma, emphysema, COPD, or a history of a collapsed lung (spontaneous pneumothorax)

2. severe anemia, recent or chronic, including sickle cell anemia

3. a recent heart attack, history of angina, or other heart problems

For any of these conditions, check the elevation of

stopovers on your scheduled itinerary. Every year a few travelers are literally stunned to learn that La Paz, Bolivia, sits at 12,000 feet (3,660 meters) above sea level. A few have required continuous hospitalization from arrival at the airport until their departing flight. For a list of high altitude destinations, see Appendix C, p. 463–464.

Prevention of High Altitude Illness

Acclimatization

Acclimatization is the gradual normalizing adjustment the body makes to higher altitudes where less oxygen is available. To minimize ill effects, allow your body to adjust by making a slow ascent. A 2–4 day rest is recommended at 6,000–8,000 feet (1,800–2,400 meters) and again at 10,000-12,000 feet (3,050–3,660 meters). Rapid ascent, especially by flying or driving from low to high altitude, increases your risk for illness. Changes due to acclimatization are lost after staying at lower elevations for 10 or more days (de-acclimatization).

If rest days are not possible at higher elevations, the following measures will help prevent or minimize altitude sickness:

1. Make a slow ascent — 2,000 feet/day (610 meters/day) between 5,000 and 10,000 feet (1,526–3,050 meters) and 1000 feet/day (305 meters/day) from 10,000 to 15,000 feet (3,050–4,575 meters).

2. "Climb high, sleep low." Make the final and highest parts of a climb quickly and early in the day. Get down off the mountain to minimize exposure.

3. Drink plenty of nonalcoholic fluids to avoid dehydration. Fluid loss increases with altitude.

4. Avoid alcohol, cigarettes, sleeping pills, narcotics, and tranquilizers.

5. Carry medications for high altitude illness.

6. Avoid diets high in salt since this may exacerbate fluid retention at high altitudes.

7. Wear appropriate clothing and avoid hypothermia. The temperature drops 3.5° F. for every 1000 feet (0.65° C. per 100 meters).

Physical conditioning at sea level does not reduce the need for acclimatization.

Diamox is prescribed to help prevent symptoms of acute mountain sickness. Diamox may have significant side effects (see Part III). It should be taken only on the advice of a medical practitioner. It's prescribed for travel above 8,000 feet (2,400 meters) or for rates of ascent greater than 2,000 feet/day (610 meters/day). For a quick one day ascent/descent, a single 500 mg. sustained release dose is taken the day before the climb. Otherwise take 125 - 250 mg. at bed time, starting 24–48 hours prior to arrival at altitude or prior to starting your ascent (and daily throughout your ascent), and for 2–3 days at elevation. Discontinue Diamox after 2–3 days at elevation or upon descent. Take the Diamox twice a day if you have previously experienced altitude sickness or if symptoms of altitude sickness occur.

Don't take Diamox if you're allergic to sulfa drugs, have kidney or liver disorders, take high dose aspirin , or are pregnant or breast-feeding. Diamox causes fluid loss and dehydration must be prevented by increased fluid intake. Don't take Diamox with sedatives or barbiturates.

Other preventive measures

Gingko biloba, aspirin, and ibuprofen may help prevent symptoms of AMS. Nifedipine and dexamethesone may also be prescribed by a medical specialist, but both have potentially serious side effects.

High altitude and the unacclimatized traveler.

Above 8,000 feet (2,400 meters) there is an increasing risk of altitude sickness among physically active but unacclimatized people. This frequently happens on trekking, hiking, skiing, or backpacking trips planned on a tight schedule. The incidence and severity of illness is increased by higher and/or more rapid ascents and by greater physical exertion.

Acute mountain sickness (AMS) — This term refers to the mildest and most common symptoms. Headache, weakness, loss of appetite, insomnia, nausea, fatigue, and a rapid pulse are characteristic. Of these, headache is the most severe and disabling symptom. There may be vomiting, irritability, dizziness, shortness of breath, even hallucinations. These usually begin within 6–48 hours of ascent to high altitude but may occur later.

Treatment — Either descend or halt the ascent. Symptoms usually subside in 1–7 days as acclimatization occurs. If symptoms persist or worsen descend immediately. You can gradually resume activity, including further ascent at a slower rate. Drink plenty of fluids to avoid dehydration. For headache, take 1 or 2 Tylenol every 4–6 hours as needed. Don't take aspirin. Don't attempt to climb to higher altitudes until the signs of AMS completely disappear. If not taking Diamox, you can treat AMS with 250 mg. of Diamox at bedtime or by taking 125 mg. twice a day.

Other minor forms of high altitude illness.

Rapid ascents above 8,000 feet (2,400 meters) sometimes cause a progressive swelling (edema) of the face and eyelids, hands, ankles, and legs. This occurs within 2–4 days of arrival at elevation. Women are more commonly affected than men. Further ascent should not be attempted.

Unless disabling, however, the condition does not require medical attention or descent to a lower altitude. Decreased salt intake or the use of Diamox will reduce symptoms. Avoid treatment with diuretics as they can cause dehydration or salt imbalance.

Flatus, or the uncontrolled passage of gas, occurs

more commonly at high altitudes. It's of no medical consequence. If symptoms are bothersome, reduce them by avoiding foods that cause gas, such as beans, cabbage, broccoli, cauliflower, onions, and cucumbers. Use of an antacid which contains simethicone may also be helpful.

Around 14,000 feet (4,270 meters), heavy exertion may cause bleeding from vessels behind the eye (high altitude retinopathy, or HAR. "Floaters," blind spots, or blurred vision may result. *If visual disturbances occur, further ascent should be halted.* Although permanent damage is rare, it does sometimes follow the development of blind spots. Above 18,000 feet (5,490 meters) retinal hemorrhages are common, especially with rapid ascent and strenuous exertion. These usually resolve within 7–10 days.

High Altitude Sickness: Emergencies

High Altitude Cerebral Edema (HACE)

HACE is a severe form of AMS usually with the additional symptoms of sleepiness followed by problems with balance and coordination. Individuals who cannot "walk a tightrope" with one foot ahead of another should descend immediately.

High Altitude Pulmonary Edema (HAPE)

Occasionally, high altitude exposure can lead to fluid accumulation in the lungs (high altitude pulmonary edema, or "HAPE"). This is a potentially life-threatening condition. It's associated with heavy exertion, usually above 12,000 feet (3,660 meters) but occasionally at elevations down to 8,000 feet (2,440 meters). It's more frequent in young adults under 21 and recently deacclimatized persons. Recurrent episodes are common.

Symptoms begin 1-3 days after arrival at higher elevation. They are worse at night. Early symptoms are fatigue, shortness of breath, an aching chest, a dry, unrelenting cough, and difficulty sleeping. Respirations may become rapid, shallow, and gurgling. A low fever up to 101°F (38.3°C), an increase in pulse rate, and mental confusion may accompany these symptoms. In later stages sputum becomes frothy, pink, and tinged with blood. Coma and death may follow. **Anyone with a dry cough and a resting pulse of over 100 at altitude should assume HAPE and descend immediately**.

Treatment and Prevention

At the earliest sign of HAPE, descend immediately to below 8,000 feet (2,440 meters). Give supplementary oxygen at a rate of 6-12 liters a minute if available. Nifedipine 10 mg. orally every 8 hours can help prevent or treat HAPE. Use a hyperbaric bag if available. Get to the nearest treatment center as quickly as possible for ongoing medical care. Use of salmeterol (Serevent), 5 inhalations every 12 hours, may help prevent HAPE.

Deep Places: Diving and Underwater Safety

Scuba diving requires mastery of special skills and knowledge to be done safely. Certification by trained instructors is an absolute prerequisite. Be wary of outfits that offer to "show you the ropes" in an hour and then strap a tank on your back. In Scuba diving, even shallow water affords no margin of safety. An ascent holding compressed air in your lungs can cause rupture of lung tissue (alveoli) in as little as *4 feet of water*! The two largest and most respected organizations which certify divers in the United States are the National Association Of Underwater Instructors (NAUI- tel. 800-553-6284 or http://www.naui.org/) and the Professional Association of Diving Instructors (PADI- tel. 800- 729-7234 or http://www.padi.com/).

It is a good idea to obtain dive insurance, which includes both emergency evacuation and treatment at the nearest decompression chamber. Divers Alert Network is an excellent insurance and emergency evacuation company for divers. They can be contacted at 919-684-8111 or through their website at http://

diversalertnetwork.org/. A list of insurers can be found in Chapter 1, p. 53–56.

Certified divers should observe the following medical precautions for safe diving:

1. Never dive when ill. Increased barometric pressure during a dive can make an infection worse. Allergies or infections involving the sinuses, ears, nose, throat, or lungs are especially hazardous. They may trap air, causing pain or injury during descent or ascent.

2. If ear pressure can't be equalized during a dive, stop the dive. Middle ear squeeze, or barotrauma, will show escalating symptoms from a sensation of pressure to pain, hearing loss, and finally rupture of the ear drum. Indications of the latter include abrupt relief of pain, followed by dizziness and loss of equilibrium. Treatment usually requires nasal and oral decongestants, analgesics, antibiotics if a colored discharge indicating infection is present, and- worst of all- no more diving. Persistent vertigo, hearing loss, or ringing in the ear may indicate inner ear barotrauma and require medical evaluation, preferably with an ENT (ear, nose, and throat) or diving medicine specialist.

   Prior to diving, also consult a specialist for any chronic conditions involving the sinuses, ears, or nose.

3. The only medications approved for use during a dive are decongestants, specifically the oral decongestant pseudoephedrine and the long-acting nasal sprays with oxymetazoline such as Afrin. The use of any other medication may be hazardous, and a diving medicine specialist should be consulted. Even the use of nasal sprays must be restricted, as use of oxymetazoline for more than 3 consecutive days can cause rebound congestion. This could be disastrous during a dive.

4. To prevent chilling use an insulating suit when the water temperature is 75° F (24° C) or less. If shivering occurs, stop diving. It's an indication of excessive heat loss.

5. Incompletely filled tooth cavities may cause problems while diving, although the incidence of dental problems is fairly low. Dental discomfort is most often due to a sinus squeeze in the jaw, close to the nerves and roots of the teeth. Avoid diving after dental extractions or surgery.

6. Decompression sickness (the "bends") is primarily a hazard of repetitive dives or when a diver surfaces too fast. However, there are other contributing factors that should be avoided. These include alcohol consumption, dehydration, exposure to cold, and physical injuries (such as a sprain). Avoid airline flights 24–48 hours following repetitive dives, or ascents higher than 200 meters above sea level for 12 hours.

7. Avoid diving throughout pregnancy.

8. Knowledge of CPR, especially mouth-to-mouth resuscitation, is recommended. Coping with wounds, injuries, seasickness, sunburn, and marine animal hazards is covered in Part II of this book.

9. Medical attention must be obtained for any of the following symptoms that occur while diving:

   Persistent ear pain, hearing loss, or ringing in the ears; dizziness or loss of equilibrium, or bleeding from the ear;

   Difficulty breathing or shortness of breath;

   Neurological symptoms, including stroke-like symptoms, visual disturbances, pain, numbness, tingling, or other abnormal sensations anywhere in the body;

   loss off consciousness.

Other safety precautions:

1. Divers who haven't been diving in several years are especially prone to accidents. No matter how expert you think you are, consider a refresher course if it's been a year or two since your last dive.

2. In unfamiliar locations, contact a local dive center for an orientation dive, and for information on nearby dive sites including local conditions or special hazards.

3. Some environments require advanced training. These include caves, shipwrecks, cold water or ice, and rapidly flowing water. Diving at altitudes above 1,000 ft. (305 meters) elevation, or to water depths greater than 100 feet (30.5 meters), requires additional certification.

Dark Places: Caves, Tunnels, and Mines

In these places, unlike diving, it doesn't take a lot of specialized training, skill, and equipment to get into trouble. Curiosity and a flashlight often suffice. To be explored safely, however, caves require special knowledge, skills, equipment, physical conditioning, and one more essential: the company of an experienced guide already familiar with the area to be explored.

Be aware of potential health hazards from places inhabited by bats. There is a risk of rabies and other diseases from inhaling aerosolized bat droppings.

Other Preventive Health Issues

Special Health Problems

If you have a medical condition, chronic illness, or regularly take medications, discuss travel plans with your doctor in advance. Inquire about aspects of travel that may affect you medically. For instance, some people with anemia or chronic heart or lung disease may not tolerate high altitudes. If you anticipate using new medications during travel, including any suggested in this book, find out if there are any contraindications. If so, have your doctor recommend an alternative. For chronic medical conditions ask your doctor to provide you a written medical summary to carry on your trip. It should be written on letterhead stationery, and include current therapy as well as copies of recent EKG results, lab reports, diagnostic tests, or other relevant data. This information could be of great value if you develop or exacerbate medical problems while traveling. Other conditions which may require medical consultation prior to travel include a recent heart attack, angina, pregnancy, diabetes, asthma, drug and food allergies, or a previous allergic reaction to insect bites or stings

Medical Precautions While Flying
Preventing Blood Clots

Sitting on long plane flights without moving may contribute to the formation of blood clots in the lower extremities (deep vein thrombosis or DVT). A clot that migrates to the lungs will block blood flow there — a pulmonary embolus. To reduce the risk, stand up and walk around at 30 – 45 minute intervals, and do isometric exercises when sitting down. If necessary, use support hose during the flight. If after an airplane flight you develop leg swelling, calf pain, or shortness of breath, seek medical attention.

Sinus and Ear Conditions

Flying with clogged ear, nose, or sinus passages can cause symptoms which vary from annoying to painful. Most problems occur during descent, but ascent can also produce symptoms.

Avoid flying if you have a cold, ear or sinus infection, or severe sinus and nasal congestion. If flying is unavoidable, use a decongestant, such as Humabid LA, or Sudafed (pseudoephedrine HCl) 60 mg. about 45 minutes before departure. Then use a .25% Neosynephrine nasal spray 15-30 minutes before takeoff and landing.

Wait 5–10 minutes after using the nasal spray, then clear your ears. Close your mouth, pinch your nose shut and pop your ears gently by blowing outward against the closed passages. Blowing your nose, swallowing, yawning, and chewing gum may also help clear air passages. If ear or sinus pain persist after flying, or for recurrent problems, obtain medical evaluation.

Medical Alert Tags

We strongly recommend wearing a medical identification bracelet or necklace for certain conditions. These include:

1. common drug allergies (such as penicillin);

2. allergies to stinging insects;

3. conditions such as diabetes or epilepsy;

4. use of certain medications, such as the anticoagulant Coumadin (warfarin).

Remember that a card in a wallet may not always be found, or may be indecipherable in a foreign country. For the conditions mentioned use a medical alert tag during travel — even if you don't use one at home.

Many pharmacies carry medical identification tags, and there are a plethora of web sites selling medical ID tags and jewelry. A possibly better option is to contact the nonprofit MedicAlert Foundation at 1-888-633-4298 or http://www.medicalert.org/. They provide a bracelet or necklace and a wallet card with current medical information. Their 24-hour hotline, with instant computer access to members' medical records, accepts collect calls in a medical emergency from anywhere in the world. There is a very reasonable annual fee for the service.

Allergies to Stinging Insects

If you have had a generalized reaction to the sting of any flying insects (wasps, bees, etc.), **wear a medical alert tag and carry emergency medications as part of a**

sting or anaphylaxis kit when traveling. It could save your life.

Commercial kits are available, or one can be assembled with your doctor's help. It should contain:

1. injectable epinephrine;

2. oral Benadryl or other antihistamine;

3. a strip of material for a loosely constrictive band;

4. any other medications your doctor advises.

Always have a prescription for any kit which contains needles and syringes. If you have angina, use epinephrine only with the prior consent of your physician.

Traveling companions should also be made aware of your situation. They must know how to use the kit on your behalf in any environment where you might encounter stinging insects. Always carry your kit with you while traveling. It does no good in your luggage or hotel room.

Auto-injectable Epinephrine

For the injectable epinephrine in your kit, the EpiPen or Anakit is highly recommended. The EpiPen contains a premeasured dose of epinephrine with an auto-injector that is simple and easy to use in an emergency. Push the pen against the skin- epinephrine is automatically injected. For severe reactions (i.e. continuing symptoms) a second dose should be given 15-20 minutes afterward.

Other Recommendations

Because the "Extractor" can be used to remove venom from stings, we recommend it along with an allergy kit. See "First Aid Kit," p. 51.

Precautions for Hypersensitive Individuals

Observe the following precautions to minimize the chance of an insect sting:

1. Avoid shiny jewelry and floral or scented perfumes, deodorants, soaps, or hair sprays outdoors.

2. Avoid wearing dark clothing outdoors. Brown, black, dark red and floral prints are said to be the most attracting, while white is the least.

3. Never go barefoot or wear sandals outdoors especially in clover or grass. Bees are attracted to flowering ground cover and yellow jackets are burrowing ground dwellers.

4. Avoid orchards and ripe fruit. Do not kick dead logs.

5. Use hair spray to quickly immobilize an insect. This works both outdoors or in a closed space such as a car. As an alternative, use a knock-down spray (Raid, Ortho).

6. Always carry an allergy kit when hiking, camping, or traveling where stings can occur. It's best to keep the kit on your person, rather than in luggage or a backpack. Replacement may be difficult if these are lost or stolen.

7. If you have a history of anaphylactic reaction to stinging insects, avoid the use of " beta-blockers." These medications, used to control blood pressure and certain heart conditions, may block the effect of epinephrine in an emergency.

Birth Control Measures for Men

Men who take responsibility for contraception have only 2 viable alternatives, and withdrawal is not one of them. Unless you have had a vasectomy, there is little choice but to use a condom during sexual intercourse. Whether you normally disdain them or have never given them a thought, seriously consider their use. Whatever reluctance you have should be measured against your feelings about unintended pregnancy, and the array of circumstances, foreseen and unforeseen, this consequence entails.

Condoms have other advantages as well. Use of a *latex* (not lambskin) condom provides good protection against sexually transmitted infections such as gonorrhea, chlamydia, herpes, warts, and HIV. Condoms are also inexpensive and widely available throughout the world. They come plain or lubricated, and in a variety of colors and styles. Know how to use them before departure.

Condoms should be stored in a cool, dry place — never in a wallet. Don't use a condom that was carried in a wallet. Condoms are disposable — never attempt to reuse one.

When putting on condoms with a reservoir tip, gently press the tip to expel air. Air interferes with sensitivity and safety. Condoms without a receptacle tip need $1/2$ inch free on the end. Place the condom on the erect penis, and roll it all the way down to the base. Following intercourse withdraw gently, holding the base of the condom to avoid either leaving the condom behind or spilling the contents.

It's appropriate and desirable to use a water-based lubricant in conjunction with the condom. Don't use Vaseline or other oil-based lubricants. Lubricants with the spermicide nonoxynol-9 may add a further degree of protection against pregnancy and disease, including HIV, but should not be used if local soreness or irritation occurs.

Concurrent use of a vaginal spermicide foam raises the effectiveness of condoms to a level approaching that of birth control pills. For the touch of thoroughness, add spermicide to your packing list. In addition to being effective, it makes customs inspections a lot more interesting.

Birth Control Measures for Women

See Chapter 4 , "Women and Travel", pp. 114 – 128.

Glasses and Contacts

Glasses

If you wear prescription glasses, it's a good idea to carry a spare set. Write the lens prescription down and put it in a safe place, such as a money belt or on your yellow International Vaccination card. Optometry services are available in major cities or most countries. New lenses can be made if yours are lost or damaged.

Contact Lenses

Contact users should carry lens prescriptions for both contacts and glasses. New contacts can usually be made in a day in any major city worldwide. However, replacements bought in a foreign country are not always satisfactory. Take a backup pair of glasses. These will save the day in case of an eye infection, scratched cornea, lost contact, inadequate replacement, or inability to find cleaning and rinsing solutions. Use of extended-wear or disposable contacts will avoid the increased risk of infection from improper cleaning.

Whether you're using hard, soft (including extended wear), or gas permeable contacts, carry enough cleaning and rinsing solution for the entire trip. These solutions may be difficult or impossible to find during travel, especially outside major cities.

Heat sterilizers

Carry the appropriate electrical conversion unit (adapter) for the countries you're visiting. Carry cold sterilization solutions as a backup in case of current incompatibility, electrical failure, or other electrical problem. Make sure you're not allergic to the sterilization solution prior to travel.

Infection precautions

Use of contacts increases the risk of bacterial or parasitic eye infections when exposed to contaminated water.

Avoid swimming with contacts in place in swimming pools, lakes, rivers, or the ocean.

When rinsing contacts, it pays to be cautious. We know one optometrist who carries plastic containers of sterile normal saline solution and tubing on backpacking trips for this purpose. Whether or not you use sterile normal saline, use only a pure water source. Never use tap water or saliva- a good way to get eye infections, including parasites. Use boiled water, or bottled water if the producer's seal on the container is intact. Water purified with iodine can be used on hard or gas permeable contacts, but is not recommended for soft contacts as it may stain and ruin them.

Air travel

When traveling by air, consider wearing glasses instead of contacts. The low humidity is very drying. Alternatively, take along artificial tears.

The Nutshell™ Guide To Healthy Traveling

Observe the following precautions in developing countries:

Beverages — Don't :
- drink tap water, or use it for rinsing your mouth, brushing your teeth, cleaning dentures, or rinsing contact lenses
- consume drinks prepared with unpurified water, such as smoothies or cocktails
- use ice cubes, eat frozen confections such as popsicles or snow cones made from unpurified water
- drink local brands of sweetened bottled beverages
- drink unpasteurized milk or dairy products
- drink water served in hotels or restaurants
- drink from a wet can or bottle or from a glass wet from washing

Beverages — Do drink:
- purified bottled water
- water purified by boiling. If unavailable, treat water with iodine or filter
- internationally recognized brands of soft drinks
- bottled carbonated water or bottled mineral water
- tea or coffee made with boiling water
- bottled or canned juices, canned milk, bottled or canned beer or wine

Food — Don't eat:
- raw fruits that you cannot peel yourself, or with broken skins
- raw vegetables that you cannot peel yourself, including salads
- foods likely prepared far in advance of eating, especially with chicken, eggs, or mayonnaise
- custards and cream or custard-filled pastries or other deserts
- raw or rare meats, poultry, fish, or shellfish
- with silverware or plates that are wet from wash-

ing

Food — Do eat:

- raw fruits and vegetables with intact skins you can peel yourself
- well-cooked vegetables, meats, poultry, fish, or shellfish served hot
- canned or packaged foods
- freshly cooked beans, rice, or other grains served hot
- bread and other baked goods

Milk Products — Don't:

- consume unpasteurized milk or dairy products

Milk Products — Do:

- use pasteurized milk products. Raw milk can be pasteurized by heating to 143°F. (62°C.) for 30 minutes, or by "flash" heating almost to boiling for just under a minute
- substitute powdered milk, mixed with purified water, or canned milk

Other Guidelines

Don't go barefoot outdoors

Don't swim, bathe, or wash in contaminated fresh or salt water. Avoid fresh water streams, rivers, or lakes where schistosomiasis is a potential hazard.

Do take precautions against biting insects. Use insect repellent containing 35% or less DEET. Wear appropriate clothing and use a permethrin clothing spray. Use mosquito netting treated with permethrin when necessary

Do take precautions against sexually transmitted diseases

Do protect yourself from sunburn and excessive sun exposure with clothing, sunscreen, lip balm and sunglasses

Women and Travel 4

by Susan Anderson, MD

Introduction

Women at all stages of life are traveling to every corner of the world. The nature of trips and destinations is wide-ranging. Whether an executive on business, researcher in a remote area, newly single elderly woman planning a world tour, or teenager on a school-sponsored volunteer mission, all women have special travel health needs.

Pre-trip Planning

The following are important questions for women to consider. If sexually active, are you taking appropriate measures for contraception and prevention of sexually transmitted diseases? Have you ensured access to emergency contraception if needed? Do you know how to recognize and treat infections of the urinary tract and vagina?

Pre- trip Preparation

Adequate preparation is important. Routine health care such as pap smears, breast exam, and mammograms should be up to date. Make breast self exam a personal skill, especially for extended travel. If sexually active or potentially sexually active during travel obtain appropriate contraceptive measures. Carry and use condoms which also prevent sexually transmitted diseases. Prepare a practical first aid kit (see pp. 46 – 51). Consider learning the basics of self-defense techniques.

Get prepared and have fun!

Gender Related Issues in Tropical Disease

Until recently there has not been much information on gender specific medicine. Most research has been done on men. Now we realize there may be gender specific issues with regards to tropical disease, such as susceptibility to disease, response to treatment, and long term complications.

Certain tropical diseases carry special risks for women. They may run an accelerated or more severe course, especially during pregnancy. Infections that may have more severe or potentially fatal complications during pregnancy include malaria, typhoid and amebiasis. Women of any age who are exposed to schistosomiasis through an adventurous kayaking, canoeing, or rafting trip may suffer from female genital schistosomiasis with vulvar lesions and future infertility. Thus exposure to certain pathogens at a particular stage of life may lead to more severe consequences in women.

With knowledge, risks can be evaluated and minimized. It's all about knowledge and personal choice.

Menstruation and Menstrual Irregularities

Traveling may affect your periods in many different

ways. Be prepared during travel for the possibility of either the worst menstrual periods of your life with increased cramping and more bleeding then usual, or for periods to vanish completely. They may cease or become irregular during travel for a number of reasons. The mere stress of traveling, changes in sleep patterns, diet, activity and time zones, or illness, can easily disrupt menstrual cycles. If you are not menstruating it does **NOT** mean you are not ovulating. *You can still ovulate and get pregnant if you are sexually active.* Unless you are postmenopausal or have another reason you can not get pregnant, definitely use a method of contraception to prevent an unplanned pregnancy.

Supplies

Carry enough disposable sanitary napkins or tampons for your entire trip. They may not be available in many countries or remote regions. As an alternative, look into one of the new products for menstruation that have recently been developed. A disposable menstrual cup and a rubber device that may be reused for up to 10 years, called The Keeper, are available through Eco Logique (1-800-680-9739 or *http://www.eco-logique.com*). Carry hand wipes and plastic bags to dispose of sanitary supplies if no other method is available.

Irregular or excessive vaginal bleeding

Medical evaluation is recommended for any of the following:

1. unexpected vaginal bleeding after the first 3 months of birth control pill (BCP) use;

2. unexpected vaginal bleeding in anyone not on BCPs;

3. a period that is prolonged or excessive;

4. any vaginal bleeding that occurs after menopause.

Immediate medical attention should be obtained for

continuous or heavy vaginal bleeding if it is accompanied by signs of excessive blood loss: a rapid heart rate, dizziness, light-headedness, or passing out. You made need administration of intravenous conjugated estrogen (Premarin) in a dose of 25 mg. every 4 to 6 hours until bleeding stops for 24 hours. Once the bleeding is controlled, start a regimen of oral contraceptive (birth control) pills.

Pregnancy should always be considered a possible cause of irregular bleeding. If you are sexually active and not on contraceptives or your contraceptives could have failed, obtain a pregnancy test (see pregnancy tests below).

Treatment of irregular vaginal bleeding in remote areas when medical care is not available

A pregnancy test should be done if there is a risk for pregnancy. If you are actively bleeding (without signs of excessive blood loss) and taking birth control pills (BCPs) try one of the following:

1. take 3 birth control pills a day for 3 days and 2 pills a day for the rest of the cycle; *or*

2. take 1 birth control pill 3 times daily for 3 days followed by 1 birth control pill twice daily for 2 days and 1 birth control pill daily until completion of the active pills in the packet, then followed by a second packet of birth control pills, taking one pill per day; *or*

3. take 1 birth control pill three times per day for 3-5 days or until bleeding stops, then 1 pill a day for the remainder of the package. This regimen is usually effective in stopping the bleeding. If bleeding persists after the first 3 days, treatment can be extended to three times daily for 7 days, twice daily for 7 days, and then daily as previously described.

When using BCPs, it is always a good idea to carry at least one extra pack of pills for emergency use.

If abnormal vaginal bleeding occurs and you are *not* using BCPs, take Provera 10 mg. daily for 10 days. After finishing the Provera, your period will start and may be heavy. If you are not menopausal and have no contraindications to BCP's , an alternative is to start BCP's.

After starting medication, medical evaluation should still be obtained.

Missed period(s) and pregnancy tests

A missed period or irregular bleeding may indicate the possibility of pregnancy if you have been sexually active with a man. Most of the time a missed period during travel is due to changes in sleep pattern, diet and other stresses that might suppress your ovulation hormones. The chance of pregnancy increases if you are not using contraceptive measures or contraceptive measures could have failed- you took your BCPs late due to time changes, missed a pill, the condom broke, etc.

We suggest the following:

1. If you are using birth control pills:

    • regularly with no missed pills- no pregnancy test should be needed unless 2 consecutive periods are missed, or if you feel pregnant.

    • with two or more missed pills: a pregnancy test is advised.

    • if recent episode of morning sickness or vomiting- obtain a pregnancy test

2. If using an IUD obtain a pregnancy test immediately. If test results are positive, indicating pregnancy, obtain medical care as soon as possible.

3. If using other forms of birth control (except Depo Provera injections) or no birth control, a pregnancy test is advised.

Pregnancy Tests

Urine pregnancy tests can detect pregnancy as soon as 10 days following conception. These should be available in all western countries and most urban areas of developing countries. When using a urine pregnancy test kit follow the instructions on the package. To be accurate a urine test should not be dilute. Avoid drinking large amounts of liquids prior to collecting the urine. Collect the first voided urine in the morning. This morning sample is thought to have the highest concentration of bHCG (the hormone that is secreted during pregnancy) and thus to give the most reliable results.

Blood tests (for bHCG) are more expensive though no more reliable then urine tests for a simple "yes" or "no" answer. The blood test is available in many developing countries.

If the pregnancy test is negative, and contraceptive techniques have been faultless, (no missed pills, IUD string in place, use of condom, diaphragm, foam, etc.) repeat the test in 7-10 days. If a second test is negative, pregnancy is extremely doubtful . Missed periods may be secondary to stress from travel or other sources as previously discussed.

Medical evaluation is required if missed menstrual cycles are accompanied by breast discharge and/or headache with visual changes. Otherwise obtain medical evaluation if normal periods do not resume within 6 months.

Even when periods are irregular and abnormally spaced, pregnancy is still possible. Don't dismiss the need for contraceptive measures.

Pregnancy

If urine tests indicate you are pregnant, consider your diet, medication, lifestyle and travel plans to avoid hurting the fetus. Prenatal care should be obtained as soon as possible. If traveling it may be best to return home for prenatal care. If you will continue to travel while pregnant, see "Pregnancy and Travel", pp. 130–142. If considering an abortion, bear in mind that it is safest when done within 7-11 weeks after the first day of your last period. If you are taking birth control pills, stop them immediately. If you have an IUD in place seek medical evaluation as soon as possible (see IUD'S p.119–120).

Delaying menstrual periods

Women who want to delay their menstrual period for a month or more due to a trek or other activity while traveling can take birth control pills continuously for 2-4 months. Instead of taking the sugar pills (the last seven days of pills) or stopping your pills for a week between packages, start the next package of pills as soon as you finish the previous one- that is, following the first 21 pills in the package. This will prevent your menstrual period. There are no known negative short or long-term side effects from doing this. A new oral contraceptive product has been submitted to the FDA ("Seasonale") that will be packaged so that a woman will take the pill continuously for 3 months with only 4 withdrawal periods a year.

Menstrual cramps (dysmenorrhea)

Cramping occurs just before and during menstruation. Carry medication for menstrual cramping in your travel medical kit, even if you have not experienced cramps before!

Treatment

A number of medications have proven effective in reducing the discomfort. Use *one* of the following until cramps are gone and take with food:

1. ibuprofen (Motrin, Advil, or Nuprin)- take 600 mg. (3 of the 200 mg. tablets) orally 3 times a day; *or*

2. indomethacin — take 1 or 2 of the 25 mg. tablets orally 3 times a day; *or*

3. naproxen (Naprosyn) — take 1 of the 375 mg. or 500
mg. tablets orally twice a day, or 1–2 of the 220 mg.
Aleve orally twice a day.

Birth Control

All women of reproductive age at risk for pregnancy
should obtain contraceptive advice prior to travel. Men
who might put women at risk for pregnancy should also
obtain pre-travel contraceptive advice. This is especially
important if the man's partner is in a country without
easily accessible contraception. Don't ignore the reality
of your sexuality, especially given the stress that traveling and living in a foreign country can sometimes produce. Make good preparations in this area. The reward
will be a safer and happier experience.

The number of women traveling who become pregnant as a result of a lack or misuse of contraception is
higher than might be expected. Whether or not you are
using a birth control method, you will need to make
preparations for contraception prior to departure. Some
methods of birth control are not suitable for extended
travel. Others should not be implemented either during
or immediately preceding a trip.

If you are already using a contraceptive method, it
should be evaluated for ease of use and reliability during travel. Check for any special recommendations concerning its use while traveling.

If you wish to try a new contraceptive method ideally you should begin at least 3 months prior to travel, especially if planning to be overseas long term or living in
a remote area. Make back up plans if for whatever reason you are no longer able to use your present method.
For example, if using oral contraceptives and they are
lost or stolen, what should you do? You can obtain

information about or access to contraceptives worldwide through a regional office of the International Planned Parenthood Federation. The Federation address is :

International Planned Parenthood Federation
120 Wall Street 9th Floor
New York, NY 10005.
Web: www.ippf.org

The International Planned Parenthood Federation also keeps a world-wide guide to contraceptives and an address list of international family planning agencies.

The "World List of Family Planning Addresses" is available from the Planned Parenthood Federation of America. The address is :

Planned Parenthood Federation of America
810 Seventh Ave
New York, NY 10019
(212) 541-7800
http://www.plannedparenthood.org

Birth Control Methods

Women have a variety of alternatives for birth control. This discussion focuses on their safety, availability, convenience and appropriateness for travel. This should help you to choose the method best for you. Most forms of birth control require a trial period of at least 3 months prior to departure as protection against unexpected problems while traveling.

Barrier methods

Barrier methods of birth control include the diaphragm, cervical cap, and condom. All are well suited for travelers. They're noninvasive, easy to use, and take up little space in a backpack or suitcase and help prevent some sexually transmitted diseases. All barrier methods except condoms are contraindicated if you have ever had toxic shock syndrome.

Diaphragms

Diaphragms can cause recurrent urinary tract infections in some people. If you have more then 3-6 urinary tract infections in a year you might want to consider another type of birth control. If planning to use a diaphragm it is a good idea to be fitted prior to departure and to consider the possibility of weight change during travel because diaphragms must be refitted if there is a weight gain or loss of 10 lb. (4.5 kg.). If you have had a diaphragm for a long time you should have the fit checked prior to long term travel and possibly obtain a new one. Take along a spare diaphragm and carry enough spermicide jelly or cream for the whole trip. They are usually available in bigger cities but hard to find in smaller towns or rural areas.

Cervical cap

The cervical cap has the advantage of not needing to be refitted during normal changes in body weight. It may also be left in place for 48-72 hours. For extended travel take along a spare and a sufficient supply of spermicide jelly. Many women find their cap effective even without spermicide. This is an advantage during extended travel if spermicide is not readily available.

Condoms

Talk to your partner about what you will do if the condom breaks or slips off. A recent study found that 23% of men did not tell their partner about a broken condom. Reasons given were an unwillingness to interrupt intercourse because orgasm was approaching, an attempt to avoid responsibility for the break and the desire to minimize the anxiety of the partner. Obviously none of these are appropriate reasons and can put you at risk for pregnancy and sexually transmitted diseases. *Emergency Contraception (EC) is available but must be taken as soon as possible within 72 hours (see pp. 126– 128).* If the condom break occurs with a casual sexual partner, you may want to consider treating yourself for certain sexually transmitted diseases and obtaining blood tests for HIV, syphilis and Hepatitis B.

Birth Control Pills (BCPs)

In developing countries you can usually purchase birth control pills at pharmacies without a prescription. Only use birth control pills that have 35 micrograms (mcg.) or less of estrogen. Many low income countries may have only higher dose contraceptives available. These can increase the risk for side effects. Trying to obtain your brand while traveling can be difficult and time consuming. Your particular pill may not be available locally. Another problem is that brand names change from country to country, making identification difficult (see Internet Resources, p. 457). If possible always take an adequate supply of your birth control pills and backups- at least one extra package- for the entire trip. If lost, have a copy of the generic names of the pills so that the closest match can be made. An empty birth control package can be carried with you in case you need help from a local pharmacist to find a match or a close alternative. If there is a change in BCP dosage necessary while traveling, you may experience some minor side effects. These usually resolve after two to three months. If they persist, consult a medical provider.

The International Planned Parenthood Federation (IPPF, p. 115) book on Hormonal Contraception is useful to see what forms and where contraception is available.

Remember that any barrier method is a good backup if oral contraceptives are lost or stolen and no replacement can be found.

Special considerations for women on oral contraceptives.

Time zones

When traveling, especially across many time zones, it may be difficult to remember to take your oral contraceptive pill on time. A good idea is to carry a special wrist watch, dedicated to oral contraceptive dosing control. Set the alarm for every 24 hours. When the alarm buzzes take your pill. This is especially important with the low dose combination pills and the progestin only mini-pills. Although not a cause for concern, some temporary spotting may occur for a few days if your dosing schedule is significantly altered due to time zone changes.

Illness

If while traveling medical attention is required for any reason, be sure to inform the physician that you are taking birth control pills.

If vomiting and/or diarrhea occurs there may be decreased absorption of the pill. If vomiting occurs within 1 hour of taking a pill you should take another. If vomiting and/or diarrhea are persistent, use a backup method of birth control for the duration of the month. If you have had intercourse during this period of decreased absorption and don't use a back up birth control method, you might also want to consider the use of Emergency Contraception (see pp. 126 – 128). This will help prevent pregnancy. Discuss this option with your physician prior to travel.

There are a some new methods of contraception that may be used if nausea and vomiting are a persistent problem. These include the contraceptive vaginal ring and contraceptive patch (see chart p. 122).

If you develop hepatitis or become pregnant, birth control pills should be discontinued for the duration.

Complications of oral contraceptives

Though uncommon, significant complications may occur from the use of birth control pills. Stop taking the pills and seek medical help for a thorough evaluation if any of the following symptoms develop:

1. severe headache;

2. severe abdominal pain, especially in the right upper quadrant;

3. chest pain which doesn't stop and/or shortness of breath;

4. eye problems, such as blurred vision, flashing lights, or blindness;

5. severe leg pain, especially in the calf or the thigh.

Contraceptive patch

Ortho-Evra patches are formulated to release a combination of estrogen and progesterone hormone for 1 week at a time. Wearers use 1 patch a week for 3 weeks followed by 1 patch-free week. Withdrawal bleeding is expected during the fourth week so that regular menstrual cycles are maintained. The patch should be applied to a slightly different spot each week on the lower abdomen, buttocks or upper body- never on the breasts. It is designed to stick to skin despite bathing or swimming. If a patch should fall off for more than a day, start a new 4 week cycle of patches and use a backup method of contraception for the first week. The patch carries the same risk as the pill; some users may experience skin irritation at the patch site. May not be a good choice for women weighing more than 198 lbs. due to decreased absorption.

Intrauterine device (IUD)

If considering IUD use, or if the replacement interval of your IUD is going to expire during your travels, have the IUD inserted or replaced at least one month prior to travel.

Women traveling with an IUD in place must be aware of the signs and symptoms of possible complications. *Pelvic pain* or *lower abdominal pain, severe cramping,* and *unusual vaginal bleeding or discharge* may all be signs of infection or other problems. These can occur *with or without fever* and ***require immediate medical evaluation.*** If untreated for even a short time, pelvic infections (PID) may lead to permanent sterility from infection and scarring.

When pregnancy occurs with the IUD in place there can be a risk of ectopic pregnancy. This is pregnancy outside the uterus and can be a life threatening emergency. Because of this, a missed period with an IUD in place calls for a pregnancy test and exam as soon as possible. If pregnancy is confirmed, the risk of spontaneous abortion is increased if the IUD is left in place. Consult a medical provider immediately for possible removal of the IUD.

Summary of danger signs requiring immediate medical evaluation when using an IUD:

1. missed period;

2. lower abdominal pain, whether alone or with a fever and chills;

3. vaginal discharge with a foul odor, alone or with fever and chills or abdominal pain;

4. abnormal bleeding between periods.

Depo-Provera

This is a highly effective form of birth control, good for short or long term travel. The contraceptive injection is available in more than 80 countries. The contraceptive effect lasts at least 3 months. An additional form of contraception, such as condoms, should be used for 2 weeks after the first injection. Depo-Provera may stop your periods, which can be an advantage when traveling. It may also decrease premenstrual symptoms, and decrease blood flow, cramps, and pain if periods do occur. A disadvantage is that periods may be irregular, meaning they could occur at any time- requiring extra menstrual supplies. It would be best not to start the injections just prior to travel.

When using Depo-Provera, seek medical attention for any of the following danger signs:

1. heavy menstrual bleeding;

2. depression;

3. severe headaches;

Vaginal suppositories/withdrawal
    Not recommended due to the high risk of pregnancy.

New options for contraception
    In case of an emergency need for contraception while traveling, there are a number of new methods of contraception available in other countries. These may be available in the US in the future.
    Lea's Shield is available in Canada and Europe. It is a silicone rubber cap that looks like a loose fitting cervical cap.. Because "one size fits all" it does not require a clinician fitting and is available over the counter. It has a loop for easy removal. The shield can be worn for 48 hours and should be left in place for at least 8 hours after intercourse. It is recommended for use with spermicidal jelly. Rubber may deteriorate in heat, so carry in a climate resistant case.
    Gyneseal is made in Australia. It is a unique two part chamber that is designed as either a menstrual blood collection device (like a tampon) and/or a contraceptive barrier. For travelers, this means less to carry!
    Oves is made in France. It is a disposable device made of softer silicone rubber designed for one time use with a spermicide.
    Protectaide sponge is available in Canada. It is a soft polyurethane sponge impregnated with a gel dispersing agent and 3 spermicides. Leave in for at least 6 hours after intercourse. It is easy to use, easy to carry in individual packets, and available without a prescription.

Contraceptive Failure

Emergency contraception
    The potential for being or becoming a pregnant

Contraceptive Choices for Travel

Barrier Methods	Advantages/Disadvantages	Travel Issues
Spermicides: Creams, Jellies, Foams, Melting suppositories. Sponges, Foaming tablets, Films	Chronic exposure may cause mucosal injury that increases risk of HIV transmission.	Easy to carry Readily available Bring own supplies Female controlled
Cap	Less concern with weight loss. Can use for up to 48 hours. Needs practice to use. Requires spermacide. Needs clinician fitting.	Easy to carry Rubber may deteriorate in heat and humidity — carry in climate resistant case. Spermacide may not be available in developing countries
Sponge	One size fits all, over the counter. Protects for 24 hr. no matter how many times intercourse occurs. Moisten with water prior to use and insert; leave in place for 6 hours after intercourse. Loop for removal. Do not wear longer than 24 - 30 hrs due to risk of Toxic Shock Syndrome.	Easy to carry, use Use bottled water for moistening in countries with questionable water supply

Barrier Methods	Advantages/Disadvantages	Travel Issues
Diaphragm	Requires clinician fitting. Must use with spermicide. Insert extra spermicide with repeated intercourse. After use leave in for 6 hrs.	Carry in climate resistant case. Spermicide may not be available in developing countries.
Female Condom (Reality)	Can be inserted 8 hours prior. Spermicide not required. One use only.	Female controlled. Bring supply from home. Does not deteriorate in heat and humidity
Male Condom	Latex- possible allergy. Do not use oil based lubricants. Polyurethane - thinner/stronger, more resistant to deterioration. Lambskin/natural: can use oil based lubricants, but smallpores permit passages of viruses - Hep B, HIV. Use only for contraception. Brands and materials differ in quality.	Male controlled. Quality varies country to country. Bring supply from home of latex and polyurethane types. May break down in heat and humidity. Carry in special cases, store in cool, dry place. *Use Emergency Contraception if condom breaks or slips and no backup method in place (BCPs, diaphragm, sponge, etc.)*

Hormonal Methods	Advantages/Disadvantages	Travel Issues
Progestin only birth control pills (BCPs)	Use if can't take estrogen. Take pill every day–no sugar pills or pill free week. Decreased menstrual cramps, less bleeding. Can use when breast feeding.	Must take pill same time every day; set alarm watch to help with time zone changes. Must use additional method for protection against STDs (condoms, etc.) Need to be prepared for irregular bleeding.
Combined birth control pills Estrogen, Progesterone	Increased menstrual cycle regularity. Less blood loss. Less cramping. Fewer ectopic pregnancies. Less PID. Fewer cysts. Fewer fibroids. Less endometriosis. If nausea and vomiting, need to take back up method. May use as emergency contraception: check instructions.	Convenient, effective, easy to carry. Need to take every 24 hours. Must use additional method to prevent STDs (condoms, etc.). May use to delay menses by starting next pkg of active pills following 3 wks of previous pkg. Consider drug interactions. Bring supply from home. Research availability of BCPs and or other method to use if BCPs lost or stolen. See IPPF guide to Hormonal Contraception; check Princeton website for availability. http://ec.princeton.edu/worldwide/default.asp

	Advantages/Disadvantages	Travel Issues
Depo-Provera Intramuscular injection (shot)—150 mg. dose given every 3 months.	Side effects: weight gain, menstrual irregularities, acne, mood changes. decreased libido, osteoporosis. Good for women who can't take estrogen.	Good if unable to remember BCPs. Great if travel is for <3 months–may be difficult to get on longer trips. Need to be prepared for irregular bleeding.
Norplant 1 and Norplant 2	Menstrual irregularities–varies from un-predictable irregular bleeding to no menstrual period. Implants difficult to remove, may be broken. No protection against STDs. Side effects: weight gain, acne, hair loss.	Long term protection 3-5 years. May be difficult to remove when traveling. Need to be prepared for irregular bleeding, carry pads / tampons / menstrual cups). Periods may stop–may be a positive side effect, needing fewer menstrual supplies.
IUD Intrauterine devices Only 2 approved for use in U.S., others available worldwide	Main risk: IUD induced infection at insertion. Only 2 approved for use in US, others available worldwide. Good method for women who have already had kids, have one sexual partner.	Great for travel as lasts for 1–10 years depending on type of IUD. Need to use additional method to prevent STDs (condoms, etc.). Need to know how to check for string. Need to know warning signs and what to do in an emergency.

traveler exists for most women of reproductive age. Contraceptive failures are common. Condoms break, diaphragms slip, contraceptive jelly runs out. Oral contraceptives may be missed due to changes in time zones, or may be inadequately absorbed due to vomiting, diarrhea, or concurrent use of certain medications. Contraceptive products may be lost, stolen, or ignored in the heat of the moment. A women may experience a rape.

If any of the above occur then emergency contraception (EC) may be needed. Emergency contraception is defined as a method of contraception that a women can use after known unprotected intercourse to prevent pregnancy. It is important for women who may be at risk for an unwanted pregnancy to obtain a prescription for emergency contraceptive pills prior to travel.

Data suggests that the primary mechanism of these pills is to delay or prevent ovulation (release of the egg). Emergency contraception does *not* cause an abortion.

Worldwide the availability of emergency contraception varies greatly. If you lose your prescription or it is stolen contact the Consortium for Emergency Contraception, at http://www.path.org/cec.htm. They can advise you on contraceptive methods that might be available where you are traveling. It is best to check their website prior to travel. Their toll free number nationwide:

1-800-584-9911 or 1-888-NOT-2-LATE

The EC hotline: http://opr.princeton.edu/ec/.

Treatment of contraceptive failure

Emergency contraception is most effective if initiated within the first 12-24 hours following intercourse and is unlikely to work after 72 hours. It is imperative that you obtain and carry the medication with you before the need arises.

Emergency contraception will not stop your pregnancy if you are already pregnant from previous intercourse. *Prior to taking EC it is always best to do a pregnancy test. If your pregnancy test is positive, do not take the EC pills.*

There are a number of options for post-coital contraception. The easiest method is to use an oral contraceptive pill that contains the combination ethinyl estradiol and norgestrel. Two doses (totaling 200 micrograms (mcg.) of ethinyl estradiol and 1.0 mg. of norgestrel) should be taken 12 hours apart as soon as possible after unprotected intercourse.

Possible pill choices include:

Type of pill	First dose	Second dose (taken 12 hours after first dose)
Ovral	2 white pills	2 white pills
Lo/Ovral	4 white pills	4 white pills
Levlen	4 light-orange pills	4 light orange pills
Tri-Levlen	4 yellow pills	4 yellow pills
Triphasil	4 yellow pills	4 yellow pills
Alesse	5 pink pills	5 pink pills

A second choice is to use Progestin only pills containing levonorgestrel. Take "Plan B," one pill (0.75 mg.) and repeat after 12 hours. An alternative is to take the Ovrette minipills, 20 yellow pills totaling 0.75 mg. levonorgestrel, and repeat after 12 hours. This regime is often better tolerated and may be more effective. "Plan B" is available outside the U.S. under a variety of names.

Side effects of the oral EC methods are generally confined to nausea in 50% and vomiting in 18% of women using the combined pills. Side effects are lower with the progestin only pills- 23% of women have nausea and about 6% vomiting. These side effects usually last a few hours but may last up to 1-2 days. If vomiting occurs within 1 hour after taking either dose, an extra dose of pills should be taken.

One of the following medications to prevent nausea and vomiting may be taken one hour before each EC dose, although there is no data to support this practice:

1. Dramamine 50 mg., 1-2 tablets orally every 4-6 hours; **or**

2. Benadryl (diphenhydramine) 25-50 mg. orally every 4-6 hours; **or**

3. Compazine 10 mg. orally every 6-8 hours *or* 25 mg. suppositories rectally twice a day;   **or**

4. Phenergan 25 mg. orally *or* suppositories rectally every 8-12 hours; **or**

5. Tigan 250 mg. orally *or* 200 mg. suppositories rectally every 6-8 hours.

Post Emergency Contraception Treatment

After treatment withdrawal bleeding similar to a menstrual period should occur within 21 days. If it does not, obtain a pregnancy test. If pregnant there is no data indicating any adverse effects on pregnancy carried to term after EC use.

If pregnancy does occur and you decide to terminate the pregnancy it is probably best to return home. Over half of the 128 countries listed by the International Planned Parenthood Federation (IPPF) prohibit abortion except in extreme circumstances such as rape and life threatening illness.

Urinary Tract Issues

Urination in difficult situations.

It's sometimes a challenge to pee in the wilderness and/or exotic or not so exotic environments. Not many people think about bathrooms when preparing for their trip. Consider what sort of facilities will be available and plan accordingly. The ideal outfit to facilitate inconspicuous voiding is a free flowing skirt or similar attire that makes it easy to urinate in the squatting position, whether in a pit toilet or the wilderness. This technique may require some practice so you can get in and out of position to urinate without difficulty or embarrassment.

There are also a number of plastic and paper funnel devices that have been designed so you can urinate while standing. These also require some practice to avoid spills. They are especially useful in extremes of cold weather and altitude when you might not want to wear a skirt or pull down your pants in zero degree temperatures.

Treatment of urinary tract infections (bladder infections) see pp. 351 – 355.

Sexually Transmitted Diseases (STDs)

For certain groups of female travelers, local males in the destination country are an important source of sexually transmitted infection. During tourist season these males may seduce female tourists on a regular basis. During off season when there are no tourists these same men may have sexual encounters with local or migratory prostitutes. As a result a link between nonpaying sexual contacts and sex for pay exists.

Sexually transmitted diseases are a risk with any new partner during travel. Some women may assume that men from their own culture are "safer." In reality, studies have shown that travel promotes more risk taking behavior in both men and women resulting in a higher risk of unexpected and possible life threatening STDs for all.

Sexually transmitted infections and other diseases can also be transmitted through needle sticks. These include needles used for blood drawing and injections, dental work, tattooing, and ear piercing instruments. Non-tested blood for blood transfusions and unsterile instruments used in surgery and dental work may also be a route of transmission.

Sexual contact between women has long been considered low risk. However, woman to woman transmission of sexually transmitted disease can happen via skin to skin contact and use of sex toys.

Prevention of STDs

To prevent acquisition of sexually transmitted diseases, avoid casual sex or practice safe sex by using condoms, no matter what other means of contraception is being used simultaneously. High quality latex condoms are an essential part of the modern adult traveler's personal medical kit regardless of gender and regardless if sexual activity during travel is planned or unplanned. A female condom made out of polyurethane is an effective alternative for persons allergic to latex. Another alternative would be the use of a vaginal contraceptive film.

Treatment of sexually transmitted diseases — see Chapter 16, p. 351.

HIV Prophylaxis

The use of HIV preventative medications for high risk exposure due to unprotected intercourse including rape is important for women travelers to know about and have access to if needed. There is an increased rate of HIV transmission from an infected male to an uninfected female which is estimated to be at least equivalent to a needle stick. Seek medical attention as soon as possible. HIV prophylaxis should be considered in these situations. Consider immediate evacuation to the nearest modern medical facility. Treatment should be started as soon as possible.

Pregnancy and Travel

Healthy women with uncomplicated pregnancies can travel freely to most areas of the world. When traveling it is important to consider both the particular risks specific to a itinerary and the quality and availability of healthcare en route. Travel is safe throughout pregnancy, although

Medical Travel Kit for Women

Menstrual and illness/medication calendar.

Enough disposable sanitary napkins or tampons for your entire trip. They may not be available in many countries or remote regions. Consider menstrual cups or the Keeper. Towelettes/ plastic disposal bags.

Medications for menstrual cramps — nonsteroidal anti-inflammatories (see p. 437).

Personal safety: alarms, whistles, pepper spray (illegal to carry on planes), consider lessons in self defense prior to travel.

Urinary tract infections — if susceptible, carry an antibiotic and pain relief medication (see p. 353–354).

Urinary voiding — toilet tissue, towelettes, funnels — paper or plastic.

Urinary stress incontinence — adult diapers, Tampax, Kegel exercises.

Vaginitis — if prone to yeast infections carry either oral or vaginal anti-yeast medications (see pp. 357–359) and possibly hydrocortisone cream for external itching.

Contraception — carry enough supplies for your whole trip. A phone number, address or internet address of organizations that can supply options and locations of birth control methods in country(s) of destination (Appendix A, p. 459).

Emergency Contraception — (see pp. 126 – 128).

Pregnancy tests — carry extras, depending on length of trip.

Sexually transmitted infections- preventive measures-condoms, barrier methods. If a history of herpes consider carrying medications for treatment (see pp. 210–211).

Perimenopausal/menopausal — hormones; for vaginal dryness — estrogen creams; vaginal moisturizers and lubricants.

Pregnancy supplies.

Supplies for lactation — breast pump/nipple cream/absorbent pads.

the period from the fourth-sixth month (second trimester) is usually the safest. The first trimester carries the highest risk of danger to the fetus from possible exposure to exotic infections as well as from required vaccinations and drug prophylaxis. During the second trimester the risk of miscarriage is less and a woman usually feels more energetic. During the third trimester there is an increased risk of complications such as hypertension, preeclampsia, phlebitis, and pre-term labor. It would make sense to be close to home and/or have access to high quality health services at this time.

Decision to travel

Your itinerary should be reviewed with a travel medicine specialist and your obstetrician. During the consultation, the specialist can help to weigh the risk vs. benefit to you and your fetus of your particular destination. By changing one stop, you may be able to greatly increase the safety of your trip. A brief trip to Europe represents a far safer trip than hiking the Annapurna circuit in the Himalayas. If traveling to a remote area with poor access to quality health care, your trip should probably be deferred. It's a personal decision but you should consider how you would feel if an unexpected emergency occurred and there was a bad outcome such as miscarriage or fetal damage. If your itinerary puts you at risk for exposure to tropical diseases such as malaria, schistosomiasis or leishmaniasis consider deferring your trip until after a safe delivery, due to a more rapid course of these diseases during pregnancy.

Basic Recommendations

Follow the routine preventive health measures outlined elsewhere in this book pertaining to food and water, insects, and skin exposure to contaminated soil and water. Discuss travel plans with your health care provider at least 4-6 week prior to departure. Go over all the medications you plan to take on your trip and possible ones you may need to take as outlined in this chapter and others.

Pre-travel checklist for pregnant women

Prior to departure review with both your obstetrician and travel health specialist your medical and obstetric history, present health, and the possible health and safety risks pertaining to your specific itinerary. Obtain and carry a copy of your prenatal records from your obstetrician.

Usual pregnancy related health issues

Be prepared for the usual pregnancy related health concerns and how you would deal with them away from home. Discuss with a medical provider preventive measures and possible self treatment for the following: fatigue, heartburn, indigestion, nausea, vomiting, constipation, hemorrhoids, increased frequency of urination, vaginal discharge, and leg cramps.

For example, pregnancy increases the risk of both vaginal yeast infection and urinary tract infections. Wear appropriate loose clothing (see Chapter 16, p. 349) and consider carrying medication for treatment. Hemorrhoids can be uncomfortable on long bumpy jeep rides- be sure to bring hemorrhoidal supplies such as suppositories and creams. Eat a high fiber diet and maintain fluid intake.

Prenatal Checkup — if possible you should have a prenatal checkup prior to your trip. This is usually somewhere around 10 weeks. You may be able to hear your fetal heart tones with a fetal heart monitor at this time. The chance of miscarriage is less once the fetal heart tones have been heard. You should have prenatal checks about every 4 weeks until week 30 then every 2 weeks until week 36 then once a week or more depending on your status. Do your best to arrange for continued prenatal care while traveling.

A pelvic ultrasound is recommended prior to long term travel to check for more then one fetus (multi-fetal pregnancy), placental abnormalities, or ectopic pregnancy. If possible carry a copy of the ultrasound on the trip.

Avoid travel if:

1. multiple births are expected

2. you have a history of pregnancy induced high blood pressure, sometimes called toxemia

3. your pregnancy is considered high risk. If you have a high risk pregnancy and choose to travel during the last 3 months of pregnancy carry urine dipsticks to check for sugar and protein. Carry a portable blood pressure cuff to check blood pressure weekly, more often if abnormal. An unexpected elevation in urinary glucose or protein levels or an increase in blood pressure requires medical attention as soon as possible.

4. your itinerary presents an increased risk of exposure to infectious disease

General Recommendations for Travel

Women seem to be more prone to falls during pregnancy especially during the third trimester. These falls can be due to a variety of causes including a general lack of balance, as the center of gravity is thrown off by your protuberant abdomen, and increased joint mobility, especially of the pelvic joints as you try to navigate a narrow path or cobble-stoned walk to explore an area you have never been to before.

You may also be dehydrated and/or anemic which can lead to your fainting as you try to climb a set of steps to get an incredible view. Stay well hydrated and walk slowly.

Trauma to a pregnant abdomen can lead to placental damage and/or placental separation. Mild abdominal trauma rarely causes placental damage. Severe blunt trauma may cause placental separation. Seek immediate medical attention. Ultrasound and or fetal monitoring may be needed to diagnose certain placental injuries.

Seek immediate medical attention for any of the following:

1. vaginal bleeding;

2. severe abdominal pain;

3. leaking of amniotic fluid;

4. decrease or lack of fetal motion;

5. dizziness or lightheadedness.

Air Travel

If 35 weeks or more pregnant, you are not usually allowed to board international air flights. Carry a letter from a doctor on letterhead stationary stating the due date. Women with a high risk pregnancy or history of blood clots should avoid flying.

Wear the seatbelt low around the hips to avoid the possibility of injury during take off, landing or air turbulence. To help circulation, walk around every 30-45 minutes. Bulkhead and aisle seats allow more leg room and are easier to get in and out of during flights.

Drink plenty of fluids in flight to avoid dehydration. Avoid un-pressurized planes. One thing not to worry about are the metal detectors used for airport security.

Immunizations — Specific Recommendations for Pregnancy and Travel

It's prudent, if possible, to avoid all vaccinations during the first 3 months of pregnancy. Avoid certain live virus vaccines such as measles, mumps, rubella, varicella and oral typhoid, throughout pregnancy. Yellow fever vaccine can be given in high risk situations. If a vaccination previously produced a high fever, inform your physician prior to revaccination. It may be prudent to avoid that particular vaccine, as fever has been related to potential fetal injury.

Drugs during pregnancy

Most drugs have not been well tested during pregnancy due to a theoretical risk to the fetus and/or mother. Overall it is better to avoid medications during pregnancy when possible. However there are times during travel when a medication might be recommended and/or required to prevent or treat an illness. Prior to travel, consult with your obstetrician or travel medicine provider concerning the use of medications during your trip.

Malaria Prevention

There are certain special concerns for pregnant women traveling to a malarial area. Malaria infection is frequently more severe in women who are pregnant. Effects on the fetus include spontaneous miscarriage, premature delivery, stillbirths and neonatal deaths. Maternal mortality is as high as 10-30%. Thus it is best to avoid trips to malarious areas while pregnant. If you must travel to these areas it is very important to take prophylactic drugs (see pp. 34 – 36) and use mosquito precautions (see pp. 39 – 44).

Malaria Drug prophylaxis

Chloroquine is the preventive drug of choice when traveling to areas of endemic nonresistant malaria. Unfortunately that is a very small area. Chloroquine and proguanil may be taken during pregnancy but unfortunately the combination is less than 70% effective for chloroquine-resistant P. falciparum in Africa.

Mefloquine is the drug of choice for travel to areas with chloroquine resistant falciparum malaria. It can be used throughout pregnancy. It has not been associated with an increase in spontaneous miscarriage, congenital malformations or adverse postnatal outcomes. Women in the first trimester may want to consult their obstetrician prior to use.

Do not take doxycycline during pregnancy.

Treating Travelers Diarrhea

Follow food and water precautions (see pp. 67 – 82) religiously. You may use iodine for water purification during pregnancy for a maximum of three weeks. Using iodine for extended periods may increase the risk of fetal goiter. Filtering and boiling water is the best alternative if available.

A few medications for the prevention and treatment of travelers diarrhea can be used safely during pregnancy. Prior to your trip discuss the following medications with your obstetrician before taking any of them:

Azithromycin (Zithromax) — the drug of choice for campylobactor enteritis. May also have good effectiveness against salmonella, shigella and E. coli.

Furazolidone — effective against many of the usual pathogens that cause diarrhea including E. coli, Salmonella, Shigella, Vibrio cholera).

Metronidazole (Flagyl) —used for treatment of invasive amoeba or giardia infections.

Loperamide (Imodium) — may be used for severe watery diarrhea. Do not use if high fever or bloody diarrhea are present.

Paromycin — used for the treatment of intestinal noninvasive amoebas or giardia infections. It is an alternative to metronidazole, but is only 60-70% as effective.

Phenothiazines (Compazine) — May be used for severe symptoms of nausea, vomiting.

Avoid these medications for the treatment of diarrhea:

Bismuth subsalicylate (Pepto Bismol) — use of salycilates or medications containing aspirin around the time of delivery may increase the risk of intracranial bleeding or other adverse bleeding in the newborn.

Sulfa drugs by themselves (not formulated with other drugs) can be used safely in the first 8 months of pregnancy. When used close to term they may cause jaundice and other adverse effects. Avoid use after 36 weeks.

Trimethoprim/sulfamethoxazole (Bactrim, Septra-sulfa plus trimethoprim). Avoid trimethoprim/sulfa combinations (Bactrim and Septra) in the first trimester and after 36 weeks.

Quinolones — including norfloxacin and ciprofloxacin (Cipro) must all be avoided.

Altitude Illness

No definitive studies have been done to determine the risk of going to higher altitude for a few days during pregnancy. From anecdotal evidence and a few small studies the risk appears minimal. However, altitude sickness (see pp. 89 – 94) *must* be avoided. It can be especially severe during pregnancy due to changes in body chemistry. Another concern is the difficulty obtaining medical care in an emergency. Risks should be measured carefully.

Drugs for altitude illness

Likewise no large studies have been done to evaluate the safety of treatment options for women with altitude illness during pregnancy. If you have symptoms of cerebral or pulmonary edema, descent and supplementary oxygen are the treatment of choice. Options to consider *in an emergency if descent is not feasible and supplementary oxygen is not available* include:

Nifedipine (calcium channel blocker) — can be used for symptoms of HAPE (high altitude pulmonary edema)

Decadron (dexamethasone) — a short course can be used to treat cerebral edema.

Avoid the following:

Diamox (acetazolamide) — not recommended for general prophylaxis. Avoid use in pregnancy, especially in the first trimester.

Coca Tea — avoid throughout pregnancy.

Exercise and pregnancy

More women are continuing to exercise and play sports while pregnant. The pre-pregnant level of exercise should be taken into account when deciding what you can do. Discuss your level of training and fitness recommendations with your physician prior to travel. The American College of Obstetrics and Gynecology (ACOG) offers fitness guidelines. Competitive athletes can make adjustments to these guidelines. The important points are to exercise within a comfort zone. If you exceed the ACOG guidelines be careful not to become overheated, dehydrated, or hypoglycemic.

ACOG guidelines

Strenuous activities should not exceed 15 minutes in duration

Body temperature should not exceed 38° C (101.4° F)
No exercise should be performed in a lying position after one month.

SPORTS SPECIFIC RECOMMENDATIONS

WATER
swimming — one of safest sports for pregnant women
water skiing/surfing is not recommended because of the possibility of hydrostatic injury to the vagina, cervix or uterus, risk miscarriage
scuba diving — pregnant women should NOT scuba dive at any depth. No safe depth/time profiles have been established for pregnancy
snorkeling is safe!
boating -power/sail — safe, avoid long distance from shore in last month
windsurfing — if experienced, safe in first trimester if cautious and low speed wind. At high speed — risk of miscarriage
Avoid hot tubs and sauna

LAND

Weight Bearing
walking — safe throughout pregnancy
jogging — low intensity
hiking/backpacking safe, no heavy packs
aerobics — low impact, minimal bouncing, light weights
yoga-safe, avoid lying positions

Non-weight Bearing
cycling — stationary bike safer then road bicycle, though may ride road bike early in pregnancy, better if upright handlebars

WINTER SPORTS

Avoid hypothermia
downhill/cross country skiing experienced skiers can continue cautiously, in third trimester ability to balance is impaired; do not start skiing during pregnancy due to the risk of falling.
ice skating — restricted even for experienced skaters due to hard falls
sledding — avoid

OTHER

Racket Sports
Tennis, racquetball, squash, badminton - safe, use eye protection, avoid long duration at high temperatures
Contact Sports
   Football, soccer, hockey, basketball- avoid collision sports.
Horseback riding - avoid, falls may lead to miscarriage and serious injury

Travel Insurance

Check your travel health insurance for the gestational date cutoff and coverage for delivery or prolonged confinement due to premature delivery while traveling.

Consider purchasing a supplemental travel health insurance policy if going to a developing country. There are a number of companies that cover complications of pregnancies through the third trimester including the two listed here.

Worldwide Assistance Services
1133 15th Suite 400
Washington DC 2005
1-800-821-2828

AEA International
Box 11568
Philadelphia, PA
!-800-523-8930

Indications for medical attention

It is important for you to know the signs and symptoms of a possible emergency during pregnancy and to obtain medical evaluation immediately for any of the following:

1. high blood pressure;

2. elevated urine protein;

3. severe abdominal pain;

4. ruptured membranes ("water breaking");

5. headaches and visual disturbance;

6. contractions;

7. vaginal bleeding;

8. severe swelling of the face or extremities or sudden weight increase.

Breast Feeding

While a challenge, we highly encourage you to continue breast feeding during travel. Breast milk has both nutritional and anti-infective properties. Exclusive breast feeding relieves concerns about the purity of water and the need to sterilize bottles. If the child is less then 6 months no extra supplements are usually needed. If older then six months and supplementation is required, carry a powdered supplement that can be mixed with boiled or purified water. For short trips it may even be feasible to carry a supply of canned formula..

Keep well hydrated, avoid alcohol and caffeine, and get plenty of sleep to help keep a plentiful supply of breast milk.

Vaccinations — All vaccinations are considered safe during breast feeding

Medications — Most medications appear in small quantities in human milk, usually less than 1 % of maternal dosage. However because drug levels in a breast-feeding infant are not usually measured we have little data on which to make recommendations. A number of factors affect the concentration of the drug in breast milk including the characteristics of the drug, how often and where it is administered, and when. A drug taken right after breast feeding has the maximum amount of time to clear the maternal blood before the next feeding. Frequency of feedings and age of the infant are also factors. The American Academy of Pediatrics Committee on Drugs has reviewed the excretion of chemicals into human milk. The rule of thumb is if an antibiotic can be given directly to the infant the nursing mother can also take it.

Guidelines for medication use during breast-feeding

Use medication only if absolutely necessary
Take the lowest does possible
Avoid sustained release preparations
Watch for untoward reaction in the infant such as a

change in feeding or sleeping habits, rash, colic or fussiness

Use a breast pump if you must take a contraindicated drug for a short time

Supplies — Carry a breast pump, nipple cream, and absorbent breast pads.

Summary

Travel during pregnancy can be extremely rewarding. Please take a little extra time to consider the risk benefit ratio of a particular itinerary, plan accordingly and have fun!

Travel With Children

5

by Sheila Mackell, MD

"What was the best part of the summer your family spent in Peru?" — The author
"They had McDonald's!!" — Aisa, age 6

Traveling with children? How? Why? What can I do to minimize the risks?

These questions are all part of preparing for and actually experiencing the world with children. The ambassadorial nature of children will expand the cultural interfaces of your journey dramatically. With thoughtful preparation and planning, it can be an enriching adventure, like few others. Stay flexible! *Keep your expectations appropriate (and low!) for small children in a new environment.* Each child adapts differently and factoring that into your travel plans will make a smoother trip for all.

This chapter explores the aspects and challenges of traveling with children. The relevance of some specific medical recommendations will need to be confirmed with your pediatrician or travel medicine provider. Careful preparation will be greatly rewarded.

Air Travel

Long airplane rides often prove the biggest challenge for families. Keeping children occupied, with age-appropriate games or drawing/coloring felt boards, cards, or books is the best way to cope with the physical constraints of the airline cabin. Seats at the airplane bulkhead may have extra floor space where young children can play and nap. Bulk head seats are also often equipped with a wall cot or foldout table where a safe cot can be secured for infants.

On night flights, many families find that young children sleep spontaneously. Parents frequently ask whether or not to use a sedating anti-histamine, like diphenhydramine (Benadryl), before a flight so their child will sleep. If you choose to do that, try it at home first using the recommended dose from your pediatrician. A small percentage of children have the opposite reaction to this type of medicine and become irritable and hyperactive. It's certainly better to cope with this at home rather than mid-flight!

Child car seats can and should be brought along on your trip. Airlines will often give discounted seats for families traveling with a child requiring a car seat. The car seat must adhere to federally approved aviation standards. Approved car seats have a sticker on them stating FAA approval or may say "certified for use in motor vehicles and aircraft". Most car seats produced since 1985 have been made to conform to these standards. Check with the airline regarding their car seat rules before purchasing your tickets.

Ear Pain

Young children may develop ear pain with air travel. Have your child either breast feed, drink from a bottle, swallow liquids, suck on a pacifier or lollipop, or chew gum (if old enough!) during these times to help the eustachian tubes to equalize. Older children can be taught to hold their nose and "pop" their ears by gently breathing out through their nose with their mouth closed. When all else fails calmly reassure your child that the pain will go away soon. Additionally, people have anecdotally reported that giving a dose of over-the-counter liquid or tablet decongestant shortly before the flight helps when children have colds and fluid in their ears, though a recent medical study did not confirm this.

Many parents wonder whether their child should fly if he/she has an ear infection. Though there have been no actual case reports of eardrums rupturing on airplanes, an ear infection can be very uncomfortable due to the pressurization inside the cabin. To help alleviate the pain and discomfort use the above recommended measures, plus a dose of a mild pain medication, like acetaminophen (Tylenol).

Food

For short trips, bring a stash of different types of foods your child eats, especially if you have a toddler. The often unpredictable nature of travel and schedules away from home can make regular mealtime a challenge. You can request meal substitutions, when flying, that your children may prefer- such as peanut butter and jelly sandwiches. Make that request in advance of your flight! Carry snacks and water, especially if you have stopovers or potential customs delays.

Diapers

Plan ahead! Disposable diapers are essential, yet may be unavailable at many destinations. Don't forget to take extra diapers for use in the airport, on the airplane, and for possible transportation delays. Disposable diaper liners can help with stool disposal when using either cloth or paper diapers. If you use cloth diapers and plan to wash them while away, be aware of the Tumbu and Botfly (see pp. 207 – 208) in Africa, Central and South America. When hanging diapers outside to dry in

Africa, these flies can lay their eggs on the diaper. When the eggs hatch, the larvae then burrow under the skin forming a raised red lesion. Ironing the diapers after drying will destroy the eggs.

If traveling around the time of toilet training your toddler, the change in routine could prove too much stress for continuing the newfound skill away from home. Lower your expectations and bring along diapers.

Safety

In traveling to a new and unfamiliar environment , parents and care givers need to heighten their awareness and steer kids clear of dangers that may not be in their usual routine at home.

Identify the children!- label their clothes, backpacks, etc. Carry at lest one full-face photograph of all children. Teach them to sit down ("Hug-a-tree"program in wilderness settings) if lost or separated. Older children can be taught to use a whistle. Many families develop a code to use if separated. Avoid the strangulation risk of attaching a whistle on a cord around the neck of toddlers and small children.

Never leave children alone to watch luggage or keep places in line. A CAR SEAT is recommended to bring for infants and children under 40 pounds. Bring a nylon strap (available at outdoor equipment stores) to attach to rental cars that may not be equipped with seatbelts.

Alert children to different traffic direction/rules abroad. Avoid bare feet *everywhere,* including beaches. Many countries have parasites that can burrow into the feet and cause annoying rashes. Never leave a child alone while they are swimming or playing near water.

If renting or using bicycles, always wear a helmet. Make an evacuation plan with your family and discuss what you would do if you got separated or some unexpected disaster occurred.

Tell children not to eat strange plants (a common cause of hospitalization of children in the tropics). Teach them not to pet or play with dogs, cats, monkeys, or other pets.

Teach them to avoid placing their hands and other objects in their mouth, swallowing bath water, or eating sand. Keep their fingernails trimmed.

Other recommendations: bring electrical outlet covers; childproof your hotel room/vacation lodgings; be extremely vigilant about keeping children and curious toddlers away from hotel balconies; bring a medical kit.

Recommended Medical Kit for Travel with Children

This is a general list of recommended items for a medical kit. You may need to customize the kit to meet your child's needs and your destination. Always store medications in child proof containers and keep out of reach of the children.

Medical card with age, weight, any important medical history, allergies, blood type, if known
Immunization records

Over-the-counter medications:
Tylenol/Advil (acetaminophen/ibuprofen) or other non-aspirin medication – for fever, pain, teething (*always avoid the use of aspirin in children*)
Antihistamine - Benadryl (diphenhydramine)- for allergic reactions, itching, hives, motion sickness or cold symptoms, sleep
Cough suppressant – any over-the-counter brand
Antibacterial skin ointment (bacitracin) – for cuts and scrapes
1% hydrocortisone cream for itching, heat rash, minor skin irritation
Anti-fungal cream – an over-the-counter brand containing clotrimazole or any other recommended by your provider, for diaper rash or athlete's foot and ringworm

Prescription medications:
Any regularly taken, with adequate supply for the trip. Take the generic name of the medication with you in case the medication is lost or stolen.

Antibiotic treatment dose for traveler's diarrhea

Antimalarial medication, if indicated

Consider antibiotic for ear infections if your child is prone to them and your medical provider agrees

Injectable epinephrine, if your child has had a history of severe allergic reactions to insect stings or foods.

Antibiotic eye drops

Medication for motion sickness if your child is susceptible (see p. 150).

First aid supplies:
Mosquito repellent 50% DEET or less for children. Do not use DEET on children younger than 2 months. For a list of products safe for children, see p. 160 – 162).

Thermometer- whatever type you are most comfortable with for your child. Consider digital thermometers, as they don't break easily.

Sun screen (at least SPF 15 with both a UV-a and UV-b block), lip balm with a sun block, sunglasses, and a wide brimmed hat

Safety pins

Disposable wipes

Colorful Band-Aids (p. 181)

Ace wrap

Oral rehydration salts

Syrup of ipecac, and a bottle of charcoal mixed with sorbitol, available from your pharmacy, with instructions from your physician or poison center on how to use. Do not use in children under 6 months old and never give for ingestion of caustic substances (like drain cleaner) or hydrocarbons (gasoline, kerosene).

A water purification plan

Whistles, bells for shoes of toddlers

Electrical outlet covers

Bulb syringe - for infant nasal congestion

For wilderness travel add:
Low/high registering thermometers
Reflective fold-up blanket
Sam splint (see p. 51).

Motion sickness

Preventing motion sickness is definitely more effective than trying to treat it once symptoms occur. Children may be more prone to motion sickness than adults. Over-the-counter antihistamines are safe for use in children over 2 years of age, but have not been proven effective. On winding roads, children susceptible to motion sickness should sit facing forward and close their eyes or wear dark sunglasses. Eating lightly can also help. For children over 12 years of age, there's a prescription medication available in a patch that can be applied behind the ear, called Transderm scopolamine.

Animals

Children are often magnets for animals and more prone to bites. In developing countries, few domestic pets and virtually no strays will have been vaccinated. Do not permit your child to pet, feed, or play with any stray dog, cat, monkey, or other animal. Bites can be fatal if the animal is carrying the rabies virus (see rabies below). Animal bites and scratches can also cause skin infections and other diseases (see monkey bites, pp. 405–407). A bite, scratch, or even exposure to saliva can be deadly! Basic first aid is extremely important. If your child is bitten or scratched by an animal, immediately and vigorously wash the bite with soap and water. Seek medical attention, including rabies vaccination as soon as possible *(within 24 hours)* in the nearest large hospital, or contact your embassy to locate a safe source of rabies vaccine.

HIV counseling

Many trips to developing countries are being taken

by groups of teens, under supervision, for projects or educational purposes. Even teens that travel with their parents need to be educated regarding HIV risk factors. Don't forget to include dental work, tattoos, and piercing as having HIV transmission risk.

Sun protection

Recent medical evidence suggests that the risk of skin cancer is directly correlated to the amount of sun exposure before the age of 18 years. Clothing and hats are the first line of defense. Several children's clothing lines have been developed that have an SPF rating. (see pp. 29 – 30). Don't forget sunglasses and lip balm.

Many chemical based sun screen products are available for use. For infants under 6 months old, clothing, hats with brims, umbrellas and shade are preferable. Sunscreen can also be used but the physical barriers are important for their young skin. For older children, choose a sun screen that blocks the damaging UVA and UVB rays. An SPF factor of at least 15 is best. Several newer products contain a pulverized physical barrier, titanium dioxide. This is not absorbed and is an excellent choice for any child, even young infants. PABA, a component of some sun screens, can cause a skin rash and should be avoided.

Carry a sun screen you have used before. If you are taking a new type of sun screen, try using it prior to your trip to assure that there is no allergic reaction. For more information on sun screens, see pp. 30– 32.

Immunizations

Traveling is an excellent time to update you child's "regular" shots as well as prepare for the extra protection you may need for your trip. Discuss these with your travel health provider and pediatrician. Start at least 2–4 weeks prior to travel.

Preventive Health
Strategies for Parents

We're going to review simple strategies to keep your children well while eating away from home. For a detailed discussion of preventive health measures for all travelers, see Chapter 3, pp. 66 – 82.

Breast-feeding (see also pp. 141– 143)

Imagine the most nutritious, germ-free food source available at almost all times and free! The safest feeding to provide your infant while traveling is breast milk. Continue to breast-feed as long as possible if you'll be traveling with an infant. The immunity transferred in the breast milk also provides additional protection from diarrheal diseases. Breast-feeding does not give protection against malaria and breast-feeding mothers taking antimalarial medications do not excrete protective amounts of medication in the breast milk.

When breast-feeding abroad, be sure to continue excellent breast hygiene. Wash your nipples with clean water and mild soap before nursing. If you are bringing along a breast pump, be extra careful to clean it thoroughly to avoid possible contamination from otherwise less sanitary conditions.

Bring along a small supply of formula and bottles (see below) for emergencies if you are unable to breast-feed for some reason.

Hand washing

Pay meticulous attention to keeping your children's hands clean. Bring along soap or pre-moistened, anti-bacterial towelettes and use them liberally! Keep their fingernails trimmed as well.

Food

Remember the simple rule: *"Boil it, cook it, peel it or forget it!"* This applies to just about everything. Kids are often finicky about the temperature of their food. Don't let that deter you! Cook all food thoroughly, then allow it to cool down (covered and away from flies wanting a nibble, of course!) before serving.

Milk

Make sure to check that the milk your children drink while abroad is pasteurized. If you are unsure, boil it for a minute (see p. 79). Much of the milk overseas is either irradiated, or purified by an ultra high temperature process . Irradiation is not dangerous to you and does not impart radiation to food. This milk is often in a box on a store shelf and does not need to be refrigerated until it is opened. Check expiration dates.

Another option many parents find convenient is to bring along a supply of powdered milk. The key with this approach is to ensure that a supply of purified water is available to use for reconstitution.

Infant formula / Bottle feeding

If you are not breast-feeding your infant, carry powdered formula with you unless assured of its availability at your destination. As stated above, it is imperative to have a source of purified water for mixing the formula to avoid transmitting harmful bacteria to your infant.

When traveling you can bring a supply of baby bottles and nipples appropriate for your child's age. Don't forget to bring an extra nipple or two. Be meticulous about cleaning the bottles with soap and clean hot water, or boiling water. Dry the bottle well before filling. More convenient would be to bring along two or three of the sleeve-type bottles that you can fit with disposable liners. The only thing that would require washing would be the nipple.

Traveler's Diarrhea in Children

In spite of precautions, your children may still develop stomach and bowel problems during travel. In many countries, the bacteria and viruses found in water and food are new to your body and can make you ill, spoil your vacation, or have even more serious consequences.

Symptoms

There are no "strict" definitions of traveler's diarrhea in children. Parents undoubtedly recognize the symptoms! Generally though, illness is characterized by:

1. Three or more unformed stools/day; or

2. Any number of unformed stools when accompanied by one or more of the following:

    fever above 38° C. (100.4° F.)

    abdominal cramps

    vomiting

    blood or mucous in the stools

Fever, bloody diarrhea, and abrupt onset are often the hallmarks. It is more common in children under 3 years old and can be more severe and prolonged. Young children and infants are at particular risk for serious complications, so prompt recognition and treatment is essential, perhaps even life saving.

Indications For Medical Evaluation

Dehydration can occur rapidly and be fatal in infants and small children without prompt treatment. When treating traveler's diarrhea in children, you must obtain medical evaluation as soon as possible if your child develops any of the following:

1. bloody diarrhea;

2. severe dehydration – no urine production in 12–24 hours, few tears, sunken eyes.

3. vomiting that is severe enough to prevent oral rehydration;

4. high stool output (more than approximately 3 oz of stool per hour for a child weighing 22 lb. (10 kilo) or less.

5. ever of more than 24 hours duration;

6. lethargy or unresponsiveness;

7. fever above 100.4° F / 38° C rectally in an infant less than 2 months old, regardless of whether or not there is diarrhea.

Treatment

To prevent dehydration, fluids lost through diarrhea must always be replaced with an oral rehydration solution.

In severe cases, medical treatment is essential and an intravenous solution is required.

Antibiotics may be required if there is fever or blood in the stool. **Anti-motility drugs, such as loperamide (Imodium) can be dangerous in children and are not recommended, except in older children (over 8 years) who do not have fever or blood in the stools.**

Hydration

Fluid losses in the stool can be deceiving, especially when infants and children wear absorbent diapers. Start hydration with oral rehydration solution immediately, once the symptoms of diarrhea begin.

Diluted fruit juices and sports drinks generally lack the necessary sodium and potassium and are too high in sugar. The standard formula from the World Health Organization (WHO) is available in packet form that can be purchased easily and inexpensively abroad in most pharmacies and even airports. Powdered oral rehydration packets can be found in selected pharmacies and outdoor equipment stores, if you'd rather have a supply before you leave. There is also a rice-based electrolyte solution available in packets, called Ceralyte (call the company at 310-490-4941 for availability). Oral rehydration solutions (ORS) are simple and effective in treating the dehydration that occurs with traveler's diarrhea. Always use purified water (or less preferably, canned juices) to mix the rehydration packets.

If you are unable to locate the pre-mixed formula and you have the right ingredients, you can make your own ORS. The recipes rely on exact proportions of salt and sugar, so use a measuring spoon. *Too much or too little salt or sugar can have serious consequences in infants and children when replacing diarrhea fluid loss.*

1 Liter/quart of purified water +
$1/2$ tsp table salt
$1/2$ tsp baking soda
8 tsp sugar or 2 Tbsp Karo syrup
$1/4$ tsp salt substitute (provides potassium)

OR (food based):

1 Liter/quart of purified water +
8 oz (approximately $1/2$lb) mashed potatoes, boiled, then cooled
$1/2$ tsp table salt
$1/4$ tsp each baking soda and salt substitute

When initiating oral rehydration, start with small volumes given by teaspoon every 15–20 minutes. Volume can be increased as tolerated by the child. During the first 4–6 hours, a one year old child should use at least 4 ounces per hour (two tablespoons equals one ounce). After the initial 4 hours, the one year old (about 22 pounds) should take about $1/2$ cup of ORS per diarrheal stool in addition to routine amounts of fluids. Infants should take less.

In the initial 4 – 6 hours, older children should take about $3/4$ to 1-$1/2$ oz for each pound (that's 8 oz per hour for a 40 pound child!) as tolerated. After that, $1/2$-1 cup of ORS per diarrheal stool is recommended.

Practical tips for getting children to drink oral rehydration solutions:

1. consider adding pre-sweetened drink mix as some of the sugar source- children often like the   color as well;

2. make it into popsicles;

3. spoon it in;

4. use a syringe or a straw.

Anti-motility agents

Hydration is the primary therapy. Anti-motility agents can mask the need for hydration in children and can be dangerous. They should never be used in infants or in any child who has a fever or bloody diarrhea.

Bismuth subsalicylate (BSS), the ingredient in Pepto-Bismol, contains salicylates which are similar to the ingredient in aspirin. Aspirin-containing products are not recommended for use in children because of the rare possibility of interacting with a virus to cause a severe liver and brain condition (Reye's syndrome). While bismuth subsalicylate has not been reported as causing this problem, most pediatricians advise against the use of BSS for treating diarrhea. It can be used in older children (over two years old) who have no fever and no blood in the stools, in circumstances such as the need to take a long bus or car ride with limited access to toilet facilities. It is not recommended for preventive or frequent use in children and should not be given to children with a viral illness or who have been recently exposed or infected with the chickenpox virus.

Another common anti-diarrheal agent often used in adults is Imodium (loperamide). It actually works by stopping the motility of the intestines. Again, caution **must** be exercised in considering its use in children and it should not be routinely used in young children. Discuss this with your pediatrician and never use this medication if there is fever or bloody diarrhea present. Severe side effects have been reported in young infants and this medication is best avoided until further information on its safety in children is available. *Remember hydration is the most important component of treating diarrhea in children and adults!*

Antibiotics

There is little published in the medical literature regarding antibiotic treatment of traveler's diarrhea (TD) in children. Several additional dilemmas exist because the most common class of antibiotics (quinolones) used to treat adults with traveler's diarrhea is not, at the time of this publication, approved for use in children under the age of 18 years old. Another antibiotic, Bactrim (same as Septra, a trimethoprim/sulfa combination) has been proven safe for children over 2 months of age. However it is not as effective, especially against the bacteria E. coli., a common cause of traveler's diarrhea. Azithromycin (Zithromax) is a better choice for children. It is pleasant tasting and needs to be given only once daily. It can be dispensed in powder form for reconstitution when needed. Another choice to treat traveler's diarrhea in children is Furizolidone. This drug comes in a liquid form and the dose is 8 mg/kilogram/day divided into 4 doses.

It's time to consider taking antibiotics when diarrhea is accompanied by fever and blood in the stools. It might be wise to carry along an antibiotic prescription for use in your child *if* **fever and bloody diarrhea occur**. Check with your medical provider. Be sure your child is not allergic to the medication prescribed and that you give it exactly as directed. Antibiotics are usually given to treat traveler's diarrhea in kids for 3 to 5 days. Review instructions with your medical provider before departure.

You'll also want to be sure that any medication you carry along on your trip is labeled and in its original container. Keep both prescription and nonprescription medications safely out of reach of your children.

Resuming meals

It was common practice in years past to keep

children on liquid diets as long as they had diarrhea. We have learned, however, that early feeding stimulates the cells of the intestine to renew themselves more rapidly. Eating food provides energy and improves the nutritional outcome. Current recommendations now include:

1. Continue breast milk feedings, or restart full strength lactose free or lactose reduced formula in bottle-fed infants as soon as initial rehydration has occurred.

2. Resume solid feedings early with a regular diet. There is no evidence that bland foods speed recovery. **Your child's appetite is a good indicator. Start slowly, especially if he or she has been vomiting in the previous 12 hours.**

3. If tolerated, add starches, cereals, yogurt, fruits , and low fiber vegetables to start with.

4. Initially, avoid foods high in simple sugars (e.g., sweet juices). Some fat in the diet is fine.

There is always some controversy about reintroducing milk. Some children have lactose intolerance after a bout of diarrhea, which may increase their symptoms. However most have no problem with milk digestion. Gradually reintroduce milk and see how it is tolerated. If symptoms seem to worsen, wait and try again in a few days. Yogurt and cheese are usually well tolerated.

Unfortunately, there are no vaccines for the majority of germs that cause traveler's diarrhea. So remember:

1. Excellent and frequent hand washing for all members of the family;

2. Meticulous attention to drinking, using only purified water;

3. Cooking all food well and eating raw fruits and vegetables only when you can peel them yourself (see **the Nutshell Guide,** p. 104 – 106).

Insect Precautions

Insect Repellents

When your trip involves journeying to places where malaria, dengue fever (see p. 261), or other mosquito and insect diseases occur, there are several preparations to make. First, buy an insect repellent with the active ingredient "DEET". It is the most effective repellent against these insects. Check the amount of DEET in the product you purchase, and make sure it has a concentration of 50% or less for children. The higher concentrations don't offer any advantage and they can potentially be more toxic (see pp. 40 – 42).

When applying mosquito repellent, put it only on exposed skin. If your child has sensitive skin, test for sensitivity prior to your trip. Apply a small amount inside the child's arm to see if there is any skin reaction. Skin rashes are very uncommon, and insect repellents with less than 50% DEET are considered safe for use in children older than 2 months. Do not permit children to apply it themselves! Avoid applying it to their palms, so they don't rub it into their eyes. Remember, dusk until dawn is the time that the malarial mosquitoes bite. Use good sense when going out at night- protective clothing and insect repellents are essential. To minimize the amount of repellent that may be absorbed wash the repellent off at night, if sleeping under repellent-treated mosquito netting. Otherwise wash it off first thing in the morning. If you are using it during the daytime, put your child's sun screen on first, then put on the insect repellent. Less of the repellent will be absorbed with this method.

Do not put DEET insect repellents on infants less than 2 months old. It is not recommended, due to the lack of research on the effects of this chemical in young infants. Protect your babies by limiting outdoor exposure at night, treating their clothing with permethrin, and using permethrin-treated netting at night.

Store these repellents with care. They are poisonous and can cause serious side effects, such as seizures, if swallowed. Be sure to keep the insect repellent away from curious small children who may want to take a taste!

Many natural products used to avoid insect bites, such as grapefruit extracts and bath oils are available on the market. Most of them haven't been tested and/or proven to protect against the bite of malaria mosquitos, or protect for only brief periods of time. Travel medicine experts recommend that you use a DEET containing repellent. Remember, malaria and other insect borne diseases can be deadly and effective prevention is your best defense.

Permethrin

Permethrin is used to treat clothing and mosquito nets. Treat some of your clothing with permethrin prior to your trip. Treated clothes remain effective for 2- 4 weeks even with repeated washing. This is a safe way to use insect repellents for children. By treating the clothes they wear at night, you'll need to apply less repellent to their skin.

You can use the spray form of permethrin and slowly spray clothes or mosquito nets for 30 to 45 seconds. An entire net will use about half of a 6 oz spray can. To treat clothing and netting with permethrin solution, you'll need the following items:

Concentrated permethrin 13% (This can be purchased commercially as Tick repellent at outdoor stores or through travel catalogs)

A basin or plastic bag

Clean water and the clothes or night time mosquito net you want to treat.

Either way, the entire process takes about 10 minutes. A few hours after the garments dry, they are ready to go. Keep these treated clothes and the mosquito net in a separate resealable bag. If anyone develops a permethrin allergy, they will have "uncontaminated" clothing to wear.

Use the permethrin impregnated bed-netting over baby carriages and cribs to cover up your children's exposed skin in the evening hours. Use a permethrin impregnated mosquito net over each bed, especially if you have babies or young children. Since the malaria mosquito bites at night, the mosquito net is a safe, effective and non-toxic way to avoid the bites.

Other preventive measures: see pp. 39 – 44.

Malaria see pp. 32 – 39.

Prevention

The best prevention is to avoid getting bitten by mosquitoes. The mosquitoes that cause malaria bite at specific hours- between dusk and dawn. Because of this, it's vital to pay attention to where you sleep and what you do at night to protect yourself and your children. With the measures previously described you can dramatically decrease your chances of getting bitten.

Medications for Malaria Prevention

When traveling to areas of the world where malaria is a risk, your travel medicine provider may decide that your child requires a medication for malaria prevention.

In the USA for children 8 years of age or less there are three medications available for malaria prevention: chloroquine, Malarone (atovaquone and proguanil), or mefloquine. They only come in pill form in the USA, so the pill may need to be split and crushed up depending on your child's weight. In Europe you can find chloroquine as a syrup, but if you choose to use it, it's best to check with a health care provider to be sure that the dose and medication are correct. **Chloroquine is extremely poisonous in overdose and must be stored away from inquisitive toddlers.**

Proguanil is commonly prescribed in countries out-side the USA and can be given to children of any age. It is not available by itself currently in the USA. It must be given daily and in conjunction with the weekly anti-malarial, chloroquine. This regimen is more complicated **and has a high failure rate.** If there are strong medical reasons that your child absolutely cannot take meflo-quine or Malarone, this regimen is a less effective alter-native for travel to areas where chloroquine- resistant malaria exists.

For children over 8 years old who can not take the above medications there is a medication called doxycy-cline (an antibiotic) that can be taken for malaria preven-tion. This is taken as a daily dose based on the child's weight. **This should not be taken by children under 8 years old because it can stain their permanent teeth.** For children over 8 years of age see section on malarial prevention for adults pp. 32 – 39. Remember that no ma-larial medication is 100% effective in preventing malaria. Always take precautions to prevent mosquito bites!

Breast-feeding mothers still must administer antimalarial medications to their children, since breast- feeding does not provide protection.

Most kids can't swallow pills! So, how can you give the medication to them? Here are a few ways:

1. Cut the pill into the correct dose that's been pre-scribed. Ask your pharmacist if you should save the other parts of the pill for the next doses. In the US, the pills to prevent malaria are quite expensive , so you may want to save the other pieces for future doses.

2. Next, crush the pill up and put it into something very sweet, like chocolate syrup or jam. Certain pills are very bitter and your kids will appreciate the strong flavor of the jam or chocolate.

3. Sometimes, your pharmacist will cut the pill up ahead

of time and even crush it. That makes your job a lot easier, so ask if you can have this done ahead of time.

4. For older kids, you can break their doses up into small chunks and sneak it into a candy bar or a sandwich.

5. Check with your physician, nurse or pharmacist.... you may have different directions based on the weight of your child.

Some children vomit shortly after getting this medication. If this happens within the first hour, it's safe to repeat the dose. After 1 hour, do <u>not</u> repeat. Keep this and all medications in child-proof containers, especially when you travel. The malaria prevention pills are highly poisonous and even deadly if taken accidentally by a small child (*even one adult tablet can be fatal for a small child!*). Remember to carry along Syrup of Ipecac in your medical kit in case of accidental poisoning.

Post malarial exposure

Upon returning from your trip, if your child develops fevers or any illness, at any time in the next 6 months, be sure to tell your medical provider that you have traveled in a malaria area and what you did to prevent malaria!

Altitude

Many trips involve journeying to cities or mountains where altitudes can be over 8000 feet (see Appendix C). Limited research available on children traveling to altitude suggests that they may be just as susceptible as adults, possibly even more so. Signs of altitude sickness include irritability, headache, restless sleeping, cough, difficulty breathing, abnormal behavior, unsteady gait. Because children often cannot express their problems in words, it is necessary to be aware of the various possibilities and be ready to descend to lower altitude immediately if worrisome signs develop.

Treatment for altitude sickness is *descent* (usually at least 1000 ft.)! Other treatments involve oxygen and steroid medications.

Acetazolamide (Diamox), a mild diuretic, is a preventative medication that can help the body adjust more rapidly to high altitude. There is no data on the use of Diamox to treat or prevent altitude sickness in children. It is not essential to take medication, as most symptoms will be mild and treatment with rest, fluids and mild analgesics will suffice. A weight-adjusted dose can be considered (2.5 mg./kg. orally every 8-12 hours, maximum 250 mg. per dose). Diamox is started 1-2 days prior to going to altitude and continued daily for 2-3 days while at altitude. Diamox is a sulfa drug. Do not take if sulfa allergic.

Prevention

Prevention of altitude sickness can be done with a combination of strategies. Slow, gradual ascent to altitude and sleeping at a lower altitude is a wise start. This allows your body to adapt to the changes a lot better than if you ascent rapidly or fly in to a high altitude destination. Don't over exert yourself. Drink plenty of fluids. Avoid caffeine, as dehydration can make the symptoms more prominent.

Fever – Indications for Medical Evaluation

When traveling to tropical destinations fevers in children become more worrisome. Malaria, dengue fever and typhoid fever are a few of the more exotic diseases children might be exposed to. Remember though that when fevers do occur in children they are often due to the same causes you would find at home.

Seek medical evaluation immediately for any of the following that are accompanied by fever:

1. high fever and headache - possible malaria;
2. any fever in an infant < 2 months old, regardless of symptoms

3. severe headache, neck stiffness and vomiting - possible meningitis;

4. cough with rapid breathing - possible pneumonia;

5. abdominal pain - appendicitis, intestinal blockage, malaria.

Chronic Diseases

Many children with complicated or chronic medical problems travel. Talk with your medical provider prior to the trip to discuss how travel and travel related health problems may effect your child's health. There are special needs that should be thoroughly reviewed with the child's regular physician or medical provider. For example, children with sickle cell disease may need oxygen during a long plane flight. Children with diabetes will need to learn how to adjust their medication for travel (see "Diabetes and Travel," pp. 168 – 171). They should have special diets ordered on the airplane.

When traveling with children who are taking medication for chronic health problems, always carry enough medication for the whole trip, plus at least a few days extra.

Consider purchasing a Medic Alert bracelet for your child to wear if chronic disease or allergies to medications are present.

Check your medical coverage and purchase evacuation insurance in case of serious medical problem occurs while away from home.

Asthma

Prior to your trip review asthma plans with your pediatrician or medical provider. Discuss bringing along a course of prednisone for severe symptoms. Take all medications on the plane with you. On the airplane be sure that your child drinks plenty of fluids. Remember that asthma can be triggered by pollution often a severe problem in foreign countries, change in weather , humidity, stress or a change of environment as well as by colds.

Conclusion

Traveling with children has tremendous rewards. We have reviewed some of the more predictable challenges in this chapter. Be sure to check your child's particular medical needs with your physician or nurse practitioner before leaving home. Being prepared will enable the entire family to have a more enjoyable adventure!

Special Concerns of Travelers

6

Diabetes and Travel

Travel presents some challenges to diabetics who use medications to control their blood sugar level. This is due to changes in time zones, irregular meal schedules, unfamiliar food, varying levels of physical activity, and other factors. With a little effort and preparation it should be possible to keep blood sugar levels under control and travel safely almost anywhere. Get off to a good start by ordering a diabetic diet from the airline 24 hours in advance. It's also important to avoid nausea, vomiting, and diarrhea. Take preventive medications as needed. Know how to treat low blood sugar and ketoacidosis prior to travel. Traveling companions should be familiar with the early signs of hypoglycemia and know when to administer oral glucose tablets or drinks.

Insulin

The most important issue for anyone using insulin is to *avoid hypoglycemia.* We highly recommend that glucose monitoring be increased during travel across time zones. Remember that travel is often more wearing than anticipated. Be sure to eat sufficiently or slightly lower your insulin dose during plane travel, transport, airport hassling, etc. This is not the time to try to maintain the tight control one usually tries to achieve.

There have been some recent advances made in insulin formulation which should be discussed with your treating physician. Cartridge pen systems that deliver NPH, regular, or 70/30 insulin are available from Eli Lilly and Novo Nordisk. These systems are disposable or can be replaced by new cartridges. More importantly, in the cartridge system NPH is stable for a week without refrigeration while regular insulin is stable for up to 4 weeks, although excessive heat can still render it inactive.

Lispro insulin (Humalog) is also available. It has a faster onset and is shorter acting than regular insulin. One advantage is that it can be administered just before or even at mealtime rather than 30-45 minutes beforehand, since it has an onset of 15 minutes and peak effectiveness 30-90 minutes after administration. Effects last 3-5 hours versus 6-8 hours for regular insulin.

Observe the following precautions:

1. Take enough insulin to last the entire trip. Insulin is good for 3 months unrefrigerated, but should be kept as cool as possible without freezing. Carry a prescription from your doctor for the insulin, including the type and dose. Supplies can more easily be replaced if necessary from loss or theft .

2. Carry enough of your syringes (U100) for the entire trip. In many areas of the world only U40 and U80 syringes are available.

3. Take more than enough lancets and reagent strips for blood glucose monitoring, and strips or tablets for urine ketone testing. Travel or unexpected illness usually requires more frequent blood tests to keep glucose levels under control.

4. Have packets of glucose tablets, sugar, crackers, dried fruit, or candy bars at hand for a quick snack if needed.

5. Carry a medical card with your insulin type and dosage, doctor's name and telephone number. Also wear a diabetic ID bracelet or necklace.

6. Carry a letter from your medical provider on letterhead stationary documenting the medical diagnosis of diabetes and the need to carry a supply of insulin, syringes, needles and lancets for diabetic care.

7. Carry your insulin and other supplies, including lancets, needles and syringes, in your carry on luggage when traveling by air or other means.

8. If you carry glucagon for hypoglycemia, *make sure your travel companions know the difference in use and purpose between glucagon and insulin in an emergency.*

Insulin adjustment across time zones

A recommended schedule for insulin dosing calls for a 3% adjustment in total insulin (which is calculated as both NPH and regular insulin), for every time zone crossed. Examples of this would be, if traveling eastward across 10 time zones, (where the day is shortened), you would reduce your total insulin by 30% (10 time zones times 3% equals 30%). For westward travel, (where the day is lengthened), across 5 time zones, you would increase your insulin by 15% (5 time zones times 3% equals 15%).

For travel east or west across 6 or more time zones, make dosage adjustments for a longer or shorter day. Traveling north or south, or across 5 time zones or less, does not require insulin adjustment. Monitor blood sugar levels every 6 hours and before meals.

Oral Diabetic Medications

Take an adequate supply of medications for the entire trip. When traveling by air or other means pack your medication in your carry on bags — don't risk losing them with your checked luggage. Also carry an extra prescription for each medication, with the generic name of the drug as well as the trade name.

Medication timing is not crucial as it is with insulin. Take the pills according to local time, regardless of how many time zones you have crossed. It's prudent to carry extra snacks, as well as a medical ID card with your doctor's name and phone number, and a diabetic ID necklace or bracelet.

Foot Care

Feet require even greater attention and care when traveling than at home. In all likelihood you will be using them more. Good walking shoes, well broken in, are a must. New shoes require close monitoring of your feet for blistering or possible infection. Carry mole skin, antifungal cream, and powders for foot care. If signs of infection or skin breakdown are noted, obtain medical evaluation at the earliest opportunity.

Travel Services for Diabetics

The names and addresses of local diabetes associations can be obtained from the International Diabetes Federation (IDF), on the web at: www.idf.org. Local associations can provide contact information for physicians specializing in diabetes. The information is also available at: www.diabetesnews.com. The IDF address is: Rue Washington 40, B-1050 Brussels, Belgium. Their address in England is at 10 Queen Street, London W1M OBD.

The American Diabetes Association (ADA) provides a wallet-size alert card with emergency information in 13 different languages. They have an extensive web site with a lots of good information: www.diabetes.org. Their address is 1660 Duke St., Alexandria, VA 22314.

Excellent annotated links for diabetic resources on the web can be found at www.mendosa.com/diabetes.htm.

Corporate and Business Travel

As the world increasingly heads towards a single marketplace, the need for international business travel commensurately rises. Similarly, extended travel can be required or desired for educational or philanthropic purposes.

Air Travel

Business trips of short duration, requiring travel over three or more time zones, should factor in the effects from jet lag on mental performance (see jet lag, pp. 21 – 24). It is wise to avoid critical decision making and meetings until one has had a chance to acclimate to the new time zone. Plan to arrive a day or two early. Consider making an extra stop partway to your destination. This is the reason why Presidential stopovers to Europe often include overnight stays in Reykjavik.

Due to increased security measures following 9/11, you will need a photo I.D. to board aircraft on domestic and international flights. Carry a backup photo I.D. separate from your passport or have it available (along with your birth certificate) at home to be sent by overnight mail in an emergency.

Vaccinations

Business related travel often occurs on relatively short notice. In order to receive all the needed vaccinations for travel, early planning and preparation is essential. While most vaccines are administered as a single dose, the protective effect may take several weeks to develop. For other vaccines such as hepatitis B, oral typhoid, Japanese encephalitis and rabies, multiple doses over many weeks are required before an appropriate immune response occurs.

Many business travelers do not consider these issues unless duly prompted. Companies with affiliates in different countries should try to anticipate which employees could be called to travel and have these employees obtain vaccinations. Such planning is important to assure full vaccine protection. In situations where advance planning is not easily facilitated, administrative assistants or travel agents who schedule business trips for a specific employer can help initiate early medical planning. Referral for appropriate pre-trip health care can be made at the same time as travel reservations.

Business travel is frequently to repeat destinations. This necessitates the consideration of cumulative time spent in a particular destination. When a company has subsidiaries in several countries requiring the business traveler to make two week trips every six months to a specific city, the total time spent in a potentially high risk area will be several months when viewed over the course of several years. This approach will prompt consideration for vaccinations not usually considered for a single two-week trip. The following is a case in point.

Of 20 U.S. employees making multiple trips during the course of a year to their company's Asian factories, four developed hepatitis B. The human resource director wondered why hepatitis B vaccination had not been initially recommended by their corporate medical clinic.

In another instance, a business traveler working in Nairobi, Kenya was bitten by a rabid dog. Two local residents were bitten by the same animal and died after developing rabies. Our traveler was fortunate to have been able to afford treatment at Nairobi Hospital and survived. In this case, the pre-exposure rabies vaccination should have been considered and would have eliminated the need for rabies immune globulin (which is from pooled human blood products or even horse serum).

Visas and Permits

Early planning and preparation are also needed when arranging for passports, visas and work permits. Work permits can be particularly delayed depending on the country of destination. Prior to approving entry for work or educational purposes, some countries may require physical examinations and testing for HIV, syphilis, tuberculosis, and other diseases. Although there may be no clear rationale for these tests, the rules of the foreign country must be followed if one desires entry.

Cultural and Social Issues

Long-term assignments to foreign destinations can frequently include family members. This raises specific questions regarding children and pregnancy (see chapters on pediatrics, p. 144 and women's health p. 107). Social, cultural, and educational issues can arise in these situations. In some cases spouses are not allowed to work. They must navigate daily living in situations where the customs and living arrangements are stressful and difficult. These cultural, social, and language differences can increase the risk for depression, anxiety, and increased alcohol consumption.

Studying the language, educating one self on the local social and cultural differences, as well as discussion with those who have traveled and lived in these areas can help make the transition from a developed to developing area easier. Linking up with others travelers upon arrival to a new city, including those from other countries, is another way to help make social adjustments. For further discussion on foreign cultures and culture shock see pp. 62 – 65.

There are often various educational options available depending on the foreign city. Children are often the most adaptive to new environments and language situations, particularly if given strong support by their parents.

Health Risks

Business travelers like all travelers are at risk for health problems usually not present at home.

Malaria and Dengue fever are commonly found in many countries. Taking preventative medication and using insect precautions are very important (see malaria, pp. 32 – 39, and insect precautions, pp. 39 – 44).

Travelers diarrhea is the most common traveler's malady (see pp. 44 – 46). Using good food and water hygiene and carrying medication for self treatment of diarrhea is crucial. It is hard to transact business from one's bathroom.

Sexually transmitted diseases are a consideration for business travelers. One's host in a foreign country may offer you the services of a prostitute or masseuse. Drinking too much alcohol at a dinner party may lower your inhibitions and common sense. Being in a foreign country where sex is easy to come by, as in the sex clubs of Thailand, may make for bad judgement and even worse results. Always use condoms if having intercourse while traveling. Avoid prostitutes, sex clubs, and contacts with the local population due to the high risk for HIV, as well as hepatitis B and C infection. If you are sexually active while traveling, be sure to have a medical evaluation and testing upon return from your trip. One business traveler we heard about developed herpes from getting a massage. The businessman denied ever having any sexual contact. Upon further questioning it was learned that the masseuse used her genital area to massage the traveler. Explain that to your spouse or partner.

Another consideration for individuals living abroad on long-term assignments is side trips to other countries in the region. This will often necessitate concerns about malaria for rural tropical travel, high altitude health concerns for travel above 8 thousand feet, and other vaccinations specific for the countries of destination (see the respective chapter on these topics). This is particularly true for those business travelers living and working in major urban areas where many of these illnesses are not present. Often, a generous estimate of the time spent on side trips as well as potential destinations is useful when planning for these additional medical needs.

Terrorism and Safety

Terrorism or the risk of criminal attack was an

increasing concern among those traveling for business purposes even prior to the events surrounding the World Trade Center in September 2001. While the actual risks during overseas travel are usually not significantly higher than in most major cities in the United States, there are many ways to reduce these risks. These techniques are useful for all travelers regardless of the reasons for travel. It is a good idea to maintain a low profile when transiting through airports, train stations, and other areas where travelers are often targeted. Avoid business dress, highly visible jewelry and clothing, corporate logos on luggage tags, and other visible signs associated with the United States or your corporate affiliation. While it is often difficult to mix in with the local population, casual dress can make one less visible or desirable target for attack. Vary your daily routine regarding leaving and returning from work, as well as your route to work. If held up, do not resist, and readily hand over all cash or valuables (which presumptively you cherish less than your life).

It is also a good idea to have friends or family know your travel itinerary. Keep in touch with them during travel in order to have someone monitor your whereabouts. In some cases, it is reasonable to notify the local consulate when traveling in potentially dangerous regions. The U.S. State Department keeps a list of high risk regions for American travelers that can be accessed though the CDC website:

http://travel.state.gov/travel_warnings.html.

Otherwise, use basic common sense. Avoid those areas which appear dangerous. Do not walk in unlighted or out of the way places at night. Only use cab companies that are well known. One of our clients, a business traveler, was recently robbed on his way to a train station in Arequipa , Peru. The cab suddenly pulled into an alley where the driver and his partner robbed him of everything, even his International shot card which he needed to cross the border to Bolivia.

Corporate Traveler's Medical Kit (see also p. 46–51)

A nonsteroidal anti-inflammatory agent
Antibiotics for travelers diarrhea
Antimotility medications for travelers diarrhea
Short acting sleep medications (such as Ambien, Sonata, or melatonin)
Condoms
Antimalarial medications (if traveling to malarious areas)
DEET insect repellent, permethrin clothing spray if traveling to tropical regions
Sunscreen if spending time outdoors in sunny areas

Disabled Travelers

Travelers with mobility, sight, or hearing impairment have special needs that are beyond the scope of this book. Resources are available on the internet. See p. 458.

Part II

Diagnosis and Treatment of Medical Disorders

In spite of precautions, illness and injury may occur. Part II will help you with the interpretation of symptoms and identification of commonly encountered illnesses. Use the table of contents and the index to locate specific information quickly. To identify possible causes and find relevant information when you know only the symptoms, consult the Quick Reference guides in each chapter. A guide to identification of a mysterious rash, for example, will be found at the end of Chapter 7. There are guidelines to help you determine when medical evaluation is mandatory.

We provide treatment schedules in Part II for use when medical care isn't available. Also use this information to ensure that when care is available, the medications prescribed for you are appropriate and safe.

Preventing and Treating Skin Problems 7

There are literally hundreds of kinds of skin problems. Some are common and easy to recognize. Others are difficult to identify without considerable experience. Unfortunately, the more you travel, the greater the chance of acquiring some unfamiliar, uncomfortable, possibly scary, skin problem. This is especially true in tropical countries. Warmth and moisture are ideally suited to fungal, viral, bacterial, and parasitic skin infections. Wounds that would heal without treatment at home may inevitably become infected in the tropics.

Some disorders affect only the skin surface, such as fungal rashes, scabies, crabs or warts. Others are a result of an internal viral infection like measles or chicken pox. Still others may have environmental causes, such as food and drug allergies. And occasionally, a rash can signify a serious disease such as lupus, syphilis, or leprosy.

We cover only the most common and easily treatable skin disorders. See a doctor, preferably a dermatologist, if you have a rash that:

1. cannot be identified;

2. becomes worse — with or without treatment;

3. looks as if it's found a permanent home.

Minor Skin Wounds

Wound Care

Many wounds are minor and you can treat them yourself. Whether minor or major, the steps involved in treating all wounds are:

1. stop the bleeding — use direct sustained pressure if necessary;

2. clean the wound;

3. bandage the wound to help prevent infection.

Tetanus Boosters

For any deep and/or dirty wound, especially puncture wounds, obtain a tetanus-diphtheria shot if it's been more than 5 years since the previous booster.

Wounds Requiring Medical Attention

Get immediate medical help for:

1. bleeding not controlled by simple pressure;

2. injuries in individuals with increased susceptibility to infection (diabetics, young children, the elderly, or those who are immune suppressed);

3. foreign bodies which cannot be easily removed; or

4. loss of sensation or function (mobility) in an affected area.

Care of Minor Skin Wounds

Minor cuts, scrapes, and abrasions that don't cause severe bleeding you can generally treat yourself. The goal is to prevent wound infection, and the key to this is proper cleaning and care until the wound is healed.

As soon as possible, wash the wound with soap and clean water. Scrub dirt out of abrasions. Deep, dirty wounds should be soaked in Betadine solution when available. Then consider applying a topical antibacterial ointment. If necessary, cover with a sterile bandage and obtain a tetanus-diphtheria shot.

Topical antibacterial ointments

Using a topical antibacterial ointment will often help prevent wound infection. Almost any of the available products will do. These include:

Polysporin ointment

Betadine (providone-iodine) ointment

Neosporin ointment

Triple antibiotic ointment

Bacitracin ointment

Bactroban ointment

Unless specified, any of these or an equivalent medication can be used when "topical antibacterial ointments" are referred to in this chapter. However, be alert to the possibility of allergic reaction, indicated by the sudden onset of itching with redness. Some products may contain either neomycin or iodine, both of which can produce an allergic response. If a reaction occurs, switch to a product without the offending ingredient.

Regardless of the medication used, watch carefully for signs of secondary bacterial infection following any break in the skin. These include redness, swelling, tenderness and drainage or pus from the wound site.

Wound bandaging

Most abrasions and lacerations heal faster if you cover them. Cover other wounds to protect them from irritation from shoes or clothing, or from dirt or other contamination. A Band-Aid or other sterile dressing can be used. Don't use cotton — the fibers are difficult to remove from the wound.

Dressings should be kept dry and changed daily until the skin is healing and clean. If sterile dressings are not available, use clean fabric. This can be either ironed, scorched with a flame, heated in an oven, or boiled for at least 5 minutes.

Use of steri-strips and butterfly bandages — Some cuts, especially lacerations, may need suturing (stitches) or other measures to bring the edges together to promote healing. Steri-strips or butterfly bandages are available commercially and can be used for small, deep cuts. They can also be used on larger or more extensive lacerations when you're traveling in isolated areas where suturing is not available.

To use steri-strips, you must first prepare the skin so that the strips will adhere. Shave any excess hair around the wound. Skin must be clean and dry for proper adherence. Starting from one side, put down one end of the steri-strip and gently pull it across the laceration. Bring the edges of the wound closely together and press the strip down on the other side. Repeat the procedure, placing the strips next to each other so that the entire wound is closed.

Butterfly bandages are applied the same way. If butterfly bandages are not available, they can be made from Band-Aids. Cut away both edges of the padded area with sterilized scissors, leaving a narrow padded central strip.

Other Skin Wounds and Injuries

Bruises (Contusions)

A bruise is a common injury, usually from contact with a blunt object, in which the skin remains intact. The skin is often discolored from small broken blood vessels beneath the surface. Bruises usually look purple, or "black and blue."

It's normal for some people to get small bruises on their legs from minor bumps and scrapes which they may not notice at the time. As a rule, though, **if extensive bruising occurs spontaneously — without known injury — it requires immediate medical evaluation**.

Treatment

Apply cold compresses for 10–15 minutes several times during the first 24–48 hours. Then switch to hot soaks, 2–3 times a day. For pain take 1 or 2 acetaminophen (Tylenol) or aspirin every 4–6 hours, or a nonsteroidal anti-inflammatory such as ibuprofen or naproxen. Tetanus-diphtheria shots are not necessary if the skin is unbroken.

Puncture Wounds

A puncture wound is caused by a sharp penetrating object, such as a splinter or nail. These rarely bleed much but are very prone to infection and difficult to clean.

Treatment

Remove small, accessible foreign particles with tweezers or a straight pin. The tweezer ends or pin should be sterilized first with a match flame or by boiling in water. Clean the site well with soap and water, then rinse thoroughly with hydrogen peroxide. This is especially important with puncture wounds. Obtain a tetanus-diphtheria booster if needed.

Indications for Medical Assistance

If the penetrating object is long or very deep, don't attempt to remove it. Obtain medical help instead. Medical assistance should also be obtained for all penetrating injuries to the chest, abdomen, head, or eye.

Deep Cuts (Lacerations)

A laceration is a deep cutting wound through the tissues beneath the skin, into the fat or muscle. These usually require suturing.

Treatment

First, apply direct pressure to the wound to stop the bleeding. Then clean the cut thoroughly with soap and water. **Don't use hydrogen peroxide on deep lacerations involving muscle tissue**, as it will damage the tissue. These cuts are best cleaned in a medical setting using a sterile normal saline solution. Sterile normal saline is simply a dilute (.9%) solution of salt in sterile water. When not available, you can make your own. Add 1 teaspoon of salt to a pint of water, boil for 5 minutes, and let it cool. Don't apply any ointment to deep cuts.

Suturing is usually best done within 8 hours of the injury to be most effective. If medical care cannot be obtained within that time, bring the edges of the wound together and tape them in place with steri-strips or a butterfly bandage as previously described. Scalp wounds can be closed by tying hairs together across the wound. Cover all wounds with a sterile dressing, tape the dressing in place, and get medical care as soon as possible.

Gouging Wounds (Avulsions)

An avulsion is a cutting or gouging injury in which a piece of the skin is dug out. If the wound is very wide or deep, it may need suturing or other professional care. Otherwise treat it in the same manner as a minor cut or abrasion.

Bacterial Skin Infections

The bacteria most often responsible for skin infections are "staph" (Staphylococcus aureus) or "strep" (Streptococcus), both of which normally reside on the skin. Treatment usually requires a topical antibacterial ointment and may require oral antibiotics as well. In isolated areas when medical attention isn't available and antibiotics are indicated, you can treat cellulitis, folliculitis, boils, impetigo, and secondary bacterial infections with one of the following antibiotics. They're listed in order of preference:

1. cephalexin (Keflex) 250–500 mg. orally, 4 times a day for 10 days (avoid if allergic to penicillin or cephalosporins); **or**

2. dicloxacillin 250–500 mg. orally, 4 times a day for 10 days (don't use if you're allergic to penicillin); **or**

3. erythromycin 250–500 mg. orally, 4 times a day for 10 days; **or**

4. clarithromycin (Biaxin) 500 mg. orally, 2 times a day for 10 days; **or**

5. azithromycin (Zithromax) 250 mg. orally, 2 pills together initially and then 1 pill daily for 4 days; **or**

6. amoxicillin/clavulanate (Augmentin) 500 mg. orally, 2 times a day for 10 days (don't use if you're allergic to penicillin); **or**

7. ciprofloxacin 500 mg. orally, twice a day for 10 days (*only if the above antibiotics are not available*).

More severe infections require the higher dosages. After starting antibiotics, medical attention should be obtained if there is no improvement within 48–72 hours.

Secondary Bacterial Infections

Any wound can become infected with bacteria, especially if not taken care of properly. This is called "secondary" bacterial infection because it follows rather than causes the original injury. The injury could be from a cut, scrape, abrasion, puncture wound, insect bite, rash, burn, or frostbite.

Symptoms

Secondary infections are characterized by redness and swelling, increasing tenderness or pain, red streaks running up the skin, or pus forming at the wound site. Fever may also be present.

Treatment

Treat a small infection with hot soaks for 10–15 minutes, 3 times a day. Change the dressing and reapply antibiotic ointment after each soak. If unable to do soaks, change the dressing and reapply ointment at least twice a day.

Add oral antibiotics to the above measures if the

infection grows worse or fails to improve after 2–3 days. Any of the following indicate a worsening infection:

1. increase in swelling, tenderness, and discharge of pus, or enlarging red area of inflammation;

2 fever greater than 101° F (38.3° C);

3. red streaks running up an extremity from the site of infection.

Cellulitis

Cellulitis is a secondary bacterial infection which fails to be localized or confined to a small area. Instead, infection spreads outward through connective tissue beneath the skin, producing an expanding area of inflammation.

Symptoms

The reddened, inflamed area of cellulitis usually doesn't have a clearly demarked edge or border. The skin is red, warm, swollen, and tender to touch. As the area enlarges, fever can develop and there may be swollen lymph nodes or red lines running up the skin. This indicates infection of the lymph channels. Untreated, infection may reach the blood stream causing a systemic infection. In the event of spreading cellulitis, medical attention must be obtained as soon as possible.

Treatment

Cellulitis should be treated initially with oral antibiotics. In addition, apply hot soaks to the affected area for 10–15 minutes 3 times a day. Keep an affected arm or leg elevated as much as possible.

Barber's Itch (Folliculitis)

Hair follicles sometimes become infected, commonly by "staph" bacteria. Infection causes itching or burning, with discomfort or pain if the hair follicle is touched. The base of the follicle is red and contains pus. The infection looks exactly like a pimple with a hair follicle in the center. Folliculitis can appear anywhere on the body, most commonly under the arms, on the face or neck from shaving, or on the buttocks, thighs, or groin. Tight jeans, wet trunks, or wet suits increase heat, moisture, and skin irritation and contribute to folliculitis.

Although these infections frequently go away on their own, it is best to treat them aggressively to avoid complications. This is particularly true in the tropics where bacteria thrive and are prone to spread. Infected follicles which don't heal, with or without treatment, often develop into boils.

Treatment

Apply warm soaks or compresses to the affected area for 15 minutes, 3 times a day. Keep the area clean and dry. Apply a thin layer of topical antibiotic ointment after each soak, or at least twice a day. If the beard is affected, skip shaving for a few days. If you do shave, avoid shaving closely, and use an antiseptic soap before and after. Change the razor blades daily until the infection clears. If these measures don't lead to improvement, consider use of the oral antibiotics previously mentioned.

Indications for Medical Attention

Increasing pus, redness, swelling, and tenderness indicate a progressing infection — get medical attention. Treat infections near or around the eyes in the same manner, **except medical attention is mandatory and you must obtain it as quickly as possible. The presence of a spreading infection or inflammation near the eye is a medical emergency.**

Boils (Furuncles)

An abscess of an infected hair follicle is a furuncle or boil. Infection of the follicle extends below the skin, forming a pus sac beneath it. Boils are red, warm, painful and tender when touched. They may cause fever or swelling of local lymph nodes.

Small boils may heal by themselves or they may

quickly enlarge and cause the formation of additional boils. These can pop up in areas such as the hands, face, back, buttocks, or legs. Frequently boils enlarge, forming pus pockets which soften and open spontaneously. These may drain pus for a few days to a week or more. Occasionally several adjacent boils join, forming a conglomerate mess with several points of drainage.

Treatment

Any skin infection which becomes abscessed should receive medical attention. Large or persistent boils usually need to be surgically opened, drained, and packed. The infected area must be washed and kept clean and dry. Hot soaks for 10–15 minutes, 3 times a day, are essential. Oral antibiotics may be considered.

Indications for Immediate Medical Attention

Boils that develop on the face or in the rectal area require **immediate** medical care. These can have potentially dangerous complications, including scar formation.

Impetigo

Impetigo is a superficial skin infection, caused by "staph" or "strep" bacteria usually found on the chin or around the nose. It's characterized by multiple, separate sores (lesions), pea size or larger. The lesions are raised and have a red base. They sometimes appear as circular red patches and may resemble ringworm.

The lesions form sacs or blisters, occasionally filling with fluid or pus. These break open, dry, and form a honey-colored crust. If the crust is removed the underlying skin is red. The lesions can spread to other parts of the face or to other areas of exposed skin. The lesions are both itchy and contagious. Infection is easily spread via wash cloths or towels.

Treatment

Apply warm soaks to the affected area for 15–20 minutes, 3–4 times a day. Spread a thin layer of antibiotic ointment to each lesion twice a day or after each soak. This may be sufficient to cure the infection. If there is no improvement in 3 days, or if the infection becomes worse, oral antibiotics may be required. Obtain medical attention. The medications usually prescribed are:

1. penicillin VK 250–500 mg. orally, 4 times a day for 10 days (don't use if you're allergic to penicillin); **or**

2. cephalexin (Keflex) 250–500 mg. orally, 4 times a day for 10 days (avoid if allergic to penicillin or cephalosporins); **or**

3. erythromycin 250–500 mg. orally, 4 times a day for 10 days; **or**

4. clarithromycin (Biaxin) 500 mg. orally, 2 times a day for 10 days; **or**

5. azithromycin (Zithromax) 250 mg. orally, 2 pills together initially, then 1 pill daily for 4 days.

Infections of the Nail or Nail Margin (Paronychial Infections)

The most common causes of nail margin (cuticle) infections are bacteria. Prolonged contact with water often makes the nail margins prone to infection. Such exposure must be reduced when it's implicated as a cause of infection.

Nail margin infections which are red, tender, and swollen with pus are treated with hot soaks for 15–20 minutes, 3–4 times a day. Apply an antibiotic ointment twice a day or after each soak. Open a pus pocket carefully with a sterile knife blade or pin, inserted and inscribed in an arc under the infected skin along the nail edge. Cover with a Band-Aid and keep the area clean. Get medical attention if there is no improvement in 3–4 days. If oral antibiotics are necessary use **one** of the following:

1. clindamycin 300 mg. orally, 4 times per day for 10 days; **or**

2. erythromycin 250–500 mg. orally, 4 times a day for 10 days; **or**

3. clarithromycin (Biaxin) 500 mg. orally, 2 times a day for 10 days; **or**

4. azithromycin (Zithromax) 250 mg. orally, 2 pills together initially, then 1 pill daily for 4 days.

If no pus is present, treat with one of the topical antifungal ointments or creams listed on p. 193.

Care of the Feet

Except for diabetics, foot problems are rarely life-threatening in healthy adults. For the traveler with limited time in a foreign city, however, a minor problem like a hangnail or blisters is a major annoyance. It may even spell disaster for someone hiking in a remote area. Because they're potentially disabling, foot problems must be prevented if at all possible.

A good pair of walking shoes or hiking boots, with support and cushioning, is essential. Always break in new shoes *prior to travel*. When hiking, wear 2 pairs of socks. The inner pair should be a wicking sock that carries moisture away from the feet. Carry extra socks to change into if needed to keep your feet dry.

Preventing Infection

Travelers should avoid going barefoot in developing nations. Infection is always a possibility following any cut, scrape, or other break in the skin. In addition to bacterial infections, there is a risk of acquiring hookworm and other parasitic infections from going barefoot.

Many cities, towns, and rural villages throughout the world lack adequate sewage treatment facilities. Local water supplies are frequently contaminated as a result. This is also often true of rivers, lakes, and coastal areas. Water reaching the ocean or even the ocean itself can be contaminated. Cuts from coral, shells, rocks, glass, or metal hidden along banks or beaches commonly become infected.

In Salvador, Brazil, one of the authors was disabled for a week with a severe foot infection after stepping in contaminated water that flowed across a beach. This occurred in spite of the fact that he had no known open cuts or breaks in the skin.

Treatment of Minor Cuts and Wounds

Feet require the same conscientious care recommended for any wound, only more so. Thoroughly remove all splinters, glass, or other foreign bodies. Clean the wound carefully as previously described. Watch for development of secondary bacterial infection or cellulitis and treat as required. If these develop, pain can be quite excruciating when pressure is applied to the foot. In addition to antibiotics and hot soaks, keep the affected leg elevated. For pain or fever take 1 or 2 aspirin or acetaminophen (Tylenol) up to 4 times a day, or a nonsteroidal anti-inflammatory such as ibuprofen or naproxen.

Blisters

Whether hiking in remote mountains or exploring a new city, a blister may be calamitous if you're unable to walk without pain or discomfort. Friction against the skin from poorly fitting shoes or socks and/or excessive moisture buildup is the usual cause of blistering.

Treatment

Immediately stop walking and take care of any developing blister. Dry your feet well and pack around the sore or blister with a doughnut-shaped ring of moleskin or gauze and tape. Leave the blister intact if possible to prevent infection. If no padding is available, or if the blister interferes with walking or is likely to break from further rubbing, use a sterile needle to puncture it at the edge. The needle can be sterilized with a match flame until red hot, then allowed to cool. After the blister is pierced and drained, cover it with a thin layer of topical antibiotic ointment and a Band-Aid 2–3 times a day or as needed to keep it clean and dry. If the blister becomes infected, treat with oral antibiotics as indicated for secondary bacterial infection, described earlier in this chapter.

Hangnails (Ingrown nails)

In addition to being painful, hangnails are a potential site of infection. They're largely preventable. Usually they're a result of improper nail cutting or shoes that don't fit. Accumulation of debris under the nail, prolonged exposure to moisture in damp climates, or injury to the nail or toe are other contributing factors.

Hangnails cause pain with redness and swelling around the nail bed, sometimes with bleeding. Secondary bacterial infection with pus formation may follow.

Prevention and Treatment

To avoid hangnails, toenails should never be cut very short. Leave the edges square, not rounded. If dampness or sweating is a problem, wear socks made of cotton rather than synthetic materials. Change them often.

It's also important to wear well-fitting, comfortable shoes that allow the feet to breathe. Avoid high-top boots which cause more dampness to accumulate. Open-toed shoes will help prevent hangnails, or wear 2 or more pairs of shoes in rotation allowing each pair to dry out between use. Antifungal powders such as Tinactin, Zeasorb, or Desenex will help decrease dampness. If redness and swelling occur without infection, place several layers of thin, twisted cotton fibers (from a cotton ball or swab) between the toe and nail, near the sides of the nail. Tamp them gently but firmly into place with something thin and blunt so as not to cut the skin. The cotton will buffer the skin and elevate the nail, allowing it to grow out without causing further injury.

If infection occurs, hangnails can become very painful. Use warm soaks, topical antibacterial ointment, dressing changes, and oral antibiotics as described for secondary bacterial infection. Obtain medical help to have the hangnail removed in severe infections, or if no improvement is noted in 2–3 days.

Superficial Fungal Skin Infections

Superficial fungal infections, like athlete's foot, jock itch, and ringworm, are relatively common. They thrive on moisture and can pop up like mushrooms almost overnight. Both prevention and cure require keeping the affected area as dry as possible.

These infections are usually moist, red, itchy, and annoying. They sometimes lead to secondary bacterial infection, especially athlete's foot which can progress to severe cellulitis. Avoid scratching to prevent secondary infection.

Use of Antifungal Medications

In addition to other measures, you usually require antifungal medications to speed relief from athlete's foot, ringworm, or jock itch. Use any of the antifungal preparations listed below twice a day. Wash the affected areas beforehand with soap and water, and dry thoroughly before applying medication.

These preparations come in different formulations, such as creams, lotions, solutions, or powders. They may also be designated for specific infections, such as "jock itch" or "athlete's foot." Use whatever is available and/or works. If there is no relief after 7-10 days of treatment, seek medical attention.

1. clotrimazole (Mycelex 1% cream or solution, Lotrimin 1% cream, lotion, or solution);

2. tolnaftate (Tinactin cream, solution, or powder);

3. undecylenate (Desenex cream, ointment, liquid, or powder);

4. miconazole (Monistat Derm cream);

5. ketaconazole (Nizoral cream);

6. miconazole (Micatin cream or ointment);

7. clotrimazole plus a topical corticosteroid - betamethasone dipropionate (Lotrisone cream);

8. terbinafine HCl (Lamisil cream).

Athlete's Foot (Tinea Pedis)

This common rash usually starts between the toes. It may spread to the sides, tops, or soles of the feet. The affected skin feels itchy or burning, and appears cracked and peeling. Clear, fluid-filled blisters may form. These are subject to secondary bacterial infection when they break.

Occasionally the hands or groin are also affected. Once established, athlete's foot may be impossible to eliminate without reducing sweaty activity or relocating to a drier climate.

Prevention and Treatment

Preventing the spread of athlete's foot requires diligent attention. Sandals, thongs, and open-toed shoes are the preferred footwear for everyday use provided they don't irritate the feet. It's also a good idea to wear thongs or sandals in a public or community shower to prevent acquiring or spreading infection.

Carefully dry between the toes after showering or swimming. A hair dryer works wonders. Socks, if worn, should be made of cotton rather than nylon or other synthetics. Liberally anoint their interiors with an antifungal powder. Change socks as often as necessary to keep the feet dry. If wearing tennis shoes, thoroughly wash and dry them to eliminate fungus and prevent reinfection.

Use a topical antifungal cream, lotion, or ointment to control athlete's foot not responsive to the above measures. Severe infections may require the placement of small wads of cotton between the toes at night.

Ringworm of the Body (Tinea Corporis)

This infection is characterized by one or more ring-shaped lesions that usually appear on areas of exposed skin or the torso. The ring develops as the fungus grows outward in an enlarging circle while dying in the center. The "rings" are usually itchy and scaly, with small raised, possibly fluid-filled lesions appearing on the well defined outer border. The central area is flat and scaly to clear or clearing. Cats or puppies may be the source of infection.

Treatment

Treat with any of the topical antifungal medications. Treatment may take weeks to clear the infection.

Jock Itch (Tinea Crusis)

"Jock itch" is an extremely itchy, red, raised, slightly scaly rash of the groin and inner thighs. It sometimes extends to the edges of the buttocks. The rash has a sharply defined border which may have clear central areas. There may be small fluid-filled blisters along the outer edge.

The rash spreads quickly with small red, raised spots (satellite lesions) frequently occurring adjacent to the central rash. Tinea crusis commonly affects men. It can occur in women, often associated with a vaginal yeast infection (see p. 357–359 for vaginal yeast infections).

Treatment

Keep the area dry (hair dryers work well) and clean. Avoid over bathing and irritation. A drying antifungal powder should be dusted on 2–3 times a day. Don't use underwear or pants made of synthetic or rough materials. Wear shorts to allow air to reach the groin. Men may need to wear an athletic supporter to decrease irritation.

Tinea Versicolor

This fungal infection is usually noticed because of skin discoloration. Rashes appear white, pink, or tan, often as spots or patches on the back, chest, or arms. They can cover large areas, extending to the abdomen, neck, and occasionally the face. Itching is absent or minimal. Scales can be obtained by scraping with a fingernail.

Recurrences are common even after treatment. The rash causes no harm and isn't very contagious. With treatment the scaling will stop, although the discolored areas remain until either tanned or until the surrounding tan fades.

Treatment
Topical treatments

Selsun solution (selenium sulfide) - Scrub the lesions with a stiff brush after bathing, then apply the solution to all areas of the body with discoloration. Avoid the eyes and genitals. Wash the medication off after 15 minutes. Repeat treatments daily for 2 weeks.

If an allergic reaction occurs, discontinue use.

If Selsun solution is not available, try one of the following topical antifungal preparations:

1. tolnaftate (Tinactin) solution; **or**

2. miconazole (Monistat Derm Cream); **or**

3. clotrimazole (Mycelex 1% cream or solution, Lotrimin 1% cream, lotion, or solution)

Oral medications (if topical unavailable):

1. ketoconazole 400 mg. orally, as a single dose; **or**

2. fluconazole 400 mg. orally, as a single dose.

Allergic and Hypersensitivity Reactions

Changes in the skin, usually some form of rash, often reveal allergies. The reaction may be localized — confined to a small area of affected skin — as in contact dermatitis. It can also be systemic, affecting the whole body and producing generalized symptoms such as itching wheezing, throat tightness or difficulty breathing.

Systemic Hypersensitivity Reactions

Systemic reactions may occur from medications, insect stings, animal dander, pollen, food, and other causes. Rashes due to systemic reactions are usually either red and flat, or red and raised in the form of welts (hives). They're frequently symmetrical, affecting right and left sides of the body equally. The skin may also appear flushed. There may be moderate to severe itching.

Rashes due to systemic reactions are sometimes, though not always, accompanied by other signs of allergic response. These can include sneezing, runny nose, nausea, vomiting, diarrhea, fever or headache, lethargy, and a tickling or lump in the throat which cannot be cleared by coughing.

Occasionally, systemic reactions result in respiratory symptoms:

Wheezing, throat tightness, or labored breathing indicates a potential emergency, requiring immediate medical help, possibly including injectable epinephrine from an allergy or medical kit if available.

Drug Reactions

When a skin rash or any other symptom of allergy follows use of a medication, stop taking the medication immediately.

Treatment

For skin rashes or other mild allergic reactions, the usual treatment is an antihistamine. Take **one** of the following until the rash and itching subside:

Non-sedating antihistamines

1. fexofenadine (Allegra), 60 mg. orally twice a day; **or**

2. loratadine (Claritin), 10 mg. orally once a day; **or**

3. cetirizine (Zyrtec), 10 mg. orally once a day; **or**

   Antihistamines that may cause drowsiness:

4. Benadryl (diphenhydramine HCl), 25–50 mg. orally every 4–6 hours; **or**

5. Atarax (hydroxyzine HCl),10–25 mg. orally every 4–6 hours.

Hives (Urticaria)

Hives are large, red, raised round areas of skin (welts) which itch moderately to severely. They're usually an allergic response to some environmental factor and develop very quickly. Factors that may induce hives during travel include extreme changes in temperature and humidity, insect bites, medications, and new foods, especially fruits. Parasites and hepatitis are other possible causes.

Hives disappear on their own schedule once the cause is removed— in as little as 2–3 hours from some food and drug allergies or up to several days or even weeks. If you started a new medicine or ate a new food, discontinue it immediately. If diarrhea or abdominal cramps accompany hives, take a stool sample to the nearest medical laboratory to check for parasites. If there's yellowing of the skin (jaundice) or right upper abdominal pain just below the rib cage, then hives may be due to hepatitis.

Treatment

Treat itching with an antihistamine as indicated above for mild allergic reactions. Cool compresses, showers, or baths will help. One cup of cornstarch (Aveeno powder) or Domeboro's solution added to bathwater twice a day will also help to relieve symptoms. When swelling occurs around the eyes and/or mouth, obtain medical evaluation and treatment. A steroid injection or oral prednisone may be necessary.

Contact Dermatitis (Localized Allergic Reaction)

Hypersensitive skin reactions can follow direct contact with chemicals or other irritants, such as the oils from certain plants. The resulting rash is usually red, flat or raised, and may be blistery with clear fluid (vesicular). Rashes from plants often follow lines where the plant has brushed against the skin.

Severe itching, burning, or stinging frequently accompany skin lesions. The area may be hot and swollen, and sometimes appears crusty after blisters break open.

Prevention

The key, of course, is to avoid exposure or re-exposure to the irritating substance. If you have sensitive skin or known allergies to certain products such as soaps or perfumes, carry enough of your own non-allergenic supplies with you. Soaps made in developing countries are often particularly harsh and irritating.

When the cause is unknown, a rash's location often provides a clue. A new shampoo, soap, hair spray, dye, or other hair product may cause rashes of the scalp. Soap, cleansers, moisturizers, suntan lotion, DEET containing repellents, or shaving cream are possible causes of a facial rash. For rashes on the hands or wrists, consider rings, bracelets, soap or other chemicals. Sometimes protective gloves or other covering can be used to avoid contact, especially in work situations.

Treatment

For relief of itching, use one of the antihistamines listed previously for mild systemic reactions. Hydrocortisone 1% cream applied sparingly on the rash twice daily is also helpful. However, **if a rash becomes infected, don't apply hydrocortisone or other steroid ointments.** Treat as indicated for secondary bacterial infection.

Indications for Medical Attention

Obtain prompt medical attention for any of the following:

1. wheezing, shortness of breath, or other respiratory difficulty;

2. symptoms unimproved after 4–5 days, with or without treatment;

3. large areas of swelling, especially of the face, eyes, neck, or genitals;

4. swelling with itching or pain unrelieved by antihistamines.

Medical treatment for these symptoms may include oral or intramuscular steroids, which should be taken only under medical supervision.

Creature Discomforts: Scabies, Lice, And Other Pests

Rashes Caused by Parasites

Creeping eruption (cutaneous larva migrans)

Larvae of hookworms that infest dogs and cats cause this rash. Infection is spread by contact with the feces of infected animals. There is a high risk of infection in moist, sandy areas, especially for several days following a rainfall. Though the larvae don't cause hookworm in humans, they do produce a rash. On contact, larvae penetrate areas of exposed human skin, usually the feet, legs, buttocks, or hands.

The larvae burrow through the top layer of skin. This leaves a winding, threadlike red trail of inflamed tissue, visible just under the skin. The trails can look quite bizarre. Itching is moderate to severe and secondary bacterial infection is common. When the rash appears on the buttocks or around the anus it may be caused by another parasite called strongyloides (see "Common Intestinal Parasites," p. 244).

Prevention

Don't go barefoot in tropical and subtropical countries. In sandy areas, avoid skin contact. Wear gloves for digging and use a blanket or other groundcover when sitting or lying down.

Treatment

For itching take one of the previously listed antihistamines. Infection is treated with **one** of the following:

1. Thiabendazole lotion (10%) applied topically four times a day until rash clears (usually 2–7 days).

2. Ivermectin taken as a single dose (note: each tablet contains 6 mg. Take twice the dose if using the 3 mg. tablets).

If your weight is		
	15-25 kg.	Take $1/2$ tablet
	26-44 kg.	1 tablet
	45-64 kg.	$1^1/2$ tablets
	65-84 kg.	2 tablets
	above 85 kg.	200 micrograms/kg.

3. An alternative is albendazole, 200 mg. orally twice a day for 3 days.

Scabies

Scabies is a mite that produces red, raised lesions, occasionally with small clear fluid-filled blisters. These lesions sometimes appear as straight lines. They're usually found in the webs between fingers, or on the wrists, elbows, belt line, ankles, legs, breasts, or genital region. They're very itchy, especially at night.

Travelers are most likely to encounter scabies in cheap hotels from contaminated beds, sheets, or blankets. Scabies can also be acquired from sleeping bags or from intimate contact with an infected individual.

Treatment (except during pregnancy)

Use Elimite (5% permethrin) cream. Thoroughly

massage into the skin from the neck down to the soles of the feet. Leave on for 8–14 hours, then wash off. May repeat treatment in one week.

Alternative treatments

Lindane lotion (1%) is an alternative treatment. Apply in the same manner as Elimite, avoiding contact with eyes and mucous membranes. Wash off after 8 hours. Lindane is related to the pesticide DDT and is toxic if used more frequently. Lindane can also cause rashes or allergic reactions (contact dermatitis), in which case discontinue it and thoroughly wash it off.

Ivermectin taken as a single dose (note: each tablet contains 6 mg.; take twice the dose if using 3 mg. tablets)

If your weight is 15-24 kg.	Take $1/2$ tablet
25-35 kg.	1 tablet
36-50 kg.	$1 1/2$ tablets
51-65 kg.	2 tablets
66-79 kg.	$2 1/2$ tablets
above 80 kg.	200 micrograms/ kg.

During the first 8 hours of treatment, wash in hot water all recently used sheets, clothing, or other fabrics that have been in contact with your skin, and use a clothes dryer if available. If washing by hand, use gloves and the hottest water tolerable. Alternatively, boil clothes and dry with direct exposure to sunlight. Sleeping bags and other large articles should be dry-cleaned if possible, or bagged in plastic and left for 48–72 hours.

After treatment, itching may persist for up to 2 weeks due to residual parasitic proteins. Treat itching with an antihistamine as indicated previously for mild allergic reactions. Repeat treatment after 7 days, but only if new lesions are noted at that time.

Treat close traveling companions even if they show no symptoms of infection. While this sounds simple, under travel conditions it can be a major hassle. One of the authors and a friend were obliged to spend an entire day in a Quito, Ecuador hotel room in undergarments after entrusting all of their other clothing to the single washing machine and dryer located across town. Two more days were spent patiently anticipating the demise of scabies larvae in their sleeping bags which had been isolated by bagging and sealing in plastic.

Treatment in Pregnancy

Don't use lindane or Ivermectin during pregnancy. Use Elimite as directed above or use Eurax (crotamiton) instead. Eurax is applied to the entire body from the neck down. Repeat the application in 48 hours. Wash off thoroughly 48 hours after the second application.

Head and Body Lice

These lice look similar. Head lice can be found in the hair, along with their small, white egg nits which are attached to the hair shafts. You can distinguish nits from dandruff because they can't be pulled off the hair with fingers. Dandruff is easy to remove.

Body lice are somewhat harder to find, frequently hiding in clothing seams. Their nits are also found on body hairs, including the eye lashes. Itching from both head and body lice is intense.

Treatment

1. **for head lice**- permethrin 1% cream rinse ("Nix"), applied to all affected areas and washed off after 10 minutes; **or**

2. **for head or body lice** - pyrethrum and piperonyl butoxide ("RID" or "R and C Shampoo"), applied to all affected areas and washed off after 10 minutes.

As an alternative (this may be less effective) :

For head lice, use 1–2 ounces of lindane shampoo before showering, with special attention to head and facial hair. Leave on for 4 minutes, then rinse thoroughly. A capful of lindane in a sink of warm water is sufficient for sterilizing combs and brushes. Let them soak for about 2 hours, then rinse well. **Don't** use lindane around the eyes. **Don't** use lindane during pregnancy.

For body lice, use lindane lotion and treat clothing as indicated for scabies. Clothing can also be treated with 1% Malathion powder.

Itching

To control itching, take one of the above listed anti-histamines.

Nit Removal

Nits are easy to remove after treatment. Hair should first be soaked for 30 minutes in a solution of hot water and white vinegar. Then comb thoroughly with a fine-tooth comb. Eyebrows or lashes can be treated with petroleum jelly or an occlusive eye ointment twice a day for 10 days.

Crabs

These critters can take up anonymous, quiet residence in private places, causing barely an itch before their offspring overrun the entire neighborhood. The presence of white nits (eggs) on the hair shafts is a clue to keep looking. As we said earlier, nits can be distinguished from dandruff because they resist being pulled from the hair.

If you find black spots at the base of the hair, they may scamper away on little legs if you watch carefully. Pick one up with tweezers to examine closely if you are feeling brave. Personally, we have always felt that if you held a mirror to your groin, the crabs would probably commit mass suicide upon seeing their true appearance.

Treatment

Before showering use *either*:

1. Permethrin 1% cream rinse ("Nix") as described above for head lice; **or**

2. Pyrethrum and piperonyl butoxide ("RID" or "R and C Shampoo"), applied to all affected areas and washed off after 10 minutes.

An alternative treatment would be the use 1-2 ounces of lindane shampoo as follows: lather and leave on for 4 minutes, then rinse thoroughly. Pay special attention to all hairy places below the neck, although beard and head are occasionally involved. If shampoo is unavailable, substitute lotion. It must be left on for 8 hours. Don't use lindane during pregnancy. RepeatlLindane after 7 days, but only if new crabs are seen

Another medication which should not be used during pregnancy is 6% precipitated sulfur in petrolatum. This is a medication some pharmacists might prepare for treating crabs.

Treat clothing and bedding as for scabies.. The nits will eventually fall off, or can be pulled or combed out with a fine tooth comb dipped in white vinegar and water. Clean combs and brushes as for head lice.

Fleas

Fleas are often encountered in older hotels, from old or dirty mattresses, bedding, or carpeting. They may also be found in grassy areas around campgrounds where pets or other animals are present.

Bites result in small, red, raised, itchy lesions, especially on the arms, legs, feet, and ankles. For severe itching, apply 1% hydrocortisone cream twice a day or use "Itch Balm Plus".

It's sometimes difficult to identify the source of bites. If you put on white socks, fleas show up easily against the white background. If a suspected flea bite doesn't get better, but instead spreads and gets very itchy, especially at night, consider the possibility of scabies.

Ticks

You can acquire ticks by brushing against vegetation while walking or hiking. On rare occasions, they cause a paralysis of an arm or leg which slowly ascends the body, and which disappears when you remove the tick.

If symptoms of illness, including fevers or rashes, arise following tick exposure, be sure to mention this fact when seeking medical evaluation.

Prevention

Wear protective clothing or tuck socks over pant legs. Treat clothing with repellent chemicals such as permethrin (see "Mosquito and Tick Precautions," pp. 39 – 44). Inspect skin closely after potential exposure since diseases such as Lyme disease require tick adherence for over 24 hours to transmit the spirochete.

Treatment

Remove ticks with blunt tweezers, or with your fingers protected by a rubber glove, paper towel, or Kleenex. Grasp the tick as close to the skin as possible and pull straight back gently but steadily. If necessary lift the tick upward and pull parallel to the skin until the tick is freed. Don't yank or twist, as this risks leaving the head imbedded in the skin. Wash the wound with soap and water or hydrogen peroxide, then apply antibacterial ointment to prevent secondary infection.

Don't apply gasoline, rubbing alcohol, ether, nail polish, or the hot end of a match or needle to the tick! These methods don't work well and can cause pain or skin damage.

Baby ticks can attack in great numbers — several hundred to a thousand, all at once. This befell one of the authors at the Mayan ruins of Palenque, Mexico. Freshly hatched and ravenous, they rapidly ascended under both pantlegs.

There was nothing to but strip on the spot and brush them off as quickly as possible. A nearby pool provided a chance to try drowning the 40 or 50 that remained, and those still lurking in the jeans. The attempt was totally ineffective, but felt good anyway. Back in the hotel room there was ample opportunity to practice every known method of tick removal, and invent a few more (tequila doesn't work). In an ongoing debate between the authors over the usefulness of underwear, score one or more points for the "pro" side, depending on your degree of modesty.

Personal experience attests that itching can be intense, lasting up to 2 weeks. Use oral antihistamines (see p. 197), 1% hydrocortisone cream, Calamine lotion, cool wet compresses, or "Itch Balm Plus" to relieve symptoms. Treat for secondary bacterial infection if necessary.

Chiggers

Chiggers are also known as harvest mites or red bugs. They live on grasses and shrubs, where the larvae attach to passing humans or animals. After obtaining a blood meal, the larvae are courteous enough (usually) to drop off. Within hours you may notice an extremely itchy red raised lesion, occasionally with a larva still visible in the center. Lesions are most frequently found on the ankles and legs, especially where clothing is snug against the skin, impeding larval movement. Severity of the reaction depends on your allergic sensitivity. In severe reactions, the rash is more extensive.

Most lesions resolve on their own within a week. Treatment is symptomatic. For itching, apply a topical steroid cream to the rash twice a day. You may also use an oral antihistamine as indicated previously for mild allergic reactions.

Prevention- see insect precautions pp. 39 – 44.

Myiasis- botflies and tumbu flies

Myiasis is the term used for the invasion of living tissue by the larvae (maggots) of various two-winged (dipterous) flies. Two common localized forms of myiasis affecting the skin are caused by botflies and tumbu flies.

Botflies

Found in the tropical Americas, botflies are known in some countries as mosquito worms or "gusano de zancudo". They deposit their eggs on mosquitoes, biting flies, or ticks. When these insects land to feed, the eggs hatch and penetrate the feeding site.

The larvae develop for 2-3 months within the skin of the host before dropping off. Larvae are seen to develop most often in lesions on unprotected areas, such as the hands, arms, neck and head. During the first week of infection there is an itchy lesion which resembles a mosquito bite. As the larva grows it begins to move, producing severe itching and pain, until the lesion finally resembles a boil. A central opening develops in this "botfly boil" through which the tail end of the larva protrudes, along with a discharge containing weepy fluid and pus.

Prevention- see insect precautions pp. 39 – 44.

Treatment

Most larvae can be removed by applying lateral pressure with the fingers around the opening of the lesion. The larvae will pop out. Caution should be taken since other fluid may squirt out. Tweezers may be needed to assist this evacuation.

Alternative removal techniques can include:

Applying a small adhesive bandage over each lesion, and removing in 3-4 days.

Drawing the larvae out by applying raw bacon over the lesion (which may require tweezer assistance).

Suffocating the larvae with paraffin, Vaseline, petroleum jelly, mineral oil, or kerosene. This is followed by removal using lateral pressure or tweezers.

In Brazil tobacco juice is sometimes applied, causing the larva to protrude so it can be squeezed out.

Tumbu Flies.

In Africa a lesion similar to the botfly is produced by the tumbu fly. These flies deposit their eggs on sandy soil or laundry, such as diapers, laid out to dry. When newly hatched, the larvae invade unbroken skin on contact, causing boil-like lesions.

Prevention- see insect precautions pp. 39 – 44. Diapers or other clothing left out to dry must be ironed to kill the tumbu fly eggs.

Treatment- same as for botfly.

Viral Skin Infections

Genital Herpes

The herpes simplex virus, similar to the one that causes cold sores, causes genital herpes. Normally, herpes lesions go away by themselves without treatment. However, they can be quite painful and mortifying.

Genital herpes may be your first encounter with a sexually transmitted disease. It doesn't help to know that no cure has yet been found. This has led one to ask, "What is the difference between herpes and true love?" Answer: "Herpes is forever." Although a first attack of genital herpes may feel like the end of the world — the end of innocence, sex, and perhaps mobility — it is in fact not cause for despair.

Herpes sores appear first as raised, pimple-like lesions (small vesicles) with white tops and a red base. They're usually grouped together. The lesions break open, releasing clear fluid. They then form small ulcers which crust over.

The first occurrence of herpes is frequently very painful. Women, in particular, can find it incapacitating. An initial attack may last 1–2 weeks. Recurrences are less frequent, of shorter duration, and produce much less discomfort.

After an initial attack there may never be a

recurrence. If there is, it may be due to stress, exposure to heat or sunlight, trauma, or minor infection.

The herpes virus is usually contagious only while a lesion is present. Avoid sex during this time. Likewise if you have oral herpes, avoid kissing or sharing drinks, glasses, or cigarettes.

While most herpes infections have no harmful or lasting consequences, women should be aware of two facts about genital herpes. As with venereal warts, once you contract it, herpes is associated with an increased risk of cervical cancer. It's thus prudent to have a yearly Pap smear. An open herpes lesion is also potentially very dangerous to a baby during delivery. If you become pregnant, inform your medical provider that you have had herpes. If herpes occurs for the first time during pregnancy, consult your medical provider.

Treatment

With first occurrences of genital herpes, oral antiviral medications decrease pain and speed the rate of healing by approximately 5 days. The oral medication works much better than topical acyclovir ointment. Both are expensive and may be hard to find outside of major cities while traveling. If prone to outbreaks due to stress, take medication with you. Even on vacations, travel can be stressful.

Oral antiviral medications are used for all *initial* outbreaks *except during pregnancy*. Use *one* of the following:

1. acyclovir, 400 mg. orally 3 times a day for 10 days; **or**

2. valacyclovir (Valtrex), 1000 mg. orally every 12 hours for 10 days; **or**

3. famciclovir (Famvir), 250 mg. orally every 8 hours for 5 – 10 days.

Don't take oral antiviral medications during pregnancy. If you are pregnant and have a history of herpes, discuss with your obstetrician what to do for an outbreak while traveling.

For frequent recurrences, obtain medical evaluation. Most recurrences don't benefit from oral medications. If used, the usual doses are:

1. acyclovir 400 mg. orally 2 times a day for 5 days *or* 800 mg. twice a day for 5 days; **or**

2. famciclovir 125 mg. orally twice a day for 5 days; **or**

3. valacyclovir 500 mg. orally twice a day for 3 days.

For discomfort during an acute attack of genital herpes, try shallow cool baths with baking soda applied to the genital area. Avoid warm water, as heat activates the virus. Cool water applied during urination (or urinating in a bath tub) helps to alleviate burning.

The lesions should be washed with soap and cool water 3 times a day to help keep the affected area dry. If tight underwear must be worn, apply talcum powder or cornstarch to the area. Women, especially, may benefit from the drying effect of a blow dryer (air only, no heat), or exposure to light (but not a heat lamp) several times daily.

Indications for medical attention — Anyone with an active herpes lesion who develops an eye infection should seek medical help immediately.

Other Skin Problems

Sunburn

Sunburn occurs very quickly at tropical latitudes, higher elevations, and near reflective surfaces. Preventive measures are important (see Chapter 1, pp. 29 – 32). Minimizing sun exposure also helps retard the skin's aging process and reduces the risk of other problems such as skin cancer.

Treatment of Sunburn

For sunburn, take 2 aspirin tablets up to 4 times a day as necessary for discomfort, or try a nonsteroid anti-inflammatory medication such as ibuprofen or naproxen. Apply cool wet compresses to the worst areas. Plain water is best, as vinegar and other home remedies may be irritating. Skin lotions may sound soothing, but oils can increase discomfort by trapping heat. Some people swear by the aloe vera plant as a means of soothing sunburns.

Don't use anesthetic sprays or ointments. These may sensitize the skin to allergic reaction. If blisters occur, don't break them. Avoid re-exposure to sunlight, and watch for secondary infection.

Skin Cancer

Repeated exposure to sunlight can lead to dangerous skin changes, including the uncontrolled growth of abnormal cells (skin cancer). Of these, malignant melanoma is the most life-threatening.

Skin cancers are largely avoidable by reducing sun exposure, using sun screens (see pp. 30 – 32), and preventing sunburn They're also curable. Even melanomas, if detected and treated early, are completely curable.

Risk Factors

People with fair skin, light hair and eye color, or who sunburn easily, are typically more prone to skin cancer. A family history of skin cancer, or a prior occurrence of melanoma, are also considered risk factors.

Danger Signs

Melanomas, in particular, often appear around existing moles, birthmarks, or skin lesions. Examine your skin monthly for any changes. Note particularly the following "ABCDs":

Asymmetry — when one half of the mole doesn't look like the other half.

Border — irregularity. Edges may be ragged, notched or blurred.

Color — pigmentation that is not uniform. Shades of tan, brown, and black may be present. In some cases red, white, or blue discoloring add to the mottled appearance.

Diameter — greater than 6 millimeters (about the size of a pencil eraser). Any growth in size of a mole or increase in number is cause for concern.

Additional warning signs include changes in the surface of a mole — scaliness, oozing, bleeding, or the appearance of a bump or nodule; spread of pigment from the border into surrounding skin; change in sensation including itchiness, tenderness, or pain. If any of these changes are noted, **obtain medical evaluation as soon as possible.** Protection from excessive sun exposure and early detection and treatment of any abnormal skin lesion could be life-saving.

Heat Rash (Prickly Heat)

This is a rash that occurs in hot moist regions, usually in the tropics or subtropics. Obese people are most affected. The cause is blockage of the skin pores (sweat glands). The use of skin ointments or powders, or sweat mixed with dirt or sand, increases the risk of developing a prickly heat rash.

The rash is red, with slightly raised blisters. It most often occurs on covered rather than exposed parts of the body. Burning and itching may be present. The heat and reduced sweating associated with this rash are conducive to other symptoms of heat exposure. Dehydration (see pp. 223 – 226) must be avoided to prevent complications such as fever and heat prostration.

Prevention and Treatment

Gradual exposure to sunlight will reduce the risk of both sunburn and prickly heat rash. Reduce sweating by wearing cool loose-fitting clothing made from nonsynthetic material, preferably cotton. Avoid greasy skin ointments or powders. Take advantage of air conditioning when available, and bathe frequently.

Cooling lotions, with menthol, or glycerin, will reduce itching and can be used 2–4 times a day. If needed, a topical steroid cream can be applied to the rash. Use a 1% hydrocortisone cream twice a day. Oral antihistamines can also be used to reduce itching.

If none of these measures are effective, it may be necessary to relocate to a cooler, dryer climate.

Chafing

Chafing occurs most often in hot, moist climates. When adjacent skin surfaces rub against each other, the result is an irritated rash. The area affected is red, slightly tender and itchy, and flat, not raised.

Prevention and Treatment

Wear cool, loose clothing. Men may need to wear an athletic supporter to reduce chafing in the groin area. A thin coat of ointment such as petroleum jelly may also help reduce friction in this area.

Otherwise, chafed areas should be gently washed and kept dry with corn starch or talcum powder. These can also be applied at bedtime. For tenderness or itching, try applying 1% hydrocortisone cream or lotion sparingly to the affected area, twice a day.

Itching (Pruritus)

Dry skin is the most frequent cause of flaking or itching. This is sometimes due simply to climate changes. However, over bathing, by depleting the natural oils, is often the root of the problem.

Prevention of Itching Due to Dry Skin

Reduce bathing. Take a sponge bath every other day, only in the areas needed. Use tepid or lukewarm water. This is less drying than hot water.

Plain soaps may be less drying and irritating than those with added perfume or deodorant. Either Dove or Neutrogena are good nondrying soaps. It's not advisable to use an antibacterial soap, such as Betadine or Hibiclens, for general skin care unless prescribed medically for a specific condition.

Bath oils can be very helpful to prevent drying if added towards the end of the bath. Skin moisturizers and creams are most effective when used immediately after a bath or shower. They help keep in moisture, but add little or none of their own.

Hydrating baths may be helpful in very dry climates. Add $1/2$ to 1 cup of salt to a tub of cool to lukewarm water. Soak for 25–30 minutes. Blot dry and apply a bath oil or other moisturizing skin cream or lotion immediately after bathing.

Other Causes of Itching

There are other causes of itching, and related sensations of burning or crawling of the skin. These include diabetes, stress, insect bites, contact dermatitis, drug or other hypersensitivity reactions, hepatitis, and parasites including scabies, crabs, and lice. Treat the causes of itching whenever possible.

Symptomatic treatment of itching

Light stroking of an itchy area is sometimes effective without aggravating the itchy sensation. For local itching, try Calamine lotion or 1% hydrocortisone cream, lightly applied to the affected area twice a day. For severe itching take **one** of the following until the itching subsides:

Non-sedating antihistamines

1. Allegra (fexofenadine), 60 mg. orally twice a day; **or**

2. Claritin (loratadine), 10 mg. orally once a day; **or**

3. Zyrtec (cetirizine), 10 mg. orally once a day; **or**

Antihistamines that may cause drowsiness

4. Benadryl (diphenhydramine HCl), 25–50 mg. orally every 4–6 hours; **or**

continued on p. 218

Quick Reference

Bacterial Skin Infections and Other Lesions

Signs, symptoms, location	Possible cause
Mild to moderate pain or discomfort:	
small red or purplish inflamed area surrounding a hair follicle, occasionally with pus; may affect chin, scalp, armpit, groin, or any other area with hair	folliculitis
blistering lesion which opens, drains, and forms a honey-colored crust; often on the chin or around the nose	impetigo
red swollen tender area around nail margin, sometimes infection with pus	paronychial infection
previously broken skin (scratch, cut, bite, etc.) that becomes red, tender, warm to the touch; possibly with swelling, pus, or red streaks up the skin	secondary bacterial infection
flat, spreading red area, hot and tender to the touch	cellulitis
small to large sac-like area below skin, red, swollen and tender when touched; if opened will drain pus	abscess or boil (furuncle)
blistery lesion(s) in genital area that form small ulcers and then crust over; pain may be intense, especially in women	herpes
Nonpainful skin lesions:	
groin: small raised cauliflower-like lesion(s) in genital area	warts
mole, scar, birth mark, or other skin feature that changes color, shape, texture, or size	possible melanoma

Quick Reference

Common Causes of Itching and/or a Rash

Signs, symptoms, location	Possible cause
Itching *without* a rash:	
rectal area, increased itching at night	pinworms
rectally, with painful bowel movements and blood on toilet paper	hemorrhoids
rectally, after recent episode of diarrhea	normal reaction, usually lasting 1-2 days
dark urine, light-colored stools, nausea, yellow eyes or skin	hepatitis
flaking skin	excessively dry skin
generalized, worse at night, especially wrists, finger webs, elbow, waist, or breasts	early scabies
genital area, male	crabs
genital area, female	vaginal infection or crabs
Itching *with* a rash:	
on feet, toe webs, with cracked, peeling area between the toes	athlete's foot
small to large red, raised, welt-like lesions anywhere on the body	hives (urticaria)
small groups of blistering (vesicular), lesions sometimes linear with adjacent flat, red areas; anywhere on body but frequently on arms and hands	contact dermatitis
on scalp with small white particles resembling dandruff at base of hair follicle which cannot be pulled off	head lice
one or more red raised lesions frequently on feet or ankles	flea bites
small red, raised lesions in webs of fingers, elbows, waist, breasts, groin, and/or thigh; itching worse at night	scabies

Signs, symptoms, location	Possible cause
groin: with white particles like dandruff that don't pull off hairs, black spots at the base of hairs	crabs
groin: flat red lesion affecting labia or scrotum, spreading to adjacent skin; well-defined border with small red spots adjacent to central rash	fungal infection (jock itch or jock rash)
flat, discolored (usually whitish) patches on the back, chest, and arms	tinea versicolor
occasionally itchy, circular lesion or lesions with red, raised, well-defined outer border; scaly or clearing in the center	ringworm
on feet or buttocks with red, thread like winding trails	strongyloides or cutaneous larva migrans

5. Atarax (hydroxyzine HCl),10–25 mg. orally every 4–6 hours.

For intense localized itching (from insect bites, etc.), try direct application of a cold water compress, ice bag, Domeboro's solution, or Itch Balm Plus. The latter is an over-the-counter medication from Sawyer products (www.sawyerproducts.com) containing hydrocortisone, Benadryl, and tetracaine. It works well for relief of mild itching and skin irritation from insect bites, sunburn, contact dermatitis, and stings from some marine animals. One home remedy that works for insect bites is to rub lime juice on the bite. This stings initially but is followed by relief of the itching.

If there is no improvement, or if the cause is unknown, symptoms of itching require medical evaluation. When itching is accompanied by a rash, the rash must be identified and treated appropriately.

Quick Reference

Symptomatic Treatment of Itching
with or without a Rash

If a rash is present, it needs to be identified and treated. For specific causes of itching without a rash, such as heat or dryness, see recommendations in this chapter.

1. Severe, localized itching (from insect bites, etc.): Use direct application of a cold water compress, ice bag, or Domeboro's solution. Topical hydrocortisone cream or "Itch Balm Plus" can be used when the cause is not bacterial or viral.

2. Generalized itching: Take a cool bath with 1-2 cups of baking soda or mulled oatmeal added to the water.

For severe itching, systemic treatment with oral antihistamines may be needed, especially for sleep. Use one of the following:

1. Benadryl 25-50 mg. orally, 3-4 times a day; **or**

2. Atarax 10-25 mg. orally, 3-4 times a day; **or**

3. Periactin 4 mg. orally, 3 times a day.

For a nonsedating antihistamine, try one of the following:

1. Zyrtec, 10 mg. orally once a day; **or**

2. Claritin, 10 mg. orally once a day; **or**

3. Allegra, 60 mg. orally every 12 hours.

Quick Reference

Guidelines for Treating Unidentified Rashes
Indications for medical evaluation

Obtain medical evaluation and treatment for:

1. Any ulcerated lesion.
2. Any generalized body rash, especially one that involves the palms of the hands or soles of the feet (possible secondary syphilis).
3. Any persistent rash that worsens with or fails to respond to treatment.

Unless medical treatment is indicated, unidentified rashes can be treated temporarily using the following guidelines:

1. Rashes which are *not infected* (they may be red, swollen, itchy, and dry or weeping clear fluid, but don't contain pus) — treat with cool moist compresses or baths for 15–20 minutes, 2–3 times a day. Rashes due to allergic or hypersensitivity reactions respond to hydrocortisone cream and antihistamines. *Don't use antibiotics.*
2. Rashes which are *infected* (red, hot, painful, producing pus or whitish, yellow, or greenish matter) — treat with warm compresses for 15–20 minutes 3 times a day. In addition, bacterial infections will usually require topical or occasionally oral antibiotics. *Don't use hydrocortisone or other steroid cream.*
3. Lesions which are dry, keep moist. If applying a topical preparation, ointments are preferable to creams or lotions.
4. Lesions which are *moist* — keep dry. If you're using a topical preparation, avoid ointments. Creams are considered slightly drying; powders may be best.
5. Topical hydrocortisone cream may be used on rashes due to contact dermatitis or other allergic reaction. Don't use on fungal rashes, primary or secondary bacterial infections, scabies, or rashes due to viral infections.
6. Apply all topical ointments very thinly and sparingly.
7. If unsure whether a rash is due to heat or fungal infection, try applying Lotrisone cream topically twice a day. Or, try alternating a topical antifungal cream or ointment with topical hydrocortisone at 4-6 hour intervals.

Stomach and Intestinal Disorders

I am poured out like water . . .
my heart like wax is melted in
the midst of my bowels.
                    Psalms 22:14

To some travelers, midnight vigils in the water closet might seem as commonplace as passport visa applications. The price of an adventuresome spirit sometimes seems to be extracted in literal pounds of flesh. As one veteran traveler put it, "nausea and abdominal cramping should be dues enough . . . losses from diarrhea and vomiting aren't even tax deductible."

With a few exceptions these symptoms, although occasionally dire, are of minor consequence. Remember, however, that the gastrointestinal or GI tract is a meandering pathway through organs of the chest and abdomen. Almost any of these organs can cause related symptoms.

At the end of this chapter there's a chart of abdominal disorders that may cause nausea, vomiting, diarrhea, or abdominal pain. Use this to help quickly locate relevant information in the text.

Nausea, Vomiting, and Diarrhea

Although they often occur together, nausea, vomiting, and diarrhea are distinct entities. Each has many possible causes. For example, anxiety, pregnancy, and even head injury can cause vomiting. We'll discuss only the infectious causes which concern most travelers — bacteria, viruses, and parasites.

In otherwise healthy travelers, these symptoms often serve a protective function. They help rid the body of potentially harmful organisms or substances. It's worth noting that the physical stress of travel sometimes causes mild diarrhea or other minor GI disturbances. Jet lag, fatigue, new foods (especially fruits), caffeine, and alcohol may contribute to symptoms.

Most viral or bacterial causes of these symptoms are "self-limiting." Allow them to run their course and they go away with no harmful effects — *provided your fluid intake is adequate*. In general, it's wise not to treat symptoms when they first appear. However, dehydration is always a potential danger when nausea, vomiting, and/or diarrhea occur. You must completely replace lost fluids. A good rule to follow is drink enough fluid to keep your urine light in color. **If vigorous oral fluid replacement can't prevent dehydration, medical care is mandatory.**

Nausea, vomiting, and appetite loss are related, but can occur separately. In most cases due to viruses or bacteria, symptoms rarely last more than 24–48 hours. In cases of nausea alone, or mild nausea and vomiting in which adequate oral fluid intake is maintained, no treatment is necessary.

Treatment

Nausea and vomiting without diarrhea should not, in most cases, be treated with antibiotics. Obtain medical treatment for the following conditions:

1. Severe nausea and/or vomiting if oral fluids can't be taken or kept down. Dehydration must be prevented, or treated if present.

2. Symptoms of nausea and/or vomiting persisting more than 48 hours.

3. Vomiting which follows a head injury (may be accompanied by lethargy and disorientation). **This is a medical emergency.**

Treatment of Nausea and Vomiting Due to Pregnancy

Vitamin B6 supplements may help symptoms of nausea due to pregnancy. Take 50 mg. in the morning and 100 mg. at night. Discontinue these when symptoms diminish. Eating snacks at 2-hour intervals and having crackers available at the bedside in the morning can help. The "Sea Band," described on p. 25 as a treatment for motion sickness, may also be of benefit. Oral ginger root is reported to help many individuals and is available over the counter. If there's no improvement, or if symptoms are severe enough to cause dehydration, obtain medical help.

Treatment of Vomiting in Isolated Areas

Medications to stop vomiting (antiemetics) may be needed if medical help is not accessible and sufficient fluids can't be taken orally to prevent dehydration. Use these medications to stop nausea and vomiting so that fluids can be replaced. This is an interim measure only, to be used until medical help can be found.

To prevent vomiting, take Tigan 250 mg. or Compazine 10 mg. orally, up to 3 times a day. When unable to keep oral medications down, use a Tigan 200 mg. rectal suppository 3–4 times a day or a Compazine 25 mg. rectal suppository twice a day, as needed. When symptoms are due to hepatitis use Tigan, not Compazine. *Don't use these or other antiemetics during pregnancy.*

Dehydration and Rehydration

Whenever nausea, vomiting, and diarrhea occur, dehydration is a potential threat. With nausea and vomiting, fluid intake is often minimal. With severe or prolonged diarrhea, fluid loss may be substantial.

Uncorrected, dehydration can lead to internal

damage, shock, and death. **Dehydration must be prevented by drinking a sufficient quantity of liquids to replace all lost fluids. When dehydration can't be prevented by vigorous oral fluid replacement, medical attention must be obtained quickly. Intravenous fluids are required.**

Symptoms of dehydration

Decreasing urine output is one of the earliest indications of dehydration. Urine becomes very concentrated, usually dark yellow or amber in color. The mouth is often dry. As the condition progresses, there may be fatigue and light-headedness or dizziness when standing. Later signs include extreme weakness, a loss of skin elasticity (turgor), sunken eyes, and weight loss. It's this progression of symptoms which must be avoided or reversed by vigorous oral fluid replacement. If this can't be accomplished, intravenous fluids are mandatory.

Treatment of Dehydration:
Rehydration (Oral Fluid Replacement)

Measure for measure, you must replace the total volume of fluid lost from vomiting, diarrhea, sweating, and urine. You must also replace body electrolytes (sodium, potassium, chloride, and bicarbonate). It's best to drink small amounts every few minutes at a rate of about one quart or liter per hour. Drink fluids preferably from an uncontaminated or purified source (see pp.67 – 77).

Treatment of Minor Fluid Losses

For fluid losses from mild diarrhea or vomiting, ordinary carbonated soft drinks (preferably without caffeine), teas, broth, fruit juice, and purified water are adequate sources of fluid replacement.

Treatment of Moderate Fluid Losses

Take clear fluids for 24–48 hours. These include purified water, broth, Gatorade and other "sports drinks", caffeine-free soft drinks such as 7-UP, chamomile or other soothing teas without caffeine, and bottled mineral water, perhaps with a squeeze of lemon or lime juice or other caffeine- free carbonated drinks. Powdered fruit flavored Pedialyte added to water can be used by children and adults to replace salts, sugars and fluids.

When vomiting is present, make sure drinks contain sodium and chloride, or add $1/4$ teaspoon table salt to each 8 oz. of liquid. You can also try nibbling on salted crackers. When diarrhea is present, add $1/4$ tsp. baking soda to 8 ounces of water. See "rehydration formulas" below.

When you're feeling better, take bland easily digested foods such as soups, noncaffeinated soft drinks, Jell-O, or fruit juices (orange, apple, etc.) for a day or two. Slowly add bananas and other soft foods (rice, baked potatoes). Avoid dairy products, fatty or spicy foods, red meats, vegetables, caffeine, alcohol, and other fruits until fully recuperated.

Treatment of Severe Fluid Losses

For severe vomiting and/or diarrhea, use one of the rehydration formulas or products listed below. If unavailable, use any source of pure fluid to prevent dehydration. *If you can't prevent dehydration, there's no choice but to seek medical help for intravenous fluids.*

Fluid replacement when pure fluids aren't available

If required to prevent or correct dehydration, use whatever water source is available. Tap water, preferably from the hot tap, or water from a river, lake, or well, even if possibly contaminated, is justified when there are no alternatives. Progressively worsening dehydration with ongoing fluid losses is a medical emergency.

Rehydration Formulas

Some commercial products, such as Gatorade, are available to help replace electrolytes lost along with water. Powders which can be added to water include Hydra-lyte, Infalyte, and WHO (World Health

Organization) Oral Rehydration Salts. Packets of this formula ("Dialite") are available from IAMAT (see p. 52). In many tropical countries equivalent rehydration formulas are available commercially in small packets which are added to a quart of pure water. Another product is Pedialyte RS, a ready-to-use fluid replacement for children which works fine for adults. The powdered form is often convenient to pack for travel.

You can make your own electrolyte replacement drinks with a formula from the U.S. Public Health Service. Sip alternately from each glass until you quench your thirst:

Glass #1: 8 oz. orange, apple, or other pure water fruit juice (potassium source), $1/2$ teaspoon honey or corn syrup (glucose, which is necessary for absorption of salts), $1/4$ teaspoon table salt (sodium and chloride).

Glass #2: 8 oz. pure water plus $1/4$ teaspoon baking soda (sodium bicarbonate).

If fruit juice is unavailable or can't be tolerated, cream of tartar is an alternative source of potassium which you can use as follows: 1 quart water with 1 teaspoon baking soda, 1 tablespoon corn syrup, and 4 teaspoons cream of tartar.

Traveler's Diarrhea

By any name ("Delhi Belli," "Montezuma's Revenge," "Greek Gallop," "Turkey Trots," "Casablanca Crud," "Rangoon Runs," "Hong Kong Hop," "Backdoor sprint" etc.) the results are identical and all too familiar. The illness is usually caused by the bacteria *E. Coli.*, but may also be due to other bacteria, viruses, or parasites.

The source of infection is usually contaminated food, water, or beverages. High risk items include raw, unpeeled fruits and vegetables, uncooked, undercooked, or poorly heated meats, raw seafood, tap water, ice cubes, and unpasteurized dairy products. Your destination, and the precautions you take (or fail to take) against traveler's diarrhea, largely determine your risk of acquiring it. See Chapter 3, "Preventive Health Measures — Food and Water Precautions," pp. 67 – 82.

Adherence to preventive measures may require some determination. You'll have to endure the braggard testimonials of those who "ate and drank everything and never got sick." Yet even the best precautions do not confer immunity.

Symptoms

Traveler's diarrhea usually develops during the first week of travel, but may occur at any time during travel or shortly after returning home. The onset of symptoms is usually sudden. There's abdominal cramping, relieved by episodic bouts of diarrhea which are frequently accompanied by a sense of urgency. These occur about 4–5 times a day. There may also be nausea, vomiting, fever, bloating, and weakness. Symptoms usually don't last more than 3–5 days even if untreated, but occasionally persist up to a week or more.

The presence of blood in the stool, or a high fever above 102° F (38.8° C)., signals a more serious infection by organisms which cause dysentery. **These are indications for prompt medical attention.**

Treatment

Avoid dehydration! The most important measure for treating diarrhea is the replacement of lost fluids and electrolytes (see rehydration on preceding pages).

A step approach to treating traveler's diarrhea is usually best. When diarrhea develops, but is mild without severe cramping, fever, or blood in the stool, you can do one of the following:

1. nothing (except oral rehydration), or

2. take an antimotility drug such as Imodium;

For further treatment options, use the following guidelines:

If the diarrhea is persistent (i.e., more than 3 loose

stools per day), also consider taking a single dose treatment of one of the antibiotics listed below.

If the diarrhea is severe at the onset, without fever or blood in the stool, consider using a combination of an antibiotic and an antimotility drug as described below.

If diarrhea is accompanied by fever or blood in the stool, begin a three day course of therapy with one of the antibiotics listed below but do *not* use an antimotility drug.

In certain circumstances (business travelers, people who are immune suppressed, for rafting or canoeing trips, or any day when using public transportation) consider immediately starting a combination of an antibiotic and antimotility agent at the onset of diarrhea. The antimotility medication loperamide (Imodium and other brands) is initiated by taking 4 mg. followed by 2 mg. after each subsequent loose stool up to a maximum of 16 mg. per day. *Don't take antimotility medications if diarrhea is bloody or accompanied by fever.*

Antibiotics for single dose *or* 3 day treatment; use *one* of the following:

1. ciprofloxacin 750 – 1000 mg. orally one time only; *or* 500 mg. daily for 3 days; **or**

2. levofloxacin 500 mg. orally one time only; *or* 500 mg. daily for 3 days; **or**

3. ofloxacin 400 mg. orally one time only; *or* 400 mg. twice a day for 3 days.

An alternative for extended (but not single dose) treatment is Azithromycin (Zithromax) 500 mg. initially, then 250 mg. daily for 2–4 more days.

If diarrhea persists for 12 hours after taking a single dose treatment consider extending antibiotic therapy for 3 days.

Persistent Diarrhea

If diarrhea lasts more than 3 days after starting antibiotics, stop taking them. Obtain medical evaluation.

Stool tests for bacteria and parasites are required to identify the cause and determine the appropriate treatment.

If traveling in rural areas where health care is not
readily available (such as trekking) and diarrhea does not
respond to the above treatment, then try Septra DS or Bactrim DS one tablet twice daily for 7 days. This will treat diarrhea due to a protozoan infection called Cyclospora. Do
not take Bactrim or Septra if allergic to sulfa drugs.

In considering antibiotic use, it's important to remember that the indiscriminate use of an antibiotic can have
serious side effects. It may cause diarrhea, and may produce strains of bacteria resistant to the antibiotic. It can
open the door to infections from organisms not affected
by the antibiotic. There is also a risk of allergic reaction.

Antimotility Medications

Don't take antimotility medications if diarrhea is
bloody, accompanied by fever above 102°F (38.8°C), if abdominal pain is unrelieved by the passage of stools or gas,
or if symptoms worsen despite treatment. In these circumstances if severe cramping or dehydration occur, you may
consider using Imodium. In all other cases of diarrhea
where antimotility drugs are desired, use either Imodium
(the drug of choice), or Lomotil. These reduce movement
of food through the intestinal tract. The dosages are:

1. *Imodium AD* — 4 mg. initially (2 capsules or 4 teaspoons), then 2 mg. after each loose stool. *Don't* exceed 16 mg. per day (8 capsules or 16 teaspoons).
   Don't use for more than two days.

2. *Lomotil* — 1 or 2 tablets orally as needed every 4–6
   hours up to 4 times a day, for a maximum of 2 days.
   Lomotil should be used cautiously by elderly
   individuals due to possible side effects including urinary retention and dry mouth.

If Imodium AD and Lomotil aren't available, paregoric, tincture of opium, or codeine may be used. These

will reduce bowel cramping and the number of bowel movements. All antimotility medications must be used cautiously as excesses are often constipating.

Some situations confronting travelers have their own compelling arguments for the use of antimotility medications. If there's a Murphy's Law of Foreign Transportation, it undoubtedly reads: "Lengthy travel on any vehicle lacking toilet facilities will inevitably induce diarrhea." Riding through remote areas on horseback, mule, or camel, rafting down the Amazon, or touring the game parks of Africa, for example, are activities that may require the use of antimotility medications if diarrhea occurs.

Alternative treatment

If antibiotics and antimotility drugs are not available, try Pepto-Bismol as an alternative. Expect the number of stools to be reduced by half. When diarrhea starts the dosage for Pepto-Bismol is 1 ounce (2 tablespoons) every half hour for 8 doses (one 8–ounce bottle). Tablets can also be used — 4 tablets 4 times a day for 1 or 2 days. Don't exceed this dosage if symptoms persist.

Tongue and stools may appear black from this medication, and mild constipation may occur. Don't use Pepto-Bismol during pregnancy. It's contraindicated for travelers with kidney impairment and for those taking Coumadin or salicylates (aspirin) regularly for other medical conditions. It shouldn't be used by travelers taking doxycycline or for those who cannot take aspirin.

Use of Prescribed and Over-the-Counter Medications

It's not unusual for useless or potentially dangerous medications to be recommended for gastrointestinal tract disturbances in some countries. **Check medications for appropriateness, contraindications, warnings, and side effects (See Part III). For your own protection, this should be done for all medications prescribed during travel.**

Useless medications

Kaopectate (kaolin plus pectin), traditionally given for diarrhea, is of no therapeutic value. It doesn't shorten the course of illness or diminish diarrhea. It doesn't alleviate abdominal cramps. It gives stools a little more consistency — that's all.

A lactobacillus preparation (yogurt or acidophilus) won't help in the treatment of travelers diarrhea. It may be of benefit if diarrhea occurs as a side effect of antibiotic use. It may help to replace lost intestinal bacteria, which are beneficial to our health.

Dangerous prescriptions

Avoid certain drugs altogether. **Don't** take *Enterovioform, MexaForm, Intestopan, chloramphenicol (Chloromycetin* and other brands), *clioquinol,* or *iodoquinol* for undiagnosed disorders. These drugs are dangerous with potentially serious side effects. They're popular in some countries for treating and preventing various gastrointestinal, respiratory, or other disorders. If prescribed, ask for something else. There are safer and more effective alternatives.

Don't take Lomotil or other antimotility medications if they are combined in a single medication with neomycin, sulfa drugs, aminopyrine, butazolidin, or any other medicine or antibiotic. Don't combine antibiotics, or take medications which combine antibiotics, unless prescribed by a doctor for a diagnosed condition. See the Quick Reference guides on the following pages.

Specific Infectious Causes of Diarrhea

Viral gastroenteritis ("stomach flu")

One or more viruses are capable of causing mild symptoms of diarrhea, nausea, and vomiting. These are often accompanied by muscle aches, a slight fever under 101° F (38.3° C) or abdominal cramping. Symptoms usually disappear in one to three days, but may persist up to a week.

Quick Reference

Treatment of Traveler's Diarrhea

For initial treatment of diarrhea:

1. prevent dehydration by replacing lost fluids (pp. 223 – 226). If you are unable to keep fluids down or keep hydrated then obtain medical evaluation immediately.

2. Step approach:

   When diarrhea develops, but is mild without severe cramping, fever or blood in the stool, you can do one of the following:

1. Nothing except oral rehydration; or

2. Take an antimotility drug such as Imodium).

If the diarrhea is persistent (i.e., more than 3 loose stools per day):

1. Consider the above

2. Consider using one of the antibiotics listed on p. 228.

If the diarrhea is severe with cramping at the onset, *without* fever or blood in the stool:

Use a combination of a single dose antibiotic and an antimotility drug as listed on p. 228.

If diarrhea is accompanied by fever or blood in the stool, begin a three day course of an antibiotic *without* the use of an antimotility drug.

In certain circumstances (business travel, immune suppression, rafting or canoeing trips, or any travel day/use of public transportation) consider immediately starting a combination of an antibiotic and an antimotility drug at the onset of diarrhea.

Don't take antimotility medications if diarrhea is accompanied by blood or fever above 102° F (38.8° C), or abdominal pain unrelieved by the passage of stools or gas. Instead, obtain medical evaluation.

After 3 days of antibiotics if diarrhea persists, stop taking the antibiotics and obtain medical evaluation.

Note: a particular form of diarrhea (pseudomembranous colitis) may occur following treatment with many antibiotics, especially clindamycin, cephalosporins, and penicillins. If diarrhea develops after beginning antibiotics and persists after antibiotics have been discontinued, medical evaluation is required.

Quick Reference

Nausea, Vomiting, and Diarrhea:

Conditions Requiring Immediate Medical Attention

When nausea, vomiting or diarrhea are accompanied by any of the following conditions, get medical help quickly:

1. severe or progressive dehydration when adequate oral fluid replacement isn't possible;
2. weight loss greater than 5% of body weight;
3. chest pain;
4. vomiting which lasts more than 48 hours;
5. projectile vomiting or vomiting which follows a head injury (often accompanied by lethargy or disorientation);
6. bright red blood or "coffee ground" material from vomiting;
7. acute abdominal pain not relieved by the passage of stool or gas;
8. diarrhea, treated or untreated, which lasts longer than 3–5 days;
9. a fever with gradual daily elevations (possible typhoid);
10. bloody stools, either bright red (unless due to hemorrhoids) or black and tarry (unless color is due to iron tablets or Pepto-Bismol).

Treatment

For headache, muscle aches, or mild fever, take 1–2 aspirin, or Tylenol or a nonsteroidal medications such as ibuprofen or naproxen as needed. Symptoms of vomiting and diarrhea should be treated as required to prevent dehydration. Antibiotics are of no benefit in viral illnesses.

Shigella

Food handlers are sometimes to blame for the contaminated food or utensils through which this bacterial infection is spread. Shigella is highly contagious and good hand washing is essential to prevent spreading the disease.

Following exposure, illness develops within 1–4 days. In adults most cases of Shigella are mild and resolve on their own in 4–8 days.

Symptoms

The earliest symptom is often painful, colicky cramping relieved with passage of stool. Sensations of urgency may accompany these episodes. They become more frequent and severe with increasing diarrhea. Later, blood and pus are often seen in the stool.

High fevers, up to 104° F (40.0° C), follow the onset of diarrhea. Chills, headache, and loss of appetite may accompany these. Nausea and vomiting are absent or minimal.

Treatment

Dehydration can be a dangerous complication and may develop quickly. *Oral fluid replacement must be vigorous.* Relieve abdominal cramping with a hot water bottle or other source of heat. Apply it locally. Antibiotics aren't usually necessary.

Lomotil should not be used for Shigella infections. Its use may prolong infection. It may also result in severe intestinal damage or infection that spreads throughout the body (septicemia).

Treatment in isolated areas when medical help isn't available

In isolated areas, the occurrence of bloody diarrhea or a fever above 102° F (38.8° C) warrants the use of antibiotics as directed for traveler's diarrhea (see pp. 228 – 229).

Conditions requiring immediate medical treatment

The following require prompt medical intervention:

1. dehydration;

2. severe abdominal pain unrelieved by the passage of stool or gas or by applications of heat (and not related to menstruation);

3. any severe or continuous bleeding;

4. symptoms that fail to improve within 4–8 days;

Cholera

Travelers rarely encounter this bacterial illness. It's transmitted through contaminated food and water. Avoid cholera by following the food and water precautions recommended pp. 67 – 82. With adequate replacement of lost fluids, infection is usually mild and self-limiting. Even in severe cases, cholera is completely curable in otherwise healthy adults if treated early. Nevertheless, severe untreated cases, especially in children and the elderly, can have high death rates.

Symptoms

Symptoms are often confined to a mild episode of diarrhea which doesn't need treatment, except for fluid replacement. Severe cases, however, are capable of producing massive water loss and dehydration. There may be frequent episodes of severe, painless, watery gray diarrhea, described as "rice water" stools. These are odorless and *don't* contain blood or pus. In severe cases, symptoms are usually of abrupt onset and may be accompanied by vomiting.

The huge amount of water lost results in intense

thirst. Oral fluid replacement must be extremely vigorous. Early signs of inadequate fluid intake include a diminished output of dark colored urine. There may be fatigue, muscle cramps, and light-headedness or dizziness when standing. Later signs of dehydration are loss of skin tone, sunken eyes, extreme weakness, and weight loss. **In such cases hospitalization with intravenous (IV) fluid replacement is required.**

Treatment

In areas where cholera is known to exist or an epidemic occurs, symptoms require immediate medical evaluation. A stool culture and sensitivity should be done prior to starting antibiotics, whenever possible. In addition to antibiotics, treat diarrhea with oral fluids. The rule of thumb is to take in at least as much fluid as is lost. (See "Dehydration and Rehydration," pp. 223 – 226.) If these measures can't prevent dehydration, intravenous fluids are necessary.

Treatment in isolated areas

If you suspect cholera and medical evaluation is unavailable, start one of the following antibiotics:

1. Cipro (ciprofloxacin) 500 mg., 2 tablets orally once; **or**

2. Noroxin (norfloxacin) 400 mg. orally twice a day for 3 days; **or**

3. doxycycline 100 mg., 3 pills orally once.

Obtain medical help if antibiotics do not reduce symptoms dramatically. It's essential to drink lots of fluids, even when taking antibiotics.

Food Poisoning

"Food poisoning" isn't a precise term. We use it here to refer to certain bacterial causes of acute nausea, vomiting, and diarrhea. Illness follows ingestion of contaminated food, usually when it's left unrefrigerated for long periods. This allows the growth of bacteria and/or the accumulation of bacterial toxins. These conditions don't normally require antibiotics.

"Staph" Food Poisoning

Staphylococcal bacteria are present on the skin. They cause common infections like pimples and boils. When spread to foods such as fish, processed meats, milk, custard, and cream-filled pastries, especially when unrefrigerated, they can produce a potent toxin.

Soon after eating (usually within an hour or two) there's an abrupt onset of intense, violent vomiting. This lasts for several hours, rarely more than 6 or 8. Abdominal cramping may occur; fever and diarrhea don't. The experience is awful but recovery is rapid and complete. No treatment is usually necessary.

Salmonella Food Poisoning (Non-typhoid)

Foods high in protein are the usual source of salmonella infection. These include chicken, fish, meat, eggs, and dairy products.

There's an abrupt onset of mild to severe nausea, vomiting, and diarrhea, usually 8 to 48 hours after eating. Abdominal cramps, fever, and chills may be present.

The severe vomiting and diarrhea are characteristic of salmonella poisoning. They don't often occur together in other bacterial infections of the intestinal tract. The intense symptoms are usually self-limiting, though they may persist for a while in milder form.

Treatment

Keep hydrated by drinking plenty of fluids. Except for rare occasions under medical supervision, avoid antibiotics. Obtain medical attention for:

1. dehydration;

2. fever persisting more than 36 hours;

3. localized abdominal pain.

Following (p. 239) is a list of potential laboratory findings *after stools have been sent for culture and sensitivity*, along with the indicated treatment.

Note: a stool culture and sensitivity test will only reveal bacterial causes of diarrhea. Intestinal parasites may also be a cause of persistent ongoing symptoms. Other tests are required to identify parasites.

Intestinal Parasites

Intestinal parasites are common in regions with inadequate sewage treatment, water purification, and personal hygiene. Most are transmitted through fecally contaminated food and water, from food handlers and other sources. They're largely avoidable (see Chapter 3, "Food and Water Precautions", pp. 67 – 82).

An occasional parasite isn't cause for undue alarm. Problems usually arise from prolonged or massive infections. However, some parasites can be dangerous if they escape the digestive tract to other parts of the body. To avoid potential problems, always treat parasites promptly.

Parasites are often comparatively shy. They may signal their presence, if at all, through vague, fleeting symptoms which are usually slow to develop. The time interval between exposure and development of first symptoms for some parasites can be months to more then one year. Symptoms are frequently recurrent and may include one or more of the following:

1. mild constipation or diarrhea, sometimes alternating;

2. abnormally foul stools or gas;

3. decreased appetite;

4. abnormal sensations of fullness or bloating;

5. occasionally, nausea and vomiting.

Quick Reference:

Treatment of Bacterial Causes of Diarrhea

The indicated treatment for diarrhea from most bacterial causes is R & R: rest and rehydration. For persistent diarrhea (see. p. 228), following are the usual treatments when stool cultures result in positive identification of:

Organism	Indicated treatment (unless organism shows resistance on the stool culture and sensitivity)
E. Coli	Mild diarrhea: Cipro (ciprofloxacin, two 500 mg tablets once orally; severe diarrhea: Cipro 500 mg. orally twice a day for 3 days, or Zithromax (azithromycin) four 250 mg. tablets once orally or 2 tablets day one and one tablet daily for 4 more days.
Shigella	Cipro 500 mg. or ofloxacin 300 mg. orally twice a day for 3 days; or Septra DS twice a day for 3 days; or Zithromax 2 tablets day 1 and one tablet daily for 4 more days.
Staphylococcus	Rehydration only
Salmonella typhi	Cipro 500 mg. orally twice a day for 10 days, or Zithromax four 250 mg. tablets on day 1, then 2 tablets daily for 6 days.
Salmonella (other)	For mild illness or no symptoms (carrier only): no treatment. For severe diarrhea: Cipro 500 mg. orally twice a day for 5–7 days, or Zithromax four 250 mg. tablets orally on day 1, then 2 tablets daily for 6 days.
Clostridium dificile	Flagyl 500 mg. orally 3 times a day for 10 – 14 days.
Campylobactor jejuni	Cipro 500 mg. orally twice a day for 3 days, or Zithromax 500 mg. orally once a day for 3 days.
Yersina enterocolica	Cipro 500 mg. orally twice a day for 3 days.

| Vibrio cholerae | Rehydration. If needed, Cipro 500 mg. orally for one day, or doxycycline 300 mg. for one day, or Septra DS twice a day for 3 days. |
| Vibrio parahemolyticus | No treatment |

Over the course of weeks or months you may finally identify the faint signals of an E.T. (Extra-inTestinal) trying to phone home.

Even without symptoms, a parasite may be passed in the stool. For this reason, many travelers make a habit of visual inspection. If a parasite is found, save it in a jar or other container and take it to a laboratory for identification. Many other parasites can be identified by careful microscopic examination of the stool in a stool ova and parasite ("O & P") test.

Guidelines for Identifying and Treating Suspected Parasites

When symptoms suggest parasites, there are several options. One is to see a doctor. A single stool sample is ordered for "culture and sensitivities," to check for bacteria. At the same time, samples can be ordered for "ova and parasites" (for parasites and their eggs). These should be as fresh as possible. In cities of most developing nations, money can be saved by going directly to a medical laboratory for these tests. While awaiting lab results, certain home remedies such as chamomile tea or garlic cloves may help reduce intestinal symptoms. They won't, however, eliminate the parasites.

Once a parasite is identified, further information and treatment schedules can be found in this section. With the lab results, you can obtain appropriate medication from a local pharmacy. If symptoms persist and stool samples don't reveal parasites or bacteria, obtain medical evaluation.

Two weeks after completing treatment, repeat the

stool exams. If parasites are still present, either repeat treatment, try an alternative medication, or see a doctor. If no parasites are found but symptoms persist or recur, obtain medical advice.

Common Intestinal Parasites

Roundworms

Ascaris or giant roundworm (Ascaris lumbricoides)

Giant roundworm infections are common among travelers, though seldom harmful. Minor infections are usually without symptoms. Suddenly encountering a fat, spaghetti-like adult worm in one's stool can nevertheless be quite traumatic.

Roundworms are spread through fecally contaminated food and water. Irrigated, low-growing vegetables such as lettuce are a frequent source of infection.

After ingestion, roundworm eggs hatch into larvae. These migrate from the intestines through the lymph and bloodstream to the lungs. In sufficient numbers they may cause fever, coughing with blood-tinged sputum, and hives or other allergic reactions.

The microscopic larvae ascend the respiratory tract in coughed secretions. Some are inevitably swallowed and grow to adult size in the small intestine.

Symptoms

When numerous, roundworms cause vague, generalized abdominal discomfort and cramping. There may also be nausea, vomiting, decreased appetite, weakness, and weight loss. Most commonly, though, symptoms are absent and the worms first appear in the stool.

On occasion, their size and migratory habits can make these worms particularly unsettling. One of the authors, admiring the spectacularly scenic Iguasu Falls between Brazil and Argentina, was startled to find an Ascaris disembarking from his pants cuff . . . presumably to get a better view.

Treatment

When lab results show the presence of other parasites in addition to Ascaris, always treat the Ascaris infection first. This is necessary to prevent the migration of these worms outside the intestines.

Take *one* of the following:

1. albendazole 400 mg. orally as a single dose; **or**

2. mebendazole (Vermox), either 500 mg. orally once; **or** 100 mg. orally twice a day for 3 days.

Alternative medication

There is one other drug which you can use for Ascaris — pyrantel pamoate —although the dosage is computed according to body weight measured in kilograms. Convert your weight in pounds to kilograms by using the conversion table in Appendix D or dividing your weight in pounds by 2.2. The dosage is 11 mg. per kg. of body weight, taken as a single oral dose. The maximum dosage is 1 gram. This should not be exceeded by those weighing more than 90 kg. (198 pounds).

Whipworm (Trichuris trichiura)

Whipworm is another common roundworm that causes symptoms only when numerous. Symptoms include abdominal pain, diarrhea, bloating, and gas. Nausea, vomiting, and weight loss occur only in very severe infections.

Treatment

The drugs of choice are:

1. mebendazole (Vermox), 500 mg. taken orally as a single dose, or 100 mg. orally twice a day for 3 days; **or**

2. albendazole 400 mg. orally once daily for 3 days.

Pinworm (Enterobius vermicularis)

Pinworm infections occur throughout the world. Rectal itching, usually worse at night, is the main symptom. Itching may lead to insomnia, restlessness, and irritability. In severe cases there may be vague abdominal pain, nausea, vomiting or diarrhea, and decreased appetite. In women itching and inflammation can spread to the vulva/vaginal area..

Treatment

Treat pinworm infections with one of the following:

1. pyrantel pamoate, 11 mg./kg. of body weight, up to a maximum of 1 gram. Take it in a single oral dose and repeat in 2 weeks; **or**

2. mebendazole 100 mg. orally once; repeat the same dose again 2 weeks later; **or**

3. albendazole 400 mg. orally once; repeat the same dose again 2 weeks later.

Hookworm (Ancylostoma duodenale or Necator americanus)

Unlike other roundworm infections, hookworms are transmitted from skin contact with larvae in fecally contaminated soil. Infection is therefore most likely outdoors in areas that lack sewage and toilet facilities.

Hookworm larvae, microscopically small, burrow through the skin. This causes an itchy local rash, usually on the feet. Wear shoes! Don't go barefoot! Since the larvae are capable of wriggling through layers of cloth, care must also be taken when choosing a spot to sit down.

Once in the body, larvae reach the lungs in the same manner as *Ascaris*. There may be a cough, sore throat, and blood-tinged sputum in severe infections. Larva reach the digestive tract after being swallowed. They then hook into the intestinal lining in order to feed on blood and mucosal substances.

Blood is often detectable in stools. Other symptoms include abdominal discomfort or pain, increased gas, diarrhea, and weight loss. Weakness, fatigue, and anemia can occur after prolonged infection.

Treatment

Keep skin lesions clean, dry, and covered to prevent secondary infection. Treatment is indicated only after the worms are identified by microscopic examination. Lab reports positive for hookworm may read either "*Necator americanus*" or "*Ancylostoma duodenale.*"

The usual treatments, in order of preference, are:

1. albendazole, 400 mg. orally in a single dose; **or**

2. mebendazole, 500 mg. taken once orally, **or** 100 mg. orally twice a day for 3 days; **or**

3. pyrantel pamoate orally, 11 mg./kg. of body weight per day, up to a maximum of 1 gram daily for 3 days.

Threadworm (Strongyloides stercoralis)

The life cycle of this threadworm closely resembles that of hookworm. The disease is widespread throughout the tropics, and is found in the same climatic and sanitary conditions that favor hookworm infections. A rash on the buttocks or anal area is one manifestation of infection.

Severe infection may cause stomach pain, just below the breastbone (sternum), as well as vomiting and diarrhea. Diagnosis is made from microscopic examination of stool. Prevention is the same as for hookworm.

Treatment

The usual treatment is *one* of the following:

1. Ivermectin taken as a single dose (note: each tablet contains 6 mg., double the dose listed if taking 3 mg. tablets).

If your weight is	15-24 kg.	Take $1/2$ tablet
	25-35 kg.	1 tablet
	36-50 kg.	$1^1/_2$ tablets
	51-65 kg.	2 tablets
	66-79 kg.	$2^1/_2$ tablets
	above 80 kg.	200 micrograms/kg.

2. Or, take thiabendazole 25 mg./kg. of body weight orally twice a day for 2 days. Don't exceed a total of 3 grams a day (1.5 grams per dose).

Protozoa

"Giardia" (Giardia lamblia)

Of all parasites which infect travelers, the protozoa giardia is the most common. Infection is known medically as "giardiasis" or "lambliasis." Giardia inhabit the small intestine just below the stomach, where they adeptly sabotage fat digestion and absorption. Initially stools may be watery and profuse. They then become characteristically foul-smelling, bulky, yellow, and frothy with undigested fats. This frequently causes them to float.

Bloating sensations are common. Giardia also cause burping that smells sulfurous, like rotten eggs. This is known among the initiated as the "Purple Burps."

Other possible symptoms include nausea, occasional vomiting, and pain in the right upper part of the abdomen. There may be cramping and intermittent diarrhea, sometimes alternating with constipation.

Indications for medical attention

Symptoms accompanied by the characteristic burping and digestive disturbances strongly suggest giardia infection. When fever, yellowing of the skin or eyes, or severe abdominal pain are also present, there may be another cause and **immediate medical evaluation is required.**

Treatment

The usual treatments for giardia in adults are:

1. Flagyl (metronidazole) 250 mg. orally, 3 times a day for 5 days; **or**

2. Fasigyn (tinidazole) 2 grams orally in a single dose; **or**

3. Quinacrine 100 mg. orally 3 times a day for 5 days; **or**

4. Paromomycin 500 mg. 4 times a day for 7 days (can be used in pregnancy).

Amoebas

Found worldwide, amoebas cause a potentially serious infection of the large intestine. Although rare, amoebas sometimes reach the liver or other organs where they can be very damaging. More likely is the development of a chronic carrier state, in which highly infective cysts are passed in the stool.

Symptoms

Amoebas produce symptoms slowly and gradually. Diarrhea occurs intermittently, worsening over several days, sometimes alternating with constipation. Stools may contain strands of mucus or blood. If there's a fever it's usually slight, less than 101° F (38.3° C). There may be lower abdominal pain or cramping, usually on the left side. All of these symptoms may disappear, only to recur at varying intervals.

Diagnosis

Diagnosis is made by examination of stool for ova and parasites. If taking Pepto-Bismol (bismuth subsalicylate), kaolin products, or castor oil, wait 3–4 days after stopping their use before submitting a stool specimen. These products make it difficult to find amoebas under microscopic examination. Start treatment if the lab report lists any of the following: "*Entamoeba histolytica*", "*Entamoeba dysenteriae*", "*Endamoeba histolytica*", or "*Entamoeba polecki*."

Treatment

The treatment for symptomatic amoebas is Flagyl, 750 mg. orally 3 times a day (every 8 hours) for 10 days. Alternatives are tinidazole 1 gm. orally twice a day for 3 days **or** omidazole (Tiberal) 500 mg. orally twice a day for 5 days. These are often better tolerated than Flagyl. Whichever drug you use, follow it with either iodoquinol (Yodoxin) 650 mg. orally 3 times a day for 20 days, **or** paramycin (Humatin) 500 mg. orally 3 times a day for 7 days. Follow up with repeat stool tests 2 weeks after finishing treatment.

Cyclospora

A recently identified organism, cyclospora, has been found to produce symptoms similar to Giardia and has been linked to infections worldwide. Cyclospora needs to be diagnosed with special microscopic stains (called acid-fast) and can be treated with Septra DS or Bactrim DS one tablet orally twice daily for 7 days.

Other Parasitic Infections

You can acquire a variety of flukes, tapeworms, and other diseases from eating raw or undercooked beef, pork, or seafood. Another source of infection is contaminated water. These illnesses are preventable by avoiding raw or undercooked meat and seafood, and by boiling or purifying drinking water.

If lab reports indicate the presence of tapeworms or flukes, **obtain medical attention immediately**. See chart on pp. 301–302 for reference.

Parasitic infections requiring immediate medical attention

If stool samples sent for examination (ova and parasites) show any of the following, get immediate medical evaluation and treatment.

1. all tapeworms;

2. all flukes;

3. all forms of schistosomiasis;

4. hookworms, Ascaris, and strongyloides if accompanied by respiratory symptoms (coughing, shortness of breath, coughing up blood);

5. strongyloides if accompanied by severe abdominal pain or bloody stools.

Noninfectious Abdominal Disorders

Ulcers, appendicitis, and minor gastrointestinal problems are discussed in the following pages. Moderate to severe abdominal pain unrelieved by the passage of stool or gas (and not related to menses), **requires immediate medical attention.** As the "Quick Reference Guide to GI and Abdominal Symptoms" indicates on pp. 255–257, there are many possible causes for these symptoms. Some are life-threatening. Only a qualified medical practitioner can provide a reliable diagnosis and adequate treatment for disorders with these symptoms.

Appendicitis

Appendicitis may develop very quickly. It's potentially life-threatening. When suspected, get immediate medical attention.

Symptoms

Pain often, but not always, begins near the navel or belly button. Usually, within 2–12 hours it moves toward the right lower abdomen where it settles and intensifies. **This progression of pain may be important for early recognition of appendicitis. Don't take pain medications.**

Other possible symptoms include:

1. a slight fever (less than 101° F (38.3° C);

2. decreased appetite, nausea, and vomiting, usually mild when present;

3. constipation or diarrhea.

Pain increased by coughing, jumping up and down, or releasing pressure after pressing on the abdomen ("rebound tenderness"), indicates severe inflammation and requires immediate medical evaluation. Because appendicitis may not present with typical symptoms, anyone with persistent or severe abdominal pain needs to consider appendicitis as a possible cause. Medical evaluation should be obtained.

Treatment

If constipation or diarrhea are present, these

symptoms should not be treated. **Never take laxatives or antimotility medications when symptoms suggest appendicitis**. Avoid enemas, pain medications, food, and liquids.

Unfortunately, there's little else that can be done short of surgery. Appendicitis is one condition that requires ready access to modern surgical medicine. It's definitely a hazard, though probably a small one, for anyone living, hiking, or traveling in an isolated area.

Ulcers

Pain from ulcers is often described as burning, gnawing, or aching. It occurs in the area above and over the stomach. The pain is mild to moderate, occurring typically 45–60 minutes after eating.

Pain may be decreased by taking food or antacids. Occasionally, other symptoms such as constipation, vomiting, or fatigue may be present. Stools are sometimes black and tarry, which may indicate the presence of blood.

If you suspect ulcers, **get medical help immediately**. With proper treatment complications are usually preventable. When ulcers progress unarrested they can cause severe or life-threatening damage.

Treatment in Isolated Areas

Start medications that reduce stomach acid such as Pepcid, Zantac, Tagamet, Prilosec, Aciphex, Protonix, Nexium, or Prevacid; liquid or chewable antacids are also helpful. Take chewable or liquid antacids 1 hour and 3 hours after meals, and at bedtime. Avoid aspirin, Pepto-Bismol, iron, and the nonsteroidal anti-inflam–matory agents (see. p. 437). If symptoms persist, seek medical treatment as soon as possible. Some ulcers have been found to be caused by a bacterial infection, Helicobacter pylori, which needs specific diagnostic tests and multiple medications to eradicate.

Minor Stomach and Intestinal Problems

Heartburn (gastritis, reflux, gastrointestinal reflux disease, GERD)

"Heartburn" is a painful burning sensation felt just above the stomach, beneath the sternum or breastbone. It usually occurs between meals. The cause is irritation of the lower esophagus from stomach acids. Heartburn may be associated with the use of aspirin, nonsteroidal anti-inflammatory medications, and the consumption of hot spicy food or caffeinated beverages (coffee, tea or sodas). Pregnancy or a hiatal hernia are conditions which often contribute to symptoms.

Treatment

Reduce occurrences by eating more frequent, smaller meals. Avoid irritating food and drinks and evening snacks. Since a reclining position often intensifies symptoms, elevate the head of the bed.   Start a medication that reduces stomach acid (see above). Liquid or chewable antacids are also helpful. Take chewable or liquid antacids 1 hour and 3 hours after meals, and at bedtime.

Indications for Medical Assistance

Obtain medical help immediately if heartburn is accompanied by any of the following:

1. pain radiating to the neck, arms, or jaw;

2. increasing pain and discomfort, especially with exertion;

3. pain unrelieved by antacids;

4. symptoms persisting more than 1 or 2 weeks;

5. shortness of breath;

6. evidence of blood loss, including black, tarry stools or vomited material which looks like coffee grounds.

Hiccups

Irritation of the diaphragm, or of the nerve which controls it causes hiccups. There are many possible causes, including spicy foods or an "upset" stomach.

Treatment

Most hiccup cures do work at times. Some, such as breathing from a paper bag, may correct a physiological imbalance. Other techniques physically interrupt nerve impulses to the diaphragm. This can occur through abdominal stretching, or through movement, irritation, or numbing of the throat and esophagus. Techniques which do this include eating sugar, drinking ice water, sipping from the far edge of a glass, and holding your breath.

Psychological inputs can also interrupt hiccuping. A sudden startle or scare is traditional, though frequently difficult to improvise and rarely appreciated. Another method involves "paradoxical intention" — trying to hiccup. It was used successfully with one of the authors. A friend simply promised a credible and tempting reward on one condition — hiccup just one more time. With money on the line, the hiccups vanished instantly.

On rare occasions hiccups may be intractable, defying for days all efforts to abort them. This requires medical help, which must be obtained immediately if breathing becomes labored.

Flatulence (gas)

Excessive gas in the digestive tract can cause abdominal distension, sometimes with cramping. These conditions are relieved by passage of the gas.

One cause is swallowed air. Gum chewing and anxious sighing with deep respirations are possible causes. More commonly, air is swallowed during meals. This occurs either because of talking, eating hurriedly, or sloshing the food down with lots of liquids. Smaller, more slowly paced meals are helpful.

Another cause is the activity of digestion and intestinal bacteria on certain foods. Beans are of course the most notorious. Decades ago, a wry, prematurely nostalgic obituary appeared in *Newsweek* entitled "A Farewell to Flatulence." It reported supposedly fruitful efforts to create a strain of gasless legume, a development the world still awaits with bated breath. Other implicated foods include dairy products, green peppers, broccoli, cabbage, brussel sprouts, cauliflower, onions, and radishes. Sensitive travelers can probably add many more. If symptoms warrant, remove implicated foods from the diet.

Individuals who have or develop lactose intolerance can also experience gas after consuming milk or other dairy products. Dietary changes or digestive supplements such as "Lactaid" may be necessary.

Treatment

Antacids with simethicone may provide temporary relief of symptoms. The usual dose is $1/2$ ounce (15 ml. or one tablespoon) of liquid or 1–2 chewable tablets 30 minutes after eating.

Be sure to check for parasites if:

1. gas unassociated with a particular food continues;

2. other symptoms develop, such as abdominal bloating, diarrhea, constipation, or sulfurous burps.

Get medical evaluation if no parasites are found and:

1. symptoms continue;

2. vomiting, fever, or abdominal pain occur.

Constipation

Travelers are frequently subjected to the minor indignity of simple constipation (unaccompanied by pain, cramping, or other symptoms.) Changes in body rhythm, daily routine, diet, and fluid intake are contributing factors. Another is the use of Pepto- Bismol or antimotility medications such as Lomotil, Imodium, or paregoric. These often cause excessive slowing of the bowel.

Other medications that may be constipating are codeine and aluminum-based antacids.

Prevention and Treatment

If constipation becomes a problem, it can usually be resolved with these measures:

1. Additional dietary fiber or natural laxatives. Sources include vegetables, fruit, whole grain products (especially bran) and prune juice. A supplementary fiber, such as Metamucil (psyllium hydrophilic mucilloid) or Fibercon, is also helpful.

2. Increased fluid intake. Excessively hard stools are often a result of dehydration.

3. A regular bowel habit. Reflex movement of the lower intestine often occurs after eating. This is a good time to establish a regular pattern if constipation is an ongoing problem.

4. Use of a mild bowel stimulant. Caffeine is often effective, especially after breakfast. A mild laxative, such as milk of magnesia, can be taken at bedtime.

Use enemas or stronger laxatives only as a last resort. Avoid straining as this frequently leads to hemorrhoids.

If constipation is accompanied by vague, recurrent abdominal symptoms, the cause may be parasites. Stool exams should be done, and treatment initiated if the results are positive. If exams don't reveal parasites but symptoms continue, obtain medical evaluation. Medical help should also be obtained if:

1. enemas or laxatives become routinely necessary;

2. there's nausea, vomiting, fever, or increasing abdominal tenderness, pain, or rigidity;

3. there's rectal bleeding (blood mixed in the stools or water). Blood appearing just on toilet paper and not in stools or water is probably due to hemorrhoids.

Hemorrhoids

Hemorrhoids are enlarged protruding veins of the rectum that cause itching and sometimes pain. This can be excruciating during the passage of hard stools. There may be some bleeding, with bright red blood usually appearing on toilet paper but not in the stool or water.

Hemorrhoids occur from a variety of causes including pregnancy, cirrhosis (advanced liver disease), and straining when passing stool. Travel conditions may foster symptoms. Sitting for long periods, especially on bus rides over bad roads, may aggravate existing hemorrhoids.

Prevention and Treatment

Avoid straining, or other activities that increase lower abdominal pressure. To keep stools soft and easily passed, follow the measures previously described for preventing constipation. Avoid vigorous wiping with toilet paper, which increases uncomfortable symptoms, or use moistened wipes.

For itching and discomfort, try warm soaks in a bathtub for 10–15 minutes 3–4 times a day. These are soothing and also help to shrink hemorrhoids. Hemorrhoidal suppositories such as Preparation H, Anusol, or Anusol with hydrocortisone can be used twice a day for 7–14 days. Medical help is necessary if the condition:

1. doesn't resolve with treatment;

2. becomes severe enough to interfere with normal activities.

If blood appears mixed in the stool or the water, medical evaluation is also required.

Quick Reference
GI and Abdominal Symptoms

This chart is provided to help locate relevant information in this book. It can't be used to diagnose abdominal disorders.

Symptoms	Possible cause
Acute nausea and/or vomiting with NO diarrhea:	
tiredness, right upper quadrant pain, yellowing of the eyes and skin (jaundice), mild headache, whitish clay-colored stools, brown urine, cigarettes suddenly taste bad, loss of appetite.	hepatitis
nausea and vomiting of sudden onset soon after eating; crampy abdominal pain, no fever.	"staph" food poisoning
recurrent symptoms, ear pain or ringing in the ears, room spinning.	inner ear infection or too much aspirin
high fever, chills, headache, neck stiffness, photophobia (light sensitivity), vomiting (may be projectile) with or without nausea;	meningitis*
morning nausea, weight gain, breast tenderness or fullness, late or missed period;	pregnancy
tenderness, burning centered in upper abdomen; symptoms may be relieved by vomiting or with antacids	ulcer or gall bladder*

Vomiting blood — either red or black (blood altered by digestion resembles dark coffee grounds) — is a medical emergency. Get immediate medical attention.

Diarrhea:	
with nausea and vomiting, crampy abdominal pain, often fever and chills; onset 8 or more hours after eating; diarrhea lasting 1–5 days, stools may contain blood or mucus	food poisoning — Salmonella

*Requires immediate medical attention

Symptoms	Possible cause
abrupt onset of symptoms, fever up to 104° F (40° C), lower abdominal cramps, decreased appetite, blood and mucus present in stools;	Shigella or Campylo-bacter
mild diarrhea, lower abdominal cramping relieved with passage of stools or gas, no fever, no blood, pus, or mucus in stools;	traveler's diarrhea
recurrent diarrhea and/or constipation vague abdominal discomfort, bloating, occasional foul-smelling stools or rotten egg burps;	parasites (amoebas, giardia, etc.)
low fever, muscle aches, headache, mild abdominal pain, nausea or vomiting, fatigue;	viral gastroenteritis
massive fluid loss, "rice-water" stools, dehydration;	cholera
"pea-soup" diarrhea, step-ladder fever, fatigue, flu-like symptoms	typhoid fever
diarrhea that develops after beginning antibiotics and persists after antibiotics have been discontinued, especially follow-ing use of clindamycin or cephalosporins	pseudomem-branous colitis*

Note: other potential causes of diarrhea include medications (antibiotics like ampicillin, penicillin, tetracycline), toxic chemicals, mushroom or other natural poisons, and diet (alcohol, food allergies, changes in diet or eating habits).

Abdominal Pain

mild to moderate pain, gnawing or burn-ing, located just below the breastbone; oc-curs 45-60 minutes after meals or at night, relieved with vomiting or antacids;	stomach ulcer*
sensation of pressure, squeezing to vice-like, across the chest; may move to the neck, jaw, or arms; often accompanied by shortness of breath, sweating, nausea, vomiting; symptoms increase with exex-tion;	heart attack*

(**If suspected, take an aspirin immediately**)

* **Requires immediate medical attention**

Symptoms	Possible cause
pain beginning near the navel, moving and localizing in the right lower quadrant and intensifying;	appendicitis*
slight fever, mild nausea, vomiting; pain with bloating, diarrhea or constipation, increased burping, gas;	parasites

Abdominal pain unrelieved by the passage of stool or gas (other than routine menstrual cramping), requires medical evaluation.

Abdominal pain in women (additional symptoms which may indicate specifically female disorders):

dull to sharp lower abdominal pain on both sides and/or pain with intercourse; usually with vaginal discharge, bleeding, or spotting, a slight fever, nausea, vomiting;	pelvic inflama- tory disease (PID)*
lower abdominal pain or discomfort, sometimes radiating to the groin; *missed or irregular period* with irregular vaginal bleeding or spotting.	ectopic preg- nancy, a life- threatening emergency*
dull to sharp midline lower abdominal pain, burning with urination of frequent, small amounts; possible slight fever;	bladder infection
pain with urination (may be absent) with fever, chills, nausea, vomiting, and low back tenderness or pain;	kidney infection*
with missed period, increased breast ten- derness, nausea usually in morning;	pregnancy
abdominal pain or bloating prior to or during period; with cramping that goes away on its own;	dysmenorrhea, PMS (premen- strual tension syndrome)

* Requires immediate medical attention

Quick Reference
Stool Exams for Ova and Parasites
(protozoa, amoebas, roundworms)

Exam shows: **Treatment**

Protozoa

Giardia lamblia

Flagyl 250 mg. 3 times a day for 5 days; **or** quinacrine 100 mg. 3 times a day after meals for 5 days; **or** tinidazole 2 grams once. During pregnancy: paromycin 500 mg. four times a day for 7 days.

Cyclospora cayetanensis

Septra DS or Bactrim DS twice a day for 7 days.

Isospora belli

Septra DS or Bactrim DS four times a day for 10 days, then twice a day for 3 weeks; **or** Cipro 500 mg. twice a day for 7 days (less effective).

Amoebas:

Blastocystis hominis

Flagyl 750 mg. 3 times a day for 10 days.

Dientamoeba fragilis

Iodoquinol 650 mg. 3 times a day for 20 days; **or** tetracycline 500 mg. 4 times a day for 10 days.

Entamoeba histolytica
Endamoeba histolytica
Entamoeba dysenteriae
Entamoeba polecki

For mild to moderate symptoms (diarrhea/dysentery): Flagyl 500–750 mg. 3 times a day for 10 days; **or** tinidazole 1 gram twice a day for 3 days; **or** omidazole 500 mg. twice a day for 5 days. Each of these is followed by either paromycin 500 mg. 3 times a day for 7 days **or** iodoquinol l650 mg. 3 times a day for 20 days.

Exam shows:	Treatment
Roundworms:	
Ascaris lumbricoides	Albendazole 400 mg. once; **or** mebendazole 500 mg. once or 100 mg. twice a day for 3 days; **or** pyrantel pamoate 11 mg./kg. once (maximum dose: 1 gram).
hookworm (Ancylostoma duodenale or Necator americanus)	Albendazole 400 mg. once; **or** mebendazole 100 mg. twice a day for 3 days; **or** pyrantel pamoate 11 mg./kg. once a day for 3 days (maximum daily dose: 1 gram).
pinworm (Enterobius vermicularis	Albendazole 400 mg. once **or** mebendazole 100 mg. once, then repeat in 2 weeks; **or** pyrantel pamoate 11 mg./kg. times one dose (maximum: 1 gram), then repeat every 2 weeks times 2.
whipworm (trichuris trichiura)	Albendazole 400 mg. once; **or** mebendazole 100 mg. twice a day for 3 days.
Capillaris philippinensis	Mebendazole 200 mg. twice a day for 20 days; **or** albendazole 200 mg. twice a day for 10 days.
Strongyloides stercoralis	Ivermectin 200 micrograms per kg. daily for 1 or 2 days; **or** thiabendazole 25 mg./kg. twice a day (maximum: 3 grams a day) for 2 days.

The following organisms are sometimes reported. They don't cause illness or symptoms and don't require treatment: Entamoeba dispar, Entamoeba coli, Entamoeba hartmanni, Iodamoeba butschlii, Endolima nana, and Chilomastix mesnili.

Infectious Diseases **9**

Diseases Transmitted by Mosquitoes and Ticks

Travelers face several mosquito-borne diseases of major concern. Malaria is the most significant, although dengue fever is increasingly prevalent in many areas of the world.

Malaria

The bite of a female Anopheles mosquito transmits malaria. The disease itself is caused by a parasite, Plasmodium, which infects red blood cells. Some forms of malaria are also harbored in the liver, which complicates treatment. There are four kinds of Plasmodium, and the recurring rhythm of malarial symptoms varies with the reproductive cycle of each.

Symptoms

The parasites reproduce within red blood cells. Chills lasting 15-60 minutes occur when they burst from the cell into the blood stream. Headache, nausea, vomiting, and fatigue may accompany the chills.

Release of the parasite from red blood cells is also associated with a fever which lasts several hours. It's followed by sweating and weakness. The particular Plasmodium species determines the duration of the cycle. Symptoms can recur every 72 hours, and occasionally every 48, but they usually are quite erratic.

The earliest appearance of malarial symptoms may be mistaken for the flu. There is often no identifiable pattern until the parasites are more firmly established.

Prevention

Medicines to prevent the establishment of Plasmodium infections are available. They're recommended for a stay of one or more days in a malarial area. The potential for exposure varies with both the season and elevation in a given region. See "Malaria Prophylaxis" and " Mosquito and Tick Precautions," pp. 39 – 44.

Treatment

If malaria is suspected, **medical evaluation is required**. The choice of treatment depends on the type of malaria identified on a blood smear. For best results, have blood taken during the fever cycle.

Self treatment of malaria in isolated areas

Treatment should always be done under medical supervision. Use the following guidelines for self treatment in isolated areas when medical care can not be accessed within 24 hours. After administering self treatment head immediately for the nearest medical care facility:

Treatment of acute, uncomplicated attacks in areas of non chloroquine-resistant malaria. Take chloroquine phosphate (Aralen) 500 mg. salt, 2 tablets orally, then take 1 tablet 6, 24 and 48 hours later.

Treatment of chloroquine-resistant Plasmodium falciparum malaria or acute attacks of presumptive malaria in chloroquine-resistant areas. Use one of the 2 drug regimes listed below *if not using mefloquine for malaria prevention*:

1. Malarone (Atovaquone 250 mg./Proguanil 100 mg.)

take 4 tablets orally as a single dose once a day for 3 consecutive days. This regimen is not recommended if using Malarone as prophylaxis; *or*

2. Take quinine sulfate 650 mg. orally, 3 times a day for 3 days; *plus either*

    a. tetracycline, 250 mg. orally 4 times a day for 7 days; *or*

    b. doxycycline, 100 mg. orally twice a day for 7 days; **or**

    c. Fansidar (pyrimethamine/sulfadoxine), 3 tablets in a single dose on the last day of quinine.

(Don't take Fansidar if you're allergic to sulfa drugs).

The quinine and either tetracycline or doxycycline are taken concurrently. By the third day of quinine treatment, it's not uncommon to start feeling ill as a side effect.

If using mefloquine for malaria prevention:

If symptoms suggesting malaria occur while taking mefloquine preventively, obtain medical attention. Inform the physician you have been taking mefloquine. Quinine sulfate or other malarial medications may be contraindicated or require medical supervision.

Do not use mefloquine or halofantrine for self treatment

Treatment of recurrent attacks of P. vivax or P. ovale Take primaquine phosphate 15 mg. base, one tablet orally, once a day for 14 days.

A G6PD blood test is required before taking primaquine. This drug regimen can also be used after treatment of P. vivax and P. ovale with chloroquine to prevent relapse. If treatment of recurrent P. ovale or P. vivax with this dose of primaquine fails, the dose can be doubled to 2 tablets daily for 14 days during a subsequent relapse. Treatment failure at this dosage requires renewed medical evaluation

Dengue (Breakbone or Dandy Fever)

Dengue is a viral infection transmitted by urban Aedes mosquitoes. The incidence of disease is expanding rapidly in most tropical areas of the world. It can be found in Asia, Africa, Mexico, North, Central, and South America, the Caribbean basin, and the South Pacific. It often occurs in epidemics, with numerous recent outbreaks throughout the world. The disease is seldom fatal in adult travelers.

Symptoms

Five to eight days after exposure, onset is sudden with high fever and chills. Joint and muscle pain, headache, and complete exhaustion accompany fever. Nausea and vomiting may also be present. Medical evaluation is necessary for diagnosis, as symptoms may be hard to distinguish from flu or hepatitis. In addition, malaria and Japanese encephalitis can mimic dengue symptoms.

A rash appears 3-5 days after the onset of fever. It's red, flat or raised, and may spread from the torso to the arms, legs, and occasionally the face. Also after 1-5 days, the fever abruptly stops for 24-48 hours. It then recurs in slightly milder form.

Occasionally a more severe variation called dengue hemorrhagic fever can develop. After an initial episode of dengue there is an increased risk for hemorrhagic disease with a subsequent infection. It can be life threatening and requires hospitalization and supportive care. Symptoms may include severe headache, abdominal or chest pain, nausea, vomiting, dizziness, and light sensitization. This may be followed by low blood pressure (shock) and bleeding, usually involving the nose, mouth, skin, and intestinal tract.

A good description of dengue and treatment in a Third World hospital can be found in John Grisham's book, *Testament*.

Treatment

There is currently no medical treatment available. Antibiotics are of no benefit. Recovery in otherwise healthy adults is usually complete, but may require an extended period of time. **For children under age 10 with dengue, medical care is mandatory.**

The most important supportive measure is to ensure good fluid intake. Dehydration must be avoided (see Dehydration and Rehydration, pp. 223 – 226). In severe cases hospitalization may be required for intravenous fluids. Treat fever and pain with 1 or 2 Tylenol up to 4 times a day. Avoid aspirin and nonsteroidal anti-inflammatory medications such as ibuprofen.

Prevention

The risk of acquiring dengue is low for most people unless their travels take them to an area where an epidemic is in progress. The best way to avoid dengue is to avoid mosquito bites. See Mosquito and Tick Precautions, pp. 39 – 44.

Mosquitoes that spread dengue are most frequently found in or near human habitations. Biting activity occurs chiefly in the morning for several hours after daybreak and in late afternoon for several hours before dark. The mosquitoes are more inclined to feed throughout the day when it's overcast, as well as indoors or outdoors in shady areas.

The mosquito larvae thrive in artificial water containers such as discarded tires, barrels, buckets, flower vases, cans, and cisterns. In dengue regions, keep the living area free of potential breeding places.

Yellow Fever

Yellow fever is a viral infection transmitted by mosquito bite. It 's preventable through vaccination. As with other viral infections, antibiotics are of no use in treatment.

Symptoms

Most cases of yellow fever produce mild symptoms which disappear in 3-5 days. Onset is sudden, with headache, fatigue, fever, nausea, vomiting, and constipation. More severe infections may also cause body aches and pain, especially in the neck, back, and legs. Bleeding can occur under the skin or from mucous membranes, and vomited material may be dark and look like coffee grounds. Jaundice or yellowing of the skin and eyes may also be present, hence "yellow fever."

There is a high death rate in severe cases between the sixth and ninth day of illness. Otherwise, fever returns to normal within 7-8 days and recovery is usually complete.

Treatment

Mild cases may be difficult to distinguish from severe sinus attacks, the flu, or hepatitis. Symptoms severe enough to cause concern must be treated quickly with medical care and hospitalization for supportive treatment, including intravenous fluids.

Prevention

In endemic areas, the best protection against yellow fever is vaccination, combined with insect precautions. See Mosquito and Tick Precautions, pp. 39 – 44 .

Japanese Encephalitis

This viral disease is also spread by mosquitoes and is preventable by vaccination. It occurs both sporadically and in epidemics in the tropical and temperate zones of Asia and Southeast Asia. In the temperate zones the highest risk is from June through September. In tropical zones the disease is present year round . Recently, an outbreak of encephalitis which was initially believed to be Japanese encephalitis occurred in Malaysia, leading to mass slaughtering of pigs (one of the vectors for this disease).

Symptoms

The incubation period is from 5 to 15 days. Many

infections are asymptomatic or mild or enough to escape notice, but in severe cases there's an abrupt onset of fever and headache. Mild respiratory symptoms and gastrointestinal symptoms including poor appetite, nausea, vomiting, and abdominal pain may accompany this. Illness progresses with confusion, delirium, and other symptoms. In mild cases, fever resolves after 6 or 7 days and other symptoms after about 2 weeks. Severe cases may proceed to coma and death within 10 days of onset, or to a prolonged period of recovery.

Treatment

There's no cure. Severe cases may require supportive measures including hospitalization. Death occurs in 30% of symptomatic cases while 50% of the survivors have some residual brain damage.

Prevention

Vaccination is recommended for travelers spending 4 weeks or longer in endemic rural areas. The mosquitoes responsible for infection begin feeding outdoors at dusk and continue through the evening (similar to the mosquito transmitting malaria). Observe insect precautions (see Mosquito and Tick Precautions, pp. 39 – 44).

Relapsing Fever (Tick or Recurrent Fever)

This illness occurs in many parts of the world. In the Americas, Africa, Asia, and Europe it's most likely to be spread by tick bites. It may occasionally be spread by lice. There have been recent outbreaks among travelers to Botswana and Zimbabwe.

Symptoms

The incubation period is about one week. Onset is sudden, with fever, chills, an increased heart rate, nausea and vomiting, joint pain, and severe headache. These symptoms may be hard to distinguish from a severe case of the flu or hepatitis. Within 3-10 days all symptoms abruptly cease. Unless treated, however, they continue to recur in milder form every week or two.

Treatment

Remove ticks (see p. 205) or treat lice (see p. 203). Their presence should be noted mentally in case illness follows within the incubation period. **Medical evaluation is required for any recurring fever.** Relapsing fever can be cured with 100 mg. of doxycycline taken twice a day for one day or erythromycin 500 mg. taken four times a day for one day.

Other Infectious Diseases

Hepatitis

One of most common diseases feared by travelers is hepatitis. It's caused by a virus, usually spread through contaminated food or water or sexual contact. In simpler times, there was infectious hepatitis, now hepatitis A, and serum hepatitis, now hepatitis B. Other forms of hepatitis include hepatitis C, D (delta agent), E and G. Infection by any of these viruses can cause the liver to become swollen and inflamed. The liver is unable to efficiently process and eliminate harmful substances from the body. These include the normal waste products of metabolism, as well as alcohol and medications. **When you suspect hepatitis, obtain medical evaluation.** Although potentially dangerous, with proper care most people recover completely.

Hepatitis A

Hepatitis A is the one travelers are most likely to encounter. It's excreted in the stools of infected persons and transmitted through a fecal-oral route. Food handlers who don't wash their hands are a major source of infection. Other sources are contaminated water and food, especially raw shellfish such as oysters and clams. Traveling in areas with generally poor hygiene and inadequate water and sewage facilities increases the chance of encountering hepatitis A. Sex with oral-rectal contact also spreads infection.

Hepatitis A is infectious for 2-4 weeks before symptoms develop, and for a few days afterwards. Fortunately, hepatitis A is a mild and limited infection although there is a 3.2% fatality rate in adults over age 40. Most people recover completely within 2-4 weeks.

Hepatitis B

Hepatitis B is significantly more common in Africa, Asia, and South America than the United States. Although less common than hepatitis A, it's a more severe and dangerous infection. It's spread through sexual contact, particularly between homosexual males, or contaminated blood. All body secretions are potentially infectious: saliva, sweat, semen, vaginal secretions, and blood, including menstrual blood. If not sterile, dental instruments, needles used in medical facilities and pharmacies, needles shared by drug users, and even needles employed in acupuncture or tattooing are potential sources of infection. Travelers whose lifestyles increase the risk should consider vaccinations, as should those who provide or may require medical care in endemic countries. The virus can be transmissible for weeks to months in dried blood (which is present in all medical facilities.)

Hepatitis E

This form of hepatitis is transmitted in a manner similar to hepatitis A. Person to person transmission can occur, but it's primarily spread through contaminated water. This is most likely in areas without adequate sewage disposal after heavy rains. There have been large outbreaks in India, Nepal, Burma, Pakistan, the USSR, and Mexico. Hepatitis E has an extremely high death rate among pregnant women. Food and water precautions and treatment are the same as for hepatitis A. There is no vaccine available.

Hepatitis C

Hepatitis C is found in approximately 3% of the world's population. Some regions of the world have rates estimated as high as 10%. Transmission of hepatitis C is primarily through blood or blood products; high rates have been found with intravenous drug users. Transmission also occurs from sexual contacts and improper medical and dental procedures, or non-medical procedures such as tattooing and piercing. There is a high rate of chronic disease (over 70%). No vaccine is currently available.

Signs and symptoms

The symptoms of hepatitis A, B, C and E are very much alike. They can cause any combination of the following:

headache, nausea, and possibly vomiting;

decreased appetite;

malaise or extreme tiredness;

yellowing of the eyes and skin (jaundice);

fever;

abdominal pain.

When present, abdominal pain is usually felt on the right upper side just below the rib cage.

As the liver is progressively affected, the urine turns dark, the color of cola. Stools become a clay-like greyish white. The skin and eyes may turn yellow (jaundiced). Smokers often find that cigarettes acquire an unpleasant taste.

Symptoms resembling the flu may precede Hepatitis B. Joint pain or a hive-like rash (*urticaria*) can also accompany it.

Hepatitis C may be totally asymptomatic.

Care and Treatment

Regardless of the type of hepatitis, the liver requires lots of tender loving care. **Don't** take aspirin, Tylenol (acetaminophen), alcohol, antibiotics, or **any** other drug or medication except under a doctor's order. Even after a quick recovery, it's wise to avoid such substances for a few weeks.

Women using birth control pills should stop taking them until they fully recover. To prevent spreading the virus, avoid all sexual contact until recovery is complete. If sexual contact does occur, by all means use another form of birth control, such as condoms.

Avoid exertion and dehydration. Get lots of rest and drink plenty of fluids. Fruit juices and light soup broths are usually well tolerated.

Eat whatever is appealing and stays down. If unable to eat because of prolonged vomiting or severe nausea, medication may help. Try a Tigan (trimethobenzamide HCl) 200 mg. rectal suppository once every 6-8 hours until symptoms diminish. If unavailable or further measures are needed to control nausea and vomiting, obtain medical evaluation. A dietary supplement of B-complex vitamins and vitamin C may be helpful.

Indications for Medical Assistance

In all cases of hepatitis, get medical help **immediately** for any of the following:

1. uncontrolled vomiting or dehydration;

2. spontaneous or easy bruising anywhere on the body;

3. spontaneous bleeding from the nose or gums;

4. presence of blood in the urine;

5. symptoms of hepatitis occurring any time during pregnancy.

Preventing the Spread of Illness

Observe the following measures to prevent spreading hepatitis A and E:

1. Keep your own plates, cups, and utensils separate. Wash them well with soap and hot water.

2. Wash your hands thoroughly after using the bathroom. Avoid preparing food for other people.

3. Avoid anal-oral sexual contact.

4. Don't share drinks, cigarettes, or food with others.

5. In restaurants, advise the staff of your illness and request that your utensils be washed separately.

To avoid spreading hepatitis B and C:

1. Abstain from sexual contact.

2. If you require dental work, inform the dentist of your illness.

3. Don't donate blood.

Coping with Extended Illness

Hospitalization is not usually required for hepatitis unless a bleeding disorder is present. It may be the only alternative if you are too sick to care for yourself and other assistance is not available. This is most likely when traveling alone. In such circumstances, hospitalization is reasonable and may be surprisingly inexpensive.

If there's someone to take care of you, a rented house or room will probably be cheaper than a hotel room for the length of time needed to fully recuperate. This is especially true for hepatitis B.

Vaccination for Hepatitis B

Travelers residing abroad or traveling long term (over 6 months) in high risk countries should be vaccinated against hepatitis B. Others at risk include health care workers with potential blood exposure, recurrent travelers such as business travelers, homosexual men, IV drug users, and those sexually active in a nonmonogamous relationships. There are 3 shots in the series at 0, 1, and 6 months. An accelerated series can be given at 0,1,2, and 12 months (4 total doses). Several studies have also proposed an even faster series with doses given at 0, 1 week, 3-4 weeks, and 6-12 months (4 total doses) although this is not FDA approved.

Treatment of Hepatitis B Exposure

Most exposures to hepatitis B are not clearly identifiable. If known exposure occurs while traveling, obtain hepatitis B immune globulin and start hepatitis B vaccine at the same time. Be sure to finish the hepatitis B vaccine series. If hepatitis B vaccine is not given at the time of the hepatitis B immune globulin then a second shot of hepatitis B immune globulin is given a month later. Be forewarned that this is an expensive medication (several hundred dollars), is from pooled human blood products, and may be hard to find..

If hepatitis B immune globulin is not available or you do not want to risk using a product made from pooled human blood, then start the hepatitis B vaccine series as soon as possible. This may not be as protective when given *after* exposure.

Sterile, disposable equipment must be used for any injection obtained while traveling.

Tuberculosis

Tuberculosis is not a highly contagious disease. Healthy adults rarely become ill with active TB although TB can be acquired and remain dormant in these individuals. This is the usual situation for people who skin test positive for TB with negative chest x-rays. Infection normally occurs from inhaling germs that are coughed or sneezed into the air. A variant of tuberculosis is also spread from unpasteurized dairy products, which should be avoided while traveling. Those at risk for active TB are primarily children, the elderly, or immune compromised persons who have been previously exposed to TB. Active TB usually involves infection in the lungs which can be spread to others through coughing and sneezing.

Have a TB (PPD) skin test done before and 2–3 months after extended travel (see Chapter 2, p. 61). If the first test is negative and the second is positive, exposure to TB occurred during travel. Medical evaluation and a chest x-ray are necessary. Medication is prescribed to prevent active disease.

Symptoms of Active or Disseminated TB.

Often, there are no symptoms of lung disease. When present, symptoms develop slowly. They may include weakness and fatigue, unexplained weight loss, decreased appetite, cough, fever and night sweats. Sputum is occasionally tinged with blood. If TB is suspected, get medical help immediately for thorough evaluation. **The presence of blood in the sputum always requires immediate medical evaluation including a chest x-ray.**

Rabies

Rabies is a viral infection transmitted in saliva through the bites of infected mammals, mainly carnivores. These commonly include dogs and cats, foxes, bats, skunks, raccoons, and other wild animals. It's unusual for rabbits or rodents to be infected.

Take every precaution against rabies. Treatment is possible only between the time of the bite and the onset of symptoms. Once symptoms appear there's no cure, and the outcome is almost always death. Infection can occur from exposure of a mucous membrane or fresh skin abrasion to infected saliva, as well as from a bite.

In industrialized nations because of dog vaccinations, most cases of rabies since 1960 have been due to wild animals. In developing countries domestic dogs, often homeless urban scavengers, must be considered a potential threat. In some cultures, religious strictures against the killing of animals contributes to an increased incidence of rabies. One of our patients was bitten by a rabid dog in Nairobi, Kenya. Two other victims of this dog died while our patient was fortunate enough to obtain treatment at a Nairobi hospital. He received the suckling mouse brain vaccine mentioned below, and did not receive rabies immune globulin. Needless to say, he was extremely traumatized by this experience.

In many countries dog populations are periodically reduced by aggressive eradication of strays. Poisoned meat may be widely distributed on public streets in both urban and rural areas. Anyone traveling with their own pet should keep this in mind.

Unchecked, dog populations can become frightening. Some U.S. agencies operating in foreign countries have at times armed their employees with chemical aerosol weapons. These have been issued for protection against dog packs running at night through city streets, as well as against rabies. The risk of rabies to travelers is greatest in countries where dog rabies is highly endemic. Areas of high risk include parts of Colombia, Ecuador, El Salvador, Guatemala, India, Mexico, Nepal, Peru, the Philippines, Sri Lanka, Thailand and Vietnam.

Preventive Measures

Avoid animals that behave abnormally. They may act either "mad", viciously biting and agitated, or lethargic and paralyzed, refusing to eat or drink. Excessive salivation (foaming at the mouth) may indicate rabies. Other indications may be daytime activity on the part of normally nocturnal animals like foxes, bats, skunks, or raccoons, and an absence of their usual fear of humans.

It's best to leave all stray animals strictly alone, no matter how cute, forlorn, or winsome. If camping outdoors, carefully mind clothing and other gear. One rabies victim was bitten by a rabid skunk that had crawled inside his sleeping bag.

Another important preventive measure is preexposure immunization against rabies. It should be considered by travelers who will be at high risk of exposure.

Rabies Symptoms

The incubation period of rabies in humans is 10 days to 2 years, averaging 3-7 weeks. It's shorter when bites occur on the face, head, or upper body.

Tingling and pain near the bite is an early symptom.

Malaise and fever follow, accompanied by restlessness which increases to uncontrollable agitation. A rabies victim develops excessive salivation and intense thirst. Excruciatingly painful spasms of the throat are triggered by the slightest stimulus, even swallowing: thus the term, "hydrophobia." Death follows from asphyxia, exhaustion, or general paralysis.

This is definitely a disease to avoid.

Treatment of Animal Bites

Any wound from an animal bite, or exposure to saliva, should be cleaned to excess. **Scrub the wound throughly with soap and water. Don't** attempt to close the wound. Medical help may be necessary to adequately flush a deep puncture wound. **Good cleansing may be the most important factor in preventing rabies.**

Rabies Antiserum and Vaccine

In the United States, rabies immune globulin (antibodies) and vaccine are normally given only under the following conditions:

1. If the animal is obviously rabid or develops rabies during a ten day confinement period following capture;

2. When the animal can't be observed or examined and if the bite was unprovoked or the animal was behaving unusually, and rabies is known to be present in the area.

As a traveler in a foreign environment, however, assume that **any animal bite carries the risk of rabies**. Never rely on assurances to the contrary, no matter how official. The only exceptions are in the handful of countries considered rabies-free, listed at the end of this section (p. 281).

After thoroughly cleaning a bite, scratch, or abrasion exposed to saliva, get immediate medical attention where rabies vaccine is available. The sooner treatment is started, the better the chance of preventing rabies.

Animal quarantine is not available in most developing countries. Even when the animal can be confined and observed for ten days, treatment should be initiated immediately. It can be discontinued if the animal proves healthy. **You require treatment even if you have had pre-exposure rabies vaccine**.

The human diploid cell rabies vaccine (HDCV) is a vast improvement over its predecessor. Discomfort and side effects aren't a concern. The full series of HDCV consists of only 5 shots given over 4 weeks. In addition to the vaccine, rabies immune globulin must be taken to provide immediate protection *if* no pre-exposure rabies vaccine was obtained.

Many developing countries use vaccines other than HDCV. They may have inactivated nerve tissue vaccine (NTV) or inactivated suckling mouse brain vaccine (SMBV). Both carry an increased risk of potentially harmful reactions. If given a choice, use HDCV. Otherwise, use whatever is available. It's better than getting rabies. None of these vaccines are contraindicated during pregnancy.

If human rabies immune globulin is not available, it should be possible to obtain antibodies derived from horses. A skin test is required before taking these antibodies because horse serum carries a high rate of allergic reactions.

Rabies treatment schedule:
   following possible exposure with no pre-exposure vaccination:

1. 5 intra-muscular (IM) injections of HDCV, 1 cc. each. The first dose is given as soon as possible after exposure. Subsequent shots are given on days 3, 7, 14, and 28 following the initial dose. All injections should be given in the upper arm (deltoid muscle).

2. In addition, 20 IU / kg. of body weight of HRIG (human rabies immune globulin) should be given immediately. As much of the dose as possible is infiltrated into the

wound area; the remainder is given IM into the buttock.

following pre-exposure vaccination:

1. 2 IM doses of HDCV are needed, 1 cc. each. The first is given as soon as possible, the second 3 days later. No HRIG is necessary.

Side effects HDCV may cause pain, redness, swelling and itching at the injection site. Less commonly there's headache, nausea, abdominal pain, muscle aches, or dizziness. For headache or localized symptoms, take 2 aspirin or Tylenol every 4-6 hours as needed. Cold packs to the injection site are also helpful. The same measures are useful for any local pain or low-grade fever that develops from HRIG.

Typhoid Fever

The culprit in typhoid is the bacteria *Salmonella typhi*. Infection is spread primarily through contaminated food, water, or milk. Outbreaks can often follow earthquakes, floods, hurricanes, drought, and other disasters. World wide there are 16-17 million cases annually with about 600,000 deaths. **Take special precautions to purify water following any disruption of normal water supplies.**

Vaccination is not as good a preventive measure as water purification and good hand washing by infected individuals. Vaccination is 70-90% effective. High risk areas include India, Pakistan, Bangladesh, Peru and Senegal.

Signs and Symptoms

Untreated, typhoid fever sometimes shows three characteristic stages. The first is marked by flu-like symptoms. These include increasing fatigue, headache, cough, general body aches, sore throat, and often nose bleeds. There may be abdominal pains, constipation, diarrhea, or vomiting. There is a classic "stepladder" fever, with the maximum temperature increasing daily for seven to ten days. It's generally highest in the evenings.

In the second stage the fever stabilizes. There may be "pea soup" diarrhea or constipation, possibly with abdominal distention. Severe weakness with delirium or coma may result. There may also be a characteristic rash, with rose-colored spots that turn white (blanch) with pressure. Fever is accompanied by a pulse which is markedly slow. If there are no complications, symptoms slowly subside over another 7-10 days. The fever decreases, again in step-ladder fashion.

Sometimes these classic stages are not present. There may only be milder symptoms with recurrent fevers. **All recurrent fevers require medical evaluation.**

Treatment
If typhoid is suspected, get medical treatment as soon as possible. Blood cultures, stool tests, and/or urine tests are required to identify typhoid.

Adults are usually treated with ciprofloxacin, ceftriaxone, or chloramphenicol. The latter can be given either intramuscularly (IM) or intravenously (IV). **By any route chloramphenicol should never be taken except under medical supervision.** Its side effects are dangerous and can be life-threatening.

Bed rest and adequate hydration are important. High calorie, low residue foods are likely to be the best tolerated. Reduce fever by applying cool compresses as needed.

Preventing the Spread of Illness
To prevent infecting other individuals observe good hand washing, especially after using the bathroom. Avoid preparing foods for others, as well as handling plates or utensils. Avoid intimate or sexual contact until treatment is complete. Keep food screened from flies, which may also spread the disease.

Mononucleosis

Mononucleosis is a viral infection. It's transmitted

directly through kissing, and indirectly through coughing, sneezing, and sharing food, utensils, or cigarettes.

The incubation period is 5-15 days. Signs of infection
include fever, sore throat, fatigue, and increased sleepiness. Lymph nodes may be enlarged and slightly tender,
especially in back of the head and neck. There may be
muscle aches and decreased appetite. At times there's a
red, flat or slightly raised, generalized body rash. If a lab
is available, diagnosis can be confirmed with a blood test.

Treatment

The main requirement is rest and increased fluid intake. For pain or fever, take one aspirin orally four times
a day. For a sore throat, use warm saline gargles three
times a day. If unable to maintain a nutritional diet, vitamin supplements may be useful. Avoid contact sports
until recovery is complete. There's an increased possibility of injury to the spleen during illness. Complete recovery may require up to 4-6 weeks.

Brucellosis (Malta or Undulant Fever)

Brucellosis is a bacterial infection that occurs worldwide. It's contracted from ingesting contaminated, unpasteurized milk or dairy products from cows, sheep,
and goats. It's also an occupational hazard for people
who work with these animals, or with pigs, dogs, cats,
or wild animals. The bacteria can enter the body and
cause infection through broken skin.

Symptoms

Onset is slow with increasing tiredness, weakness,
loss of appetite, headache, stomach ache, swollen lymph
nodes, and possibly joint pain or constipation. Fever
may be absent or severe. When present, one's temperature may be normal in the morning and elevated in the
afternoon and evening, or have no particular pattern.

Acute cases without complications may resolve
completely in 2-3 weeks. Often the fever recurs after

short periods of absence. **Any recurrent fever requires prompt medical evaluation.**

Treatment

Obtain medical help to distinguish brucellosis from other causes of fever. **This is especially important during pregnancy.** Spontaneous abortion is a frequent complication of brucellosis. Brucellosis is usually treated with combination antibiotic therapy. Usually treatment will require at least 8 weeks to completely eradicate the infection.

This illness is preventable. **Avoid unpasteurized dairy products.**

Plague, Typhus, and Leprosy

These diseases are virtually nonexistent among travelers. Plague in recent years has emerged in India although it can be prevented by treatment with tetracycline antibiotics for those at risk. The last reported case of typhus in a U.S. traveler was more than 30 years ago.

Leprosy, too, has vanished as a concern among travelers . . . almost. If you travel in northern Mexico or the southwestern U.S. (Texas, New Mexico, and Arizona), armadillos have been found to carry leprosy. Several recent cases of leprosy were traced to this source, and the organism which causes leprosy has been isolated from the paw pads of local armadillos.

Quick Reference
Countries Reported Free of Rabies

(does not include rabies transmitted by bats)

Americas Bermuda, Saint Pierre, Miquelon
Caribbean: Antigua, Aruba, Barbuda, Bahamas, Barbados, Cayman Islands, Grenadines, Guadeloupe, Jamaica, Martinique, Saint Christopher (St. Kitts) and Nevis, Saint Martin, Saint Vincent, Virgin Islands (U.K. and U.S.) Netherlands Antilles (Aruba, Bonaire, Curacao, Saba, St. Maarten, and St. Eustatius)

Europe Albania, Denmark, Cyprus, Faroe Islands, Finland, Gibraltar, Greece, Iceland, Ireland, Isle of Man, Malta, Italy, Jersey, Macedonia, Malta, Monaco, Jersey, Norway (mainland), Spain except Ceuta and Melilla), Sweden, United Kingdom (Britain and Northern Ireland),Bulgaria*, Portugal*

Asia Bahrain, Brunei, Japan, Hong Kong, Republic of Korea*, Kuwait, Malaysia (Malaysia Sabah*), Maldives, Oman,* Qatar, Singapore, Taiwan

Oceania American Samoa, Australia, Cook Islands, Federated States of Micronesia (Kosrae, Ponape, Truk, and Yap), Fiji, French Polynesia (Tahiti), Guam, New Zealand, Papua New Guinea, Indonesia (with the exception of Java, Kalimantan, Sumatra and Sulawesi),

Kiribati, New Caledonia, Niue, Solomon Islands, Tonga, Vanuatu.

Africa Cape Verde, Reunion, Libya*, Seychelles*, Mauritius*

*Denotes countries that have only recently reported an absence of rabies. This should be considered a provisional status.

Tropical Diseases by David Spees, M.D. 10

With few exceptions, travelers in urban areas infrequently encounter the diseases we discuss here. Many tropical diseases are really hazards of rural areas, poverty, and native lifestyles. Schistosomiasis, for example, mostly affects rural agricultural workers exposed to canal and irrigation water. It's also prevalent in villages near rivers and lakes where sanitation facilities and potable water systems don't exist. By the same token, travelers to these areas — dependent on the same water supply — are definitely at risk for schistosomiasis. Anyone who travels in a predominately rural area must be aware of local health hazards and precautions. This is especially true for missionaries, field researchers, service volunteers including Peace Corps members, agricultural workers, or others living in a rural setting.

It's also important to document or make a written note of travel in endemic areas where exposure to infection may have occurred. Delayed symptoms are sometimes possible months or even years after leaving the area. **Any recurrent fever or ulcerated lesion or sore which doesn't heal requires medical evaluation as soon as possible.**

Protozoan Infections

Leishmaniasis

Leishmaniasis is a protozoan infection transmitted by certain biting sandflies. Different forms of the disease appear in different parts of the world. When the infection is generalized (spread throughout the body), it's called visceral or systemic leishmaniasis. When localized (limited) to the skin or mucous membrane, it's called cutaneous or mucocutaneous leishmaniasis.

Systemic Leishmaniasis

The systemic form, known as Kala-azar or dum-dum fever, occurs in several South and Central American countries. It's also found in Africa, India, southern Russia, the Near and Middle East, and along the Mediterranean coast.

The incubation period varies widely, averaging 3–8 months. Symptoms have a gradual onset. There may be vague abdominal pain, fever, weakness, decreased appetite, coughing, weight loss, muscle aches, and constipation or diarrhea. The skin may be pale, dry, and scaly. It sometimes acquires a gray tone, particularly on the hands and feet ("Kala-azar" means literally "black disease"). Fever may be recurrent, or high and spiking, with chills, sweats, and even nose bleeds. The liver and spleen are enlarged. A primary skin lesion at the site of the sandfly bite is rare.

Because most of the symptoms are nonspecific, identification of the disease requires laboratory testing. Antimony compounds and other medications are available to treat the disease. **Any recurrent fever requires medical evaluation.**

Cutaneous and Mucocutaneous Leishmaniasis

Cutaneous leishmaniasis, affecting only the skin, is known outside the Americas as oriental sore, tropical sore, Bangladesh or Delhi boil. It occurs in China, India,

Africa, the Mediterranean, and the Near and Middle East. In these areas it's predominantly an urban disease. It's common in the larger cities of the Middle East such as Teheran, Baghdad, Aleppo, and Damascus. It's also found in northwest India and Pakistan and around the Mediterranean, including Italy and North Africa. In urban areas, the lesions are dry and usually occur singly. They grow slowly and may persist a year or more unless treated.

In the Americas, leishmaniasis of the skin is a predominantly rural infection. It's common among people living or working near the edge of jungles and forests. Several forms occur from Mexico and Central America south to northern Argentina. The disease is prevalent in Chile and Uruguay. The authors have seen several cases in Guatemala, where tourists camping at the popular Mayan ruins of Tikal were affected. In the Americas, lesions are moist rather than dry and multiple lesions occur more often.

Lesions may take weeks to months or even years to develop. They can occur anywhere on the body, including the mouth, nose, and face. They may vary in appearance, even on the same person.

The lesion begins as a small, sometimes itchy nodule. It grows, becomes encrusted, and ulcerates. The ulcer is usually shallow and circular, with a well-defined hard, raised, red border. There may be a discharge, either clear or with pus. The ulcer may grow to an inch (2–3 cm) or more across. Sometimes new smaller lesions spring up around it.

The lesions are painless and are neither tender nor itchy unless secondary infection occurs. Lesions around the nose may produce nose bleeds or nasal obstruction.

Prevention

Use a DEET containing insect repellent and wear permethrin treated clothing to minimize exposure to sandflies. Sleep under permethrin impregnated mosquito netting (see insect precautions, pp. 39 – 44).

Treatment

All forms of leishmaniasis require medical attention. Skin lesions usually spread and may be disfiguring. Although lesions may eventually heal after many months, they almost inevitably become infected if not treated.

Leishmaniasis is often more quickly identified in the regions where it's known and can be diagnosed virtually on sight. Back home it may be quite mysterious, requiring weeks and repeated biopsies to identify. **Any persistent lesion that does not heal requires medical evaluation.** Formerly, lesions were treated with a locally injected antimony compound. They're now usually treated with oral antimony medications such as meglumine antimonate (Glucantime) or stibogluconate sodium (Pentostam). One of the authors recently encountered a researcher who had contracted mucocutaneous leishmaniasis with a nasal ulceration while studying primates in Ecuador. His original treatment had not included an antimony compound leading to a recurrence of disease.

Trypanosomiasis (sleeping sickness & Chagas disease)

Sleeping Sickness

Sleeping sickness, transmitted by the tsetse fly, occurs in West, Central, and East Africa. It ranges between 20°N. and 20°S. latitudes, where the tsetse fly lives only in scattered localities near certain lakes and rivers with damp, shady vegetation.

There are two forms of sleeping sickness, both bad. The nasty Gambian form is found in West Africa, Zaire, Uganda and the southern Sudan, with strongholds along the main branches of the Congo and Niger rivers. It's also found in Gambia, Guinea, Ghana, and Sierra Leone.

The even nastier Rhodesian form is largely limited to East Africa, including Kenya, Uganda, Tanzania, Zambia, Malawi, Mozambique, and Zimbabwe National

Park in Rhodesia. It is responsible for several deaths among travelers on safari in East Africa.

Although the risk of infection is small, travelers entering endemic areas should know both preventive measures *and* early signs of disease. The latter is necessary so that effective treatment can be obtained. **Early treatment is essential.** The longer treatment is delayed, the less likely it is to be effective.

Typically, tsetse fly bites are painful. After a bite from an infected fly, local redness and swelling may appear within minutes, subsiding in a few hours. This is followed in several days by a characteristic reddened, firm, raised nodule or tumor. It's usually about one inch (2–3 cm.) across. It may be accompanied by swelling, or surrounded by a diffuse, reddened, raised or thickened area. This is the so-called "trypanosomal chancre."

The chancre usually occurs on exposed parts of the body — often the legs, but also the hands or head. It's sometimes said to resemble a boil. Although itchy and tender to mildly painful, the chancre is never as painful as a boil. The nodule subsides spontaneously in 1–2 weeks, with no apparent scarring.

The chancre is an identifying sign of infection that almost always occurs in travelers. (It does not necessarily occur in local inhabitants, who have some immunity.) It's especially severe with the Rhodesian form of sleeping sickness.

Once alerted by development of the chancre, quick medical attention will prevent the infection from spreading. If neglected, the second phase of the disease occurs with dissemination of the parasites throughout the blood stream.

Symptoms of generalized infection usually develop within 10-21 days of the bite. The protozoa cause recurrent fever, tiredness, insomnia, and headache. The fever is irregular, accompanied by a fast pulse which may persist after the fever subsides. Lymph nodes are often enlarged, soft, rubbery, and painless. They can frequently be felt high in the back of the neck. The face, feet, and legs may appear swollen. Six to eight weeks after the onset of illness, a patchy red rash may develop on the chest, back, or elsewhere. Untreated, progressive damage occurs to the heart, nervous system, and other organs.

Prevention

Some protection from tsetse flies can be provided by protective clothing and repellents. There's also a chemical prophylaxis for individual travelers, given in the form of intramuscular injections. However, it's not recommended. This is because the length of effective protection against the Rhodesian form of sleeping sickness is uncertain. The procedure also masks the trypanosomal chancre, which otherwise provides a reliable early warning of infection. Without this sign, diagnosis is vastly more complicated if an illness accompanied by fever does occur. Normally diagnosis and treatment of early sleeping sickness is easy, rapid, and effective.

American trypanosomiasis (Chagas disease)

Chagas disease exists throughout rural areas of southern Mexico, and in Central and South America. The "kissing bug" or "assassin bug" that spreads the infection is large and nocturnal. It usually inhabits only the poorer adobe and thatch-roof huts in tropical areas.

Victims of the "kissing bug", usually asleep, are often bitten about the face. When the bite occurs near the eye, there may be a characteristic one-sided conjunctivitis ("pink-eye") and swelling of the eyelid and face. This is called "Romana's sign." Otherwise the bite causes local redness and swelling.

Symptoms of infection which may occur 2–3 weeks following the bite include daily fever, and a rash on the chest and abdomen. The rash consists of pinhead small red spots; there is no pain or itching.

Symptoms diminish over several months. There may or may not be further symptoms or damage to internal organs, especially the heart. Congestive heart failure and a large, poorly contracting heart can develop. In addition, Chagas disease can be transmitted through blood transfusions.

Prevention and treatment

Mosquito netting is an effective barrier against kissing bugs at night. The bugs can also be controlled with insecticides. Although contact is unlikely, travelers should choose their sleeping quarters carefully with an eye for prevention. This disease has long been considered incurable, although new drugs appear promising. Treatment requires medical supervision.

Blood Flukes and Other Parasitic Worm Infections

There are a variety of parasitic worms that infect the blood and lymphatic system, or organs such as the liver, lungs, bladder, and intestines. These are not your run-of-the-mill intestinal parasites discussed in Chapter 6, "Stomach and Intestinal Disorders." Rather, they have complex life cycles involving intermediate hosts. They are commonly transmitted by insects or contact with fresh water, not by ingestion of contaminated food.

Repeated exposure and reinfection is generally necessary to produce symptoms of disease from these parasites. Anyone living or traveling where these diseases are widespread should take precautions against them. This is especially true for extended visits. On rare occasions even minimal exposure to some diseases, such as schistosomiasis, can have devastating consequences.

Filariasis

Filariasis is an infection of the lymphatic system with tiny threadlike nematode worms. Several species of mosquitoes transmit these. The disease occurs in scattered urban and rural areas of the tropics and subtropics worldwide. The disease is slow to develop, usually no earlier than 8–12 months after infection. Signs and symptoms, caused by inflammation and obstruction of lymph channels, include swelling of lymph vessels and glands. There may also be swelling of the scrotum, arms, or legs.

Swelling may be preceded or accompanied by fever, sweating, malaise, loss of appetite, nausea, and vomiting. After leaving an endemic area, early symptoms which may have arisen during an extended stay gradually disappear. Occasionally, though, the initial symptom is a recurrent fever that develops within a few months of leaving an endemic area.

Elephantiasis, the gross enlargement of a leg, arm, scrotum, or other part, is still frequently seen among natives where infection is widespread. This rarely occurs without a decade or more of chronic disease.

Ocular form

Two eye infections are caused by filaria. The first is *Loa Loa*, transmitted by the deer fly. The infection presents as a visible worm crawling across the outside of the eye, but under the conjunctiva or clear membrane covering the eyeball. Though frightening, the worm causes little harm and is allowed to crawl out of the eye before treatment.

The second, *onchocerciasis* or river blindness, is transmitted by black flies. Infection may be symptomless, or range from mild or severely itchy skin to blindness brought about by invasion of the eye. These filaria are too small to be seen without special magnification. Short term travelers bitten by the infected black fly usually develop a transient itchy rash, characteristically with fine bumps or papules, that causes little discomfort.

Prevention and Treatment

Mosquito precautions (see pp. 39 – 44) will help reduce exposure. People who face years of continuous mosquito exposure, such as missionaries, Peace Corps volunteers, or field researchers, might want to consider a prescription drug regime (diethyl-carbamazone) to prevent infection.

The vague symptoms, especially in travelers who spend a short time in an endemic area, make an early diagnosis difficult. Anyone with recurrent fever should seek medical help for diagnosis and treatment. The drug of choice, diethyl-carbamazone, should only be taken under medical supervision. Full control of infection may require repeated treatments over a period as long as one year.

Schistosomiasis (Bilharziasis)

This is a potentially dangerous infection from trematode worms known as blood flukes. It's a rural disease, transmitted through an intermediate host, the fresh water snail. These snails generally require standing or slow-moving water, usually dirty or muddy, with aquatic vegetation and exposure to sunlight. They are found commonly in streams, ponds, small dams, shores of lakes, lazy rivers, and canal or irrigation water. However, we have treated a white water rafting guide who spends time on the Omo River in Southern Ethiopia for two infections from schistosomiasis.

The snails become infected from eggs passed in human urine and feces. In time, they release free-swimming larva. These are capable of penetrating the skin within 15 minutes of contact. In such areas, it's hazardous to drink, wade, or bathe in untreated water.

Contact frequently causes a mild form of "swimmer's itch." This is an itching, prickling sensation with local redness or swelling at the site of entry of the parasite that lasts up to three days Usually within 2–8 weeks a general allergic reaction begins with fever, malaise, muscle pains, and often hives (urticaria).

The severity of all schistosome infections in most cases depends on the degree of exposure to larvae. Although frequent re-exposure is usually necessary for symptoms to develop, this is not always true. Adult worms live up to 20 years in the body. Because tissue damage occurs from the myriad eggs produced over this time, long term consequences can easily accrue. In addition, some individuals with minimal exposure have developed paralyzing spinal cord disease.

Additional symptoms vary according to the type of schistosomiasis responsible. There are three forms.

Urinary schistosomiasis

This variant is found throughout Africa and adjacent islands. It's heavily present in Egypt, particularly along the Nile. In the Mediterranean and Middle East it occurs only in a few scattered areas. It occurs nowhere else with the exception of Bombay province in India.

This form may cause only a mild allergic reaction. Three to six months after infection, but sometimes up to 2 years or more, there may be local symptoms of urinary frequency and urgency. Characteristically there is blood in the urine, often at the end of urination. Rectal symptoms, with blood or pus in the stools, are possible. Progressive and irreversible damage to genital, urinary, and other organs can occur if the infection is not treated.

Intestinal schistosomiasis

This one is found predominantly along the Nile valley, in Africa from the southern Sahara to about 15•S. latitude, and in Madagascar. In the Middle East it rarely occurs outside Yemen, except for a few places in Saudi Arabia. It's also common in a wide coastal band of South America, extending from near Barranquilla in northern Columbia through Venezuela and Brazil to about 20•S. latitude, or just north of Rio de Janeiro. In Brazil this region extends west across the highlands and far into the Amazon basin. The infection also exists in the Caribbean, mainly in Puerto Rico and Santa Lucia.

The general allergic reaction is often severe. Headache, nausea, vomiting, abdominal pain, severe diarrhea with bloody stools may accompany it. Six to eight weeks after infection (but sometimes up to two years or more) dysentery develops. Symptoms include severe colicy pains, diarrhea, passage of blood and mucus in the stools, fever, weakness, and weight loss. Untreated, symptoms endure for 6–12 months with increased severity at intervals of 2–3 weeks. Damage to abdominal organs is cumulative and irreversible.

Asiatic schistosomiasis

This is the most dangerous form. It's found only in southeastern China, the Philippine Islands (including Leyte, Mindanao, and southern Luzon), Sulawesi (Celebes), and a few areas of Laos and Kampuchea. It may have been eliminated in Japan.

The initial reaction is usually severe, with vomiting, diarrhea, abdominal pain and cramps. There may be a dry cough. After several weeks, blood and mucus often appear in the stools as diarrhea becomes increasingly severe. Untreated, damage is progressive not only to abdominal organs but throughout the body.

Prevention: schistosomiasis precautions

Observe the following precautions to reduce or eliminate potential schistosomiasis exposure in endemic areas:

1. Don't swim in fresh water lakes or ponds that might be contaminated by nearby inhabitants.

2. Don't swim, bathe, or drink from slow-moving fresh water rivers and streams.

3. Avoid contact with irrigation or canal water.

4. Be wary of oceans, beaches, or bays near river or sewage outlets.

5. wading is necessary to cross potentially contaminated water, use high-top rubber boots. If the skin becomes wet, dry off quickly (within 5-10 minutes) to prevent skin penetration by larvae.

6. Never drink untreated water from potentially contaminated lakes or streams. Larvae are destroyed by the water purification measures recommended in Chapter 3 — boiling, iodine, filters, or chlorine (see pp. 71 – 77.)

7. Water can be made safe for bathing by the above measures or by allowing it to stand in a container for at least 3 days.

Although fast moving clear streams and rivers may be safe, there is no practical way for travelers to distinguish infested from uninfested water. Many areas that were safe in the recent past are now considered contaminated. Swimming pools, if chlorinated, are considered safe.

Treatment

Medical evaluation is mandatory to diagnose schistosomiasis. Laboratory exams, usually of stool or urine for ova and parasites, and occasionally a rectal biopsy, may be needed to identify the parasite. In the U.S., blood tests (serologies) are best performed at the Centers for Disease Control (CDC). The earlier that diagnosis and treatment is made, the sooner potential damage can be limited.

Praziquantel is effective against all forms of schistosomiasis. The usual dose is 20 mg./kg of body weight **taken orally 3 times a day for one day.**

Other Parasitic Infections

Intestinal infections are mostly symptomless and usually go unnoticed until a worm shows up in the stool. A laboratory stool exam is necessary to identify mild infections. In general, the worms are easily treated with prescription drugs. A chart of lab results and the indicated treatment is included at the end of this chapter for reference. Exceptions to this rule are pork tapeworm and anisakiasis.

Pork Tapeworm

Acquired mainly by eating raw or undercooked pork, ingested eggs hatch in the stomach. The larvae then penetrate the stomach wall and are carried to other organs of the body where they become trapped. Unable to mature, they form cysts. In the head these may block the flow of the brain's cerebrospinal fluid (CSF)), or cause problems such as seizures or neurological deficits like those caused by brain tumors. Treatment depends on the problems caused and ranges from no intervention to drug treatment and brain surgery. To prevent the disease, avoid undercooked pork.

Anisakiasis

Anisakiasis is a nematode infection acquired by eating raw or undercooked fish or squid. The larvae then invade the wall of the stomach or intestine but don't penetrate it like the pork tapeworm. Severe abdominal pain begins a few hours later, often associated with nausea and vomiting. These symptoms gradually resolve or are intermittent for weeks to months. They can mimic appendicitis.

The worm may be spontaneously regurgitated, ending the infection. Otherwise, the worm can be removed by endoscopy (looking into the stomach with a flexible fiberoptic light) or surgery. Medications also help in heavy infections.

Guinea worm infection (Drancunculiasis, Dragon Worm, Fiery Serpent)

Nearly eradicated, guinea worm may be one of the oldest and most fascinating known parasites. These worms are encountered in West, Central, and East Afri- They can also be found in Afghanistan, Sudan, Egypt, Pakistan, Iran, Turkey, southern Russia, western and southern India, Burma, New Guinea, South America, and some of the Caribbean islands. Moses in the Bible (Numbers, 21) refers to fiery serpents which plagued the Israelites on their travels along the Red Sea.

Human infection is the result of ingesting contaminated water containing a microscopic intermediate host, the Cyclops. Freed from the Cyclops by digestive juices, larvae burrow out of the stomach or upper intestines and migrate into body tissues. After 10–14 months, the female worm is mature enough to produce young. It then burrows outward toward the skin, most commonly in the legs and feet.

Many people complain of a deep, stinging pain at the site where the worm nears the surface. When the worm reaches the surface, a raised lesion (or group of lesions that grow together into one) develops. It enlarges for 1–2 days, forming a painful blistering area. The blister bursts when it touches water. The worm then sticks out its uterus which bursts, expelling hundreds of thousands of larvae into the water. The resulting ulcer heals somewhat, reducing in size to a small hole with the head of the worm often visible within it. A frequent complication is secondary bacterial infection. Tetanus is also a concern.

Prevention

Infection is easily prevented by any of the water purification methods discussed in Chapter 3 – boiling, iodine, filters, or chlorine (see pp.71 – 77).

Treatment

Pain, tenderness, and swelling are quickly relieved with treatment. The worms will emerge or are easily removed. Use one of the following medications:

1. Flagyl, 250 mg. orally 3 times a day for 10 days; **or**

2. thiabendazole, 25 mg./kg. of body weight twice a day for 3 days.

When drugs aren't available, slow extraction taking many days is necessary. Extraction should start after 2–3 days of wet compresses to the lesion. This allows the worm to discharge its eggs, after which it's easier to remove.

One end of a thread is attached to the worm's head, the other to a stick about which the worm is gently wound, a little each day. This may take a while as the worms can be two feet long. Patience is required to avoid breaking the worm. Keep the ulcerated area clean, dry, and covered to prevent secondary infection. If this occurs, use one of the following:

1. dicloxacillin 500 mg. orally, 4 times a day for 10 days; **or**

2. erythromycin 250 mg. orally, 4 times a day for 10 days; **or**

3. Keflex or Velosef 500 mg. orally, 4 times a day for 10 days.

Obtain a tetanus booster if needed.

Parrot Fever (Psittacosis)

Many travelers are attracted to the wonderfully colorful tropical birds of the world — handling them in the markets or keeping them as pets while living or working abroad. Caution is required, as many of the birds carry *Chlamydia*, a bacteria that can cause lung infections in humans.

Fever develops 1 to 3 weeks after exposure. Onset may be slow or abrupt. It's accompanied by chills, headache, backache, fatigue, muscle aches, and sometimes a bloody nose. There is a cough, dry initially, which becomes productive as pneumonia progresses.

Treatment

Parrot fever is treated with tetracycline 500 mg. orally, 4 times a day for 2–3 weeks. Rest, fluids, and aspirin, 2 tablets up to 4 times a day for fever, headache, and muscle aches, are also appropriate. If allergic to tetracycline, an alternative medication is erythromycin 500 mg. orally, 4 times a day for 2–3 weeks.

Prevention

A course of antibiotics will rid parrots of any Chlamydia bacteria they might harbor. European formulations of injectable Vibramycin, if available, can be given to the parrot intramuscularly. These are required only once every 6 days. Unfortunately American preparations of Vibramycin for injection are considered too irritating by some veterinarians.

The full course of oral antibiotics for parrots lasts 45 days and must be adhered to rigorously. The dose for parrots is Vibramycin (doxycycline) 8–12 mg. per lb. twice a day for 45 days. Syrup formulations are the easiest to measure and handle. An alternative is chlortetracycline (syrup form), 20 mg. per lb. 3 times a day for 45 days.

Leptospirosis

In warm, humid climates, this bacterial disease can be transmitted by exposure to contaminated water through either breaks in the skin or the mucous membranes. Exposure occurs when wading, swimming, or bathing in fresh water contaminated with the urine of infected mammals such as rats, mice, pigs and cattle. Rainfall or flooding is often responsible for washing the bacteria into the fresh water source.

Symptoms

One to two weeks after exposure illness begins with a sudden onset of fever, severe headache, muscle aches and bloodshot eyes. The muscle aches are worse in the back, calves, and thighs. Symptoms resolve without treatment but reappear within 30 days in less severe form. This recurrence can last for months. Though 90% of infected persons have a mild illness, the most severe form, called Weil's syndrome, results in turning yellow (jaundice), kidney failure, internal bleeding, collapse, and possibly death.

Prevention

Avoid skin contact with freshwater and mud after

heavy rainfall or flooding. Avoid swamps and ponds. Rafters need to carefully cover all cuts and abrasions. If thrown out of a boat or raft, keep the eyes closed under water, avoid swallowing water, blow your nose, and shower off as soon as possible.

Treatment

Many of the common antibiotics (penicillin, amoxicillin, doxycycline and others) shorten the course if used within the first few days of illness. Intravenous penicillin is the treatment of choice. Rafters and visitors to areas of flooding or where leptospirosis is a known problem may consider taking 200 mg. of doxycycline once a week for prevention.

Leeches

To travelers in the tropical rain forests of New Guinea, India, Indochina, and elsewhere, it may seem like bloodthirsty little gremlins are hiding under every leaf and rock. Slithering stealthily, they attach themselves to the skin like murderous hickeys, producing a trickle of blood at the site.

There are 2 types of leeches — land and aquatic. Neither appears to cause any disease. Their bite is painless, and the main problem with leeches, after their removal, is itching and secondary infection.

Land Leeches

A photographer and an anthropologist we know trekked for 10 days in the New Guinea jungles. They pulled an average 100 leeches off each person daily. In one 3-hour stretch, they pulled 292 leeches from 1 person alone. As a result of their experiences, they provide the following information and advice:

1. Don't pull off an attached leech, or a sore will develop a few days later. Remove the leech with insect repellent, lemon juice, salt, vinegar, or tobacco juice. Or, if

you are feeling generous, let it fall off when it's finished with you.

2. DEET insect repellent is particularly effective. Put a drop on the leech and not only will it fall off, it will curl up, shrivel, and die.

3. Heat from a lighted match, applied to the body of the leech, may also be effective, but isn't recommended due to the possibility of burn injury.

4. Leeches are sticky. In removing them, they will stick to the hand. Immediately roll them between forefinger and thumb (decreasing the stickiness) — then throw them away.

5. Leeches are diurnal creatures. Don't worry about sleeping on the ground at night, even in heavily infested areas.

6. You can remove a leech from the eye by shining a flashlight close to it. The leech will move toward the light and off of the eye.

Treatment
To reduce itching, take a nonsedating antihistamine such as Claritin, Allegra, or Zyrtec. Benadryl or Atarax are other choices, but often cause drowsiness. By not scratching the chance of secondary infection is reduced. (For specific doses see p. 215.)

Prevention
Insect repellents such as dibutyl or dimethyl phthalate or DEET will help ward off leeches. The repellent should be applied to clothing as well as skin, although dimethyl phthalate should not be used on rayon. If sweating a lot or exposed to water reapply DEET every 3–5 hours or as needed.

In leech-infested territory, wear knee-high boots (preferably waterproof), and closely woven pants tucked into the boots. An Australian friend who has lived in

Africa suggests rubbing Vaseline petroleum jelly over exposed skin. This prevents leeches from attaching and resists being washed off.

Aquatic or Water Leeches

Aquatic leeches are found only in fresh water, primarily in North Africa, western Asia, Indonesia, and southern Europe. They are less common than the terrestrial variety, but more dangerous.

Water leeches are acquired by drinking or bathing in infested water. They can attach themselves to the mouth, throat, nose, lungs, vulva, vagina, male urethra, and other internal sites.

In the nose they may cause bleeding, obstruction, and persistent headaches. Lodged in the throat, they may cause continuous coughing with a bloody discharge, difficulty swallowing, hoarseness, and possibly even suffocation. In the lungs they may produce chest pain and shortness of breath. Elsewhere they cause other localized symptoms.

Treatment

Internal leeches should be removed by medical personnel. In the mouth or nose, a strong saline solution swished, gargled, or lavaged may remove leeches.

Prevention

Don't drink or bathe in infested waters. Water for all purposes should be filtered, then boiled. If you can't do both, one or the other will at least be effective in removing leeches.

See the following table for stool exams and indicated treatment.

Quick Reference:
Stool Exams for Fluke
and Tapeworm Ova and Parasites

When lab reports indicate the presence of tapeworms or flukes, medical attention must be obtained immediately. The following information is provided for reference only.

Exams show presence of:

Treatment:

Tapeworms (cestodes)

Taenia saginata
Taenia solium
Diphyllobothrium
  latum
Diphyllobothrium
  pacificum
Diphyllobothrium
  mansoni

For the treatment of all tapeworm infections, take either niclosamide, four 500 mg. tablets (2 grams chewed thoroughly, or praziquantel, 10–20 mg. per kg. of body weight, as a single oral dose (except Hymenolepsis nana).

Hymenolepsis nana

The drug of choice for Hymenolepsis is praziquantel, 25 mg. per kg. of weight in a single oral dose. The alternative is niclosamide, four 500 mg. tablets (2 grams) chewed thoroughly as an initial dose, then two 500 mg. tablets daily for 6 successive days.

Exams show presence of:	Treatment:
Blood Flukes Schistosoma mekongi Schistosoma japonicum Schistosoma haematobium Schistosoma mansoni	The drug of choice is praziquantel, 20 mg. per kg. of body weight 2 times a day for 1 day.
Intestinal Flukes (trematodes) Heterophyes heterophyes Metagonimus yokogawai Fasciolopsis buski	The drug of choice for intestinal flukes is praziquantel, 25 mg. per kg. of body weight, 3 times a day for 1 day. An alternative for Fasciolopsis is niclosamide, four 500 mg. tablets chewed thoroughly, as a single oral dose.
Liver Flukes Clonorchis sinensis Opisthorchis viverrini	The drug of choice is praziquantel 25 mg. per kg. of body weight, taken 3 times a day for 1 day.
Fasciola hepatica	The drug of choice is Triclabendazole 10 mg. per kg. of body weight once. An aternative is Bithionol, 30 – 50 mg. per kg. of body weight every other day for 10–15 doses.

Avoiding and
Treating Ear Disorders

Any ear infection is potentially dangerous and should receive treatment. When problems do occur, they can affect any part of the ear — external, middle, or inner ear structures. The risk of injury or infection is greatly increased by two activities: sticking foreign objects in the ear, or swimming in contaminated water.

The Outer Ear

Wax Obstruction

Blockage of the external ear canal with wax is a frequent problem in childhood. Adults are also susceptible. Dust is sometimes a contributing factor, and you might need protective ear covering (such as ear plugs or a bandana) in some environments. When necessary, wax should be removed regularly by washing with warm water. This is best done while showering, or with the aid of a wash cloth or bulb syringe.

Don't attempt to remove ear wax with Q-tips or other objects. A Q-tip acts as a trash compactor, often tamping the wax into an immobile brick. This may block the ear canal so that normal hearing is impossible. Other objects can scratch the canal, leading to infection. You can even puncture the ear drum (tympanic membrane).

Wax contains enzymes and other necessary substances to protect the ears, much as tears protect the eyes. Remove it only if there is:

1. a sense of fullness or feeling that the ear is plugged up;

2. a sense of hearing through water (water trapped in the ear after swimming or showering);

3. diminished hearing due to wax buildup.

There might be ringing in the ear and on rare occasions an earache, but wax alone should not cause any other symptoms.

Removal of a wax plug is often best done professionally. If no medical help is available, wash the ear out with warm water. Fill an ear or bulb syringe, if available, with equal amounts of hydrogen peroxide and warm water. Some clinics use a dental water-pik, filled with warm water, on the softest possible setting. If necessary, first soften the ear wax with Debrox. Place 5–10 drops into the ear twice daily for up to 4 days. Obtain medical evaluation if symptoms of hearing loss or ringing in the ears continue after wax removal.

In Isolated Areas

If you're unsuccessful in removing wax, medical help is unavailable, and you have no Debrox, use 2–4 drops of Cortisporin Otic solution in the affected ear 3–4 times a day for 5–7 days. This should soften and loosen the wax so it can be washed out as described above. If there is no improvement, obtain medical help.

Infection of the Outer Ear

(Otitis Externa, "Swimmer's Ear")

Infection occurs frequently after swimming in contaminated water. Q-tips or other foreign objects can also cause infection in the ear canal. They scratch the skin, creating a place for bacteria to breed.

Symptoms

Itching and pain within the ear canal are the primary symptoms. There may be decreased hearing, or a sense of fullness or obstruction in the canal. A colored, pus-filled discharge may also be present.

To distinguish between a middle and outer ear infection, pull upward and outward or down and outward on the external parts of the ear on either side of the canal (the auricle and tragus, see diagram). Pain or discomfort that is increased by this action indicates an outer ear infection. Then tap over the mastoid bone just behind the ear (see diagram). **If pain is present, this is an emergency. Get medical help immediately.**

Treatment

Treat outer ear infections with Cortisporin Otic Solution (ear drops) – a mixture of polymyxin B sulfate, neomycin sulfate, and hydrocortisone which may be available under other brand names. Apply 4 drops in each affected ear 4 times a day for 1 week. Keep the head tilted for 3–5 minutes after applying drops to allow the medication to reach the entire area. An alternative treatment is to use ofloxacin 0.3% otic solution, 4 drops twice a day.

If medicine isn't available, you can make your own ear drops. Use either a 2% acetic acid solution or mix together a combination of 1/3 white vinegar and 2/3 rubbing alcohol. Use as above: 4 drops four times a day for 7 days. As a preventive measure for recurrent infections or after swimming in contaminated water, apply homemade ear drops after exposure to water.

The ear must be kept dry for at least 1 week — no swimming, and no water in the ear when bathing. For discomfort or pain take either 1 or 2 aspirin, Tylenol, or a nonsteroidal anti-inflammatory such as naproxen or ibuprofen.

Indications for medical attention

Get medical attention promptly if there is:

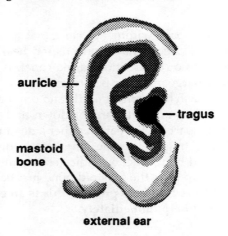

auricle

tragus

mastoid bone

external ear

**Never stick anything in your ear
smaller than your elbow.**

1. no improvement after 3-4 days, or infection occurs after a week of treatment. A laboratory culture may be needed to make sure the cause isn't a fungus;

2. swelling so severe that ear drops cannot be administered;

3. pain or tenderness of the mastoid bone (see drawing);

4. an allergic reaction to the medication;

5. concurrent diabetes.

Surfer's ear

Recurrent exposure of the ear canal to cold water may lead to progressive bone growth within the canal. Eventually this causes severe hearing loss. It also increases the risk of infection in the outer ear. The condition is preventable. Always wear good form-fitting ear plugs when swimming or surfing in cold water.

Treatment

Surgical removal of the excessive growth is the only treatment. There is no regression of the bone growth once it has taken place.

The Middle Ear

Middle ear infections may result in permanent hearing loss and other severe damage if not treated promptly. For this reason, **medical evaluation is required for any infection of the middle ear.**

Bacterial Infection (Acute Bacterial Otitis Media)

A bacterial middle ear infection is occasionally associated with bacterial infection of the nose and throat. These infections are more common in children than in adults. Bacteria can travel through the eustachian tubes to the middle ear. When this occurs, sputum or nasal discharge, usually tinged gray, green, or yellow, may accompany the infection.

Symptoms

Symptoms include earache or pain, possibly with a sense of fullness, decreased hearing, and elevated temperature. Occasionally there is headache, nausea, or vomiting. As mentioned, there may be a recent or concurrent upper respiratory infection. For treatment, obtain medical evaluation.

Treatment in Isolated Areas

In areas where medical help isn't available, start one of the following medications for **10** days. If you haven't been treated with antibiotics in the previous month, use amoxicillin. If you received antibiotics in the preceding month, do not take amoxcillin. Use Augmentin or one of the other listed antibiotics instead. If allergic to penicillin, do not use amoxicillin, Augmentin, or Ceftin. Take one of the other listed antibiotics.

1. amoxicillin 250-500 mg. 3 times a day; **or**

2. Augmentin (amoxicillin 875 mg./clavulanate 125 mg.) orally twice a day; **or** Augmentin (amoxicillin 500 mg./clavulanate 125 mg.) plus amoxicillin 375 mg. orally twice a day; **or**

3. Ceftin (cefuroxime) 250 mg. orally twice a day; **or**

4. Biaxin (clarithromycin) 500 mg. orally twice a day; **or**

5. Zithromax (azithromycin) 250 mg., 2 tablets initially then one daily for the next 4 days.

Seek medical attention as quickly as possible. If pain is still present after 48 hours and you haven't yet obtained medical care, switch to one of the other antibiotics and continue seeking medical help.

Along with antibiotics, oral decongestants or antihistamine decongestants may be used for 7-10 days. Any of the following can be used:

a decongestant:

1. Humabid L.A. one orally twice a day; **or**

2. Sudafed (pseudaephedrine) 60 mg. orally three times a day; **or**

one of the nonsedating antihistamines:

3. Allegra (fexofenadine) 60 mg. orally twice a day; **or**

4. Claritin (loratadine) 10 mg. orally once a day; **or**

5. Zyrtec (cetirizine) 10 mg. orally once a day; **or**

one of the following antihistamines which may cause drowsiness:

6. Actifed or Benadryl (diphenhydramine) one tablet orally 3 times a day; **or**

7. Drixoral or Dimetapp one tablet orally twice a day.

If any of the following conditions develop either before or after you start treatment, **medical help is urgently required:**

1. recurring or continued elevation of temperature, or lack of improvement after 2-3 days of antibiotic therapy;

2. development of a headache, stiff neck, lethargy, nausea, or vomiting;

3. development of pain over the mastoid bone (see illustration, p. 306);

4. increasing pain, possibly with a sudden decrease in pain which may be accompanied by a flood of drainage from ear canal (ruptured ear drum).

Fluid in the Middle Ear (Serous Otitis Media or Eustachian Tube Dysfunction)

A noninfectious condition of fluid accumulation sometimes occurs. This happens because of a blocked eustachian tube, often from an allergic condition (hay fever or runny nose) or an upper respiratory infection.

Symptoms

There's a sense of fullness in the ear with some hearing loss. There may be a snapping or crackling sensation when swallowing, yawning, or blowing the nose.

Treatment

Treat with an oral decongestant or antihistamine decongestant as described above for otitis media. If the condition is accompanied by a stuffy nose unrelieved by an oral decongestant, use a nasal spray such as Afrin or Neosynephrine (oxymetazoline hydrochloride) in addition to the decongestant. Wait a few minutes, squeeze your nose, hold your mouth shut, and gently blow. This should pop open the eustachian tube.

Nasal spray must be used sparingly: one whiff twice a day for no more than 3 consecutive days. It shouldn't be used for a chronic, ongoing problems since it can lead to a dependent condition. Obtain medical help if there is no improvement in 3–5 days.

The Inner Ear

Dizziness or a spinning sensation, ringing in the ears, and varying degrees of hearing loss usually indicate inner ear problems. In severe cases there may also be nausea or vomiting. **These symptoms should receive prompt medical evaluation.**

Some medications, especially some antibiotics, may cause hearing loss or ringing in the ears. These include aspirin, streptomycin, neomycin, kanamycin, vancomycin, and gentamicin. If hearing problems occur while taking any of these, stop immediately and consult a doctor.

For treatment of dizziness or a spinning sensation when medical care isn't readily available, try meclizine 25 mg. orally, 3 times a day until you can obtain medical help.

Ear Conditions Requiring Medical Treatment

1. hearing loss;
2. a ruptured or punctured ear drum;
3. bleeding from the ear;
4. earache or pain not due to outer ear infection;
5. any unexplained or persistent ringing in the ears, dizziness, spinning sensation, or difficulty with balance;
6. mastoid bone tenderness or pain;
7. an ear infection under treatment that fails to improve within 48 hours;
8. any ear infection accompanied by headache, fever, neck stiffness, nausea, vomiting, or lethargy.

Quick Reference: Ear Problems

Problem/Symptom	Possible Cause
earache	
with runny nose, sore throat, possibly fever	middle ear infection (otitis media) *or* blocked eustachian tubes
with pain when the earlobe is pulled, and/or discharge from the ear; possibly decreased hearing	external ear infection (otitis externa)
with tooth or jaw pain	possible cavity, dental abscess, sinusitis, or TMJ syndrome
decreased hearing, with sense of fullness or of water in ear after swimming or bathing	wax obstruction
hearing loss, with or without ringing	requires medical evaluation
ringing in the ears while taking aspirin or antibiotics	possible aspirin or drug toxicity

Treating Eye Disorders 12

Eye medications are extremely potent. Always observe the following precautions when using eye medications:

1. Eye drops are labeled "sterile ophthalmic solution." Be careful not to confuse them with "otic" ear medications.

2. Eye medications must be sterile. Avoid touching the container to the eye or any other surface.

3. To instill eye drops: blink after each drop, but don't close eyes tightly. Ointments: warm tube slightly in your hands, squeeze ointment onto the lower lid, then close the eyes but don't squeeze them tightly shut.

Use of Dangerous Medications

In many developing countries, antibiotic eye medications may be encountered which contain chloramphenicol (Chloromycetin or other brands). This drug can cause a severe disease of the blood.

Don't take any eye medications which contain chloramphenicol unless under the care of an eye specialist.

Conjunctivitis or "Pink Eye"

Conjunctivitis is an inflammation of the white part of the eye, the conjunctiva. Your eye gets pink or "bloodshot." It's the most common eye disease. Usually the cause is viral or, bacterial. Occasionally, chemical irritation, parasites, a fungal infection, or allergies cause conjunctivitis.. On rare occasions, most often in young men, burning on urination and joint pain may accompany it. (See "Reiter's syndrome," p. 316.)

Allergic Conjunctivitis

"Hay fever" and other allergic reactions can affect the eyes. Symptoms include itching, redness, and watering. This invariably affects both eyes, and is never accompanied by pus or other discharge. It's usually a recurrent problem and may be accompanied by sneezing and itching of the nose, ears, and roof of the mouth. Travelers with a history of hay fever should add appropriate medications to their first aid kit prior to travel.

Treatment

Oral antihistamines (see pp. 215) are usually sufficient for the treatment of symptoms. For more severe symptoms try Naphcon-A Ophthalmic Solution, 1 drop in each eye every 3–4 hours as needed. **Don't** use these medications if a rash is present around the eyes.

Bacterial Conjunctivitis

When the cause is bacterial, a discharge containing pus accompanies the inflammation — most noticeably in the morning. Waking up, your eyelids may be stuck together with encrusted, dried yellow matter. Most mild bacterial or viral types of conjunctivitis do not require treatment and resolve spontaneously. For treatment, obtain medical evaluation.

Treatment in Isolated Areas

1. Sulfacetamide sodium 10% (10% Sodium Sulamyd Ophthalmic or Bleph-10 Liquifilm Ophthalmic), 1 or 2 drops to the affected eye 4 times a day for 5–7 days. **Don't** use this medication if you're allergic to sulfa drugs.

Alternative treatments include:

2. Ocuflox (ofloxacin) ophthalmic solution or Ciloxan (ciprofloxacin) ophthalmic solution - 1-2 drops every 2-4 hours for 2 days then 1-2 drops 4 times per day for 5 days. Do not use if allergic to quinalone antibiotics.

3. gentamicin sulfate (Garamycin Ophthalmic) ointment or solution. Use the ointment or apply 1 or 2 drops of the solution to the affected eye 3 times a day for 5–7 days.

Before using any of these medications, remove encrusted matter from the eyelids. To do this effectively, first apply cool moist compresses to the eyes for several minutes. After starting treatment, make your eyes feel better with warm compresses 3 times a day.

Conjunctival infections can be very contagious. Wash your hands thoroughly before and after touching the eyes. Be careful not to pass infection from one eye to the other. **Don't** share towels, washcloths, or pillows with anyone else.

Stop treatment and get medical help immediately if there is:

1. worsening of the condition or development of vision problems after starting treatment;

2. no improvement in 2–3 days;

3. development of an allergy or sensitivity reaction to the medication. This is usually indicated by itching or a constant burning sensation;

4. sharp stabbing eye pain.

Other Eye Infections

Possible Exposure to Gonorrhea or Chlamydia

When an eye infection occurs following a casual sexual encounter or after known exposure to gonorrhea or chlamydia through sexual contact, **get medical help immediately.** Medical evaluation is always required if an eye infection is accompanied by an abnormal discharge from the penis or vagina. Gonorrheal infections usually affect only one eye, not both.

Orbital Cellulitis

Redness and swelling of the eyelid, accompanied by pain and fever, is a medical emergency. The cause is bacterial and potential complications include abscess into the brain. **Medical attention must be obtained immediately.**

In isolated areas. If medical care is not immediately available, start one of the antibiotics listed below **while seeking medical attention as quickly as possible. Orbital cellulitis requires potent intravenous antibiotics.**

1. dicloxacillin 500 mg. orally, 4 times a day for 10 days; **or**

2. Biaxin (clarithromycin) 500 mg. orally, 4 times a day for 10 days; **or**

3. Augmentin (amoxicillin 500 mg./clavulanate 125 mg.) orally, 3 times a day for 10 days; **or**

4. Cipro (ciprofloxacin) 500 mg. orally 2 times a day for 10 days (for severe cases only); **or**

5. erythromycin 500 mg. orally, 4 times a day for 10 days; **or**

6. Zithromax (azithromycin) 250 mg. orally, 2 tablets at once then one tablet daily for 4 days.

Sties

A sty is an inflammation of one of the oil glands

located on the eyelid. This results in a tender red lump or swelling on the lid margin which eventually becomes capped by pus. Pain or sensitivity to touch is proportionate to the swelling.

Treatment

Apply warm compresses to the area for 10 minutes, 3–5 times a day. Use antibiotic ointment or eye drops for 2–5 days as suggested for conjunctivitis. The sty should come to a head, open, and drain the pus with relief of symptoms. Obtain medical help if:

1. sties are a recurring problem;

2. infection spreads;

3. the sty does not resolve within 3–5 days.

Reiter's Syndrome

Conjunctivitis accompanied by painful joints (arthritis) and burning on urination (nonspecific urethritis) is usually Reiter's syndrome. It's most common in young men. The joints most frequently affected are the ankle and the knee, usually on one side only. There is often a discharge from the penis and there may also be a rash or fever. This syndrome is a reaction following venereal exposure to the bacteria chlamydia, or diarrhea caused by either shigella or yersina bacteria.

Treatment

Seek medical attention for treatment. If medical care isn't readily available, the anti-inflammatory drug Indocin helps relieve joint pain. Take 25–50 mg. orally 3 times a day. Obtain medical evaluation after starting treatment.

Physical Injury to the Eye

Foreign Bodies

Wash or flush out with water a small foreign object,

such as an eyelash or grain of sand, for 5–10 minutes as needed. An alternative is to gently flick it out with the twisted fibers on the end of a Q-tip or cotton swab. This requires the help of a mirror or another person. If a foreign object is suspected, **never rub the eyes**. This may cause further injury. If a foreign object has punctured or protrudes from the eye, **don't** attempt to remove it. Protect it from being touched or bumped if possible and get medical help immediately.

After removing any small foreign object which hasn't punctured the eye, obtain medical help if:

1. sensation of scratchiness, abrasion, or presence of a foreign body persists;

2. there is swelling, pain, or discoloration of the eye;

3. there is bleeding from the eye.

Chemical Contact

Eye injury including blindness can occur rapidly from chemical contact. Acids or bleach are common causes of eye injury; alkaline chemicals are particularly dangerous. Chemicals must be removed **immediately and thoroughly** to stop eye damage.

Immediate Treatment

Flush the eye immediately with large amounts of cool water for 20–30 minutes, or longer if burning continues. Use a gentle but sufficient stream from a hose or faucet, or water from any other available source — bucket, pan, drinking fountain, stream, or lake. Keep the eyelid open and wash under it thoroughly. Having a friend or companion perform the eye wash will often improve the ability to wash material out of the eye since they will be able to monitor the water flow and keep the eye open. **Don't** use any eye medications. Get medical attention as quickly as possible, preferably from a hospital emergency room or an eye specialist (ophthalmologist).

Quick Reference: Eye Problems

Problem/Symptom	Possible Cause
eye red, with discharge; eyelids encrusted, stuck together in a.m.; usually one eye, may spread to the other	conjunctivitis ("pink eye")
both eyes red, watery, itching	allergic conjunctivitis
scratchy or abrasive sensation and watering in one eye	foreign body
red, swollen lesion on either eyelid, often with small amount of pus	sty
tenderness around cheekbones or the eyes, or pressure behind the eyes; no no redness of the white part of the eyes (conjunctiva); with headache, nasal discharge, occasionally fever	sinusitis
light hurting the eyes, with severe, throbbing headache	migraine
light hurting the eyes, with severe headache, fever, neck stiffness	meningitis*
eye(s) red with a discharge, possibly stuck together in a.m.; joint pain, burning on urination with discharge from penis (usually affects young men); symptoms following sexual intercourse or episode of diarrhea	Reiter's syndrome
blurred vision in one eye becoming progressively worse ("A curtain came down over my eye")	retinal detachment*

*requires immediate medical evaluation

Quick Reference:
Eye Conditions Requiring
Immediate Medical Attention

1. Exposure to chemicals of any kind with burning or irritation which persists after eye washing.

2. Visual disturbances: any blind spot that develops in the field of vision; blurred vision, especially in one eye, becoming progressively worse; double vision; dimness or decreased vision. Spots (floaters) may require medical evaluation if they persist or recur.

3. Eye pain, either sudden or slowly developing, if not due to sinus problems.

4. Light hurting the eyes (photophobia) if not related to known migraine headaches, or if accompanied by stiff neck and severe headache.

5. Redness or discoloration just around the iris (colored circle) of either eye; or an irregular (not round) pupil (small black circle).

6. Uncontrolled infection, inflammation, itching, or persistent burning.

7. Presence of a rash around the eye (may indicate a herpes infection).

8. Infection following known or possible exposure to venereal disease (gonorrhea or chlamydia) through sexual contact.

9. Conjunctivitis with concurrent joint pain and burning with urination (Reiter's syndrome).

10. Development of allergy or sensitivity to any eye medication.

Treating Nasal Problems

Hay Fever (Allergic Rhinitis)

Hay fever is an allergic response to airborne irritants in the environment. These include pollen, dust, sudden temperature changes, and animal dander (bits of skin, hair, or feathers). Unfortunately, travelers usually don't have control over these environmental factors. Preventive measures that may work at home aren't always effective when traveling in new environments.

Symptoms

Symptoms of hay fever include sneezing and often itching of the ears, eyes, nose, and throat. The eyes may be red, watery, and itchy. There may be a dry (nonproductive) cough. There is usually a clear watery nasal discharge or a stuffy nose. Attempts to relieve nasal itching and congestion often result in the "allergic salute" — rubbing the nose upward and outward with the edge of the forefinger.

Treatment

Consult a doctor if the condition becomes chronic, interferes with daily activities, or is accompanied by wheezing, shortness of breath, or cough. Otherwise there are generally no serious complications.

You can treat most conditions with an antihistamine. Frequently used are one of the nonsedating antihistamines such as:

1. Allegra (fexofenadine) 60 mg. orally twice a day; **or**

2. Claritin (lovatadine) 10 mg. orally once a day; **or**

3. Zyrtec (cetirizine) 10 mg. orally once a day; **or**

4. Astelin (azelastine) nasal spray 2 whiffs in each nostril twice a day (good for itchy eyes due to allergy).

Alternatively, you may try one of the following antihistamines which often cause drowsiness as a side effect:

1. Actifed (pseudoephedrine + triprolidine) or Benadryl (diphenhydramine) one tablet orally 3 times a day; **or**

2. Drixoral (pseudoephedrine + dexbrompheniramine) or Dimetapp (brompheniramine + phenylpronanolamine) one tablet orally twice a day.

Treatment of Wheezing in Isolated Areas

In isolated areas, treat wheezing with an oral inhaler that will open the air passages. These begin working within 5 minutes and last 3-8 hours. Try **one** of the following:

1. Alupent (metaproterenol sulfate); **or**

2. Proventil or Salbutanol (albuterol).

If these aren't available, use an epinephrine inhaler 3–4 times a day until you can find medical attention. See "How to Use an Oral Inhaler," p. 446.

Sinus Problems

Sinus problems may arise from either bacterial or nonbacterial causes. Drainage passages become blocked, and pressure differences can then result in varying degrees of pain.

Symptoms

There may be a frontal headache, over or behind one or both eyes. Pain is usually greatest in the morning and

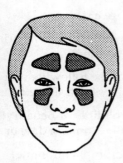

Sinus locations

lessens during the day. It's increased by moving the head rapidly up and down. There may be tenderness when tapping or pressing just above and over the eyebrows or over the cheekbones (see diagram). Sometimes the pain is in one or both cheeks. It may feel like a toothache in the upper jaw, but there's no facial swelling and no tenderness of any tooth if pressure is applied. Fever and chills, nasal discharge

and, frequently, a foul-tasting postnasal drip, cough, and headache may all be associated with sinusitis.

Nonbacterial Sinusitis

Nonbacterial sinusitis may have an allergic or viral cause. It can accompany or follow an attack of hay fever or a common head cold. *Antibiotics are of no value.* Sinusitis from these causes is characterized primarily by a nasal discharge that is frequently clear or watery.

If the cause is viral it may be associated with muscle aches, a low fever (under 101°F (38.3°C).), and a dry cough. Sneezing often accompanies it if the cause is allergic. There may also be burning, itching, and watering of the eyes and/or mouth.

Treatment

Nonbacterial sinusitis is treated with decongestants **or** antihistamines. Use **one** of the following:

A decongestant:

1. Humabid (guaifenesin) L.A., 1 orally twice a day; **or**

2. Sudafed (pseudoephedrine), 60 mg. orally 3 times a day; **or**

   A nonsedating antihistamine:

3. Allegra (fexofenadine) 60 mg. orally twice a day; **or**

4. Claritin (lovatadine) 10 mg. orally once a day; **or**

5. Zyrtec (cetirizine) 10 mg. orally once a day; **or**

   An antihistamine which may cause drowsiness:

6. Actifed (pseudoephedrine + triprolidine) or Benadryl, (diphenhydramine) one tablet orally 3 times a day; **or**

7. Drixoral (pseudoephedrine + dexbrompheniramine) or Dimetapp (brompheniramine + phenylpronanolamine, one tablet orally twice a day.

   In addition, steam inhalation (from a bowl of hot water or shower) will help loosen and clear blocked passages. Get plenty of rest and drink lots of fluids.

Bacterial Sinusitis

Sinusitis of bacterial origin may be severe. It's characterized by a thick nasal discharge which is usually colored green or yellow, has a foul taste, and which lasts for more than 7 days. It's **never** clear. There may be a cough, usually producing green or yellow sputum. Weakness, fever, nausea, vomiting, and severe sinus pain or "headaches" over the face, or with facial tenderness (see diagram p. 322), are all possible. Often there is a sense of fullness in the sinus areas. These symptoms vary individually with the degree of infection.

Treatment

In *addition* to using decongestants (#1 & 2 above), you need antibiotics to curb the infection. Use *one* of the following antibiotics, listed in order of preference, *for at least 10 days*:

1. amoxicillin 500 mg. orally, three times a day (**don't** take if allergic to penicillin medications); **or**

2. Augmentin (amoxicillin + clavulanate) 875 mg. or 500 mg. orally 3 times a day (**don't** take if allergic to penicillin medications); **or**

3. Ceftin (cefuroxime) 250 mg. orally twice a day (**don't** take if allergic to cephalosporin or penicillin medications); **or**

4. Biaxin (clarithromycin) 500 mg. orally twice a day (**don't** take if allergic to erythromycin medications); **or**

5. Bactrim DS (or Septra DS) 1 tablet orally, twice a day (**don't** take if allergic to sulfa medications); **or**

6. Doxycycline 100 mg. orally twice a day.

Rest and drink plenty of liquids. For fever or pain, take aspirin, Tylenol or a non-steroidal anti-inflam–matory such as ibuprofen or naproxen as needed.

Indications for medical treatment

Seek medical attention for any sinus condition if:

1. there's no improvement within 3–4 days of treatment.

2. there's redness or swelling around the eye.

If a sinus problem fails to improve with treatment and is accompanied by jaw pain, this may indicate a possible tooth disorder — get medical or dental help for evaluation and treatment.

Nosebleed

A nosebleed is usually due to the rupture of a small blood vessel in the sensitive inner lining of the nose. These vessels are fragile, exposed, and easily damaged. A nosebleed can occur from colds or other infections,

hay fever, exposure to dry air, irritation from nose picking, vigorous blowing, or trauma. Medical evaluation is
usually necessary only when:

1. the bleeding is very great or cannot be stopped within
   20 minutes;

2. the nose is or may be broken;

3. there's an increased tendency to bruise or bleed elsewhere on the body;

4. the nosebleeds recur frequently;

5. trauma has occurred to the head (away from the
   nose).

Treatment

Sit up in a chair, lean forward, and breathe through
the mouth. Apply pressure to the bleeding site by
pressing the nostril closed with the thumb, or by pinch-
ing both nostrils shut. If necessary, gently pack a small
amount of tissue (not cotton balls) one-half inch inside
the affected nostril, enough to make it bulge slightly.
Then apply pressure to the outside of the nose. Maintain
pressure for 5–10 minutes. Avoid blowing the nose for
several hours to keep from dislodging the clot. If available, in an emergency you can use a mini tampon in place
of the tissue.

Prevention

When nosebleeds are due to excessively dry air, you
can usually prevent them with some lubricating ointment. Place a small pea-sized amount on a fingertip or
Q-tip and rub it up inside each nostril several times a
day and at bedtime, as needed. Use any commercial
ointment, such as Vaseline, Vick's VapoRub, or A and D
Ointment. If not available, a topical antibiotic ointment
can be used.

Quick Reference:
Causes of a Runny Nose

Problem or Symptom	Possible Cause
Thick, greenish yellow nasal discharge with frontal headaches or pain behind the eyes or face which is increased by moving the head up and down rapidly	bacterial sinusitis
Clear watery or white nasal discharge with frontal headache	nonbacterial sinusitis
Clear watery or white nasal discharge with itchy eyes, nose, and mouth; sneezing	allergy (allergic rhinitis)
Clear watery or white nasal discharge with mild fever	cold
Clear watery or white nasal discharge with muscle aches, fever, chills.	flu

Dental Problems: Gum and Tooth Disease 14

Satisfactory dental care is sometimes more difficult to find than medical care in developing nations. Even in countries with superb dental schools, care may be scarce outside the urban centers. In rural areas the most sophisticated dental tool is often a pair of pliers; "anesthetic" may be the brand name of a locally distilled beverage. It's a good idea when traveling to have any required dental work performed in a large major city, after obtaining a reliable referral.

Use good dental hygiene to prevent dental problems when traveling. The risk of HIV infection from dental procedures, though small, is greater in developing countries than in western industrialized nations.

Cavities

The bacteria in plaque convert sugar to acid. As this eats through tooth enamel, cavities form. They commonly occur between the teeth, along the gumline, on molar surfaces, and behind the last molars. These are the areas that require special attention when cleaning.

Discolorations of the tooth that are soft when probed indicate cavities. If you're in an isolated rural area for an extended time, a cavity can sometimes be found early with the help of a small dental mirror, a dental pick, and a friend.

Once located, clean and fill a cavity to prevent further damage. A dentist is needed because of the technical skills, specialized tools, and anesthetic that you may require. If a dentist isn't immediately available, you'll need to provide interim care for a simple toothache and possibly emergency care for advanced disease. For new cavities, or old ones exposed when fillings are lost, use the following temporary measures.

Temporary Cavity Care

If there is no pain, scrape out all debris from the cavity. Rinse thoroughly: swish and spit, using a mixture of equal parts hydrogen peroxide and water. When pain is present, relieve it first by applying a few drops of clove oil to the affected area with a cotton swab or small cloth. Then rinse the area as previously described. "Oil of cloves" is a numbing sedative that also promotes some dental healing. Make it part of your first aid kit for travel in rural areas.

For pain, try one of the nonsteroidal anti-inflammatories such as ibuprofen or naproxen every 4-6 hours. If necessary, take Vicodin 1 tablet 3–4 times a day, or Tylenol with 30 mg. of codeine every 6 hours. One or two aspirin may also help, but **never** put aspirin directly on the painful tooth or gum. This is one home remedy that causes damaging and painful tissue burns.

After cleaning, find a dentist — within 24 hours when toothache pain is continuous or severe. If this is impossible, temporarily fill the cleaned cavity. This should be done only when:

1. pain is absent, slight, or intermittent; **and**

2. heat relieves, not intensifies pain.

Use one of the filling materials listed below. The first 2 are commercial preparations. Both are inexpensive and available without prescription from dental supply stores in the U.S. If not obtained before leaving, equivalent preparations may be available in major cities.

1. "Cavit" is a handy temporary filling that lasts 1–2 weeks — time enough to find a dentist. It's the easiest of the 3 preparations to use, and comes in a small tube.

Instructions. Before applying, add a drop of clove oil. The cavity shouldn't be dried. Contents of the tube are squeezed onto the cavity area, then patted down with a piece of moistened cotton. It can also be pressed into the cavity with a finger. In contact with saliva, Cavit begins to harden in an hour or two and sets completely in 1 day. Avoid any pressure on the new filling for 30 minutes, and avoid eating or chewing for a couple of hours.

2. "I.R.M." (Intermediate Restorative Material) is a more durable filling. It's considerably less convenient than Cavit. Add enough powdered zinc oxide to 2 drops of the liquid clove oil (eugenol) base to form a putty. After drying a few minutes, you'll have a very small window of time to press the material into the thoroughly cleaned cavity to harden. The cavity must be completely dry or bonding will not occur. Don't swallow this preparation.

3. Warm soft candle wax can also be used as a temporary filling material. It will not survive exposure to temperature extremes. Apply a few drops of clove oil before inserting the wax. Mix the warmed wax with wisps of cotton fiber from a cotton ball before using to create a slightly stronger material.

Lost Fillings

A woman we know who was traveling through South America for 4 months lost a filling midway through her travels. She spent the next two months in moderate discomfort since she did not feel comfortable with the hygienic standards of local dental care. A first aid kit with Cavit or I.R.M. would have spared her considerable pain. The above materials can be used for temporary cavity care if fillings become loosened or dislodged. Clean and keep the filling. A dentist will be able to evaluate its potential reuse.

Toothaches and Other Tooth Pains

Simple Toothache (Partial Simple Pulpitis)

Without regular dental exams, a toothache is often the first sign of a cavity. When a cavity reaches or is near the inner tooth (the pulp), injury may occur from either bacterial infection or temperature extremes. At first the pain is intermittent and slight. It's intensified by cold and relieved by heat. Dental care needs to be obtained at this stage so that the tooth and pulp can be saved without extensive procedures. Take one of the nonsteroidal anti-inflammatories such as ibuprofen or naproxen every 6 hours for pain. If necessary for extreme discomfort, take 1 or 2 Tylenol or aspirin with codeine orally 3–4 times a day, or Vicodin, one tablet orally 3–4 times a day.

Advanced Tooth Disease

Untreated, simple toothache pain becomes increasingly severe until it's intense and continuous. **It should never be permitted to reach this stage.** You'll require dental care for pain control and extraction or other procedures. Severe pain which later seems to ease off is of concern as this may indicate the death of the nerve, requiring root canal work.

Tooth abscess (periapical abscess)

Sometimes pressure builds within a tooth as a result of injury or infection. Pain is either intermittent, sharp, and throbbing, or continuous and intense, even excruciating. In contrast to simple toothache pain, it's intensified by heat and relieved by cold. Tapping on or near the tooth increases the pain.

The pressure often causes infection and inflammation in the tissues underlying the tooth. Indications are facial swelling, fever, local pus formation, and often a persistent bad taste in the mouth. **When these symptoms occur, antibiotics must be started immediately.** If uncontrolled, the infection may spread throughout the blood or to bones of the face and jaw.

Treatment in Isolated Areas

If dental or medical care isn't immediately available, start **one** of the following antibiotics, listed in order of preference. Continue taking the medication for the full 10 days, or until treatment can be found.

1. amoxicillin 500 mg. orally 3 times a day for 10 days **or** penicillin VK 500 mg. orally 4 times a day for 10 days (do not use either of these medications if allergic to penicillin); **or**

2. erythromycin 250 mg. orally 4 times a day for 10 days (only if allergic to penicillin); **or**

3. Keflex 500 mg. orally 4 times a day for 10 days (do not use if allergic to penicillin or cephalosporins); **or**

4. Biaxin 500 mg. orally twice a day for 10 days; **or**

5. Zithromax 250 mg. orally , 2 tablets initially then 1 tablet daily for 4 more days.

To relieve pain, take 1–2 aspirin or acetaminophen (Tylenol), with codeine if needed, 3–4 times a day or Vicodin, 1 tablet 3–4 times per day. This may be necessary for a day or two until the swelling subsides. By this time you should have obtained medical or dental care, but it's urgently required if the pain and infection fail to improve, become worse, or recur after starting antibiotics. Once the infection has been successfully treated, dental care is still required to remedy the underlying cause.

Tooth Injury or Trauma

Chipped or Broken Teeth

The teeth of adults are more likely to shatter from a blow than are children's teeth. A tooth that is knocked out, chipped, or broken can often be saved if it can be professionally splinted and stabilized within an hour. When help is more than an hour or so away, success rates are unfortunately too low to warrant this effort.

It's sometimes possible to press the tooth back into place, using clove oil to reduce pain if necessary. First lick the tooth clean (saliva is preferable but water can be used when the tooth is very dirty). If it will not stay in place, keep it in your mouth while en route to a dentist or emergency room. The tooth can also be kept in cold milk, or as a last resort wrapped in a damp cloth. Use a cold compress on the face to reduce swelling of the injured area. Take 1 or 2 Tylenol, with codeine if necessary, every 4–6 hours or Vicodin, 1 tablet 3–4 times per day as needed for pain.

Control of Bleeding

Following injury to the teeth and gums, excessive bleeding can be controlled by applying direct pressure with a gauze bandage or clean cloth. If bleeding doesn't stop, rinse the mouth with warm salt water and place a used tea bag (cooled after steeping in hot water for 5–10 minutes) over the area. Hold with firm pressure for 20–30 minutes. The tannic acid in the tea bag helps to stop the bleeding.

Gum Disease

Inflammation of the Gums (Gingivitis)

Inflammation or infection of the gums can sometimes be a sign of vitamin deficiency, allergic reaction, or the onset of diabetes or other disease. Usually, however, the cause is plaque. This gradually builds up beneath the gum margin. Plaque, calculus, and bacterial products all irritate the gums, causing inflammation.

The earliest and sometimes only sign of gingivitis is bleeding. In contrast to healthy gums, inflamed gums bleed readily when touched, brushed, or flossed. After a prolonged time they may become swollen, and bluish or red in color. If the condition isn't corrected, the gums become progressively detached from the teeth. The gums recede, and the underlying bone ultimately erodes away.

Treatment

A dentist must remove calcified plaque. Good diet and daily oral hygiene is required to prevent recurrence. Under normal circumstances, antibiotics and mouthwashes are of no value.

Trench mouth

Also called Vincent's infection, trench mouth is a noncontagious infection of the gums. Small ulcers form along the gum margin or between the teeth, covered with a grayish membrane. These bleed readily. Unlike gingivitis, the lesions are painful. Swallowing and talking may be difficult. Usually there's swelling of lymph nodes in the neck, but no fever.

Treatment

Have your teeth cleaned professionally to prevent infection from recurring. Plaque and calculus are the root of the problem.

Control symptoms by rinsing the mouth several times daily for a few days with a mixture of equal parts hydrogen peroxide solution (3%) and warm salt water (1 teaspoon in 1 pint of water). This preparation is available over the counter in the U.S. as "Amosan" (add one package to a glass of water, rinse or gargle). Similar preparations are available in most countries.

Conscientious oral hygiene is essential. Rest and a

good diet with vitamin supplements of B complex (1 daily) and C (500-1000 mg. daily) are also helpful.

Quick Reference:
Dental Problems

Problem/symptom	Possible cause
tooth pain	
intermittent; intensified by cold, relieved by heat	early cavity
continuous; intensified by heat, relieved by cold; possibly with fever or facial swelling	abscess
pain only when biting down on tooth	possible cracked tooth, filling, or early abscess
bleeding from the gums, without pain or fever	gingivitis
gums red, painful; bleed easily	trench mouth
sores around lips; blistering, painful	probable cold sore (herpes simplex)

Any sore or ulcer in the mouth which does not heal within 10 days requires medical evaluation. If the sore follows oral sex with a new or casual partner, medical evaluation including a test for syphilis is required.

Respiratory Problems

15

The lungs are a branching system of air passages that become progressively smaller. This system, the "respiratory tree," ends in tiny air sacs (alveoli) where inhaled air interacts with the blood.

The throat (pharynx), vocal cords (larynx), and the air passages that connect the nose, sinuses, and middle ears make up the upper respiratory system. The trachea, bronchi, and alveoli — the lungs — make up the lower respiratory system.

Upper Respiratory Disease

Viral Infections

Viruses are a frequent cause of upper respiratory infections. In order to treat these infections properly, it's important to understand the difference between viral and bacterial infections. Antibiotics work well against bacterial infections because they inhibit the ability of the bacteria to reproduce. Viruses, on the other hand, have entirely different methods for reproduction than bacteria. Therefore antibiotics have *no* effect on viruses, and will *not* help cure viral infections.

The Common Cold

Cold symptoms vary, depending partly on which of over 200 different viruses is the cause. Symptoms may include sneezing, a runny or stuffy nose, watery eyes, a mild, dry sore throat, headache, and tiredness. There may be muscle aches, nausea, or plugged-up ears. Nasal discharge is watery and either whitish or clear. There may be a mild cough with a small amount of whitish, clear, or colored sputum. A low grade fever (less than 101°F (38.3°C)) is also common.

These symptoms usually disappear in 3–14 days. Since the cause is viral, antibiotics don't help and should not be used. Symptoms can sometimes be confused with influenza, nonbacterial sinusitis, or hay fever.

Treatment

The traditional prescription is to rest and drink plenty of fluids — still good advice. Nutrition is important, and can include your favorite recipe for chicken soup. Echinacea has been reported by some to shorten the course of the illness, but this has not been validated scientifically.

Treat mild fever and aches with 1 or 2 tablets of aspirin (for adults) or Tylenol up to 4 times day, or a non-steroidal anti-inflammatory such as ibuprofen or naproxen. Do warm salt water gargles (1 teaspoon salt in 1 pint of water) several times a day for a sore throat. Avoid smoking to prevent complications.

Oral decongestants may be useful. Try Sudafed (pseudoephedrine HCl.) 60 mg. up to 3 times a day or Humabid LA twice a day to lessen secretions and to decrease any sensation of "popping" or fullness in the ears. If nasal discharge is clear and accompanied by itchy, burning, watery eyes, the cause may be allergic rather than viral (see "Hay fever," pp. 320–321).

Decongestant nasal sprays, such as Afrin or Neosynephrine, should be used only if other decongestants aren't available. Strictly follow directions on the package — usually 1 – 2 puffs in each nostril no more than twice a day. **Don't use nasal sprays for more than 3 days at a time.** Otherwise, these products may cause a "rebound" effect which makes symptoms even worse once they are discontinued.

Viral Upper Respiratory Syndrome ("Flu-like illnesses")

Cold symptoms accompanied by an elevated temperature (101°–103°F (38.3°–39.4°C)), chills, and general body or muscle aches, may indicate a flu-like virus. Fatigue can be severe. Related symptoms may include decreased appetite, nausea, vomiting, diarrhea, sore throat, and headache.

Fever can last 3–5 days, while other symptoms, including fatigue, often last 3–14 days. Recovery should be complete in 7–21 days. If symptoms persist beyond this time, or recur, obtain medical evaluation.

Treatment

The cause is usually viral and antibiotics are of no benefit. Treatment is the same as for the common cold, with bed rest recommended until the fever subsides. Drink plenty of fluids, purified if necessary, to prevent dehydration. Resume activities slowly.

Symptoms Requiring Medical Attention

Most often a cold, flu, or other viral upper respiratory infection runs its course uneventfully. **The following conditions require immediate medical attention:**

1. wheezing;

2. shortness of breath with chest pain or a dry, painful cough, with or without a fever;

3. severe pounding headache, high fever, and neck pain or stiffness increased by bending the head forward or bringing the knees to the chest;

4. coughing up blood;

5. an earache that doesn't clear with decongestants.

6. recurrent high or cyclical fevers (should prompt immediate medical evaluation for diseases such as malaria).

Other Upper Respiratory Infections

Sore Throat

The majority of sore throats are viral in origin, especially when accompanied by other head cold symptoms.
These include a dry cough, stuffy nose, and whitish-clear
sputum or nasal discharge. Sore throats with a viral cause
don't respond to antibiotics, and these shouldn't be used.

To relieve throat discomfort, gargle with warm salt
water (1 teaspoon salt in a pint of purified or boiled water) 3–4 times a day. A soft or liquid diet and throat loz-
enges such as Chloraseptic and zinc may also be helpful.
One to two aspirin 3–4 times per day will also help decrease discomfort.

"Strep" Throat

A "strep" throat is an infection due to a form of
streptococcus bacteria. You should treat it with antibiotics to prevent rheumatic fever, rheumatic heart disease,
and streptococcal kidney disease, although these complications are rare.

**A throat culture is the only way to accurately identi-
fy a strep throat.** There are no reliable physical signs or
symptoms. So-called "classic" features of strep throat occur in only a small percentage of cases. These features are:

1. fever;

2. tonsils that are swollen, red, and covered with white
   spots;

3. a beefy red sore throat;

4. tender enlarged lymph nodes in the front of the neck.

Even when all of the above are present, odds are only
about 60% that the cause is streptococcus, although these

odds are a little higher for persons under the age of 25.

Throat cultures can usually be done at a doctor's office, clinic, or medical laboratory. Results are frequently ready in 24 hours, or in a few minutes with the rapid strep tests. In developing countries it's often cheaper and quicker to go directly to a medical laboratory for the throat culture. Then take the lab report to a doctor. *This is necessary only if the report shows the presence of Group A beta-hemolytic streptococcus.* Other forms of streptococcus are often present normally and don't need treatment. If in doubt, ask a doctor.

Treatment

Obtain treatment when the lab report is positive for "Group A beta-hemolytic streptococcus." Treat with either:

1. penicillin VK 250-500 mg. orally 4 times a day for 10 days; **or**

2. erythromycin 250 mg. orally three times a day for 10 days; **or**

3. Ceftin (cefuroxime) 250 mg. orally twice a day for 4 days; **or**

4. Biaxin (clarithromycin) 200 mg. orally twice a day for 10 days; **or**

5. Zithromax (azithromycin) 250 mg. - 2 tablets orally together, then one tablet a day for the next 4 days.

Symptoms disappear after a few days, but it's important to complete the entire course of antibiotics. Medical follow-up is necessary if an allergy to the medication develops or if there is no improvement in 2–3 days.

Other causes of a sore throat

If the lab report does not show strep, and the sore throat is associated with fatigue, low grade fevers, increased sleepiness, and decreased appetite, mononucleosis is a possible cause (see pp. 278–279).

Persistent sore throat following sexual contact

If a sore throat persists following oral sex (with someone other than an established, exclusive partner), gonorrhea, chlamydia, or syphilis are possible causes. Obtain medical attention for evaluation. A blood test for syphilis and a throat culture for gonorrhea and chlamydia should be done. If any are positive, further evaluation and/or treatment are required.

Chronic sore throat

If tests for strep throat and mononucleosis are both negative and a sore throat persists for more than 3 weeks, the cause may be allergic or due to reflux disease of the esophagus (see p. 249).

If the sore throat continues, consider a trial of an antihistamine (see p. 249) and/or an antacid medication (see p. 215). If there is still no improvement, obtain medical evaluation.

Sinusitis. See pp. 321 – 324.

Allergic rhinitis. See pp. 320 – 321.

Lower Respiratory Disease

Acute Bronchitis

Bronchitis (inflammation of the bronchi) is usually caused by a viral infections. It's often accompanied by cold symptoms. It's characterized by a cough, usually dry at first but with increasing sputum production.

There may be pain centered in the upper chest with coughing, or coughing may be accompanied by a sensation of tightness in the chest. Temperature is often normal or mildly elevated, 101°F (38.3°C) or less.

Viral bronchitis

A cough which produces clear, whitish or colored

sputum without fever indicates the cause is probably viral. Antibiotics are of no benefit. Symptoms should diminish within 5–7 days, although coughing may persist a week or two. Follow the general guidelines below.

Treatment guidelines for bronchitis

The secretions that lungs produce must be kept thin and loose so they can be coughed up. Otherwise, a secondary bacterial infection can develop. Adequate fluid intake is very important. Drink at least 2–3 liters (quarts) per day. You may also need other measures, such as vaporizers and cough expectorants. See "Care of a cough" at the end of this chapter for a summary of recommendations.

In addition to drinking plenty of fluids, adequate rest is important. Take 1 or 2 aspirin (for adults only) or Tylenol as needed up to 4 times a day for fever or pain. Smokers who continue to smoke will prolong their illness and risk potential complications.

Persistent Bronchitis (cough over 2 weeks with temperature less than 101 degrees Fahrenheit)

If the cough consists of episodic bouts of non-stop coughing that persists over 2 weeks, pertussis (whooping cough) should be considered. Medical evaluation should be sought to obtain appropriate cultures.

Other causes of persistent coughing can include asthma, tuberculosis, reflux of the esophagus, post-nasal drip and certain parasitic diseases.

Treatment of suspected pertussis in isolated areas

1. erythromycin 500 mg. orally, four times a day for 7 days; **or**

2. Septra DS (Bactrim DS) one tablet orally, twice a day for 14 days (do **not** take if allergic to sulfa medications); **or**

3. Biaxin (clarithromycin) 500 mg. orally, twice a day for 7 days.

Symptoms Requiring Immediate Medical Attention

Obtain medical care immediately if a cough is accompanied by any of the following:

1. shaking chills and fever above 103°F (39.6°C);

2. fever lasting more than 3 days;

3. chest pain, not related directly to coughing.

4. wheezing, or difficulty inhaling or exhaling (these may indicate airway obstruction — a potential emergency. See "Asthma," p. 344).

5. a persistent cough with fever (temperature greater than 101°F. or 38.3°C) and pulse greater than 100 beats per minute may indicate pneumonia- see following.

Pneumonia

Pneumonia is an inflammation of the lungs. Infectious causes are usually viral or bacterial, but may sometimes be fungal. Travelers should be aware of other potential causes as well, such as inhaled smoke or chemicals, tuberculosis, and roundworm or other parasitic infections.

Symptoms

Pneumonia can occur without chest pain. More often, though, chest pain is present and may be described as "stabbing." Coughing frequently increases this pain, though it may or may not initially produce phlegm or sputum. Breathing is usually rapid and may be accompanied by shortness of breath. There is an elevated temperature that either becomes increasingly worse, or lasts more than 72 hours. **These symptoms require immediate medical attention.**

Other symptoms which may be present include headache and shaking chills. Phlegm is usually produced soon after the onset of coughing and the resultant sputum may be yellow, green, gray, or brown.

Sputum that is rust-colored, thick, and sticky is often characteristic of pneumococcal pneumonia. The onset of symptoms is extremely rapid, with increased breathing and pulse rates.

Treatment

Regardless of cause, *pneumonia always requires medical evaluation as quickly as possible.* Chest x-rays, blood tests, and occasionally sputum gram stains are useful. Severe cases may require further measures, including hospitalization. **Never** start antibiotics unless medical help is unavailable.

Initially, complete bed rest is essential. Drink plenty of fluids. For fever or pain, take 1 or 2 aspirin (for adults) or Tylenol tablets as needed up to 4 times a day or use a nonsteroidal anti-inflammatory such as ibuprofen or naproxen. **Don't take any other pain killers, cough suppressants, or other medications unless prescribed by a doctor.**

Treatment in isolated areas

In addition to the above measures, if medical help is more than 36–48 hours away, start antibiotics if signs of pneumonia are accompanied by any of the following:

1. severe shortness of breath;

2. a temperature above 103°F (39.4°C);

3. rapid progression of symptoms, with sputum that is rust-colored, thick, and sticky (suspected pneumococcal pneumonia).

The recommended antibiotics, in order of preference, are:

1. Zithromax (azithromycin) 250 mg. , 2 tablets orally together, then one tablet a day for the next 4 days; **or**

2. Biaxin (clarithromycin) 500 mg. orally twice a day; **or**

3. Ceftin (cefuroxime) 250-500 mg. orally twice a day; **or**

4. doxycycline 100 mg. orally twice a day.

Except for zithromax, antibiotics are taken for 3 – 5 days after fever subsides — usually 7 – 14 days.

Medical care must still be obtained as quickly as possible. Some strains of pneumococcal bacteria are resistant to many antibiotics. It's always best to get medical care before starting any antibiotics.

Asthma

An attack of asthma can be triggered by pollen, dust, animal dander, or other airborne particles. It can also result from viral or bacterial respiratory infections, inhaled irritants (physical or chemical), psychological stress, or vigorous exercise.

Symptoms

Asthma is characterized by shortness of breath, wheezing (a high pitched noise from the airway during inhalation and/or exhalation), and a sensation of tightness in the chest. A persistant cough can be the only symptom. Coughing may bring up thick secretions of mucus.

Asthma is usually, but not always, an ongoing condition. *Travelers with a history of asthma should carry their usual medications and know how and when to use them.* They should also consult with their doctor prior to travel regarding any special medications to take along. Medical care is necessary if asthma is not relieved with the usual medications, or if an underlying bacterial infection is the suspected cause.

Travelers with no history of asthma or chronic lung disease should get medical attention at the onset of wheezing or with development of a chronic cough.

Wheezing should be considered the first sign of a possible life-threatening emergency.

You don't need to be an asthmatic to have an asthma attack. On a camping trip, one of the authors experienced severe respiratory difficulty accompanied by wheezing — suddenly and for no apparent reason. Sitting around the campfire, a fellow camper had thrown sulfur-bearing rocks onto the fire to spark some color. Downwind, invisibly, the sulfurous fumes provoked a nearly lethal reaction.

Treatment

During a first attack of asthma, it's important to stay calm. Reduce the work of breathing: sit up, lean forward, support the upper body with arms folded across a table or desk if available. Drink lots of fluids to keep secretions thin and loose. **Don't** smoke. Get medical help as soon as possible, including a follow-up evaluation once the initial attack subsides.

Treatment in isolated areas

Asthma symptoms may sometimes accompany infection, either viral or bacterial. If symptoms of persistent cough with a fever greater than 101 degrees Fahrenheit are present and no medical help is available, then in addition to the above measures we suggest starting treatment with an oral antibiotic- see treatment schedule for pneumonia.

Get medical help as quickly as possible.

For wheezing, you may use an Alupent (metaproterenol sulfate) or Albuterol ("Proventil") inhaler. If these aren't available, you can use an epinephrine inhaler, but it has the potential for more side effects. For further information on these drugs and how to use an inhaler, see p. 446. Drink plenty of fluids, and **don't** smoke.

If none of the inhalers are available, one option is to take Alupent 20 mg. orally 3–4 times a day, or an equivalent medication such as Brethine 2.5 mg. 3 times a day. Severe wheezing with shortness of breath that doesn't respond to any of these measures is a medical emergency requiring immediate attention.

Care of a Cough

Secretions produced by the lungs must be coughed up to prevent a bacterial infection either from starting or from becoming worse. **Productive coughing (coughing which produces phlegm) should always be encouraged rather than suppressed.** The following measures will help keep secretions loose and thin so that coughing can be effective:

1. Drink plenty of fluids — 2 or 3 quarts (liters) a day.

2. Keep the room comfortably warm and humidified if possible.

3. Use a vaporizer if available, or try steam inhalations several times a day. Take hot steamy showers, or heat water over a stove and transfer it to a basin. Cover your head and the basin with a towel to enclose the steam. Be careful to avoid burns. Eucalyptus leaves added to the water will help open air passageways.

4. Cough medicines should contain an expectorant such as guaifenesin. Avoid cough suppressants as much as possible. If necessary for sleep, use a cough suppressant such as codeine or terpine hydrate.

5. Smokers must not smoke. Cigarette smoke paralyzes the structures (cilia) that sweep pulmonary secretions out of the lungs so they can be picked up and properly disposed of by a good cough.

Symptomatic Treatment of Fever and Indications for Medical Evaluation

Mild fevers (less than 102°F (38.9°C) can be treated with aspirin, Tylenol, or a nonsteroidal anti-inflammatory such as ibuprofen or naproxen. Increase fluid intake. In addition, fevers above 102°F (38.9°C) may require tepid water sponge baths.

Obtain medical evaluation for:

1. any recurrent fever;

2. any fever over 104°F. (40°C.);

3. any fever accompanied by chest pain and/or short-ness of breath, with or without a productive cough;

4. any fever accompanied by yellowing of the skin or eyes (jaundice);

5. fever accompanied by severe headache, nausea, vom-iting, and neck stiffness.

Quick Reference
Common Causes of a Cough

Symptoms	Possible Cause
Nonproductive, or dry cough	cold, flu-like illness, allergy, smoking, viral bronchitis, post-nasal drip, pneumonia, asthma, or esophageal reflux
with:	
clear nasal discharge, fever, sore throat, muscle aches	flu-like illness, cold with post-nasal drip
watery, itchy eyes, nose, mouth	hay fever (allergic rhinitis)
wheezing*	asthma
mild fever	viral bronchitis
chest pain, fever, possibly shortness of breath*, chills	pneumonia
heartburn, acid taste in mouth, indigestion	esophageal reflux

*requires immediate medical attention.

Symptoms with:	Possible Cause
productive cough with white or clear sputum	viral bronchitis, flu-like illness, cold,
slight fever less than 101°F.	cold, viral bronchitis
slight fever, muscle aches, fatigue	flu-like illness
wheezing*	asthma
with fever over 101°F.*	pneumonia
Productive cough with green or yellow sputum and nasal discharge, fever and, pain behind the eyes, forehead or cheekbones which is increased when bending over	bacterial sinusitis
Productive cough with bloody or blood-tinged sputum*	pneumonia (usually blood streaked with yellow-green sputum), tuberculosis, severe parasitic infection, tumor
Cough with shortness of breath, difficulty breathing*	asthma, pneumonia
Chronic or persistent cough*	tuberculosis, smoking, asthma, chronic bronchitis, parasitic infection, or esophageal reflux
Persistent cough often with choking or gagging	pertussis

*Requires immediate medical evaluation

Quick Reference
Common Causes of a Fever

Symptom	Possible Cause
Accompanied by a cough, with:	
chest pain, shortness of breath, night sweats, un-explained weight loss, occasional blood-tinged sputum with wheezing	pneumonia, tuberculosis, asthma*
muscle aches, fatigue, headache, chills, nausea	flu-like illness, "viral upper respiratory syndrome"
nasal discharge, headache, pain behind eyes or face increased by bending over; cough dry or productive	sinusitis
fatigue, headache, sore throat, "stepladder" fever; cough non-productive	typhoid fever
Without a cough, but with:	
chills, fatigue, sore throat, with or without cold symptoms	flu-like illness, "viral upper respiratory syndrome", strep throat, viral sore throat, mononucleosis
nausea, and/or vomiting, diarrhea; muscle pain, abdominal pain, possibly headache or chills	gastroenteritis

*Requires immediate medical evaluation.

Symptom	Possible Cause
Without a cough, but **with:**	
burning on urination, urinary frequency, small amounts **and:**	
no back pain	urinary tract infection (bladder infection)*
back pain, nausea and/or vomiting	kidney infection*
fatigue, shaking chills that come and go periodically; occasionally with headache and diarrhea	malaria*
severe lower abdominal pain	appendicitis, pelvic inflammatory disease*
bloody diarrhea	intestinal bacterial infections/dysentery, schistosomiasis,
chills, severe headache, nausea, vomiting, neck stiffness	meningitis**

*Requires immediate medical evaluation.

**If meningitis is suspected, don't take antibiotics. Get immediate medical evaluation.

Genital and Urinary Tract Infections

16

Problems Common to Women

Urinary Tract Infections (UTI's)

Urinary tract infections are very common. All things considered its remarkable that UTI's don't occur constantly. The short length of the urethra, its proximity to the bacteria of the vagina and the rectum, and the abundance of the ways bacteria can spread in the area including intercourse, all predispose to such infections.

Other contributing factors include an absence of hygienic facilities, long rides on buses and trains with an unemptied bladder, inadequate fluid intake, and an increase in sexual activity (sex with a new partner may be especially intense). Other factors that can contribute to urinary tract infections include tight fitting jeans, undergarments of non-breathing synthetic fabrics, or wearing the same underclothes day after day. Around the time of menopause, women may be more at risk for bladder infections due to vaginal dryness.

Preventive measures

Drink plenty of purified fluids (see pp. 71 – 77) and stay well hydrated. Maintain good genital hygiene. Most public restrooms do not have toilet paper or what they have is industrial strength. Carry a supply of toilet paper or paper tissues and packets of pre-moistened towelettes in your purse or backpack.

When urinary tract infections are a recurrent problem, some experts say to avoid citrus drinks, coffee, and alcohol due to their effect as a urinary irritant. On long bus or train rides it is a good idea to empty the bladder as frequently as possible. Make a habit of voiding whenever there is convenient access to a public toilet, whether the bladder is full or not. It is also a good idea to avoid any practice, sexual or other, that may transfer germs from the rectal area to the vagina/urethral area.

Use underwear made with a cotton crotch. It will absorb excessive moisture which may otherwise promote bacterial growth. Avoid irritants such as vaginal sprays or deodorants and tight clothing.

Peri-menopausal or menopausal women may experience vaginal dryness and urinary frequency or urgency without burning. Estrogen vaginal creams or even an oral contraceptive pill intra-vaginally once a week may decrease these symptoms. If any of these symptoms occur check with your medical provider prior to your trip.

Symptoms of a urinary tract infection

The symptoms of a urinary tract infection are easily recognizable and may be maddeningly familiar. The most common symptoms are a sensation of urgency and burning, associated with increased frequency and voiding of small amounts of urine. When these symptoms occur, they are treated with an antibiotic and if necessary, a urinary analgesic.

Treatment of a urinary tract infection

Simple urinary tract infections with no abnormal vaginal rash or discharge, no pelvic or back pain, no fever, and no nausea and vomiting are easily treated. Oral antibiotics are prescribed for 3 – 7 days. Drink plenty of water or other fluids throughout the course of antibiotic therapy. Cranberry juice or tablets or vitamin C tablets can be taken to acidify the urine.

Treatment of urinary tract infections in isolated areas.

When medical help isn't readily available use any *one* of the following treatments in order of preference, except during pregnancy. **Treatment is for 3 days.** If there is blood in the urine or a history of recurrent urinary infections, then treat for 7 days.

1. ciprofloxacin 500 mg., **or** ofloxacin 200 mg., one tablet orally twice a day, *or* levofloxacin 250 mg. orally once a day; **or**

2. Bactrim DS (Septra DS), one tablet orally twice a day. Recently, up to 30% of infections due to *e. coli* bacteria have been resistant to these sulfa medications. **Don't take Bactrim or Septra if you are allergic to sulfa drugs.**

3. Augmentin 500 mg. orally twice a day. **Don't take Augmentin if you are allergic to penicillin.**

If you're pregnant, use *one* of the following instead:

1. Ampicillin or Augmentin 500 mg. orally twice a day for 7 days **(don't take ampicillin or Augmentin if you are allergic to penicillin);** *or*

2. Nitrofurantoin 100 mg. orally 4 times a day for 7 days.

Do not use tetracycline or any of the quinolones (ciprofloxacin, levofloxacin, ofloxacin) during pregnancy. Bactrim or Septra should be stopped at least 2 weeks prior to delivery.

After treatment, signs of bladder infection may occasionally reappear after 2 or 3 days. If so get medical attention. In order to determine the most effective antibiotic, the bacteria will need to be identified through a urine culture and sensitivity. Then one of the above treatments may be prescribed for 7 days.

Vaginal yeast infections are a frequent side effect of antibiotic therapy. Vaginal yeast medications can help prevent yeast infection if taken concurrently with the antibiotics (see p. 358).

Urinary Tract Analgesics

The burning sensation that accompanies a bladder infection can be extremely uncomfortable. It can be relieved with:

1. phenazopyridine 200 mg. (Pyridium and other brands) 1 tablet orally 3 times a day for no more than 2 days; *or* 95 mg. (Uristat), 2 tablets orally 3 times a day for no more than 2 days.

This medication can be taken along with the antibiotics. It turns the urine bright orange, so don't panic. Some people even notice that the tears from their eyes turn orange and may stain contact lenses.

Indications for medical assistance

When accompanied by unusual vaginal discharge, symptoms of a urinary tract infection require medical evaluation. The symptoms may be due to a vaginal infection rather than a bladder infection.

Get medical attention immediately if symptoms of a urinary tract infection are accompanied by any of the following:

1. chills or fever (102-105° F or 38.9 -40.6° C.);

2. back or flank pain (a dull ache or tenderness in the back along the rib margin);

3. nausea and vomiting.

These may all be signs of a kidney infection.

Emergency treatment in isolated areas

If any of the above signs of kidney infection develop and you are close to medical care get help immediately. Don't take any medications. If unable to access medical care immediately start one of the following medications, listed in order of preference:

1. ciprofloxacin 500 mg., *or* ofloxacin 400 mg., orally twice a day for 7 days (**do not take these during pregnancy**); *or*

2. Augmentin 875 mg. orally twice a day **or** 500 mg. orally three times a day for 14 days (**don't take Augmentin if you are allergic to penicillin.**)

Head **immediately** for the nearest physician or medical care facility whether antibiotics are started or not.

Stress Incontinence

If you have a problem with bladder control or urinary stress incontinence (loss of control of urine with coughing, sneezing or laughing), consult with a medical provider specializing in female urinary tract problems in advance of the anticipated trip. For minor problems bring a supply of panty liners and learn to do exercises to strengthen bladder control (Kegel exercises).

Vaginal Infections

Women are at risk during travel for vaginal infections. These can occur for many of the same reasons as urinary tract infections, discussed above. Factors which may contribute to an increased rate of infection include pregnancy, diabetes, stress, and long hard days of travel in a tropical climate. Other contributing factors include douching and the use of oral contraceptives, antibiotics, or synthetic fabrics that trap heat.

There are four main causes of vaginal discharge. A normal clear white discharge that may vary during the menstrual cycle but is asymptomatic, bacterial vaginosis (BV), yeast, and trichomonas.

Even if a you have never had vaginitis it is important to be prepared for the possibility, especially during travel. *If you develop vaginal discharge and/or pelvic pain following intercourse, especially with a new partner, you may have a sexually transmitted disease. Seek medical evaluation and treatment.*

Use of douches

Don't douche. It washes out normal bacteria and can lead to vaginal infection. Douching may also push bacteria into the uterus. This may result in pelvic inflammatory disease (PID). Statistically, women who douche have a 4 times greater risk of developing PID.

Bacterial vaginosis (BV)

This is the most common cause of vaginal discharge and vaginal odor. Bacterial vaginosis during pregnancy may increase the incidence of pre-term delivery.

Symptoms

A thin homogenous discharge is produced, usually whitish or greyish in color with a fishy or foul odor. Mild itching may be present.

Treatment

Metronidazole (Flagyl) is usually effective. If infection recurs, consider treating your male partner(s) simultaneously. Avoid alcohol when taking this medication. Treat with *one* of the following:

1. metronidazole (Flagyl) 500 mg. orally, twice a day for 7 days; avoid use in 1st trimester of pregnancy.

2. metronidazole gel 0.75% – one full applicator applied intravaginally twice a day for 5 days; avoid use in 1st trimester of pregnancy.

3. Clindamycin 2% vaginal cream — one full applicator

applied intravaginally at bedtime for 7 days (avoid use in pregnancy); *or*

4. clindamycin 300 mg. orally, twice a day for 7 days.

For symptomatic relief of itching and irritation, see p. 359.

Yeast Infections

The second most common cause of vaginal infections is yeast. This organism usually causes a thick cottage cheese like white discharge with vaginal itching and vulvar itching, swelling, and redness. The risk of yeast vaginitis can increase with travel to warm humid tropic and subtropic regions. Infection may follow antibiotic use, such as doxycycline for malaria prevention or antibiotics for the treatment of traveler's diarrhea or respiratory, skin, or urinary tract infections. Although vaginal yeast infections are not regarded as a sexually transmitted disease, balanitis (redness, irritation, swelling and itching around the tip of the penis) may occur in men exposed to women with genital yeast infections. This is more likely to happen in the tropics. If your male partner develops a rash on the penis, scrotum, or groin area he should also be treated.

Treatment

Most yeast infections can be cured with one of the 1-3 day treatments listed below. For severe or persistent infections use a 1 week or longer treatment method. Insert the medication - suppository, cream, or tablet- into the vagina before bedtime. The medication should be put in following intercourse, not before. Otherwise it will get squashed out and not do any good. Some women feel that the vaginal creams are too messy for travel but they do help with the local symptoms of vaginal itching. A 1% hydrocortisone cream may also be used for a week or two if needed for vulvar itching. *Don't apply hydrocortisone cream if herpes lesions are present (see p. 209 – 210).*

Treatment can be with either oral medication or vaginal creams, tablets or suppositories:

Oral – fluconazole (Diflucan). Take a single 150 mg. tablet. If symptoms persist, repeat the dose one week later.

Vaginal preparations-

1. Butoconazole (Femstat) 2% cream. Apply 5 grams (one full applicator) at bedtime for 3 days, or 6 days if pregnant.

2. Clotrimazole 10% cream (Gynelotrimin, Mycelex)- apply 5 grams (one full applicator) as a single application. Alternatively, use 1% cream, 5 grams (one full applicator) applied intravaginally at bedtime for 7-14 days; *or*

   clotrimazole 100 mg. vaginal tablet- use one tablet vaginally at bedtime for 7 days, *or* two tablets at bedtime for 3 days. Alternatively, use a 500 mg. vaginal tablet one time only.

3. Miconazole (Monistat)- 2% cream. Apply 5 grams (one full applicator) intravaginally at bedtime for 7 days. Alternatives: 100 mg. vaginal suppository, one intravaginally at bedtime for 7 days; *or* 200 mg. vaginal suppository,   one intravaginally at bedtime for 3 days; *or* 1200 mg. vaginal suppository, one intravaginally as a single application.

4. Teraconazole (Terazole)- .4% cream, 5 grams (one applicator full) applied intravaginally at bedtime for 3 days; *or* 80 mg. vaginal suppository, one intravaginally as a single application.

5. Tioconazole (Vagistat), 6.5% ointment- 5 grams (one applicator full) applied intravaginally at bedtime as a single application.

Some women find that a yeast infection invariably follows the use of any antibiotic. If this is true in your case, consider treatment with one of the listed antifungal medications every time you use antibiotics. Carry antifungal medication in your first aid kit.

Any persistent or recurrent symptoms should be evaluated by your medical provider upon returning home.

Trichomonas ("Trich")

Characterized by profuse yellow -green, foamy, bubbly discharge, usually with a very foul odor. There may be mild itching of the vulva. Vaginal trichomonas may be associated with adverse effects during pregnancy, especially pre-term delivery and premature rupture of the membranes.

Treatment

1. Flagyl (metronidazole) 2 grams (eight 250 mg. tablets) orally taken in a single dose; *or*

2. Flagyl (metronidazole) 500 mg. orally twice a day for 7 days.

Don't use Flagyl during the first trimester of pregnancy without first consulting an obstetrician. Do not take alcohol with this medication.

Male sexual partners should be treated at the same time with the single 2 gram dose of Flagyl provided there are no contraindications. Left untreated, men may reintroduce the infection to their partner. Partners undergoing treatment should refrain from intercourse until they have both completed treatment. If intercourse does take place use condoms.

Symptomatic relief of vaginal infections

If vaginal medications aren't available and symptoms of itching, redness, swelling, or irritation of the labia occur, wash the area free of any discharge. Apply a thin coating of sterile lubricant such as K-Y jelly or diaphragm jelly to protect the skin. If these aren't available, use a 1% topical hydrocortisone cream to the area to reduce symptoms. *Don't apply hydrocortisone cream if herpes lesions are present* **(see pp. 209 – 210).** Aspirin or antihistamines (see p. 215) orally may give some symptomatic relief, especially if no other treatments are available.

Common Sexually Transmitted Diseases (STDs).

Sexually transmitted diseases are a major public health problem worldwide. An estimated 333 million people contract an STD annually, of which 80% are in developing countries. In parts of the world some STDs have developed resistance to commonly used antibiotics. Statistics show that up to 25% of travelers have at least one new sexual contact while abroad

Gonorrhea and chlamydia are two of the most common sexually transmitted diseases. Gonorrhea is increasingly resistant to standard doses of antibiotics, especially fluoroquinolones such as Cipro. Drug-resistant gonorrhea has been identified in Asia and S.E. Asia, Africa, the U.S.A., Canada, Europe, and Australia. The incidence of resistance is especially high in the Philippines, Thailand, Singapore, South Korea, and West Africa, especially Ghana, Cote d'Ivoire (formerly the Ivory Coast) and Nigeria.

Symptoms

A pus like, yellowish discharge from the vagina may occur. It's sometimes accompanied by urinary burning and frequency. When present, these symptoms occur from 1-3 weeks after exposure to infection. There may however be no symptoms or such minimal ones that they are easy to overlook. The first indication of infection is often from a male sexual partner who develops burning with urination and/or a discharge from the penis. If not discovered early, infection may go undetected until it produces more serious symptoms of PID (Pelvic Inflammatory Disease-see Quick Reference Chart, p. 362).

Treatment

Any vaginal discharge, especially following unsafe sexual contact, should be evaluated medically prior to treatment. Cultures for gonorrhea and chlamydia should be done, as well as blood tests for HIV, hepatitis B and C, and syphilis.

Treatment in isolated areas

When concern for a sexually transmitted disease occurs, and no medical help is available, the usual treatments for gonorrhea/chlamydia infection when there are no symptoms of PID present are:

1. ciprofloxacin (Cipro) 500 mg. orally once; *or*

   norfloxacin (Floxin) 400 mg. orally once;

   plus either:

2. Zithromax 250 mg. tablets, 4 pills orally in a single dose (1 gram total); *or*

   doxycycline 100 mg. orally twice a day for 7 days.

In areas of resistant gonorrhea (see p. 360) seek medical care for other treatment options.

Abdominal Pain

Lower abdominal or pelvic pain can be difficult to assess. **It should always be evaluated medically as soon as possible.** There can be many different causes including severe menstrual cramps, bladder infection, ectopic pregnancy, sexually transmitted disease, appendicitis, ruptured ovarian cyst, or food poisoning. Knowing if you are pregnant or not can be important in the diagnosis. If pregnancy is a possibility, obtain a pregnancy test as soon as possible, especially if you are having pelvic pain and vaginal bleeding.

Quick Reference

Gynecologic Symptoms That Require Immediate Medical Evaluation

See a physician immediately for any of the following signs and symptoms, whether already receiving treatment or not:

1. Lower abdominal pain (not associated with normal menstrual pain or diarrhea), accompanied by any of the following:

   - chills or fever;
   - pain with intercourse;
   - spotting after intercourse;
   - loss of appetite, nausea, or vomiting;
   - abnormal vaginal discharge.

These are usually indications of PID (Pelvic Inflammatory Disease). Symptoms are often, but not always, accompanied by a foul vaginal odor or discharge which may be more intense during or following menstruation.

2. Urinary urgency, frequency, and burning, accompanied by any of the following:

   - chills or fever — 101°F (38.3°C) or greater;
   - pain or tenderness in the back or side;
   - nausea or vomiting.

These symptoms usually indicate kidney infection.

3. abnormal vaginal bleeding;

4. problems with contraception (birth control pills, IUDs, diaphragms, etc.);

5. vaginal infections.

Problems Common to Men

Whether or not you acquire an infection from sexual contact, there's usually no lack of opportunity to do so. This is often truest for those traveling alone. With few exceptions, all sexual encounters carry a risk of disease.

Gonorrhea

Gonorrhea is one of the most common sexually transmitted diseases. It has been increasingly resistant to standard doses of antibiotics in many areas of the world. Among these are the Philippines, Thailand, Singapore, South Korea, and West Africa, especially in Ghana, Cote d'Ivoire (formerly the Ivory Coast), Nigeria, and Kenya.

Symptoms

Initially there's burning on urination accompanied by a clear or milky discharge. This occurs approximately 2–10 days after contact. Within a day or two the discomfort increases and the discharge turns yellow, yellow-green, or cream-colored. Urination is frequent with a sense of urgency and burning. The tip of the penis is often tender, red, and swollen.

Nongonoccocal Urethritis (NGU)

This infection is even more common than gonorrhea. Symptoms are virtually the same as for gonorrhea and can easily be mistaken for it. The discharge usually remains clear or milky. Diagnosis is based on the absence of gonorrhea bacteria in a Gram-stain of the discharge, usually caused by chlamydia.

Treatment of Penile discharge (Gonorrhea and Nongonoccocal Urethritis (NGU))

Obtain medical care for evaluation and treatment. As indicated, it's usually impossible to tell the difference between gonorrhea and NGU infections without laboratory tests. In addition, about a third of men with a urethral discharge have a combination of both gonorrhea *and* NGU. *Always have blood tests for HIV and Syphilis done.*

Treatment in isolated areas

If medical care isn't available, all penile discharges should be treated with 2 drugs to cover the possibility of infection by both gonorrhea and NGU.

During treatment for either infection, it's important to increase fluid intake. Avoid both alcohol and coffee, which are irritating to the urethra. There should also be no sexual contact until at least 3–4 days after completing treatment. If sexual contact does occur, use a condom. **Condoms are recommended for any casual sexual contact to help prevent disease.**

Treatment schedule in isolated areas for any penile discharge:

1. Take either ciprofloxacin 500 mg. *or* ofloxacin 400 mg. orally **once**

   plus either:

2 Azithromycin 250 mg. tablets - 4 tablets together (1000 mg. or 1 gm. total) **once;** *or*

   doxycycline 100 mg. twice a day for 7 days.

Treatment of gonorrhea in drug-resistant areas

In countries where antibiotic resistant strains of gonorrhea are known to exist (see p. 360), check with local medical practitioners or the public health department for the recommended treatment. If symptoms persist after treatment, or recur following treatment, medical evaluation is required.

Partner Contact

Make sure sexual partners are also treated so that infection isn't transferred back and forth, ping-pong style.

Enlarged prostate or Benign Prostatic Hypertrophy (BPH)

An enlarged prostate puts pressure on the urethra and may cause symptoms of:

1. difficulty starting your urinary stream;

2. difficulty stopping your stream (dribbling);

3. frequent urination;

4. having to get up repeatedly at night to urinate;

5. decreased force of urinary stream.

If you have any of these symptoms, see your medical provider prior to travel for evaluation and possible medication.

Prevention- Certain medications may increase the symptoms of BPH or completely stop the ability to urinate. Avoid the following medications: antihistamines, decongestants, and Lomotil. It has been suggested that regular ejaculations (2-3 times per week) will help prevent prostate enlargement. There is no proof of this, but it is risk-free....if you are practicing safe sex.

Problems Common to Men and Women

Human Papilloma Virus (HPV)

Genital warts can look like either a cauliflower growth, or a flat to raised pearly lesion. They can occur anywhere in the groin area of a woman or man including the urinary and or anal openings. They are most commonly seen on the penis in men and the vulva or cervix in women. Transmission is by skin to skin contact. *HPV is particularly important for women as it appears to one of the main causes of cervical cancer.*

Exposure and Treatment

Anyone who has been exposed to or who develops HPV infection should obtain blood tests for syphilis and HIV. Women should also get yearly pap smears. Pap smears may pick up early precancerous or cancerous changes due to HPV. Cervical cancer is a treatable disorder if caught early. In developing countries cervical cancer is a common cause of death in women due to the lack of pap smear screening programs.

Women who experience recurrent outbreaks of HPV or develop it while traveling and require treatment should ideally return home for treatment and monitoring. If you have a history of recurrent outbreaks discuss self-treatment options with your medical provider prior to travel.

Condoms can reduce but do not totally eliminate transmission as the lesions can occur in areas that are not protected by condoms. Treatment of genital warts does not eliminate the HPV infection and individuals with HPV can remain infectious after treatment even if the "wart" is gone.

Genital Herpes- see pp. 209– 211.

Scabies, Crabs, and Lice- see pp. 201 – 205.

Ulcerative Genital Lesions- all ulcerative lesions should be medically evaluated and tests for syphilis and HIV should be done.

Quick Reference

Typical Signs of Ulcerative Genital Lesions

	Syphilis	Chancroid	Herpes	LGV	Granuloma inguinale
Primary lesion	raised, smooth lesion may be pustular	red, raised lesion, blister (vesicle)	raised, pimple-like (vesicular) or pustular lesion	raised, smooth blister-like	raised, smooth lesion
Border	well defined	red, ragged	red	variable	rolled, elevated
Base	red, smooth with gray film	pus yellow to gray, bleeds easily	red, smooth	variable	red, rough
Pain	rare	present	present	variable	rare
Lymph nodes	firm, non-tender	tender, rubbery	tender, firm	tender	pseudo

Injuries to Bone and Muscle

17

Strains, Sprains, Fractures, and Dislocations

With the exception of simple sprains and strains, most acute injuries to muscles, joints, ligaments, tendons, and bones require medical evaluation. Unfortunately, many bone fractures are difficult for even the most experienced practitioner to identify. An x-ray is usually required if there is any doubt about a bone being broken.

First, some definitions:

Sprains occur when the ligaments that support the joints are torn or stretched, usually by overextending or twisting a joint beyond its normal range. This kind of injury is seen frequently in ankles, knees, and wrists.

Strains are injuries of the muscles, from over extension or overexertion. These cause swelling and moderate to intense pain with movement. Strains are common in muscles of the back and arms from lifting.

Fractures are broken bones. They are called *open* fractures if bone protrudes from the skin. *Closed* fractures do not protrude and are often difficult to detect without x-rays.

A **dislocation** is the displacement of any bone from its normal position in a joint. This occurs most often to shoulders and fingers.

Treatment of Sprains and Strains

Minor sprains and strains are treated identically. During the first 24-48 hours, a cold pack or compress, such as ice, wrapped in a towel, is applied to the area for 15-20 minutes 4 times a day. Keep cloth or other material between the ice and the skin. Elevate the injured area if this involves an extremity at least 12 inches above the level of the heart to further reduce swelling and pain. After 24-48 hours, either continue ice (especially if swelling persists) or apply heat to the area for 15-20 minutes, 3-4 times a day.

For pain and swelling, take either aspirin, 1 or 2 tablets orally every 4-6 hours, *or* a nonsteroid anti-inflammatory, such as one of the following:

1. ibuprofen (Motrin or Advil) 400-600 mg. orally, 4 times a day; **or**

2. naproxen (Naprosyn or Anaprox) 250-500 mg. orally twice a day; **or**

3. indomethacin (Indocin) 25 mg. orally 2-3 times a day; **or**

4. nabumetone (Relafen) 500-750 mg. orally either once or twice a day.

See contraindications for nonsteroid anti-inflammatories in Part III before taking any of these medications.

For severe pain not relieved by the above measures, obtain medical evaluation.

In Isolated Areas

When medical help isn't available, for severe pain take aspirin or Tylenol with 15-30 mg. of codeine, 1 or 2 orally every 4-6 hours or Vicodin, 1 tablet 3 or 4 times per day. For severe muscle spasm, a muscle relaxant may also be considered (not "necessary" since the use of muscle relaxants is probably not very helpful). Use one of the following or an equivalent muscle relaxant.

1. cyclobenzaprine (Flexeril) 10 mg., 1 tablet 3 times a day; **or**

2. methocarbamol (Robaxin) 500 mg., 2 tablets 4 times a day; **or**

3. carisoprodol (Soma) 350 mg., 1 tablet 3 times a day.

Use of an "Ace wrap" or supportive bandage or splint.
   An "Ace wrap" or elastic bandage is sometimes used to support an injured joint, most commonly the ankle, knee, or wrist. When using an elastic bandage, or a substitute such as a long strip of cloth, be sure it isn't too tight. Remove and rebind the joint less tightly whenever a wrap causes discomfort, skin discoloration, numbness, or pain in or beyond the joint. Splints, if available, will be far more supporting for a joint injury. A Sam splint can be molded to any joint or extremity and then wrapped with an ace wrap (see "First Aid Kit, p. 48 – 51).

Treatment of Other Muscle, Bone, or Joint Injuries
   Any injury more severe than a minor strain or sprain **requires medical evaluation and treatment.** Immobilize suspected fractures or injured joints with a Sam Splint, a multipurpose splint that can be molded into many shapes (see p. 51), or any other splint material, while seeking medical attention.

Quick Reference:
Injuries Requiring Medical Evaluation and Treatment

Medical evaluation and/or x-rays are required as soon as possible for the following injuries:

1. all open fractures;

2. any dislocation (any injury causing joint deformity);

3. inability to walk or bear weight after an ankle or knee injury 2;

4. a "snap, crackle, or pop" (the Rice-Krispie syndrome) heard at the time of an injury;

5. any injured area, especially a joint, that becomes hot, tender, swollen, or painful;

6. any joint injury with moderate to severe swelling;

7. any injury where there is tenderness or pain over the bone;

8. whenever there is doubt about a bone being broken;

9. any joint that becomes painful or disabling without an identifiable cause (for example, waking up in the morning with a tender, unmovable wrist or knee).

10. any injury that isn't improved after 2 weeks of treatment.

   Women fewer than 20 weeks pregnant should not have x-rays unless medically required and authorized. If x-rays are deemed necessary, have a lead apron placed over the abdomen - provided one is available and the abdomen or back are not needed in the x-ray.

Burn Injuries   **18**

Burns caused by heat are classified by the degree (depth) of injury to the skin. Treatment varies depending on the degree, extent, and location of injury. Although some aspects differ, the evaluation and treatment of external burns from electricity or acidic and alkaline chemicals is the same as for thermal injuries.

First Degree Burns

First degree burns affect only the outermost layer of skin. They cause redness but not blistering. They may be painful, but swelling is absent or minimal. A nonblistering sunburn is a common example.

Treatment

Following brief contact with a hot object, immerse the burned area immediately in cold water or apply a cold wet cloth until the pain subsides. **Never** apply butter, grease, or other home remedies to any burn.

Cool water or damp cool cloths are soothing and effective for local pain. Take one or two aspirin orally as needed or a nonsteroidal anti-inflammatory such as ibuprofen or naproxen every 4-6 hours to reduce swelling and pain. Infection is unlikely.

Second Degree Burns

Second degree burns cause incomplete injury to the skin below its surface layer. Blistering is a characteristic sign. The skin may appear moist or oozing. Redness, pain, and swelling are usually present for several days. Injuries from spilled hot liquids and severe sunburn are examples.

Treatment

Apply cold water or a cold wet cloth to the burn area until the pain subsides. **Don't** break blisters unless the areas involved would be prone to pressure or tension (e.g. a large blister on the foot). Intact skin is the best defense against infection. Some second degree burns require immediate medical care; indications are summarized at the end of this chapter.

The main goal of care in minor second degree burns is to prevent infection. Bathe the injured area for 20 – 30 minutes, using lukewarm water. If the water isn't reliably treated and clean, boil it first for 5 minutes, then allow it to cool.

After bathing, pat the surrounding skin dry, but allow the burn to air dry. Don't blow on it. Dress the burn by putting on a thin layer of Silvadene Cream, if available. Cover it with a non sticky dressing such as a Telfa pad, then wrap with sterile gauze.

Repeat this procedure every 12 hours, or more often if needed to keep the gauze bandages clean. Before changing, soak off dressings that are dry and stick to the wound. For blistering burns from a deep sunburn, apply a topical antibacterial ointment to help prevent infection.

Relieve pain with 1 or 2 aspirin or Tylenol or a nonsteroidal anti-inflammatory such as ibuprofen or naproxen every 4-6 hours as needed. For extensive burns, **don't** use aspirin. For moderate to severe pain, take 1 or 2 Tylenol with 15-30 mg. of codeine every 4-6 hours, or Vicodin, 1 tablet up to 4 times a day, as needed.

Tetanus and Wound infections

Get a tetanus booster if you haven't had one within the previous 5 years.

Infected second degree burns require immediate medical attention. Infection delays healing and increases tissue damage. Infected burn wounds need to be cultured before the appropriate antibiotics can be prescribed. Signs of infection are:

1. yellow or greenish pus draining from the burn or present on the dressing;

2. a foul odor coming from the burn or dressing;

3. fever greater than 101°F (38.3°C).

4. increased pain and tenderness with redness or swelling surrounding the burn.

Treatment of Infected Burns in Isolated Areas

If you're more than 2 days from medical care and develop signs of infection, start antibiotics and head for the nearest medical care facility as quickly as possible. Continue bathing and dressing the burned areas, with care not to spread the infection. Use one of the following antibiotics:

1. dicloxacillin 500 mg. orally, 4 times a day for 10 days; **or**

2. Keflex 500 mg. orally, 4 times a day for 10 days; **or**

3. Biaxin 500 mg. orally 4 times a day for 10 days; **or**

4. Zithromax 250 mg., two pills together initially then one a day for 4 more days.

Third Degree Burns

Third degree burns destroy all layers of the skin. Fire, prolonged contact with hot substances, and electricity are frequent causes of third degree burns. The burned area may be charred, or turn as hard and white as the edge of a fried egg. There is little or no pain because nerve endings in the skin are destroyed.

Treatment

All third degree burns, even small ones, *require immediate medical evaluation*, preferably at a hospital or burn center. If you do not have access to quality medical care, consider air evacuation. In contrast with milder burns, **don't** apply ice or cold water compresses to third degree injuries. Don't attempt to remove stuck or charred clothing or apply any ointments or medications.

While awaiting or during transportation to medical care:

1. Cover burned areas loosely with a sterile dressing if available. Otherwise, use a clean sheet or cloth, preferably ironed or dried in the sun.

2. Elevate burned extremities.

3. Keep the injured person calm and lying down, or supported with pillows if there are burns on the face or neck.

Burns Requiring Special Treatment

Second Degree Burns
Involving Adjacent Skin Surfaces

Burns to areas of the body where skin comes in contact with skin, such as the fingers, toes, armpit, or groin, require special care. Sterile Vaseline gauze dressings should be placed between the adjacent skin surfaces. *Obtain medical care immediately for these injuries.*

Electrical Burns

Electrical burns of any type must also receive immediate medical evaluation and treatment. Damage is often internal and may not be readily apparent. Electrical burns which arc across the chest can cause heart damage and are of particular concern. This can occur when electricity passes from one arm to the other and is associated with chest pain or discomfort.

Quick Reference

Burns Requiring Immediate Medical Attention

1. Any third degree burn.
2. Any electrical burn.
3. The following second degree burns:
   - of the face (including eyes, nose, and ears);
   - of adjacent skin surfaces, such as the fingers, toes, armpit, or groin;
   - covering more than 10% of the body surface. This can be quickly estimated, counting the injured person's hand (from base of palm to fingertip) as 1% of the body surface. More than 10 hand spans requires immediate care;
   - in adults over age 50, diabetics, or anyone with circulatory or immune system impairment, including those taking steroid medications.
4. Signs of secondary infection in any burn:
   - green or yellow drainage (pus) on the burn or dressing;
   - a foul smelling wound or dressing;
   - an elevated temperature greater than 101°F (38.3°C).
5. Whenever smoke, gas, or chemical inhalation has or may have occurred. The following are indications for immediate medical help even if there are no other injuries:
   - exposure to fire in an enclosed space such as a house, hotel room, subway, theater, etc.;
   - singed nasal hairs;
   - soot in the nose, mouth, throat, or sputum;
   - burns of the face, nose, or mouth;
   - hoarseness, coughing, wheezing, or difficulty breathing;
   - presence of a headache after possible exposure to fire or smoke.

Exposure to Heat and Cold   19

Heat Exposure

Problems from heat exposure — cramps, exhaustion, or "heatstroke" — are normally preventable. They're due to excessive loss of water and salt.

These conditions are unlikely except on very hot days, especially when the humidity is high. The cause is profuse sweating over an extended time (as from working or hiking), *accompanied by inadequate replacement of water and salt*. Other sources of water loss — diarrhea, vomiting, or consumption of alcoholic beverages — may intensify symptoms. Cold beer may sound great, but it will increase rather than replace body water losses.

For normal to moderate levels of activity, salt replacement shouldn't be necessary. Don't use salt tablets. Replace fluid losses with nonalcoholic drinks.

At the first sign of any heat-related symptoms, stop all activity and take preventive measures. Otherwise, symptoms may progress to heat stroke, which is often fatal.

Prevention of Heat-Related Problems

When traveling, allow yourself time to adjust to warmer climates. Go slowly and don't try to do too much too soon. Avoid serious activity for a few days after arrival in a warm, humid environment. It may take as long as 8–14 days for your body to adapt to the heat, especially if you've just flown south to escape a long, cold winter.

Drink plenty of fluids — even if you're not thirsty, but avoid alcohol and caffeine. Get enough rest and sleep. Maintain a good diet. Wear loose-fitting light colored clothing, preferably of cotton rather than stuffy synthetic materials. Above all, don't push it — but drink lots of fluids if you do.

Prickly Heat Rash (see pp. 213).

Heat Cramps

Heat cramps are painful muscle spasms, usually of the arms, legs, or abdomen. They occur when large amounts of fluid lost from sweating are replaced only by water. Heat cramps were formerly common in steel-workers, for example, who did not replace lost salts during exposure to high heat for 8–12 hour stretches.

Prevention

Acclimatization decreases the risk for heat cramps. When activities cause profuse sweating over a prolonged period, drink plenty of fluids- especially fruit juices or beverages such as Gatorade. These are preferable to water for fluid replacement. If only water is available, added salt or salt tablets may be necessary but can cause stomach upset/gastritis.

Treatment

Stop all activity. Replace lost fluids by drinking a minimum of 1 glass (8 ounces) of juice or water every 15 minutes for an hour. Add 1 teaspoon of salt per glass, or eat salted crackers or food. Gently massage and stretch the painful areas. Rest for 1–3 days.

Heat Exhaustion

Symptoms of heat exhaustion include thirst, fatigue, weakness, headache, dizziness, nausea, and possibly fainting ("heat collapse.") The skin is cool, pale, and clammy. The pulse rate is usually under 100. There may be vomiting, diarrhea, or muscle cramps. Body temperature remains normal or is only slightly elevated (less than 102°F (38.9°C)).

Treatment

Stop all activity. Get out of direct sunlight if possible and lie down in the coolest available place. Elevate and support the feet about 8–12 inches above the head. Unless there is vomiting or unconsciousness, replace fluids orally with juices or cool water: a minimum of one glass every 15 minutes for an hour. Add one teaspoon of salt per glass.

Cool down by any available means, such as wetting the skin with cool or tepid water and vigorous fanning. If ice is available, place an ice pack or cold compress in the armpits, behind the neck, and in the groin. **Don't** leave an ice pack on for more than 15–20 minutes at one time to avoid frostbite. You can reapply it after 15–20 minutes. **Don't** take aspirin or alcoholic beverages. Avoid further heat stress for the next 24-48 hours.

Indications for medical assistance

Obtain medical help immediately for any of the following:

1. vomiting or unconsciousness. Don't give oral fluids if either is present;

2. symptoms that worsen or persist beyond one hour;

3. cessation of sweating, accompanied by a sudden, rapid rise in temperature: **This is heatstroke — an emergency.**

Heatstroke (Sunstroke)

Heatstroke is a life-threatening emergency. It may occur suddenly, or follow heat exhaustion — when the latter condition is not promptly corrected.

Sweating Fails

This is sometimes an early warning that may precede other symptoms by an hour or more, although in heat stroke due to exertion sweating is still present about 50% of the time. The skin is red, hot, and dry. The pulse rate is rapid — well over 100. The person affected becomes listless, confused, or unconscious as the body temperature rises rapidly to 105°F (40.6°C) or higher.

Treatment

Cool the victim **immediately** using any means available. If possible, place the person undressed in a tub of cold water. Otherwise, bring the body temperature down with rubbing alcohol, cold packs, cool water and fanning, etc. If a hammock is available, place the person in it and spray with cool water and fan from as many sides as possible. Place ice packs in the groin and under the arms. Check the body temperature and stop treatment when it reaches 102°F (38.9°C). Recheck the temperature every 30 minutes for 3–4 hours as there will often be a rebound temperature rise. Avoid the use of Tylenol. **Get medical help as quickly as possible.**

Exposure to Cold

Like heat, cold has exacted a toll on military forces. Hannibal lost about half of his troops crossing the Alps. Napoleon nearly lost his entire army invading Russia. Unlike heat, acclimatization to cold does not occur. Adaptation to cold is based on experience and avoiding behaviors or situations that are known to increase the risk of injury.

Prevention of Frostbite and Hypothermia

Be prepared for cold, wet, or windy weather. Multi-layered clothing is your main defense. This allows the addition or removal of garments as needed to keep warm or to avoid unnecessary sweating. Wool clothing retains heat even when wet, and a wind breaker may be crucial to minimize wind chill. Wet clothing should be replaced as soon as possible with dry garments.

Protect your hands, feet, and especially your head from the cold. Mittens are better than gloves for keeping hands warm. Protect your face as well as neck, including your nose and ears. To prevent windburn, use sun screens with a cream or grease base on any exposed skin.

Stay hydrated, eat well, carry snacks, and get plenty of rest. Hunger and fatigue increase your vulnerability to cold weather. Avoid dehydration, which can be exacerbated by both alcohol and caffeine. Alcohol also contributes to heat loss by dilating blood vessels at the surface of the skin. Tobacco use may contribute to frostbite by constricting the same vessels. Avoid alcohol, caffeine, and tobacco use when exposed to the cold.

When hiking in snow, it is a good idea to carry a small camp stove for heating snow used as a water source. Trying to stay hydrated by eating snow may contribute to hypothermia.

Remember the maxim, "Keep warm, keep dry, and keep moving." Move around to keep circulation going and body heat up — don't stay in one position for a long time.

Frostbite

Exposure to freezing temperatures may cause frostbite. Predisposing factors include advanced age and diseases of the blood vessels, cigarette smoking, consumption of alcohol, and use of constrictive clothing or poorly fitting shoes.

Ice crystals form in affected tissues, most often the nose, ears, fingers, and toes. The skin is initially red, with a prickling or itchy sensation. There may be a sense of numbness and/or clumsiness. The affected area may feel like a piece of wood. Joints become stiff, their movement progressively slowed. With continuous exposure the skin turns white, yellow, or mottled blue, with a firm waxy feel. There may be paralysis, with numbness or pain.

Injury from frostbite is much like a burn and is graded accordingly:

First degree frostbite: freezing of the topmost layer of skin without blistering or peeling. Numbness, redness, and swelling are usually present. Pain is minimal or absent once the area has been rewarmed.

Second degree frostbite: freezing with blistering or peeling, usually with a risk of infection from broken skin. It's often accompanied by pain after rewarming.

Third degree frostbite: freezing that causes complete skin death, with possible injury to deeper tissues. As with burns, there is no pain once the area is rewarmed. There is also no return of color or other sensation.

All second and third degree frostbite requires immediate medical attention.

Treatment of Frostbite

Avoid treatment of frostbite if there is a risk of the thawed area refreezing. *Do not attempt to thaw a frostbitten extremity until you can assure no further risk of cold injury.* The frozen extremity should be splinted and wrapped loosely in a dry dressing. Assume hypothermia may exist and treat for hypothermia as needed before beginning frostbite treatment (see "hypothermia" below).

Seek shelter where warmth and proper care can be maintained as soon as possible when any frostbite occurs. Once in a safe environment, rewarm frostbitten areas quickly to minimize injury.

Procedure for Rewarming Frostbitten Tissue

If warm water is available, immerse the frostbitten area in warm circulating water at about 104-106 degrees Fahrenheit (40-41 degrees centigrade). This should feel hot, but not so hot that prolonged immersion causes pain or burning. Test the water first with an elbow or other area with normal sensation, or have someone else test the temperature. Rewarming takes about 20–30 minutes. Stop rewarming when the skin becomes pink or feeling returns. Encourage active motion of the frostbitten extremity. Exercising fingers and toes increases circulation. Never massage an injured area.

There may be a great deal of pain with the rewarming process. Pain medication such as Vicodin or Tylenol with codeine may be necessary.

If water is not available, wrap the affected areas in warm blankets or additional clothing. Warm fingers and hands under armpits. When toes or heels are affected, it's necessary to remove footwear, dry and rewarm the feet and re-cover with dry socks. Never rewarm frostbitten areas by rubbing them, especially with snow. Don't use dry heat from a campfire. There is decreased sensation to the injured area and either method may cause further damage.

After re-warming the injured extremity, cover it with a warm, dry, clean dressing. Keep it elevated, as swelling will progress for 48-72 hours afterward. Ibuprofen or another nonsteroidal anti-inflammatory medication can be given.

Other guidelines:

1. leave blisters unbroken to protect against infection;

2. use sterile gauze or Vaseline gauze between toes and fingers to keep them separated if needed;

3. protect against infection in the same manner as for equivalent burn injuries. If the skin is broken, apply

antibiotic ointment and cover with a sterile, non-stick dressing such as Vaseline gauze.

After rewarming get medical attention immediately , especially for second or third degree injury. Signs include:

1. blistering or broken skin;

2. moist, oozing skin with pain or swelling;

3. areas which remain white, darken in color, or become numb or cool.

Following injury from frostbite, watch for secondary bacterial infection (see p.185).

Hypothermia

Hypothermia occurs due to overexposure to the cold, when body temperature falls below normal. Alcohol consumption is frequently a contributing cause. Victims of accidents (especially near-drownings) often suffer from hypothermia. However excessive heat loss can happen to anyone who is poorly clothed, tired, and hungry on cold, wet, windy days. Diabetics, the elderly, and people with cardiovascular disease are particularly vulnerable to the cold.

The earliest sign of hypothermia is shivering. It may become uncontrollable and then, after several hours, stop completely as the stores of fuel for the muscles (glycogen) are used up. Progressive symptoms of hypothermia are lethargy, lack of coordination, not keeping up with activities, slurred speech, mental confusion, and inappropriate behavior, followed by fatigue, sleepiness, unconsciousness, and death.

Treatment

Always treat the hypothermic person gently. Never rewarm a person too quickly as this can cause heart problems which may be fatal. First obtain shelter. Replace wet clothing with dry. Insulate the person totally. Use a blanket or sleeping bag to warm the person up. Place a pad, sleeping bag, or blanket under the person to avoid contact with a cold surface. Apply insulated hot water bottles, if available, to the neck, groin, and chest. Be careful not to burn the skin. As an alternative use your own body heat by snuggling close to the person if required. Unless the victim is unconscious, warm sweet drinks may be given but avoid alcohol and caffeine, and tobacco use as well. *Obtain medical help as quickly as possible.*

Surviving Animal Hazards

20

Marine Hazards

Marine life presents a variety of challenges to the traveler. Creatures can cut, sting, bite, and puncture, frequently adding insult to injury by injecting poison for good measure. Even being at the top of the food chain does not confer immunity from contaminated sea food, which causes several types of poisoning with unique characteristics. In addition wounds acquired in the marine environment, usually while swimming or bathing in warm or tropical water, frequently become infected and require diligent care.

Wound care

Wounds should be irrigated with large amounts of soap and water. Remove all foreign material. Unless severe, closure of wounds is contraindicated and should not be attempted. If secondary bacterial infection occurs, use one of the following antibiotics:

1. Cipro (ciprofloxacin) 500 mg. orally twice a day for 10 days; **or**

2. Augmentin 500 mg. orally three times a day for 10 days; **or**

3. Septra DS (Bactrim DS) orally twice a day for 10 days (*do not take if allergic to sulfa*).

Stings and Envenomations

These can generally be prevented by being careful while engaging in water sports and activities. Avoid handling, playing with, or- whenever possible- stepping on sea life.

Stingrays and Other Fish

Stings from fish with venomous spines are fairly common. They can occur from a variety of species with local or widespread geographic distribution. All have one or more bony spines covered with an envenoming sheath.

Stingrays cause most incidents as they often nestle in shallow, sandy bays or near beaches when warm waters are likely to be shared by bathers. When disturbed, the serrated spine at the base of their lashing tail may cause either a ragged cut or a small puncture wound. Frequently part of the sheath, or on rare occasions even a broken spine, remains embedded in the tissues. All of this material must be removed.

Other species with venomous spines include dogfish, catfish, weeverfish (in the Atlantic and Mediterranean), scorpionfish (widely found in tropical and temperate seas, especially around coral reefs), and stonefish. The latter is a coral reef dweller of the tropical Indian and Pacific oceans.

Symptoms

From any of these fish, tissue damage may occur locally at the site of the sting. The main effect though is immediate and severe pain. Without treatment it may increase in intensity for up to an hour or more, then subside over several hours or even days. Deaths from stonefish have occurred.

Treatment

The toxins of all these species are *heat sensitive*. The most effective treatment for stings is immersion of the affected part in hot water. The water should be as hot as can be tolerated without causing a burn. Relief from pain is usually instantaneous.

Soaking should continue for 60–90 minutes or until most of the pain is gone. To maintain an effective but tolerable water temperature, it's best to let the injured person regulate the addition of hot water to the soaks. This reduces the possibility of a burn injury.

Take 1 or 2 aspirin or Tylenol up to 4 times a day for pain, or a nonsteroidal anti-inflammatory such as ibuprofen or naproxen. Obtain a tetanus booster if needed, and watch for secondary infection (see p. 185). If parts of the sheath or spine remain, obtain medical help for their removal. Ragged cuts may require Steri- strips (p. 182) or suturing, which should be done within 8 hours of the injury.

Prevention

If caught when fishing, cut scorpionfish off the line and never handle them. Avoid stingrays by shuffling your feet noisily through flat, sandy bottoms. Don't step, run, or jump in suspect areas.

One of the authors, crossing a shallow channel in Baja California waters known to be infested with stingrays, nonetheless suffered a sting and laceration in spite of faithfully doing the "stingray shuffle." Further protective measures were then copied from a local group of research scientists. They employed a long stick, waving it through the water and sand to clear a path ahead of them in the shallow channels.

Jellyfish

Jellyfish have tentacles covered with nematocysts –

microscopic envenomating stingers. A single tentacle may fire hundreds of these on contact. Only a few actually penetrate the skin, creating a red raised welt or lesion, usually in one or more discontinuous lines surrounded by inflamed tissue.

Symptoms

Pain may be severe and itching is common. Occasionally there may be headache, nausea, weakness, sweating, and watering of the eyes and nose.

Prevention

You can often avoid incidents by knowledge of seasonal occurrence of jellyfish in local areas, and by noting the presence of jellyfish washed ashore. These shouldn't be handled. Nematocysts are capable of discharging their poison for up to several hours out of the water.

Treatment

Pour ocean water over the injured area. Don't rinse with fresh water or let remaining bits of tentacle dry out, as this causes more nematocysts to discharge into the skin. If present, remove the tentacles with gloved hands or an instrument such as a knife blade or piece of wood. Saturate the area with either a mixture of baking soda and water for 10 minutes, or vinegar, rubbing alcohol, dilute ammonia, or Domeboro's solution for 30 minutes. Then sprinkle baking soda, flour, or dry sand on the injured area. Scrape, don't rub, this off with a knife blade or other instrument. Wash the area again with salt water. Apply Itch Balm Plus to reduce itching, swelling, and pain. In Australia, antivenom is available for treatment of stings from certain species of jellyfish.

Stinging Corals and Sea Anemones

If you touch stinging corals and sea anemones, they can produce a localized red rash. If necessary, treat as indicated for jellyfish stings.

Cone Shells

Cone shells found in tropical and subtropical regions can inject poison through a single, dart-like tooth. Shell collectors are the most frequent victims. Injuries can occur through clothing, such as a shirt, blouse, or pants pocket.

Symptoms may include localized pain, redness, and numbness at the site of injection. Giddiness, double-vision, difficulty in swallowing or speaking, and difficulty in breathing can occur in severe reactions. Recovery is usual, although fatal respiratory failure has occurred.

Treatment

First aid measures are of little value. In areas where highly toxic reactions have been noted, primarily in the Indian ocean and South Pacific, obtain medical attention.

Other Marine Hazards

Sea Urchins

Sea urchins are found worldwide. Their spines can break off in the skin, making them very difficult to remove. Symptoms include intense local pain and inflammation, with redness, swelling and local muscle aches. When multiple spines are present there may be nausea, vomiting, abdominal pain, and local numbness and tingling. There have even been a few deaths.

Prevention.

Don't walk in areas where urchins are present, especially where the bottom is rocky or there are rocky or coral patches. Never walk on coral. Most footwear will not provide protection against sharp spines if you step directly on an urchin. Don't assume that because people are surfing in an area, it's safe for bathers. Anyone with a board can float over the sea urchins you will find with your foot.

Treatment

Immerse the affected area in hot water for 30-90 minutes. Remove spines immediately or they may cause infection or destructive tissue changes. Deeply imbedded spines require surgical removal under local anesthesia.

If superficial spines can't be pulled or worked out, they can sometimes be dissolved by vinegar soaks, 3–4 times a day for 10–20 minutes. Apply wet vinegar compresses between soaks. After spines are removed, clean the wound thoroughly and watch for secondary bacterial infection.

Contaminated Sea Food

Scombroid poisoning is relatively common. It occurs following consumption of a variety of fish, including albacore, mackerel, bonita, wahoo, bluefin and yellowfin tuna, mahi mahi, sardines, black marlin and anchovies. When inadequately preserved or refrigerated, bacterial contamination of the fish results in a release of histamine-like substances which are not destroyed by cooking, canning, or smoking. Affected fish may have a sharp metallic or peppery taste, or an odor of ammonia.

Symptoms

Symptoms usually begin within 90 minutes of ingestion. They may include flushing, usually of the face, neck and upper torso, rapid heart rate, red eyes, nausea, vomiting, abdominal pain, headache, itching, and hives. Death is rare and symptoms usually resolve within 12 hours.

Treatment

Seek immediate medical treatment. In isolated areas, oral antihistamines may help alleviate symptoms. Take one of the following, listed in order of preference, while seeking medical attention:

1. Allegra 60 mg. orally twice a day; **or**

2. Claritin 10 mg. orally once a day; **or**

3. Zyrtec 10 mg. orally once a day; **or**

one of the antihistamines that produce drowsiness as a common side effect:

4. Benadryl (diphenhydramine HCl) 25–50 mg. orally, every 4–6 hours; **or**

5. Atarax (hydroxyzine HCl) 10–25 mg. orally, every 4–6 hours.

Ciguatera Poisoning

Poisoning can occur from eating certain tropical reef fish, usually between 35° north and south latitude. The fish most often involved are red snapper, grouper, barracuda, amberjack, surgeonfish, sea bass, and moray eel. Toxin is especially concentrated in the eggs (roe). Because of the way the toxin concentrates, there have even been a few cases of ciguatera poisoning passed sexually, from husband to wife.

Ciguatera poisoning occurs sporadically in all subtropical and tropical areas of the Pacific and Indian oceans, and in the West Indies. Outbreaks are episodic, often thought to occur after storms, changes in currents, or other natural or even man-made disturbances of the coral reef systems.

Prevention

Unfortunately there's no way to identify affected fish, and the toxin itself is not destroyed by heat. The only preventive measure is to avoid eating large reef fish or those fish in the area known to be toxic.

Symptoms

Ciguatera poisoning involves some very distinctive symptoms. The onset occurs from 15 minutes to 24 hours but usually within 1-3 hours following ingestion of the toxic fish. Symptoms may be more severe in individuals who have experienced previous ciguatera poisoning.

The symptoms can be quite variable and include:

- tingling or numbness of the mouth;

- dizziness, blurred vision, or temporary blindness;

- reversal of hot and cold sensations.

When present, these neurological symptoms can be disabling for weeks, months, or even years. Other common symptoms are:

- diarrhea, vomiting, and abdominal cramps;

- sweating, chills, muscle and joint pain.

Though rare, in very severe cases death may occur from respiratory paralysis.

Treatment
Obtain medical care if symptoms suggest ciguatera poisoning after eating reef fish. Treatment measures are primarily supportive.

Treatment in isolated areas
If available, use syrup of ipecac to induce vomiting. For itching take cool baths or showers and an oral antihistamine (see pp. 389 – 390); Tylenol is useful for headaches. Drink plenty of fluids. Medical care should be obtained as soon as possible.

Recovery
Avoid eating fish and shellfish products, drinking alcoholic beverages, or eating nuts and nut oils. All of these can potentially worsen symptoms. *Following recovery, ingestion of alcohol and physical or emotional stress may cause a recurrence.*

Fresh Water Hazards – See Schistosomiasis and Leptospirosis, pp. 85 – 86.

Spiders and Scorpions

Spider Bites

Spiders are almost universally venomous, but only a few have fangs long or strong enough to penetrate human skin. Among these, the two most often responsible for injury are the black widow spider and the brown recluse or violin spider. Black widows are large, shiny black spiders with a red hourglass marking on their abdomens. Brown or violin spiders are light brown in color, marked with a violin shape on their backs. They are usually less than $1/2$ inch long. Fortunately, bites can often be prevented by observing a few precautions.

Prevention

Use gloves to protect the hands when working in areas commonly inhabited by spiders. These include woodpiles, garages, sheds, barns, and other rustic structures. If living or camping in rural areas, check clothing and shoes before putting them on. Netting used at night to prevent mosquito bites will also protect against other insects, including spiders.

In some rural areas, black widow bites occur more frequently in men than women. The spiders often establish webs in the darkness under outhouse seat covers, and they are sufficiently territorial to attack any anatomy which invades their space. Use a stick or broom handle to periodically dismantle these webs. The silk is very strong, tacky, and adherent, and can be easily rolled up onto the stick and discarded. Otherwise, exercise appropriate caution. This is a rude way to start the day after leisurely morning coffee.

Treatment

Many bites attributed to spiders are actually caused by mosquitos, fleas, bedbugs, ticks, or other insects. If a spider bite is witnessed, capture the spider in a jar or other container if possible. Obtain medical evaluation, taking the spider with you for identification. Ice placed on the bite often helps to reduce pain.

Any bite which becomes ulcerated (crater-like) requires medical treatment. This may indicate a bite from the brown or violin spider. Whether or not from a spider bite **any ulcerated skin lesion requires medical evaluation.**

Scorpions

Most scorpions are small, nocturnal, and not particularly shy about sharing human space or accessories. This includes shoes, pants, sleeping bags, and bed linen. As with spider bites, many scorpion stings can be prevented by observing a few precautions.

Prevention

Encounters with scorpions are more likely at night, particularly after rain or periods of high humidity. Always check bedding at night before retiring. Anything crawling on you in the dark should be quickly flicked or brushed off rather than swatted or smashed. Mosquito netting might even be necessary at night when camping in some remote areas. In the morning, inspect and shake out shoes, socks, pants, and other apparel before use.

Most stings occur to the hands or feet. Wear gloves and boots when handling or moving rocks, logs, firewood, or lumber, or working around sheds or barns.

Treatment

The majority of stings, especially in adults, cause only a local reaction with redness, swelling, or pain. Apply ice to the sting to reduce pain, and keep the area below the level of the heart. **If more severe symptoms develop, get medical attention as soon as possible.** Antivenom is available locally in parts of the world where it's sometimes needed, primarily Mexico, North Africa, India, and the Middle East. Be especially cautious in these areas.

Stings from Flying Insects

Bees, wasps, hornets, yellow jackets, and ants of the order *hymenoptera* are a major threat to hypersensitive individuals because of anaphylaxis, a fatal allergic reaction. In the nonallergic, stings may be painful but are not life- threatening. The pain is immediate, quickly followed by swelling and redness which may last 2–3 days. Symptoms subside gradually.

The risk of stings can be reduced by wearing light colored clothing and protective footwear. Avoid open sandals, bright clothing, shiny jewelry, and perfumes.

Removal of a Stinger

Any stinger left in the skin should be carefully teased, scraped, or flicked out with a pin, pointed knife, or fingernail. **Don't** use tweezers or fingers. This is likely to squeeze out more venom from the poison sac attached to the stinger.

Treatment

Use the "Extractor" in your first aid kit to suction out as much venom as possible. Then apply an ice pack to the site to relieve pain and slow absorption of the toxin, and elevate an affected extremity to reduce swelling. For swelling and pain take an antihistamine. Try one of the non-sedating antihistamines such as:

1. Allegra 60 mg. orally twice a day; **or**

2. Claritin 10 mg. orally once a day; **or**

3. Zyrtec 10 mg. orally once a day; **or**

one of the antihistamines that produce drowsiness as a common side effect:

4. Benadryl (diphenhydramine HCl) 25–50 mg. orally, every 4–6 hours; **or**

5. Atarax (hydroxyzine HCl) 10–25 mg. orally, every 4–6 hours.

Local reactions to a sting can include localized redness, swelling, itching, and pain. After removing the stinger and cleansing the area apply ice or cool cloth to the area. Soothing lotions such as calamine, Domeboro's solution, or a paste of baking soda and water applied to the sting often help to relieve discomfort. Applying raw onion to the site is reputed to be effective — worth a try in a pinch.

For severe swelling, obtain medical evaluation and treatment.

Hypersensitivity Reactions

Increasingly severe responses to subsequent stings is an indication of a hypersensitivity reaction. Each sting further sensitizes the individual to the venom. A local reaction greater than 6 inches (15 cm) across, and redness, swelling, or itching in areas other than the sting site, are early signs of allergic reaction. Headache, nausea, abdominal pain or cramps, and weak rapid pulse, wheezing, or labored breath are signs of advancing severity. Travelers who have experienced allergic reactions in the past should carry a Medic Alert identification bracelet or necklace (see p. 99).

Even with no prior history of allergy, **it's best to get medical attention immediately for any generalized reaction**, including skin reactions away from the sting area. There's a possibility of a life-threatening progression of symptoms.

Treatment of Hypersensitivity Reactions

In addition to the measures previously described, apply a loosely constricting band 3–4 inches above a sting on an extremity. Make sure 1 or 2 fingers can easily be slipped underneath and a pulse can be felt in the hand or foot beyond. Loosen this for 1 minute out of every 10, and move it 2–4 inches above any swelling that occurs. **Obtain transportation to medical care immediately.** Obtain an allergy kit for future use.

Emergency treatment for stings in known hypersensitive individuals.

If you're stung, use your allergy kit as directed, or follow these steps:

1. Immediately give the injectable epinephrine (and repeat after 15 – 20 minutes if symptoms persist).

2. Take the oral antihistamine (usually 50 mg. of Benadryl).

3. Apply the loosely constricting band 3–4 inches above a sting on an extremity as previously described.

4. Remove the stinger if present by flicking, not squeezing. Then use the "Extractor" to remove the venom.

5. Apply ice or a cold compress.

6. Get medical attention promptly, keeping the affected area *below the level of the heart*.

Use of epinephrine

Don't use inhalants. Absorption is too low to counteract a serious allergic reaction. Epinephrine **must** be injected. If unsure about or reluctant to use the epinephrine injection, **use it anyway**. The oral antihistamine alone will not save your life in a severe reaction, but epinephrine will. In severe reactions, wheezing or respiratory difficulty is an ominous sign and can develop within 5 minutes of the sting. Oral medications will not begin to work before 15–45 minutes. Effective first aid requires both medications if you have a history of allergic reaction. After using the epinephrine, immediate medical attention is still needed for further evaluation and treatment. *If you have angina, use the epinephrine with the prior consent of your physician and only in emergencies.*

Snakebite

Like some of the tropical diseases, snakebite is primarily an occupational hazard. In industrialized countries most bites occur to snake handlers. Elsewhere, particularly in the tropics, farmers or others who work the land in rural areas are the likely victims of venomous land snakes. Net fishermen are the most frequent victims of sea snakes.

The possibility of snakebite should not be of great concern unless you plan to spend extended time traveling or working in rural areas where snakes are a known hazard. Even then, by following suitable precautions and knowing emergency medical procedures, you should be reasonably safe from this hazard.

Prevention

1. Avoid the unnecessary capture, killing, or harassment of snakes. Even after suffering fatal injuries, including decapitation, venomous snakes are capable of injecting venom.

2. Always wear closed shoes and protective clothing outdoors in rural areas.

3. Take clear paths and avoid tall grass, bushes, or heavy groundcover and walk slowly.

4. Keep hands and feet out of places that can't be seen, as when climbing ledges or stepping over logs.

5. Inspect clothes, shoes, and bedding before use when camping.

6. When walking at night, wear shoes and use a flashlight.

7. Know the first aid measures for snake bites.

8. **Know the location of the nearest clinic or source of anti-venom.**

9. When fishing, always cut sea snakes from a fishing line, **never** handle them.

Snakebite — an Unpredictable Event

The degree of poisoning from the bite of a

venomous snake isn't predictable. The amount of venom injected and the individual's response to it vary greatly. About 25% of bites from venomous snakes are "dry bites" — no venom is injected at all.

For purposes of treating snakebite assume that all bites are venomous until proven otherwise. **Medical attention should be obtained as quickly as possible.** Antivenom is always the treatment of choice when poisoning from snakebite has occurred. The quicker you obtain it, the better the chance of minimizing tissue damage or preventing death.

Types of Poisonous Snakes

There are three broad classes of poisonous snakes: vipers, cobras, and sea snakes. Vipers are represented in North America by rattlesnakes; in Central and South America by the tropical rattlesnake, fer de lance, and bushmaster; and in Central and South Africa by the common puff adder. Cobras, such as the yellow cobra, spitting cobra, Egyptian cobra, and black mamba, are present in Central and South Africa. Cobras are also found in the Far East, including India and Southeast Asia. Sea snakes are found in the Pacific Ocean, but not in the Atlantic.

Viper Poisoning

Bites that result in immediate local swelling and edema (accumulation of fluid) are usually unmistakable signs of viper poisoning. These signs appear within 3–5 minutes, often after only a minute or two. Pain, redness, and bleeding at the site of the fang marks are common. Other signs of envenomation include a metallic taste in the mouth, and tingling in the back, ears, or around the mouth. If no symptoms develop within 30 minutes following a viper bite, *it's unlikely that envenomation has occurred.*

When viper poisoning does occur, untreated cases may lead to progressive swelling and destruction of local tissue. In severe cases, there may be generalized symptoms such as vomiting, abnormal bleeding, difficulty breathing, circulatory collapse, and death.

Cobra and Sea Snake Poisoning

Unlike vipers, the bites of sea snakes and most cobras produce little or no local swelling. When these symptoms do occur, it's usually not for 1–2 hours or more following the bite.

Severe sea snake poisoning may produce generalized muscle aches within $1^1/_2 – 3$ hours. This can progress to muscle paralysis and death. Cobra venom may cause numbness or tingling and weakness of the bitten extremity. Drooping eyelids are often the first sign of general poisoning, with slurred speech, increasing muscle weakness, lethargy, and paralysis. This may progress to respiratory failure. Signs of cobra poisoning can occur within 15 minutes, or be delayed up to 10 hours.

First Aid for Snakebites

Some first aid measures formerly recommended are more likely to harm than to help. Do not use incision, suction, heat, ice or cold water, any form of electrical stimulus, or a tourniquet so tight it reduces arterial blood flow. A snakebite victim should **never** drink alcoholic beverages, which speed absorption of venom into the general circulation. Identification of the snake may be helpful, but do not waste time or risk further injury trying to capture or kill the snake. Get the victim to medical care and antivenom treatment as quickly as possible-it may be the only way to prevent significant harm or death.

Compression wraps and splints

Most snake bites occur on the extremities, especially feet, ankles, hands, and arms. The goal of first aid is to limit spread of the venom through the blood and lymph. To accomplish this *keep the victim perfectly still,* since even faint muscle movements will spread venom. A

companion should then apply a compression wrap and
splint the extremity.

For compression, use a 3-6 inch wide elastic wrap
(Ace wrap) or crepe bandage (such as Coban) and wrap
firmly just as you would to support a sprained ankle or
wrist. Bandage upwards from the lower portion of the
bitten limb. Wrap the entire limb if possible, then splint
the joints- ankle and knee, or elbow in conjunction with
a sling. Use the Sam splint or any other available splint-
ing material (branch, spade handle, walking stick, rolled
up newspaper, etc.). Once placed, the compression bandage should not be removed except by medical personnel
at a treatment center where antivenom is available.

Loosely Constrictive Bands

Never use a tourniquet — a band so tight that it interferes with arterial blood flow. However if a compression wrap and splint are not available, a loosely constricting band applied 2–4 inches above the bite may be
helpful. It's purpose is to restrict the flow of blood and
lymph back to the heart. This may delay symptoms of
general poisoning until antivenom can be obtained. The
band, preferably at least 1–2 inches wide, should be
loose enough so a finger can easily be slipped underneath. You should be able to feel a pulse in the foot, ankle, or wrist below the band.

Other First Aid Measures

In most cases of snakebite the victim will need reas-
surance and calming. After moving away from the
snake, have the person lie down and rest to avoid all
muscle movement. Remove rings, watches, and constrictive clothing from an affected extremity. Apply a compression wrap and splint, then keep the victim as still as
possible during transport to the nearest source of antivenom. Use a stretcher or help carry the person if necessary. Use blankets to prevent the victim from shivering
only in cold environments. If it is eventually established

that poisoning did not occur and antivenom is unnecessary, bites can then be treated and cleansed like any other puncture wound. Obtain a tetanus shot if necessary and watch for secondary infection.

Ticks - see pp. 205 – 206.

Animal Bites

Avoid contact with or be cautious around animals, especially mammals. Animal behavior can be unpredictable. Carnivorous (meat-eating) mammals may carry rabies. Animals may also carry both ticks and fleas which can spread a number of infectious diseases. Avoid any animals that appear sick or dead. These may be particularly infectious.

While traveling any bites from animals, including dogs and cats, should be scrubbed aggressively with soap and water as soon as possible. Then seek medical evaluation immediately for rabies vaccine and a tetanus shot if needed. Bites should also be treated with antibiotics. The recommended treatment schedules are as follows.

Dog bites

1. Augmentin 875 mg. orally twice a day for 10 days *or* Augmentin 500 mg. orally three times a day for 10 days; **or**

2. clindamycin 300 mg. orally 4 times a day for 10 days **plus** Cipro (ciprofloxacin) 500 mg. orally twice a day for 10 days. Ofloxacin 400 mg. or norfloxacin 400 mg. may be substituted for the 500 mg. of Cipro.

Cat bites

1. Augmentin 875 mg. orally twice a day for 10 days *or* Augmentin 500 mg. orally three times a day for 10 days; **or**

Quick Reference:
Emergency First Aid Treatment
of Venomous Snakebite

1. Assume that every bite is a serious medical emergency and immediately begin first aid measures.

2. Move away from the snake, then sit or lie down, remain calm, and minimize all movement.

3. Remove rings, jewelry, or any other constrictive items from an affected extremity.

4. Apply a compression dressing. Wrap an elastic or crepe bandage up an affected limb, as firmly as you would to support a sprain (p. 401).

5. Splint the limb to prevent movement.

6. Proceed immediately to a medical facility where antivenom is available.

7. Keep the victim as still as possible during transport. Use a stretcher or help carry the person if necessary. When alone, walk slowly towards help, resting periodically.

8. Do not use incision, suction, or ice on the bite, or a tourniquet on an affected limb.

2. Ceftin (cefuroxime) 500 mg. orally twice a day for 10 days; **or**

3. doxycycline 100 mg. orally twice a day for 10 days (*do not take doxycycline if allergic to tetracycline*).

Bat, raccoon or skunk bites

1. Augmentin 875 mg. orally twice a day for 10 days *or* Augmentin 500 mg. orally three times a day for 10 days; **or**

2. doxycycline 100 mg. orally twice a day for 10 days (*do not take doxycycline if allergic to tetracycline*).

Human bites

1. Augmentin 875 mg. orally twice a day for 5 days; **or**

2. clindamycin 300 mg. orally 4 times a day for 10 days **plus** *either* Septra DS orally twice a day for 10 days *or* Cipro 500 mg. orally twice a day for 10 days.

Injuries from Monkeys

Monkeys are found throughout tropical countries. They may be kept as pets, used in work (like organ grinder monkeys), or found in their natural habitat. Monkey related injuries occur more often than people think and can pose serious medical problems from infectious diseases, including rabies. Following any bite or scratch, scrub the area immediately with soap and water. Then seek immediate medical attention.

Old world monkeys found in Asia, SE Asia, and Africa that are part of the macaque family (which includes the rhesus and cynomolgus monkeys) are known to carry a form of herpes virus called herpes simian B virus or simply "B virus". It manifests in monkeys much as herpes does in humans, causing a type of cold sore in the mouth or a genital lesion. However when humans contract this virus, usually through a monkey bite or scratch, it can cause a potentially fatal infection of the brain. Unfortunately, many doctors are unaware of the B virus hazards.

If small fluid filled blisters appear at the site of a monkey bite or scratch, or if neurological symptoms (numbness, tingling, weakness, lethargy, confusion, coma) develop, immediate medical attention is required. Evaluation may include blood tests, culturing of the injured site, and consideration of antiviral medications. This is not a trivial concern since this infection can cause death or require lifelong therapy.

In addition monkeys are known to carry other diseases such as simian immunodeficiency virus (SIV), the simian version of the virus that causes AIDS in humans. While the true impact of these viruses in humans remains unknown, it is prudent to avoid contact with these closely related animals.

One of our travel patients was bitten by a monkey which was kept chained in an Indonesian hotel lobby. Another traveler in Africa was bitten on both calves by monkeys when her neighbor on an adjacent veranda was feeding the animals. Another patient was bitten on the arm while trying to feed monkeys at the monkey caves in northern Thailand. In each case various infectious diseases, including rabies, had to be considered in the medical evaluation.

Prevention

Avoid trying to feed, pet, or play with any monkey, tame or wild. This is equally advisable when visiting tourist areas where monkeys are found, such as the monkey caves in Thailand, the monkey temples in Nepal, and similar places. Do not carry food on you or with you, as the monkeys can become quite aggressive, inflicting bites and scratches while attempting to relieve you of lunch.

Treatment of Monkey Bites

Scrub thoroughly with soap and water immediately. Seek medical attention for consideration of rabies vaccine, a tetanus shot (if more then 5 years since your last one), and evaluation for herpes simian B virus exposure. The latter may require use of an antiviral medication, Valtrex (valacyclovir).

In remote areas if secondary bacterial infection occurs (see p. 185), start antibiotics. Use one of the following:

1. Augmentin 500 mg. orally, 3 times per day for 10 days; **or**

2. clindamycin 300 mg. orally 4 times a day for 10 days **plus** Cipro (ciprofloxacin) 500 mg. orally twice a day for 10 days. Ofloxacin 400 mg. or norfloxacin 400 mg. may be substituted for the 500 mg. of Cipro.

In remote areas if signs of herpes simian B virus occur such as vesicular lesions at the site of the bite start an anti-viral herpes medication as soon as possible and continue taking it while seeking medical evaluation. Take either:

1. Valtrex 500 mg. orally twice a day **or**

2. Acyclovir 400 mg. orally 3 times a day.

While monkeys are often considered cute or interesting, it probably is best to keep a distance from these as well as other wild animals, for the sake of all species concerned.

Dealing with Insomnia

21

At one time or another almost everyone experiences difficulty falling or staying asleep. Causes can be emotional (anxiety, grief, or depression), physiological (stimulants such as the caffeine in coffee, colas, or tea), or environmental (noisy neighbors, barking dogs). For jet lag related sleep disorders see pp. 21 – 24.

In new environments you may encounter unaccustomed barriers to a good night's sleep: strange hotels, dripping faucets, lumpy mattresses with sinkhole springs, hot sticky tropical nights, buzzing mosquitos, itchy bites or rashes, crowing roosters, and even intestinal parasites. Just thinking about it is enough to keep you awake at night.

Treatment

It's important to remember that a night without sleep will not cause any harm. Worrying about lost sleep can easily entertain you past daybreak.

The easiest bad habit to acquire following recurrent insomnia is the use of alcohol as a sedative at night. This produces a poor quality, unrestful sleep. The accumulating anxiety about restless sleep can continue the pattern of alcohol use in a vicious circle. Use of alcohol frequently wakes people up in the middle of the night with dehydration, thirst, and the need to urinate. Returning to sleep is often a struggle without additional quantities of alcohol. It's easy to see that this is a self-defeating and unhealthy endeavor.

Don't

1. Drink alcohol regularly as a sedative before bedtime.

2. Drink stimulants with caffeine (coffee, colas, many teas) in the evening.

3. Take an afternoon nap.

4. Use prescription or over-the-counter sleeping pills on a regular basis, as they may be habit forming.

5. Combine alcohol with sleeping pills or other sedatives — ever.

6. Exercise just prior to sleep.

Do:

1. Establish a regular time to retire for the night and a relaxing nighttime ritual. This may be showering or bathing, reading a book or magazine, or other quiet activity.

2. Get out of bed if you're not sleepy. Do something productive but not overly stimulating — listen to the radio, or do some light reading by low, soft light.

As a last resort, an antihistamine that produces drowsiness as a side effect may help. Try 25–50 mg. of Benadryl or 3 mg. of melatonin an hour or so before bedtime. This may cause a "hangover" feeling the next morning. Sleeping pills are occasionally used for treating insomnia, especially if related to jet lag (see pp. 21 – 24).

Indications for Medical Evaluation

When nothing works and insomnia continues, sleeplessness may be due to intestinal parasites. This can occur with or without other symptoms. Stool exams should be obtained (see Chapter 8, "Quick Reference — Stool Exams," p. 258–259; if positive for parasites see treatment schedules on the same page.) For chronic insomnia obtain medical evaluation.

Returning Home <u>22</u>

Following even a brief visit out of the country, travelers with symptoms of illness may require medical evaluation. Get medical attention for the following:

1. Any recurrent fever. This requires immediate evaluation. Fever accompanied by jaundice, or which occurs after handling parrots or ingesting unpasteurized milk products, also requires immediate attention.

2. Diarrhea or other intestinal problems such as bloating, abdominal cramping, nausea, vomiting, and constipation. These symptoms require stool tests for parasites (stool O & P- ova and parasites) and bacteria (stool C & S — culture and sensitivity). You may also need a blood test for hepatitis.

3. Any other symptom of illness, including a skin rash, requires evaluation.

Notify your medical provider of your travel itinerary, especially after visiting areas of risk for malaria, schistosomiasis, or other diseases. It may be helpful to see a specialist in travel medicine or infectious diseases who is knowledgeable in tropical medicine. If you took any medication prophylactically (preventively), or received treatment, vaccinations, or medications for any illness while traveling, provide this information to your physician.

Routine Tests

Even if symptoms of illness aren't present, some routine tests are desirable to make sure you weren't accompanied by unwanted stowaways.

For Brief Travel up to 3–4 weeks

No tests are necessary in the absence of any symptoms.

For Travel of 1–6 Months

The following routine tests are recommended:

1. stool test for parasites (O & P);

2. Tuberculosis (TB) skin test (PPD) 2–3 months after returning home. If positive, a chest x-ray should then be done to ensure there is no active disease.

If there were any casual sexual contacts, blood tests (RPR) for syphilis, hepatitis B and C, and HIV are also recommended. For exposure to fresh water in areas where schistosomiasis occurs, a blood test for schistosomiasis should be done.

For Travel of 6 Months or More

In addition to the above routine tests, we recommend a physical exam as well as the following:

1. blood tests — a complete blood count (CBC) and liver enzymes;

2. urinalysis;

3. dental checkup.

For Travel of More Than 1 Year:

1. If over age 50, a complete physical exam and routine laboratory tests, plus a TB test and stool tests.

For women:

1. a pap smear and breast exam;
2. if over age 50, a mammogram.

Reentry Shock:

Returning Home After Extended Travel

Coming home to familiar surroundings may seem mundane compared to the challenge of living in a foreign culture. Surprisingly, it can be just as demanding. Some studies suggest that the easier it is adjusting to life in a foreign country, the more difficult it may be readjusting to life back home. This phenomenon is called "reentry shock."

Some symptoms are remarkably similar to culture shock. These include feelings of frustration, isolation, depression, or anger, often directed at your own culture. As with culture shock, symptoms develop slowly and may intensify over time.

One source of frustration is the difficulty others, including family and friends, are likely to have relating to your experiences. No matter how intense and important these seem, they may simply strike others as irrelevant. People may treat time spent outside the country as an interruption in your life, rather than as an integral part of it.

New perceptions about your homeland and other countries are apt to be met with polite tolerance, routine indifference, or outright hostility. People may also simply fail to understand. It may be that it is inherently difficult to share the ways in which you have outgrown your own culture's biases with people who haven't.

You may also have returned to a land less familiar

than anticipated. It's not uncommon to see your own culture in a new, perhaps profoundly different light. This too can produce a sense of isolation and alienation, especially if there's no one with whom to share thoughts and feelings.

As perceptions of your own culture change, so may your role within it. Returned travelers frequently redefine their goals and priorities, or re-evaluate their educational and career choices.

It is easy to mourn for the loss of a foreign country as if for a good friend, which it may well have become. The loss of excitement and adventure, freedom and independence, responsibilities or lack thereof, may seem at first inconsolable. Thoughts of return to the foreign country are common. In fact, return trips often prove cathartic, providing a needed perspective.

As with culture shock, coping with reentry shock requires patience. It takes time to integrate "foreign" experiences, to realize the meaning of those experiences within the context of your own culture. It takes time to assimilate new perceptions, reorder priorities, gain perspective.

The discomfort of reentry shock is one measure of the magnitude of change that has taken place. It is also an integral part of an ongoing process of change and growth.

Part III

Medications and How To Use Them

The medications listed in this section should be taken under the direction of a physician, unless medical care is unavailable and circumstances warrant. General guidelines provided here cover all medications noted in Parts I and II. The prescribed doses are only for acute illness in adults. They are not intended for long term use. Know the proper use and administration of any medication taken while traveling. Be familiar with contraindications and side effects, and follow any special instructions.

When possible the generic name of a drug has been provided along with the trade or brand name. Trade names are capitalized, generic names are not. The trade names of drugs in foreign countries often differ from U.S. trade names. If trouble is encountered finding a particular medicine, show the pharmacist or doctor the generic name. With this information it is often possible to obtain the correct medication.

How To Use Part III

We provide the following information for each medication:

1. **Uses**. A single medication can often be used for a variety of conditions. The uses covered here are only for those illnesses discussed in Parts I and II.

2. **Side effects -** mentioned are the most common ones associated with the medication. They may or may not occur. **For any unusual or severe reaction, stop the medication and seek medical advice.**

3. **Contraindications.** If a condition listed under contraindications applies to you, **don't** take the medication.

4. **How To Take.** Information is provided on the best way to take the medication for the maximum benefit with the fewest possible side effects.

Important Considerations

Dosages

All dosages are for adults only. When one medication is used to treat several different illnesses, dosages may vary. Check the specific illness in Parts I and II for the exact dosage.

In some cases, dosages must be calculated according to body weight. These dosages are usually given as milligrams per kilogram of body weight. To determine weight in kilograms, divide your weight in pounds by 2.2 (there are 2.2 pounds per kilogram). A pound-kilogram conversion table can be found in Appendix C p.471. If you're unsure of a dosage or dosage calculation, get help before taking the medication.

Most of the medications discussed in the book are taken by mouth; instructions read "take orally." A few medications and vaccinations must be given by intramuscular injection, abbreviated "IM."

Use of Multiple Medications

As a general rule, don't use more than one medication for the treatment of an illness or its symptoms, unless prescribed by a doctor or explicitly recommended in the book. This is especially true for antibiotics. Drugs taken together may interact harmfully. If a drug reaction does occur there is no way to tell which drug was responsible - all must be discontinued.

When taking medications regularly for chronic conditions, check with your doctor before departure. Find out if there are any drugs which shouldn't be taken in combination with your regular medications.

Routine Contraindications

Contraindications listed as "routine" for any drug in this section include the following:

History of allergic reaction

Prior to treatment, inform the medical practitioner, dentist, or pharmacist of any food and drug allergies you have. Read the ingredients in every medication before taking it. If you have ever had an allergic reaction to a medication or to any of its ingredients, **don't** use it!

Pregnancy

During pregnancy, inform any doctor, dentist, or pharmacist you consult of your condition. Avoid all medications unless specifically prescribed by a doctor. Definitive answers about drug safety during pregnancy and breast-feeding are frequently unavailable. Under medical supervision a medication may be prescribed when the practitioner judges that it is safe or the benefits outweigh potential risks.

Breast-feeding

Avoid all medications unless specifically prescribed by a doctor.

Allergic and Other Adverse Reactions

Allergic or other adverse drug reactions can take many forms, including itching, hives or other skin rash, headache, fever, chills, wheezing or difficulty breathing. **If a skin rash or any other unexpected or severe side effect occurs while taking a medication, stop taking it immediately. Obtain medical evaluation. Wheezing or difficulty breathing or swallowing requires immediate medical attention.**

Photosensitivity Reactions

Some topical and oral medications sensitize the skin to react strongly when exposed to sunlight. There are 2 common reactions:

1. **severe sunburn** (phototoxicity) - with redness, swelling, blisters, peeling, and increased pigmentation only on light-exposed areas of skin, usually within 6 hours of exposure; or

2. **allergic skin rash -** either hives, or a red, raised, scaly or blistery rash which can occur anywhere on the body, usually within 24-48 hours of sun exposure.

Don't stop a medication because of a photosensitivity reaction. Stay out of the sun to prevent the rash from becoming worse. Photosensitivity reactions can be prevented or decreased by using protective clothing (p.29) and a sunscreen which blocks out ultraviolet "A" (UV-A) sunlight. See "Sunscreens," p.30.

Treatment of photosensitivity reactions

Use cool compresses or cool baths, topical steroid ointments (hydrocortisone), or Itch Balm Plus. For severe reactions, get medical attention for possible oral steroid therapy.

Photosensitizing medications

The following is a partial list of medications that may cause a photosensitivity reaction.

Antibiotics:
>   tetracyclines including doxycycline
>   fluoroquinolones (Cipro, Levaquin, Ofloxin,
>   Noroxin)
>   nalidixic acid
>   sulfa drugs (Fansidar, Bactrim or Septra, Gantrisin)

Anti-inflammatory drugs (non steroid), including aspirin: see list p. 437.

Antiparasitic drugs:
>   Bitin (bithionol)
>   Povan (pyrvinium pamoate)
>   quinine

Sunscreens:
>   Some sunscreens may cause photosensitivity reactions!

Other medications:
   Diamox (a sulfa drug used for altitude sickness), some anticancer drugs, diuretics, seizure medications, and diabetic (oral hypoglycemic) medications may cause photosensitivity reactions. If you're taking any of these regularly, check with your doctor prior to any intense or prolonged sun exposure.

Medications by Category

   Medications are grouped according to usage. *We caution that due to space limitations, the information provided can not be considered comprehensive. It covers only some of the major side effects and contraindications. The final determination of when to treat must be between you and the prescribing physician.*

Altitude Sickness Medications

Δ Diamox (acetazolamide sodium)

Use of this medication doesn't eliminate the need for an immediate descent if severe symptoms of altitude sickness occur, such as pulmonary edema (HAPE).

Uses - prevention of altitude sickness

Side effects - cramping in hands and feet, drowsiness, fatigue, diarrhea, decreased appetite,
skin rashes, nausea, vomiting, tingling in extremities, taste alteration, especially carbonated beverages

Contraindications - routine (see p.417.) adrenal insufficiency, allergy to sulfa medications, electrolyte imbalance, hypersensitivity to thiazide diuretics, kidney disease, liver disease, lung disease, pulmonary obstruction
use cautiously if taking digoxin or other digitalis medications

How to take - Take orally, with food if stomach upset occurs. Don't take with aspirin, Pepto-Bismol, or sedatives.

Analgesics (Pain-killers)

Δ Aspirin (acetylsalicylic acid)

Uses - mild pain relief, reduce fever and inflammation

Side effects - stomach burning (mild to severe)
stop immediately if ringing in the ears occurs while taking aspirin

Contraindications - routine (see p.417); ulcers, history of ulcers, use of other anticoagulants such as Coumadin
Aspirin should not be used by children under age 18 either during or immediately following any viral infection (may cause Reye's syndrome)

How to take - Take orally with food or milk to reduce GI side effects. If side effects occur, stop the medication.
Studies have shown that the caffeine in some aspirin preparations may increase the effectiveness of aspirin.

Δ Pyridium (phenazopyridine HCl)

Uses - to stop painful burning sensations in urinary tract infections

Side effects - mild nausea or vomiting (occasionally) turns urine bright orange (color may stain clothing)
Contraindications - routine (see p. 417), impaired kidney function
How to take - Take orally with lots of fluids.

Δ Tylenol (acetaminophen)
Uses -mild pain relief
Side effects - liver damage in high doses or prolonged therapy (especially with extra strength preparations).
Contraindications - routine (see p. 417.), liver disease (hepatitis) or impaired liver function
How to take -Take orally.

Δ Tylenol With Codeine
Uses - moderate to severe pain relief
Side effects - constipation
Contraindications -routine (see p.417), liver disease (hepatitis) or impaired liver function
How to take - Take orally with lots of fluids. You may wish to take it with prune juice or another natural laxative, as it is frequently constipating.

Δ Vicodin (acetaminophen and hydrocodone bitartrate)
Uses - moderate to moderately severe pain
Side effects - anxiety, mood changes, decreased alertness and coordination, drowsiness, sedation, nausea, vomiting
Contraindications - routine (see p.417), use cautiously with impaired liver or kidney function, hypothyroidism, or prostate enlargement
How to take- take orally; avoid alcohol; avoid prolonged use as physical and psychological dependence may occur.

Antacids

Δ Amphojel, Mylanta, Riopan, Maalox, Tums and Many Others
Uses - Relief of acid indigestion, and stomach upset from hot spicy foods. Maalox Plus and Mylanta both contain simethicone, which also makes them useful for flatulence (gas).

Side effects - Antacids with aluminum hydroxide, aluminum carbonate and calcium carbonate may be constipating. Antacids containing primarily magnesium compounds tend to work as a laxative. Read carefully all ingredients before buying.

Contraindications - Anyone on a low salt diet should be careful to avoid antacids containing large amounts of sodium, including Alka Seltzer. Those with low amounts of sodium are Maalox, Mylanta, Riopan and Tums.

How to take — Take orally.

Δ Stomach Acid Inhibitors (H2-receptor inhibitors) - Axid (nizatidine), Pepcid (famotidine), Tagamet (cimetidine), Zantac (ranitidine), and others

Uses - Relief of acid indigestion, treatment of gastric and duodenal ulcers and esophagitis (inflammation of the esophagus) by blocking stomach acid secretion.

Side effects - Headache, dizziness, constipation and diarrhea with rare cases of low red or white blood cell counts and hives have occurred with these medications

Contraindications - Anyone with a known hypersensitivity to any medications in this class of H2 receptor inhibitors

How to take - Take orally

Δ Stomach Acid Inhibitors (acid (proton) pump inhibitors), Prilosec (omeprazole), Prevacid (lansoprazole), Nexium (esomeprazole), Protonix (pantoprazole), and Aciphex (rabeprazole).

Uses - Relief of acid indigestion, treatment of gastric and duodenal ulcers and esophagitis (inflammation of the esophagus) by stomach acid inhibition

Side effects - Headache, diarrhea, nausea, abdominal pain, dizziness, rash and constipation have occurred with these medications

Contraindications - Anyone with a known hypersensitivity to any medications in this class of acid pump inhibitors

How to take - Take orally in the morning before eating

Antibiotics

Antibiotics treat only bacterial infections. They are useless for illnesses due to viruses and other causes. **Never** take antibiotics for routine colds or trivial infections! Even for bacterial infections, antibiotics are **never** to be taken casually. Besides killing bacteria which cause infection, they frequently also kill beneficial bacteria. This may result in still other infections.

Vaginal yeast infections are a common occurrence following use of antibiotics. Women prone to yeast infections may wish to add vaginal yeast medications to their first aid kit.

All broad spectrum antibiotics are capable of causing a potentially serious inflammation of the intestines called pseudomembranous colitis. The condition ranges from minor to life-threatening. It may be indicated by diarrhea which develops either during or immediately following the use of antibiotics, and which fails to respond to treatment for traveler's diarrhea. If this occurs, obtain immediate medical evaluation.

Overuse or misuse of antibiotics can also result in the creation of organisms resistant to the antibiotic, rendering it ineffective. At best, this will complicate or delay treatment. At worst, it may result in serious illness or death.

Standby antibiotics

In general, infections should be evaluated by trained medical providers. Diagnosis should be made with the use of appropriate tests and cultures to identify the infecting agent.

Standby antibiotics should only be used by travelers who can not rapidly access appropriate medical evaluation. Most healthy travelers can carry Cipro (ciprofloxacin) or one of the other fluoroquinolones (see p. 426) for traveler's diarrhea. In remote areas other general antibiotics, such as azithromycin (Zithromax), cephalexin (Keflex), or clarithromycin (Biaxin) can be carried for emergency treatment of a majority of common infections. We strongly recommend that the final decision to carry antibiotics should be based on careful evaluation of your travel plans with a qualified medical provider or travel medicine specialist.

Use of Antibiotics

Dosages are not found in this section. Check treatment schedules for specific illnesses in Part II. Once an antibiotic is started, always take it for the full length of time prescribed. **Finish it!** This helps prevent both recurrence of illness and creation of organisms resistant to the medication. It's dangerous to stop taking antibiotics just because you're feeling better. *Stop antibiotics if an allergic reaction occurs* (see p. 418).

Δ Cephalosoporins

These are broad spectrum antibiotics that resemble the penicillins. They include:
Keflex (cephalexin) and Ceftin (cefuroxime)
Side effects -
nausea, vomiting, upset stomach, diarrhea, pseudomembranous colitis
Contraindications- routine (see p. 417). If allergic to penicillin or other cephalosporins, take cephalosporins only under the care of a physician. **Don't** take if you had an anaphylactic or severe reaction to penicillin.
Use cautiously in cases of impaired kidney function.
How to take -Take orally.

Δ Chloromycetin (chloramphenicol)

This antibiotic should **never** be used in any form for the treatment of trivial or routine infections (colds, eye infections, influenza, upper respiratory diseases, diarrhea or intestinal disturbances), as a prophylactic agent to prevent infections, or for undiagnosed disorders. **Refuse this medication if prescribed for any of these conditions.** Chloramphenicol can cause a serious or fatal blood disease. **Take this medication only under direct medical supervision.**

Macrolides

Δ Erythromycin
This is a broad spectrum antibiotic.

Uses - Erythromycin is an alternative to oral penicillin when penicillin allergies are present. It's also an alternative to tetracycline when tetracycline is contraindicated (e.g., during pregnancy or breast-feeding).

Side effects - nausea, vomiting, diarrhea, and abdominal pain

Contraindications - routine (see p. 417), concurrent use of Seldane (tertenadine) or Hismanal (astemizole), which are no longer available in the U.S. and should be avoided if found elsewhere.

How to take - Take orally, preferably on an empty stomach. If nausea, vomiting, or diarrhea occur, take with food or milk.

Δ Zithromax (azithromycin)
This is a member of the erythromycin family but with better absorption and fewer gastrointestinal side effects.

Side effects - nausea, vomiting, diarrhea, and abdominal pain

Contraindications- routine (see p. 417)

How to take - take orally.

Δ Biaxin (clarithromycin)
Another member of the erythromycin family. It is also absorbed better with fewer gastrointestinal side effects than erythromycin.

Side effects - nausea, vomiting, diarrhea and abdominal pain

Contraindications- routine (see p.417), Biaxin is not to be used in pregnancy

How to take - take orally

Δ Cleocin (clindamycin)
This antibiotic is particularly useful for travelers who are pregnant, allergic to penicillin, or have *serious* infections caused by anaerobic bacteria (those that thrive in low oxygen tissues).

Side effects - abdominal pain, pseudomembranous colitis (an antibiotic-induced diarrheal illness), inflammation of the esophagus, nausea, vomiting, and diarrhea.

Contraindications - routine (see p. 417); known sensitivity to clindamycin or lincomycin.

How to take - Take orally with a full glass of water.

For Bacterial Vaginosis, use either the oral tablets or the
vaginal cream.

Δ Flagyl (metronidazole)

Flagyl is used mainly for infections by protozoa, but
can be used for some bacterial infections

Side effects – nausea, vomiting, diarrhea, gastrointestinal upset, abdominal cramping, headache, dry or metallic taste in the mouth, alcohol reaction, dark urine

stop the medication and obtain medical help for unusual
side effects, such as a rash or severe nausea.

Contraindications - routine (see p. 417), active liver disease. Do not use in first trimester of pregnancy.

How to take -Take orally with food or milk to minimize
side effects if necessary.

Don't drink alcohol. Combining alcohol with Flagyl may
cause cramps, nausea, vomiting, and severe headache.
It's best not to drink alcohol for 24 hours before taking
Flagyl and for 48 hours after finishing the medication.
Check for alcohol in other liquid medications such as
cough syrups, vitamins, or pain relievers.

Δ Macrodantin (nitrofurantoin macrocrystals)

Uses- bladder infections, especially during pregnancy

Side effects -

abdominal pain, decreased appetite, diarrhea, dizziness,
drowsiness, headache, nausea, vomiting

Contraindications - routine (see p. 417), impaired kidney function, hypersensitivity, pregnancy at term

use cautiously with anemia or diabetes

How to take - take orally with meals or milk to decrease
stomach irritation

Penicillins

There are several classes of penicillins, grouped according to what they treat.

Δ **Penicillin VK,**

Δ **Ampicillin, amoxicillin, Augmentin**

Δ **Penicillinase-resistant penicillins**

Side effects - (all penicillins)- nausea, vomiting, diarrhea

epigastric distress, black "hairy" tongue (more likely with Penicillin VK, Procaine, Penicillin G, and Bicillin)

note: diarrhea occurs much less often with amoxicillin than with ampicillin

Stop *using* **any** *penicillin immediately if a rash develops.* This is a sign of allergic reaction to the medication. Obtain medical help as soon as possible. An allergic reaction can occur at any time, even if you've taken it with no side effects in the past.

Stop using **any** penicillin if severe diarrhea persists.

Stop using **any** penicillin if wheezing or shortness of breath occur. Obtain medical help immediately. This is a potentially life-threatening emergency.

Contraindications (all penicillins)

1. **All** penicillins are contraindicated if you've had an allergic reaction to *any* penicillin.
2. **All** penicillins are contraindicated if you've had a severe allergic reaction to Keflex, Ceftin or any of the class of antibiotics known as cephalosporins. Following mild reactions to these medications, seek medical advice before taking any penicillin.

How to take (all penicillins)

Orally - It's preferable to take penicillins on an empty stomach, 1 hour before or 2 to 3 hours after a meal. If mild nausea, vomiting or diarrhea occur, try taking the medication with food.

By intramuscular injection - Take **only** in a medical setting. Wait 20 - 30 minutes after any penicillin injection to assure there is no allergic reaction.

Δ **Ampicillin, Amoxicillin**

These are wide-range, broad-spectrum antibiotics.

Amoxicillin is absorbed twice as efficiently as ampicillin.

Δ Augmentin (amoxicilllin/clavulanate)

Augmentin is a combination of amoxicillin with cla-vulanate, a compound which blocks the effect of en-zymes produced by bacteria that inactivate penicillin an-tibiotics. This expands the effect of penicillin or amoxicillin without increasing side effects.

Augmentin is an expensive antibiotic which should be reserved for injuries from bites of meat-eating ani-mals and other infections where appropriate, based on culture results.

Δ Penicillinase-resistant Penicillins
Δ cloxacillin
Δ dicloxacillin
Δ nafcillin
Δ oxacillin

These are used for infections from bacteria resistant to other forms of penicillin, usually skin infections from staph aureus and streptococcus.

Quinolones (fluoroquinolones)

Δ Cipro (ciprofloxacin)
Side effects --
oral - dizziness, lightheadedness, photosensitivity reac-tions, headache, nausea, vomiting, diarrhea
eye drops -local burning or discomfort, itching, bad taste in mouth
Contraindications - routine (see p. 417), hypersensitivity to quinolones; use cautiously if there is a history of seizures; can not be used by anyone under age 18 or during pregnancy
How to take -
oral - take orally 2 hours after eating, if possible
drink plenty of fluids while taking Cipro
avoid taking antacids with aluminum or magnesium, multivitamins with zinc or iron supplements for 2 hours after taking Cipro
eye drops - place drops in affected eye(s). Avoid

contaminating the applicator tip with material from
the eye, fingers or other source

Δ Noroxin (norfloxacin) / Levaquin (levofloxacin)
Side effects -
dizziness, photosensitivity reactions, headache, light-
headedness, nausea
Contraindications - routine (see p.417)
hypersensitivity to quinolones, nalidixic acid
use cautiously in cases of impaired kidney function or a
history of seizures
can not be used by anyone under age 18 or during pregnancy
How to take - take orally one hour before or two hours
after meals with a glass of water
don't take norfloxacin with nitrofurantoin
don't take antacids with aluminum or magnesium, multivitamins with zinc or iron or zinc or iron supplements for two hours before or after taking either antibiotic.
drink plenty of fluids

Δ Floxin - (Ofloxacin)
Side effects -
oral - photosensitivity reactions, insomnia, headache,
nausea
eye drops - local burning or discomfort, stinging or itching
Contraindications - routine (see p. 417), hypersensitivity
to quinolones; can not be used by anyone under age
18 or during pregnancy
How to take - take orally
don't take antacids with aluminum or magnesium, multivitamins with zinc or iron, or with zinc or iron supplements for two hours before or after taking
drink plenty of fluids
eye drops - place drops in affected eye(s). Avoid contaminating the applicator tip with material from the
eye, fingers or other source.
Sulfa Drugs

Δ **Bactrim, Septra (trimethoprim and sulfamethoxa-zole).**

Bactrim and Septra are identical and very useful medications. Like other sulfa preparations they may cause allergic reactions.

Both products are available in double strength preparations, designated "DS." As implied, one DS tablet equals two regular strength tablets. Regular or "DS" tablets can be substituted for one another, but be sure to adjust the number you take accordingly.

Side effects - dizziness
nausea, vomiting, diarrhea
ringing in the ears
stop taking immediately at the first sign of a skin rash, fever, jaundice, sore throat, or **any** other adverse reaction. These may be early indications of a potentially life-threatening drug reaction.

Contraindications - routine (see p. 417)
history of allergy to any sulfa medication
use cautiously with impaired kidney or liver function
How to take - Take orally with lots of fluids to help prevent kidney problems.

Tetracyclines

Δ **Tetracycline**

Tetracycline is a broad-spectrum antibiotic, one that kills many different bacteria.

Side effects - nausea, vomiting, diarrhea
photosensitivity reactions
Contraindications - routine (see p. 417)
a history of kidney problems (renal insufficiency)
How to take - Take orally on an empty stomach with a full glass of liquid. Don't take with milk or other dairy products, or with antacids, potassium, or iron. These all interfere with absorption of the medicine.
Take at least 1 hour before meals or 2 hours after a meal. If using antacids, take them at least 3 hours after the tetracycline.

Δ **Doxycycline**

This is a long-acting form of tetracycline. It can be

substituted for tetracycline in the treatment of any
disease. It doesn't need to be taken as often.. Do not,
however, substitute tetracycline for doxycycline in malaria prophylaxis. The side effects and contraindications
are the same as for tetracycline, although doxycycline
does offer a few advantages. It can be taken with dairy
products, and it's not contraindicated in cases of impaired kidney function. Do not take with bismuth (Pepto
Bismol).

Antidiarrheal or Antimotility Medications

Never take these medications if there is blood, pus, or
mucus in stools, or a high fever above 102 degrees F
(38.9° C). Never take for more than 2 days.

Uses - to help stop or slow down diarrhea

Imodium AD (loperamide HCl)
A nonopiate antidiarrheal agent.

Side effects - abdominal distension, constipation, dizziness, drowsiness, dry mouth, nausea, vomiting, skin
rash

Contraindications - routine (see p. 417)
blood in stools, fever above 102° F (38.9° C), liver disease
or impaired liver functioning

How to take -Take orally. Discontinue use after 48 hours.

Δ Lomotil (diphenoxylate HCl with atropine sulfate)
An opiate derivative that acts by slowing intestinal
motility.

Side effects - urinary retention, abdominal discomfort,
depression, constipation (frequent), drowsiness, dry
mouth, headache, nausea, vomiting, rashes

Contraindications - routine (see p. 417)
blood in stools, fever above 102° F (38.9° C), hypersensitivity, jaundice

How to take = Take orally.

Don't exceed recommended dosage
Don't take with alcohol, barbiturates, or tranquilizers.
Discontinue use after 48 hours.

Δ Pepto-Bismol (bismuth salicylate)

Uses - abdominal cramps, gas pains, nausea, upset stomach

Side effects - constipation, may temporarily discolor tongue (black), temporary darkening of stool

stop the medication immediately if you develop ringing in the ears

Contraindications - routine (see p. 417)

aspirin intolerance (or if you should avoid aspirin for any reason); don't use if taking doxycycline

How to take - Take orally. If using tablets, chew or dissolve them in your mouth - then follow with liquids. Rinse mouth and brush tongue after taking to minimize blackening of tongue.

Δ Opiate – containing Antidiarrheals
Δ Diabismul (suspension or tablets)
Δ Donnagel Pg (suspension)
Δ Paregoric
Δ Parepectolin (suspension)

Uses - abdominal cramping, diarrhea

Side effects - constipation (very frequent)

large doses can cause symptoms of opiate intoxication and may be habit-forming

Contraindications - routine (see p. 417)

How to take - Take orally with at least one glass of water or other liquid. Discontinue medication when diarrhea subsides. **Don't exceed recommended dosages.**

Antiemetics

These medications are for nausea and vomiting due to illness or motion sickness.

Δ Antivert, Bonine (meclizine HCl)
Δ Marezine (cyclizine HCl)

Uses - prevention and treatment of nausea and vomiting due to motion sickness.

Meclizine can also be tried for dizziness (vertigo).

Side effects - blurred vision, drowsiness, dry mouth, rashes

Contraindications - routine (see p. 417); use cautiously with asthma, glaucoma, or enlarged prostate
How to take - Take orally. **Avoid** alcohol and other depressants (may increase drowsiness).

Δ Compazine (prochlorperazine) – capsules or suppositories
Uses - severe nausea and vomiting due to illness or motion sickness
Side effects - blurred vision, dizziness, drowsiness, photosensitivity reaction, pink or reddish-brown colored urine. If twitching or spasms of tongue, head, and neck occur, stop taking the medication immediately and get medical help. If medical help is not available, treat these side effects with 50 mg. of Benadryl orally every 6 hours until they subside, while seeking medical care.
Contraindications - routine (see p. 417)
How to take - Take capsules orally, or use a rectal suppository. **Avoid** alcohol and other depressants. Avoid sunlight as a rash may occur.

Δ Dramamine (dimenhydrinate)
Uses - prevention and treatment of nausea, vomiting, or dizziness due to motion sickness
Side effects - drowsiness (frequent), headache, insomnia, nervousness
Contraindications - routine (see p. 417), asthma, enlarged prostate, glaucoma
How to take - Take orally. **Don't** use alcohol while taking this medication. To prevent motion sickness, the first dose should be taken $1/2$ - 1 hour before activity or travel.

Δ Pepto-Bismol see "Antidiarrheals"

Δ Phenergan (promethazine HCl)
Uses - motion sickness, nausea, vomiting , sedation
Side effects - drowsiness, dry mouth, twitching or spasms of tongue
Contraindications - routine (see p. 417), asthma attack, concurrent use of MAO inhibitors, hypersensitivity to antihistamines, hypertension, narrow angle

glaucoma. Cardiovascular disease or impaired liver function: use cautiously.

How to take - Take orally. **Don't** take with alcohol or sedatives.

For motion sickness, take one hour before travel.

Δ Tigan (trimethobenzamide HCL)

Uses - severe nausea and vomiting

rectal suppositories are especially useful for symptoms due to hepatitis

Side effects - diarrhea, dizziness, drowsiness, headache, twitching or spasms of tongue

Contraindications - routine (see p. 417)

How to take - Take capsules orally, or use rectal suppositories.

Δ Transderm-scop (scopolamine)

Uses - prevention of nausea and vomiting due to motion sickness

Side effects - - blurred vision (occasionally), drowsiness, dry mouth

stop the medication if hallucinations, confusion, disorientation, memory loss, or restlessness occur.

Contraindications - routine (see p. 417)

liver disease (hepatitis), glaucoma, kidney disease

How to take - Apply disc to a clean area of skin behind the ear 4 hours before travel. Avoid placing on hair. You can bathe with the disc, and it may be left in place for up to three days. If it comes off, simply replace it with a new one. Always wash your hands after touching the disc to remove any scopolamine. If you rub scopolamine into your eye it will cause a painfully dilated pupil. Transderm comes with step-by-step instructions - read them carefully.

Antihistamines and Decongestants

Sedating antihistamines

Δ **Actifed (pseudoephedrine HCl and triprolidine HCl)**

Δ **Dimetapp (brompheniramine maleate, phenylephrine HCl**

Δ Drixoral (pseudoephedrine HCL and dexbrompheniramine maleate)

Uses - colds (as a decongestant), eustachian tube blockage, hay fever symptoms (sneezing, runny nose, watery itchy eyes, itching of the nose or throat), nasal congestion, other upper respiratory allergies, sinus infection

Side effects - drowsiness, thickening of bronchial secretions, kidney disease

Contraindications - routine (see p. 417)

Medical supervision is required for use with the following chronic conditions: asthma, diabetes, glaucoma, heart disease, hypertension, thyroid disease

How to take - Take orally. **Don't** use alcohol while taking any of these medications (may increase drowsiness).

Δ Atarax (hydroxyzine HCl)

Uses - insomnia, itching due to hives or other causes

Side effects - drowsiness, mild sedation (frequent), dryness of the mouth (frequent)

Contraindications - routine (see p. 417)

How to take - Take orally. **Don't** use alcohol while taking this medication (may increase drowsiness).

Δ Benadryl (diphenhydramine HCl)

Used chiefly to control symptoms of allergies, especially itching, and to decrease nasal secretions.

Uses - hay fever and similar allergic reactions, itchy allergic reactions to medications, itching from insect bites, itchy rashes from scabies and lice, upper respiratory illnesses (as a decongestant), insomnia (may be used occasionally for its chief side effect, drowsiness)

Side effects - drowsiness (frequent), dryness of mouth, nose and throat (frequent), nausea, vomiting, diarrhea (rare)

Contraindications - routine (see p. 417), narrow angle glaucoma, asthma, prostate enlargement, peptic ulcer

How to take - Take orally. **Don't** use alcohol while taking this medication (may increase drowsiness).

Non-sedating antihistamines
Uses - symptomatic relief of hay fever/allergy symptoms, itching, allergic reactions

Δ Allegra (fexofenadine)
Side effects - (infrequent) drowsiness and headache
Contraindications - routine (see p. 417)
How to take - take orally

Δ Claritin (loratadine), Clarinex (desloratadine)
Side effects - (infrequent) drowsiness and headache
Contraindications - routine (see p. 417), lower dosage should be used for those with liver or kidney disease
How to take - take orally

Δ Zyrtec (cetirizine hydrochloride)
Side effects - tiredness, fatigue, dry mouth
Contraindications - routine
How to take - orally

Decongestants
Uses - symptomatic relief of sinusitis, colds, ear aches eustachian tube blockage; injuries due to changes in pressure (barotrauma), especially of the ear

Δ Humabid L.A. (guaifenesin)
Side effects - headache, dizziness, nausea, vomiting
Contraindications - routine (see p. 417)
How to take - Take orally

Δ Sudafed (pseudoephedrine hydrochloride)
Side effects - possible mild stimulant
Contraindications - routine (see p. 417), use with caution for the following: hypertension, taking antidepressive medications
How to take - Take orally.

Anti-inflammatory Medications
(Oral, Nonsteroid)

Δ **Aspirin** - see "analgesics"
Δ **Feldene (piroxicam)**
Δ **Indocin (indomethacin)**
Δ **Motrin/Advil (ibuprofen)**
Δ **Naprosyn, Anaprox, Aleve (naproxen)**
Δ **Relafen (nabumetone)**
Uses - mild to moderate pain from menstrual cramps, muscle spasms, strains and sprains
Side effects - constipation, dizziness, drowsiness, headache, nausea, vomiting, diarrhea
stop the medication if any of the following occur:
black tarry stools, itching, edema (swelling in the extremities from fluid accumulation), persistent headache, rash, severe nausea, visual disturbances, vomiting, diarrhea, abdominal pain
Contraindications - routine (see p. 417); allergy to aspirin or when aspirin is contraindicated, history of asthma or ulcers, hypertension (use cautiously), impaired kidney function, runny nose, or other allergic reaction from aspirin or other nonsteroid anti-inflammatory medications
How to take - Take orally. Don't take aspirin along with these medications. Take with food, milk, or antacids if gastrointestinal upset occurs.

Antimalarial Medications

Δ **Aralen (chloroquine phosphate) / Plaquenil (hydroxychloroquine)**
These are the primary antimalarial medicines for non-chloroquine-resistant areas.
Uses - prevention of malaria caused by Plasmodium ovale and Plasmodium vivax, as well as nonresistant P. falciparum
Side effects - itching, especially in blacks, dizzines, headache, nausea, vomiting, rashes, diarrhea, weight loss, possible worsening of psoriasis, eczema, and other rashes

Contraindications - hepatitis, hypersensitivity
How to take - Take orally once a week on the same day
  (we suggest you take it religiously, on Sundays).
  There are no restrictions on food or liquids.
Start one to two weeks before entering a malaria area.
  Continue taking while in the malarial area, and for
  four weeks after leaving the area.

Δ Doxycycline (see "Antibiotics")
Uses- malaria prophylaxis

Δ Fansidar (pyrimethamine and sulfadoxine)
Uses - Standby treatment of chloroquine-resistant P.
  falciparum malaria
Side effects - abdominal cramps, headache, nausea,
  vomiting, hepatitis, diarrhea
Contraindications - routine (see p. 417)
anyone with severe allergies or bronchial asthma should
  consult their doctor before taking this medication.
history of allergic reaction to sulfa drugs
How to take - Take orally. Drink lots of fluids to help
  prevent kidney stones. **Don't take other sulfa drugs
  (Septra, Bactrim) while taking Fansidar**
Take as a single dose (3 tablets) for febrile illnesses that
  occur while taking chloroquine and or Paludrine
  (during short stays in areas of chloroquine-resistant P.
  falciparum).

Δ Lariam (mefloquine)
Uses - prevention of malaria, especially in chloroquine
  resistant areas of P. falciparum
Side effects -
The following may occur briefly but usually resolve
  quickly: dizziness/disequilibrium, headache, light-
  headedness, nausea/vomiting, upset stomach
More serious side effects - convulsions (seizures), mental disturbances, including severe anxiety, psychosis,
  hallucinations, depression
Contraindications - routine (see p. 417), history of seizures, severe psychiatric disorders including psychosis, depression and anxiety; concurrent use of quinine,

quinidine or halofantrine; persons with cardiac conduction abnormalities

How to take - Take orally.

Δ Malarone (atovaquone/proguanil)

Uses - prevention of malaria, especially in chloroquine resistant areas of P. falciparum

Side effects - few side effects with prophylaxis: possible abdominal pain, nausea, vomiting, headache. Higher risk of side effects with treatment dosages: diarrhea, weakness, loss of appetite, dizziness, and potential liver damage.

Contraindications - routine (see p. 417),

concurrent use of tetracycline, doxycycline, Reglan (metoclopramide) and rifampin.

oral typhoid vaccine must be finished at least 10 days before starting Malarone.

How to take - Take orally with dietary fat (i.e., dinner or pasteurized dairy products that contain fat). If vomiting occurs within one hour of taking, repeat the dose.

Δ Plaquenil (hydroxychloroquine) -see profile on Aralen

This can be interchanged with Aralen (chloroquine) and has the advantage of lower rates of gastrointestinal side effects as well as lower cost

Δ Primaquine Phosphate

Uses - prevention of malaria caused by P. ovale and P. vivax

Side effects - abdominal cramps, hemolytic anemia in G6PD deficiencies, nausea, vomiting

stop the medication if jaundice develops, or if urine turns dark or red, and obtain medical help.

Contraindications - routine (see p. 417); G6PD blood deficiency (requires blood test to determine), rheumatoid arthritis, lupus

How to take - Take orally. Take daily during the last 2 weeks of antimalarial treatment. *Never take till after obtaining a G6PD blood test.*

Always take this medication under medical supervision.

Δ Quinine Sulfate

Uses - Treatment of chloroquine-resistant P. falciparum malaria, in combination with either Fansidar or tetracycline/doxycycline.

Side effects - abdominal pain, dizziness, ringing in the ears, headache, visual disturbances, nausea

Contraindications - routine (see p. 417); history of blood disorders from previous quinine therapy, hypersensitivity, G6PD deficiency (requires a blood test to determine), ringing in the ears

How to take - Take orally with food or after meals

Don't take with antacids

Antiparasitic Medications

Uses- see specific diseases in Part II.

Δ Albenza (albendazole)

Side effects - The following occur occasionally: abdominal pain, reversible hair loss, elevated liver enzymes, nausea/vomiting, dizziness, fever, rash, low white blood cell counts, kidney abnormalities

Contraindications - routine

How to take - Take orally

Δ Antepar, Vermizine (piperazine citrate)

This medication paralyzes worms, allowing them to be expelled.

Side effects – The following occur occasionally: abdominal pain, cramps, dizziness, hives, nausea, vomiting, diarrhea

Contraindications - routine (see p. 417); epilepsy, impaired kidney or liver function

How to take - Take orally on an empty stomach

Δ Antiminth (pyrantel pamoate)

Side effects - The following occur occasionally:
abdominal pain, dizziness, decreased appetite, fever, headache, insomnia, nausea, vomiting, rash, diarrhea

Contraindications - routine (see p. 417)

How to take - Take orally on an empty stomach.

Δ Biltricide (praziquantel)

Side effects - Usually mild and transient, but may be more severe when large numbers of worms are present: abdominal discomfort, dizziness, drowsiness (may interfere with driving or other tasks requiring alertness) headache, malaise

Contraindications - routine (see p. 417); don't treat cysticercosis with this medication if symptoms of eye involvement are present

How to take - Take orally with liquids during meals. Don't chew tablets; swallow quickly as bitter taste may produce gagging or vomiting

Δ Diodoquin, Floraquin, Yodoxin (diiodohydroxyquin or iodoquinol)

Side effects - nausea, vomiting, constipation, diarrhea, gastritis, skin rashes, including hives and generalized itching, headache, malaise

Contraindications - routine (see p. 417); iodine sensitivity, liver damage (including active or chronic hepatitis); thyroid disease: use with caution

How to take - Take orally. If gastrointestinal symptoms occur, take with food. If diarrhea continues, stop the medication.

Δ Fasigyn (tinidazole)

This drug is available in many countries outside the U.S. It hasn't yet been approved for use in the U.S.

Side effects –decreased appetite, metallic taste in the mouth, nausea, vomiting, diarrhea, alcohol reaction less severe than with Flagyl

Contraindications - routine (see p. 417); history of blood disorders; history of central nervous system disease

How to take - Take orally with food to help minimize side effects. **Don't consume any alcohol while using this medication** Avoid alcohol for 24 hours before starting and 48 hours after finishing the medication. Be sure to check for alcohol in other liquid medicines such as cough syrups, vitamins, or pain relievers.

Δ Flagyl (see "Antibiotics")

Δ Hetrazan (diethylcarbamazine citrate)
Used for some ascaris and onchocerciasis infections. Must only be taken under medical supervision as severe allergic reactions can occur after a single dose.

Δ Humatin (paromomycin sulfate)
Side effects – nausea, vomiting, cramps, diarrhea, headache, vertigo (spinning sensation), rash

stop taking the medication and notify the doctor if hearing impairment, ringing in the ears, or dizziness occur.

Contraindications - routine (see p. 417); intestinal obstruction

How to take - Take orally with food.

Δ Mintezol (thiabendazole)
Side effects - any of the following may occur, usually 3 – 4 hours after taking the drug: decreased appetite, dizziness, nausea, vomiting

Contraindications - routine (see p. 417)

How to take -Take with food to decrease gastrointestinal side effects. Chew tablets thoroughly before swallowing.

Δ Vermox (mebendazole)
This medication is very effective and has few side effects. It kills worms by blocking their sugar intake.

Side effects - If there are many worms, there may occasionally be transient symptoms of abdominal pain and/or diarrhea.

Contraindications -routine (see p. 417)

How to take - Take orally.

Δ Yomesan, Niclocide (niclosamide)
This medication is used primarily for intestinal tapeworms and some flukes.

Side effects - constipation, dizziness, drowsiness, headache, nausea, vomiting, rectal bleeding, diarrhea

Contraindications - routine (see p. 417)

How to take - Take orally with food to minimize side

effects. Chew tablets, then swallow with a small amount of water. Use a mild laxative if necessary to relieve constipation.

Antispasmodics

Uses - relief of abdominal cramps caused by diarrhea

Δ Belladenal (phenobarbital and belladonna)
May be habit forming due to phenobarbital (a barbiturate).
Side effects - blurred vision, drowsiness, dry mouth, flushed skin, urinary retention
Contraindications - routine (see p. 417); advanced kidney disease, glaucoma
How to take: Take orally.

Δ Donnatal (phenobarbital, hyoscyamine sulfate, atropine sulfate, and scopolamine hydrobromide; in addition, the elixir contains alcohol)
Side effects - blurred vision, dry mouth, flushed skin, skin dryness, urinary retention
Contraindications - routine (see p. 417); glaucoma, liver impairment, kidney impairment
How to take - Take orally.

Antiviral Medications

Δ Symmetrel (amantadine) and Flumadin (rimantadine)
These medications are useful in the prevention and treatment of influenza A (but not influenza B) infections. Influenza is an acute respiratory tract illness with fever, often accompanied by a prominent headache and muscle achiness. Elderly patients (over age 65) and those with chronic diseases are at highest risk during outbreaks of influenza. Vaccination is the preferred method for controlling this infection. These medications can be used during outbreaks of influenza A and are usually given for 2 weeks after administration of the vaccine (the time it takes to get antibody protection from the vaccine) or can be given for prevention if the vaccine is not

available. They can also be used for treatment of the illness if administered within 24 to 48 hours of onset, but reduce the duration of illness by only 1–2 days.

Δ Symmetrel (amantadine)
Uses - Prevention and treatment of influenza type A infections.

Preferably used for two weeks after administration of the flu vaccine during outbreaks.

Used in high risk individuals (those over 65 years or with heart, lung or chronic disease) with influenza illness. It needs to be started within 48 hours of the beginning of flu symptoms.

Side effects - nervousness, anxiety, difficulty concentrating, insomnia, lightheadedness or dizziness, mental confusion, seizures, nausea and loss of appetite

Contraindications - routine (see p. 417)

Those with liver or kidney disease and those over age 65 should take lower doses of the medication.

How to take - take orally.

Δ Flumadine (rimantadine)
Uses - Prevention and treatment of influenza type A infections (see Symmetrel above). Usually preferred over Symmetrel due to decreased side effects.

Side effects - see Symmetrel above. Substantially lower nervous system side effects than Symmetrel although higher in cost.

Contraindications - routine (see p. 417); those with severe liver or kidney disease and chronically ill elderly patients may need to consider lower doses.

How to take - take orally

Δ Relenza (zanamivir) and Tamiflu (oseltamivir)
Both medications may be used for treatment of uncomplicated influenza types A and B, if administered within 30–36 hours of onset. They reduce the duration of illness but only by 1–2 days. Use has not been found to reduce serious complications from influenza. The recommended duration of treatment is 5 days.

Relenza (zanamivir)
Side effects - the inhaled drug may increase respiratory problems in people with asthma or emphysema. Use cautiously.
Contraindications - routine (see p. 417)
How to take - this drug is inhaled twice a day (2–5 mg. each dose)

Tamiflu (oseltamivir)
Side effects - taken orally, it does not have the respiratory side effects of Relenza.
Contraindications - routine (see p. 417). Individuals with kidney disease need a reduced dosage.
How to take - take orally twice a day (75 mg. each dose)

Δ **Famvir (famciclovir)**
Uses - symptomatic relief of genital herpes or herpes zoster (shingles) infections. Take when you first notice symptoms of infection, such as tingling, itching, or pain in the affected area.
Side effects
Contraindications - routine (see p. 417).
How to take - take orally with a full glass of water

Δ **Zovirax (acyclovir), Valtrex (valacyclovir)**
Due to higher blood medication levels with Valtrex, this may be a more useful medication with certain monkey bite injuries.
Uses - initial or recurrent herpes simplex
monkey bites (see p.403 – 405)
Side effects - fatigue, headache, menstrual abnormalities, insomnia, joint pain, nausea, vomiting, rash, diarrhea, vertigo
Contraindications - routine (see p. 417)
How to take - Tablets - take orally. Avoid sexual contact while herpes lesions are present.

Bronchial Dilators

How To Use an Oral Inhaler

The assembled inhaler should form an "L" shape. Put the inhaler next to your mouth, not inside it. Don't seal your lips around it. Exhale, then squeeze the inhaler and breathe in the medicine. The extra air inhaled with the medicine helps drive it deeply into the lungs. Hold the medication in for 10-20 seconds, then breathe out. Wait 5-10 minutes and repeat the procedure.

Δ Alupent (metaproterenol sulfate) inhalant or tablets

Uses - reversible wheezing associated with bronchitis, bronchial asthma, or emphysema

Side effects - increased heart rate, nausea, nervousness, tremors

Contraindications - abnormally rapid heart rhythms (tachycardia)

How to take- inhalant- see above; tablets - take orally

don't overuse the medication

Δ Proventil, Ventolin (albuterol/salbutanol), inhalant

Uses - reversible wheezing associated with bronchitis, bronchial asthma, or emphysema

Side effects - apprehension, insomnia, nausea, palpitations, rapid heart rate (tachycardia), restlessness, tremor

Contraindications - routine (see p. 417)
abnormally rapid heart rhythms (tachycardia)
use cautiously with the following conditions: diabetes, heart disease, hyperthyroidism

How to take - see "how to use an inhaler" above.

don't exceed recommended dosage, as excessive use decreases effectiveness and may lead to adverse effects

Contraceptives - Oral

Uses -preventing pregnancy

Combination Pills (estrogen and progesterone)

These work by inhibiting ovulation and implantation

of a fertile egg, and by creating a thick cervical mucus.
There are many different types. Try to use only low-dose
pills (those with 50 micrograms or less of estrogen).

Side effects - multiple (beyond the scope of this book)

Contraindications - routine (see p. 417); coronary artery
disease, history of heart problems, history of or active
breast or reproductive system cancer, history of embolus or thrombosis (material blocking a blood vessel), impaired liver function including hepatitis, liver
cancer, pregnancy

How to take - Take orally, 1 pill each day at approximately the same time of day.

Diarrhea which occurs while using the pill may have the
same effect as missing one or more pills. If you miss 1
pill, take 2 the next day. If you miss 2 pills, take 2 pills
the next day and 2 pills the day after that. Use a backup form of birth control for the rest of the month. If
you miss 3 pills, stop taking them altogether. Throw
away the package with the remaining pills. Start a
new package on the first day of bleeding or on the
Sunday after your next period or 5 days after the
bleeding begins. Use a backup form of birth control
(condoms, foam,) for one month.

If you miss a pill or pills while sexually active and have
no period for 45 days, get a pregnancy test (see pp.
111-112).

Δ Progesterone Only Pill ("mini- pills," Micronor, Nor-QD, Ovrette)

These are primarily used by people who can't use the
combination pill due to hypertension, headaches,
breast feeding, or any other reason.

Side effects - absence of periods, bleeding between periods, irregular periods

Contraindications - pregnancy, coronary artery disease
history of heart problems, history of an active breast or
reproductive system cancer, history of embolus or
thrombosis (material blocking a blood vessel)
impaired liver function, including hepatitis, liver cancer

How to take - Take orally, one each day. **Never** miss a

pill as you may ovulate and become pregnant. If you
miss a period, obtain a pregnancy test.

Ear Medications

Uses -external infections of the ear canal (otitis externa)

**Δ Cortisporin Otic Drops (polymyxin B sulfate, neomy-
cin sulfate, and hydrocortisone)**
This medication combines two antibiotics with an anti-
inflammatory agent.
Side effects - neomycin may be sensitizing; if rash/
redness occurs, discontinue use
Contraindications - herpes infections (including chickenpox)
How to take - After putting drops in the ear, keep head
tilted for 3-5 minutes. This allows the medication to
work all the way down the canal. **Don't** get water in
the affected ear(s) during the course of treatment.

Δ Ofloxacin - see Floxin under antibiotics.

Emetics
Emetics are used to induce vomiting in cases of accidental poisoning. Emetics should **not** be given to unconscious victims, or when poisoning is due to petroleum-
based products, acids or alkalis, or strychnine.

Δ Ipecac Syrup
Uses - accidental poisoning
Side effects - none
Contraindications - as indicated above
How to take - Take orally with lots of fluids (7-Up
works especially well). Repeat dosage in 20 minutes if
vomiting does not occur.

Eye Medications

Δ Antibiotic Eye Drops - Uses - conjunctivitis (pink eye)
**Δ Bleph 10/Sodium Sulamyd (sulfacetamide sodium
Side effects -** none

Contraindications - routine (see p. 417); history of allergic reaction to sulfa drugs
How to take - See instructions for ophthalmic solutions on the next page.

Δ **Garamycin Ophthalmic Eye Drops and Ointment (gentamicin sulfate)**
Side effects - burning and stinging of the eyes (occasionally)
Contraindications - routine (see p. 417)
How to take:

Ophthalmic solution:
Lie down or tilt head backward, hold dropper above eye and put drops inside lower lid. **Don't** touch dropper to eye, fingers, or any surface. Keep eye open, avoid blinking for 30 seconds. After instillation, don't close eyes tightly. Try not to blink excessively.

Ophthalmic ointment:
Hold tube in hands for several minutes to warm it before use. Tilt head back or lie down. Squeeze a small amount of ointment ($1/4$ inch to $1/2$ inch) inside the lower lid. **Don't** touch tip of tube or cap to eye, finger, or any surface. Close eye gently and roll the eyeball in all directions while eye is closed. Temporary blurring may occur.

Δ **Ocuflox (ofloxacin)** ophthalmic solution - see Floxin under antibiotics

Δ **Ciloxan (ciprofloxacin)** ophthalmic solution - see Cipro under antibiotics

Δ **Antihistamine eye drops**
Δ **Naphcon- or Naphcon A (naphazoline HCl and pheniramine maleate)**
Uses - eye irritation from allergies
Side effects - mild transient stinging, burning, tearing
Contraindications - routine (see p. 417); concurrent use of MAO inhibitors, narrow angle glaucoma; use cautiously with the following conditions: cardiac rhythm disturbances, diabetes, hypertension, hyperthyroidism
How to take - apply 1 drop in each eye every 3-4 hours

Menstrual Cramping (Dysmenorrhea) Medications

Δ **Motrin, Advil, Nuprin (ibuprofen)**
Δ **Naprosyn (naproxen)**
Uses - to relieve or reduce the pain of menstrual cramps
Side effects - blurred vision, dizziness, edema, rash, nausea, vomiting, diarrhea
Contraindications - routine (see p. 417); hypersensitivity to other nonsteroid anti-inflammatory medications
How to take - Take orally. Begin taking the medication either before cramps start or just as they begin. Take with food to help minimize side effects.

Muscle Relaxants

Δ **Flexeril (cyclobenzaprine HCl)**
Uses - severe muscle spasms only
Side effects - dizziness, drowsiness, dry mouth
Contraindications - routine (see p. 417)
How to take - Take orally. **Don't** use alcohol while taking this medication. **Don't** take for longer than 2 weeks.

Δ **Soma (carisoprodol)**
Uses - mild to severe muscle spasms
Side effects - nausea, drowsiness, dizziness, headache
Contraindications - routine (see p. 417)
How to take - Take orally. Avoid alcohol. Take with food or milk

Robaxisal (methocarbamol and aspirin),
Δ **Robaxin (methocarbamol)**
Uses - mild to severe muscle spasms, muscle-skeletal sprains and strains
Side effects - dizziness, drowsiness, light-headedness, nausea
Contraindications - routine (see p. 417); aspirin allergy (Robaxisal), ulcers, history of ulcers
How to take - Take orally. Take with food if nausea occurs. **Don't** use alcohol with these medications.

Nasal Medications

Δ Afrin or Neosynephrine Nasal Spray
These medications constrict the smaller arterial blood
   vessels of the nasal passages.
Uses relief of nasal congestion due to allergic or infectious disorders of the nose (hay fever, colds, sinusitis)
Side effects - headache, sneezing, burning, stinging,
   dryness of nasal membranes, "nasal rebound" - a reaction that occurs when you stop using the spray. The
   nasal membranes puff right back out worse than before starting the medication. Be very aware of this important side effect.
Contraindications - routine (see p. 417)
How to take – Drops or spray are put in one or both nostrils. **Don't** use more often than the instructions indicate. To avoid nasal rebound, **don't** use for more than
   3 days at a time.

Other Nasal Decongestants - see "Antihistamines and
   Decongestants," pp.434–436.

Skin Medications, Topical

   These medications are applied to the skin. In developing countries many topical medications are combined
with antibiotics. Don't use these products. They frequently cause allergic reactions.
   Almost all topical medicines are available without
prescription in developing countries. Be careful not to
overuse them.

Antibacterial Ointments

Δ Bacitracin
**Δ Neomycin Triple Antibiotic (polymyxin b, bacitra-
   cin, neomycin)**
Δ Neosporin
Δ Bactroban
   These are the most common. Always read the ingre-
dients on the label. If allergic to any of them (particularly
neomycin), don't use the medication.

Uses - minor skin infections (folliculitis, infected insect bites, cuts, abrasions)
Side effects - none
Contraindications - routine (see p. 417)
How to take - Rub in lightly and gently on the affected area.
Don't use in eyes.

Antifungal Preparations
(Creams, Powders, and Lotions)

Δ **Desenex (undecylenic acid)**
Δ **Monistat Derm (miconazole nitrate)**
Δ **Mycelex, Lotrimin (clotrimazole)**
Δ **Mycolog (nystatin, triamcinolone)**
Δ **Nizoral (ketaconazole)**
Δ **Nystatin, Mycostatin (nystatin)**
Δ **Tinactin (tolnaftate)**

All of the above can be used more or less interchangeably. However, some preparations may be more effective than others for specific disorders. Check treatment recommendations (Chapter 7).
Uses - fungal rashes: athlete's foot, ringworm
Side effects - possible skin irritation with redness, blistering, stinging, swelling or itching (infrequent)
Contraindications - routine (see p. 417)
How to take - Spread thinly and rub in lightly to the area of rash. **Don't** overuse.

Δ **Selsun Solution (selenium sulfide)**
Uses - tinea versicolor
Side effects - possible oiliness or dryness of the skin
Contraindications - routine (see p. 417)
How to use - Apply to rash, rubbing in gently. Leave on 15 minutes, then wash off. Repeat daily for 2 weeks.

Antiparasitic Preparations

Δ **Elimite (permethrin)**
This is the preferred treatment for scabies and is the same

medication (although in a different formulation) as the spray for mosquito and tick protection on clothing.

Uses -scabies

Side effects – skin irritation

Contraindications - history of allergic reaction to the ingredients

How to use - Don't use near the eyes or mouth. Rub in thoroughly on entire body from the neck down and leave on skin for 8-14 hours. One application is generally curative. Persistent itching is often present for up to 2 weeks due to residual killed mites under the skin. Nursing mothers should temporarily discontinue nursing during application or avoid use. Use during pregnancy should only be done with approval from a treating physician (see Eurax below).

Δ Eurax (crotamiton)

This is an alternative to Kwell and Elimite, usually preferable during pregnancy and breast-feeding.

Uses -scabies

Side effects - skin irritation

Contraindications - history of allergic reaction to the ingredients

How to use - Don't use near the eyes or mouth. Rub in thoroughly on entire body from the neck down, but avoid use on the nipples when breast-feeding. Repeat application in 24 hours. Don't wash off until 48 hours after the second application.

Δ Lindane or gamma benzene hexachloride lotion and shampoo

This medication is a derivative of the pesticide DDT - handle with care. Avoid use on children or infants and overuse by adults.

Uses:

Lotion - scabies, crabs, and body lice

Shampoo - crabs and head lice

Side effects - rash (usually occurs only from overuse)

Contraindications - routine (see p. 417); use Eurax instead during pregnancy and breast-feeding.

How to take - Don't take orally.
Don't use near the eyes. **It's very poisonous.**
Lotion - Don't bathe before use. Shake the bottle well and apply lotion to entire body below the neck. Leave on for 8 hours, then wash off thoroughly (the lotion can't be seen or smelled when on the skin).
Shampoo - Apply to hairy areas of the body, add a little water, and lather thoroughly. Leave on for 4 minutes, then rinse off even more thoroughly.

Δ **Rid (pyrethrin)**
Uses - head and body lice, crab lice (including eggs)
Side effects - none
Contraindications - Don't use if allergic to ragweed.
How to use - Apply to affected areas undiluted (no wa-ter) until entirely wet. Allow to stay on for 10 minutes **only**. Then wash off thoroughly with water and either soap or shampoo. Repeat treatment in 7 – 10 days.
 Don't use on eyebrows or eyelids.

Steroid Creams

Δ **Aristocort .1% or .5%**
Δ **Kenalog .1%**
Δ **Halog .1%**
Δ **Lidex**
Δ **Hydrocortisone 0.5 or 1%**
There are many. These are some of the more widely used.
Uses - inflammation and itching due to insect bites, con-tact dermatitis (see p. 199).
Side effects - burning, itching, dryness of the skin, follic-ulitis, secondary bacterial infection
Contraindications - Don't use on any rash caused by a virus (herpes, chickenpox).
How to take - Apply thinly to skin and rub in lightly.
Don't put in or around the eyes.
Don't use on the face.

Don't use in genital region for more than three days.
Sleep Medications
Uses - jet lag and short-term treatment of insomnia

Δ Ambien (zolpidem)
Frequently preferred for travel due to its short duration of action and fewer "hangover" effects.
Side effects - daytime drowsiness, dizziness, headache, nausea and vomiting. May cause confusion and impaired movement in elderly patients where lower doses are recommended
Contraindications - routine (see p. 417). Use with caution and lower dosages in the elderly.
How to take - take orally
Don't exceed the prescribed dose.
Don't take with alcohol. Take only short-term as physical and psychological dependency may occur.

Δ Sonata (zaleplon)
Short acting. Effects last for about 4 hours.
side effects -constipation, dry mouth, difficulty concentrating, drowsiness, dizziness,
contraindications - routine (see p. 417)
how to take - take orally

Benadryl (see "Antihistamines")

Vaginal Medications

Δ Cleocin (clindamycin)
Uses - bacterial vaginosis
Side effects - appetite loss, diarrhea, fatigue, headache, nausea, vomiting, rash, itching, pseudomembranous colitis, sore throat
Contraindications - routine (see p. 417); use cautiously with: impaired kidney or liver function, stomach or intestinal disorders, history of asthma
How to take – take orally with a full glass of water

Δ **Flagyl - see "Antibiotics"**
Uses - bacterial vaginosis, trichomonas vaginitis
Δ **Diflucan**
Uses - vaginal yeast infections
Side effects - headache
nausea
abdominal pain
Contraindications - routine (see p. 417)
How to take- take orally as a single dose

Vaginal Antifungal Creams

Δ **Femstat (butoconazole)**
Δ **Monistat (miconazole)**
Δ **Mycelex, Gynelotrim (clotrimazole)**
Δ **Mycostatin (nystatin)**
Δ **Terazol 7 (teraconazole)**
Uses -vaginal yeast (monilia) infections
Side effects - none
Contraindications - routine (see p. 417)
don't use in pregnancy after membranes have ruptured
How to use:
Cream: use the applicator to place the cream as high up
   and far back in the vagina as possible
Suppository: place the suppository as far back in the va-
   gina as possible. The medication should be applied or
   reapplied following intercourse. Otherwise, it gets
   squashed out and does you no good. If there is any irritation on the outside of the vaginal opening, spread
   some cream thinly over the irritated area twice a day.

Internet Resources for Travelers

Health Information

Note: most web browsers no longer require typing http://
ahead of the web address. For older browsers you may need to
add it as a prefix to the addresses listed below.

The first internet stop for most travelers should be the CDC
(Centers for Disease Control) at: www.cdc.gov/travel/. You'll
find country specific information on health hazards and recommended or required vaccines, the latest bulletins on disease
outbreaks, including SARS, information on specific diseases,
and more. SARS (or severe acute respiratory syndrome) is a
respiratory illness with fever, dry cough, shortness of breath
and pneumonia (seen on chest x-rays) recently identified in
Asia. While most healthy individuals recover, severe problems
or death can occur in a significant percentage of those who
contract the illness. For updates, check the CDC website at
www.cdc.gov/ncidod/sars/ or the WHO site below.

For general health information check the following web sites
and their links to other helpful web pages: World Health Organization homepage: www.who.int/home-page/–search the
site for travel health information, (www.who.int/ith/
index.html/), data on specific diseases, disease outbreaks
(SARS: www.who.int/csr/sars/en), and more. The Pan American Health organization has similar information for Central and
South America and the Caribbean: www.paho.org/. The Merck
Manual has long been a standard medical reference for doctors
and other health professionals:
www.merck.com/pubs/mmanual_home/ or for general information: www.merck.com/disease/travel/.The Medical College of Wisconsin: health information at healthlink.mcw.edu/
content/topic/Travel Medicine and links at health-
link.mcw.edu.travel-links.html.

For country by country health risks plus general information

see Travel Health Online: www.tripprep.com/. At
www.travelsafely.com/, sponsored by GlaxoSmithKline, you'll
find country by country health risks, including information on
hepatitis and hepatitis vaccines. Other sources of health information for travelers: www.TravelHealth.gc.ca (a Canadian
site) and the UK based Medical Advisory Services for Travelers
Abroad (MASTA):
www.masta.org/about/index.html;

Two excellent sites for drug information:
www.medscape.com/; cp.gsm.com/. The latter, Clinical
Pharmacology Online, requires a subscription.

High Altitude health and medical concerns: www.high-
altitude-medicine.com/; www.ciwec-clinic.com/.
The latter is the online site of the travel medicine center in
Kathmandu- a good resource for anyone traveling in Nepal or
the Himalayas.

First aid advice: www.healthy.net/clinic/firstaid/index.asp.
First aid and drug information: www.mayohealth.org/
Diving Medicine: Links page: www.gulftel.com/~scubadoc/
lnks.html; www.diversalertnetwork.org/.
Handicapped travel: lots of good information plus links-
    www.mossresourcenet.org/;
Access-Able Travel Source: www.access-able.com/.
Diabetic travel: diabeticresource.com/; www.mendosa.com/
diabetes.htm.
Gay travel: deals with health and travel issues including HIV:
www.outandabout.com/.

Facts, travel advisories, and country information:
The State Department issues travel warnings by country as
needed and also maintains consular information sheets with
descriptions of entry requirements, currency regulations or unusual health conditions, the crime and security situation, politi-
cal disturbances, areas of instability, driving and road conditions, etc. They also provide addresses and emergency
telephone numbers for U.S. embassies and consulates: trav-
el.state.gov/. The World Factbook, published online by the
CIA, has maps and thumbnail country descriptions some travelers find useful: www.odci.gov/cia/publications/factbook/.
The Canadian Bureau of Foreign Affairs maintains country by
country travel tips and cautions: www.voyage.gc.ca/
destinations/menu_e.htm.

Other useful sites:
Local times in any country: <u>times.clari.net.au/index.htm;</u> or
  <u>timezoneconverter.com/</u>
Currency conversion: <u>www.bloomberg.com/markets/</u>
<u>currency/currcalc.html.</u>
Language translation: <u>www.virtualtourist.com/.</u>
Insurance needs: <u>www.worldtravelcenter.com/Eng/</u>
<u>index.cfm.</u>
Location of some internet cafes around the world:
<u>www.indranet.com/potpourri/links/cybercafe.html.</u>
For returning U.S. travelers, customs information and border
wait times can be found at <u>www.customs.gov/travel/</u>
<u>travel.htm.</u>
For sustained release DEET repellant, the Extractor, Itch Balm
Plus, and other useful travel products, log onto: <u>sawyerpro-</u>
<u>ducts.com.</u>

Women and Travel: Resources
on Reproductive Options
The Contraceptive Research and Development (CONRAD)
program – links to sites for general contraceptive information
<u>www.conrad.org/general.html.</u>
Office of Population Research Emergency Contraception:
<u>ec.princeton.edu/worldwide/default.asp</u> information on
emergency contraception. Click on country of destination to
see available options.

PATH (Program for Appropriate Technology in Health) Consortium for Emergency Contraception <u>www.path.org/cec.htm</u>
or <u>path.org/</u> – health information on EC for providers and patients. Available in many different languages.

International Planned Parenthood Federation – <u>www.ippf.org</u>

Marie Stopes International – <u>www.mariestopes.org.uk/</u>
<u>abortion.html</u> –provides country information on the availabili-
ty of emergency contraception, contraceptive methods and
abortion, along with help line numbers for advice and services
related to family planning and sexual health.

The Center for Reproductive Law and Policy –<u>www.crlp.org/</u>
<u>abortionl_icpd.html</u> –provides country by country information
on the legality of or restrictions placed on abortion.

Travel Clinics   <u>B</u>

Clinics run by the authors or contributors are listed here. For complete country by country, state by state listings see the homepage of the International Society of Travel Medicine at: www.istm.org/; The American Society of Tropical Medicine and Hygiene at: www.astmh.org/; or at: www.travelhealth.com/clinics/.

Fujimoto, Gary R., MD
Medical Director, Travel Medicine Department
Palo Alto Medical Foundation
795 El Camino Real, Palo Alto, CA 94301
Phone:1- 650-853-2970

Robin, Marc., Nurse Practitioner
International Travelers Clinic
3309 4th Ave., San Diego, CA 91977
Phone: 1-619-698-6736;
Fax: 1-619-698-8538
Languages: English (principal), Spanish
Pre-Travel Vaccination, Official Yellow Fever Vaccine Center

Spees, David N., MD
Traveler's Clinic
Sharp Rees-Stealy Medical Group
16950 Via Tazon,San Diego, CA 92127
Phone: (858) 521-2322
Fax: (858) 521-2388
Hours Available: 8:00 am - 5:00 pm.
Description: All immunizations including Yellow Fever

Anderson, Susan, Dr.
Stanford Travel Service
Office of Medical Education
MSOB x365 Stanford, CA 94305-5409
Phone: 1-650-723-1283
Language: English
Pre-Travel Vaccination, Official
Yellow Fever Vaccine Center
Post-Travel Medical Consultation,
On-Site Diagnostic Laboratory

Mackell, Sheila, MD
Kaiser Permanente Pediatric Travel Medicine
280 W. MacArthur Blvd., Oakland, CA 94611 USA
Phone: 1-510-596-1200
Limited to members of Kaiser health plan
Languages: English (principal), Spanish, Cantonese, Mandarin
Pre-Travel Vaccination
Official Yellow Fever Vaccine Cente,
Post-Travel Medical Consultation
On-Site Diagnostic Laboratory

Keystone, Jay S., MD FRCPC MSc
(CTM) Centre for Travel and Tropical Medicine
Toronto General Hospital
200 Elizabeth Street, EN g-208
Toronto, Ontario M5G 2C4 Canada
Phone: (pre-travel appointments): 1-416-340-3000,
(post-travel): 1-416-340-3675;
Fax: 1-416-595-5826**Web**:
http://start.tripprep.com/travel/
Language: English
Pre-Travel Vaccination
Official Yellow Fever Vaccine Center
Post-Travel Medical Consultation
On-Site Diagnostic Laboratory

Jong, Elaine, MD
Hall Health Travel Clinic
University of Washington
UW Box 354410
Seattle, Washington 98195-4410 USA
Phone: 1-206-685-1060;
Fax: 1-206-685-1853
Web http://depts.washington.edu/hhtravel/
Language: English
Pre-Travel Vaccination
Official Yellow Fever Vaccine Center
Post-Travel Medical Consultation
On-Site Diagnostic Laboratory

Jong, Elaine, MD
University of Washington Medical Center
Travel and Tropical Medicine Service
1959 NE Pacific Street
Box 356123, Seattle, Washington 98195 USA
Phone: 1-206-598-6205;
Fax: 1-206-598-4569
Web http://depts.washington.edu/travmed/
Language: English
Pre-Travel Vaccination
Official Yellow Fever Vaccine Center
Post-Travel Medical Consultation
On-Site Diagnostic Laboratory

High Altitude Destinations, Map Resources

C

To find the altitude of any city not listed here, check www.calle.com/world. You will also find the latitude and longitude, weather and temperature information, forecasts, maps, and links to photographs as well as google searches for further information. A great website. Other map sites: www.un.org//depts/cartographic/english/new.htm; http://www.lib.utexas.edu/maps/index.html

Travel Destinations Above 1800 Meters / 6000 Feet.

City	Meters	Feet
Arosa, Switzerland	1847	6059
Asmara, Ethiopia	2325	7628
Bogota, Columbia	2645	8678
Cajamarca, Peru	2640	8662
Cochabamba, Bolivia	2550	8367
Cuenca, Ecuador	2530	8301
Cuzco, Peru	3225	10,581
Darjeeling, India	2265	7431
Durango, Dgo., Mexico	1889	6198
Erzurum, Turkey	1951	6402
Flagstaff, AZ, U.S.A.	2137	7012
Grand Canyon NP, AZ, U.S.A.	2015	6611
Guanajuato, Gto., Mexico	2500	8202
Kabale, Uganda	1871	6138
Kerman, Iran	1859	6100
Kitale, Kenya	1920	6299

City	Meters	Feet
La Paz, Bolivia	3658	12,001
Leh, India	3506	11503
Lhasa, Tibet, China	3685	12090
Morella, Mich., Mexico	1941	6368
Narok, Kenya	1890	6200
Nanyuki, Kenya	1947	6389
Nuwara Eliya, Sri Lanka	1880	6188
Pachuca, Hgo., Mexico	2426	7959
Puebla, Pue., Mexico	2162	7093
Queretaro, Qro., Mexico	1842	6043
Quito, Ecuador	2879	9446
San Antonio de los Banos, Cuba	2509	8230
San Cristobal de Las Casas, Chis., Mexico	2276	7467
San Luis Potosi, S.L.P., Mexico	1859	6100
San Miguel de Allende, Gto., Mexico	1852	6076
San'a',', Yemen Arab Republic	2377	7800
Simla, India	2202	7224
South Pole Station, Antarctica, U.S.A.	2800	9186
St. Moritz, Switzerland	1833	6013
Toluca, Mex., Mexico	2680	8793
Zacatecas, Zac., Mexico	2446	8025

Conversion Charts

D

Pound/Kilogram Conversions for Dosage Calculations
I Kg = 2.2 lbs, 1 lb =.45 Kg

lb.	Kg.	lb.	Kg.	lb.	Kg.	lb.	Kg.
80	36.3	115	52.2	150	68.0	185	83.9
85	38.6	120	54.4	155	70.3	190	86.2
90	40.8	125	56.7	160	72.6	195	88.5
95	43.1	130	58.9	165	74.8	200	90.7
100	45.4	135	61.2	170	77.1	205	93.2
105	47.6	140	63.5	175	79.4	210	95.5
110	49.9	145	65.8	180	81.6	215	97.7

Fahrenheit/Celsius Temperature Conversions

$$^{o}C = (^{o}F-32) \times 5/9; \quad ^{o}F = (^{o}C \times 9/5) + 32$$

^{o}F	^{o}C	^{o}F	^{o}C	^{o}F	^{o}C
90	32.2	96	35.6	102	38.9
91	32.8	97	36.1	103	39.4
92	33.3	98	36.7	104	40.0
93	33.9	99	37.2	105	40.6
94	34.9	100	37.8	106	41.1
95	35.0	101	38.3		

Index

About the Authors

Gary R. Fujimoto, MD has been the Medical Director of the Travel Medicine Department at the Palo Alto Medical Foundation for over 14 years and a Clinical Associate Professor of Medicine at Stanford University. He received his undergraduate degree at Oberlin College and his medical degree at Albert Einstein College of Medicine in New York. He is board certified in both internal and occupational medicine and specializes in biological and chemical hazards, including laboratory exposure to tropical diseases. He is a member of the International Society of Travel Medicine and the American Society of Tropical Medicine and Hygiene and lectures frequently on travel medicine.

Dr. Fujimoto has volunteered teaching other physicians in Thailand and met Marc Robin over 20 years ago while volunteering at the Beach Area Community Clinic during his Internal Medicine residency at the University of California, San Diego. He recently joined Marc and Dr. David Spees (chapter on tropical diseases) on a whale watching expedition in Baja.

Marc R. Robin, ANP, is the coordinator of the International Traveler's Clinic in San Diego, California. He received his Registered Nurse degree at Grossmont College, El Cajon, California and his Adult Nurse Practitioner license at the University of Oregon. He is a member of the International Society of Travel Medicine. He is also a freelance writer and photographer, specializing in wilderness subjects. He is an avid explorer by foot, mule, and with backpack of Baja California. He has traveled extensively in Latin America. He also writes on prehistoric rock art of Baja California.

Bradford L. Dessery, RN, is a former Peace Corp Volunteer who served in Honduras, Central America from 1966–1968. He holds a B.A. degree in English Literature from Stanford University. He received his Registered Nurse degree in San Diego and currently works at the University of California Medical Center in San Diego. He has lived in Guatemala and traveled extensively in Mexico, Belize, and Costa Rica. In his spare time he enjoys SCUBA diving, most recently in the Bahamas and Bay Islands, Honduras.

Contributors

Sheila Mackell, MD is a pediatrician who is certified in travel and tropical medicine. She has published numerous articles in the Journal of Travel Medicine. Founder of the Pediatric Travel Medicine service at Kaiser Permanente in Oakland, she has lectured internationally on advice for the pediatric traveler.

Susan Anderson, MD, MPH, has served as Director of Research, Child Family Health International. She is on the faculty of Stanford University Hospital and a member of the Stanford Medical Center Bioterrorism and Emergency Preparedness Task Force. She is a frequent lecturer on women's travel health issues.

David N. Spees, MD, is certified in Family Practice, Tropical Medicine, and Traveler's Health. He was a family physician for the Department of State, and a Regional Medical Officer for the Middle East and Central Africa. His numerous publications include articles or chapters in *Family Medicine: Principles and Practice*, the *American Journal of Tropical Medicine and Hygiene*, and *State*. Professional associations include the International Society of Travel Medicine, the American Society of Tropical Medicine and Hygiene, the Society of Vector Ecology, and the California Academy of Family Practice.